LAW IN A CULTURE OF THEOLOGY

Law in a Culture of Theology: The Use of Canon Law by Parisian Theologians, ca. 1120–ca. 1220 considers the study of law within its intellectual environment. It demonstrates that theologians associated with the schools of Paris in the twelfth century, particularly Peter the Chanter and his circle, had a working knowledge of the Roman-canonical tradition and thought about the human context of the law, which, in turn, reflected the environment in which each master worked. It begins by showing the extent to which law was woven into the fabric of the schools of Paris and follows with individual case studies.

These case studies—marriage in Hugh of St. Victor's *De Sacramentis* and Peter Lombard's *Sententiae*, excommunication in Peter the Chanter's *Summa de sacramentis et animae consiliis*, crusade activity and heresy in Robert of Couçon's *Summa penitentiae*, homicide in Robert of Flamborough's *Liber penitentialis*, and the faces of greed in Thomas of Chobham's *Summa confessorum*—demonstrate how each theologian drew upon legal thought, for what end he was using it, and how his use of law fit into contemporary legal thinking. A competency in law proved valuable to, and was tailored for, different types of ecclesiastical roles: teachers showing students how to analytically navigate complex questions of pastoral care, papal judge-delegate on the cusp of full-time administration on behalf of the papacy, *penitentiarius* of St. Victor and the students at the University of Paris, or diocesan management.

This book will be a useful resource for all students and researchers interested in medieval canon law, medieval theology, and pre-modern law.

Melodie H. Eichbauer is Professor of Medieval History at Florida Gulf Coast University, Fort Myers, U.S.A. Her research focuses on the dissemination of legal knowledge; the interpretation of law; and the ways in which social, political, and intellectual developments and trends shaped both between ca. 1000 and ca. 1500. She authored the second edition of *Medieval Canon Law*, an expanded and revised version of the first edition by James A. Brundage (2023). She is the editor of *A Cultural History of Genocide, Vol. 2: The Middle Ages* (2021), the co-editor with Danica Summerlin of *The Use of Canon Law in Ecclesiastical Administration, 1000–1250* (2018), and the co-editor with Kenneth Pennington of *Law as Profession and Practice in Medieval Europe: Essays in Honor of James A. Brundage* (2011).

LAW IN A CULTURE OF THEOLOGY

The Use of Canon Law by Parisian Theologians, ca. 1120–ca. 1220

Melodie H. Eichbauer

Routledge
Taylor & Francis Group
LONDON AND NEW YORK

Designed cover image: Meeting of doctors at the University of Paris. ©
Jimlop collection / Alamy Stock Photo 2E4NKT0

First published 2025
by Routledge
4 Park Square, Milton Park, Abingdon, Oxon OX14 4RN

and by Routledge
605 Third Avenue, New York, NY 10158

Routledge is an imprint of the Taylor & Francis Group, an informa business

British Library Cataloguing-in-Publication Data
A catalogue record for this book is available from the British Library

Library of Congress Cataloging-in-Publication Data
Names: Eichbauer, Melodie H., author.
Title: Law in a culture of theology : the use of canon law by Parisian theologians, ca. 1120-ca. 1220 / Melodie H. Eichbauer.
Description: Abingdon, Oxon [UK] ; New York, NY : Routledge, 2025. | Includes bibliographical references and index. | Identifiers: LCCN 2024046306 (print) | LCCN 2024046307 (ebook) | ISBN 9781032736099 (hardback) | ISBN 9781032736082 (paperback) | ISBN 9781003465096 (ebook)
Subjects: LCSH: Canon law--History--12th century. | Religion and law--France--History--12th century. | Theology--France--Paris--History--12th century. | Pastoral theology--Catholic Church. | Catholic Church--Doctrines--History--12th century. | Theologians--France--Paris--History--12th century. | Christian heresies--History--12th century. | Petrus, Cantor, approximately 1130-1197.
Classification: LCC KBR160 .E323 2025 (print) | LCC KBR160 (ebook) | DDC 262.90944/09021--dc23/eng/20241008
LC record available at https://lccn.loc.gov/2024046306
LC ebook record available at https://lccn.loc.gov/2024046307

ISBN: 978-1-032-73609-9 (hbk)
ISBN: 978-1-032-73608-2 (pbk)
ISBN: 978-1-003-46509-6 (ebk)

DOI: 10.4324/9781003465096

Typeset in Times New Roman
by SPi Technologies India Pvt Ltd (Straive)

CONTENTS

ACKNOWLEDGMENTS

This book has been a *long* time in the making. Initial thoughts began during the project *Codes, Communities, and Church: The Cultural Contexts of Medieval Law* with Abigail Firey, a project funded by the American Council of Learned Societies between 2016 and 2018. I cannot thank Abigail enough for the conversations that connected people and ideas. I also want to thank Danica Summerlin, Greta Austin, and Kathleen Cushing for their questions and support throughout the project. They had a way of taking my thoughts, clarifying them, and putting them into understandable words. Of course, FGCU's University Library, especially Peggy Glatthaar, deserves my deepest thanks. The number of interlibrary loans and, more importantly, the number of extensions requested went even beyond what I consider to be reasonable.

Work on the project stalled following the conclusion of the fellowship when the realities of academic life resumed; teaching and other projects all took their toll. Its completion, coincidentally enough, coincided with an interim administrative appointment. I found myself empathizing with those whom I was studying. The bonds of partnerships made across campus led to shared knowledge, documents, and ideas. Questions arose for which nothing could have prepared me to answer. I found myself conducting research in completely new fields, learning the lay of a different scholarly landscape. Stepping out of our disciplinary boundaries lies at the heart of administration, but that does not mean we step away from our training. In both instances, we are faced with questions, need to conduct a survey of the literature and what has and has not been done in the past, frame our thesis for moving forward based on the evidence, shape a plan to bring the project to completion (being willing to change the thesis and plan as new evidence arises), and disseminate our findings to stakeholders.

I found myself wondering if those whom I studied also questioned the nature of power and the ability of some to competently execute their office.

Throughout all of the adventures this project has taken me on, my husband Paul has been by my side: tolerating odd hours, weekends, airport runs, listening to my frustrations at the office, celebrating the wins which were neither guaranteed nor rarely came easy, and pretending to listen to me as I talked through my research. It is to him that this book is dedicated...not that he will ever know because he probably will never read it.

ABBREVIATIONS

The following sigla are used without further explanation:

Bartholomew	Adrian Morey, ed., *Bartholomew of Exeter, Bishop and Canonist: A Study in the Twelfth Century* (Cambridge: Cambridge University Press, 1937).
BAV	Biblioteca Apostolica Vaticana
Bk.	Book
BMCL	*Bulletin of Medieval Canon Law*, New series
BnF	Bibliothèque nationale de France
BVM	*Hugonis de Sancto Victore De beatae Mariae virginitate*, in *L'oeuvre de Hugues de Saint-Victor, Vol 2: Super Canticum Mariae; Pro Assumptione Virginis; De beatae Mariae Virginiate; Egredietur virga, Maria porta*, ed. Patrice Sicard with intrucitonn notes, and French translation by Bernadette Jollès, Sous la règle de saint Augustin series (Turnhout: Brepols, 2000). English translation in Hugh Feiss, OSB, ed. *On the Sacraments: A Selection of Works of Hugh and Richard of St. Victor, and of Peter of Poitiers*, Victorine Texts in Translation, 10 (Turnhout: Brepols, 2020).
C.	Causa (case), Gratian's *Decretum* (subdivision of part 2)
c.	*capitulum* (chapter) or canon
CCL	*Corpus Christianorum, Series latina*
CCCM	*Corpus Christianorum, Continuatio mediaevalis*
Cdp	*Collectio decem partium* in Berlin, Staatsbibliothek Preußischer Kulturbesitz, Phill. 1746, fol. 107v–130v.

Chanter	Pierre Le Chantre, *Summa de sacramentis et animae consiliis*, ed. Jean-Albert Dugauquier, Analecta Mediaevalia Namurcensia, 4 (Lille: Librairie Giard, 1957).
Chobham	*Thomae de Chombham Summa confessorum*, ed. Revd. F. Broomfield, Analecta Mediaevalia Namurcensia, 25 (Louvain: Éditions Nauwelaerts, 1968).
CHR	*Catholic Historical Review*
Cod.	*Codex*, *Corpus iuris civilis* (part 3)
COGD	*Conciliorum oecumenicorum generalium-que decreta*, 2.1*: The Oecumenical Councils of the Roman Catholic Church*: *From Constantinople IV to Pavia-Siena (869–1424)*; 2.2*: From Basel to Lateran V (1431–1517)*, eds. Alberto Melloni et al. (Corpus Christianorum; Turnhout: Brepols, 2013).
Courçon	Robert of Courçon, *Summa penitentiae* in Paris, BnF, lat. 14524, https://gallica.bnf.fr/ark:/12148/btv1b100363481/f2.item.
CSEL	*Corpus scriptorum ecclesiasticorum latinorum*
CSV	*Collectio canonum of St. Victor* in Paris, Bibliothèque de l'Arsenal, ms. 721, fol. 244r–277r.
D.	*Distinctio*, Gratian's *Decretum* (subdivision of Part 1 and the *Tractatus de penitentia* [C.33 q.2])
De Sacr.	*Hugonis de Sancto Victore De sacramentis Christiane Fidei*, ed. Rainer Berndt (Münster: Aschendorff, 2008). English translation in Hugh Feiss, OSB, ed. *On the Sacraments: A Selection of Works of Hugh and Richard of St. Victor, and of Peter of Poitiers*, Victorine Texts in Translation, 10 (Turnhout: Brepols, 2020). English translation in Roy J. Deferrari, *Hugh of Saint Victor On the Sacraments of the Christian Faith (De Sacramentis)* (Cambridge, MA: The Medieval Academy of America, 1951).
DDC	*Dictionnaire de droit canonique*
Dig.	*Digesta*, *Corpus iuris civilis* (part 2)
d.p.c.	*dictum post capitulum* (Gratian's comment after a chapter)
edF.	Emil Friedberg, *Corpus iuris canonici*, 2 vols. (Leipzig: Tauchnitz, 1879).
Flamborough	Robert of Flamborough, *Liber poenitentialis: A Critical Edition with Introduction and Notes*, ed. J. J. Francis Firth, Studies and Texts, 18 (Toronto: Pontifical Institute of Mediaeval Studies, 1971).
fol.	*folium* (*folia*), in a manuscript
GD	*Decretum Gratiani*, ed. Emil Friedberg, *Corpus iuris canonici*, vol. 1 (Leipzig: Tauchnitz, 1879).

HMCL 2	*The History of Medieval Canon Law in the Classical Period, 1140–1234: From Gratian to the Decretals of Pope Greogry IX*, eds. Wilfried Hartmann and Kenneth Pennington, History of Medieval Canon Law (Washington D.C.: The Catholic University of America Press, 2008).
HMCL 3	*The History of Courts and Procedure in Medieval Canon Law*, eds. Wilfried Hartmann and Kenneth Pennington, The History of Medieval Canon Law (Washington D.C.: The Catholic University of America Press, 2016).
I Comp.	*Compilatio prima*
II Comp.	*Compilatio secunda*
III Comp.	*Compilatio tertia*
IV Comp.	*Compilatio quarta*
V Comp.	*Compilatio quarta*
ID	Ivo of Chartres, *Decretum*, eds. Martin Brett et al. available at https://ivo-of-chartres.github.io/decretum.html
Inst.	*Institutiones*, *Corpus iuris civilis* (part 1)
JEH	*Journal of Ecclesiastical History*
JK, JE, JL	Jaffé, *Regesta pontificum romanorum* ... ed. secundam curaverunt F. Kaltenbrunner (JK: an. ?–590), P. Ewald (JE: an. 590–882), S. Loewenfeld (JL: an. 882–1198)
Kéry	Lotte Kéry, *Canonical Collections of the Early Middle Ages (ca. 400–1140): A Bibliographical Guide to the Manuscripts and Literature* (Washington D.C.: Catholic University of America Press, 1999).
Lombard	Magistri Petri Lombardi, *Sententiae in IV libris distinctae*, Vol. 2 [of 2], Spicilegium Bonaventurianum, 5 (Rome: Collegii S. Bonaventurae ad Claras Aquas Grottaferrata, 1981). English translation in Peter Lombard, *The Sentences. Book 4 On the Doctrine of Signs*, trans. Giulio Silano, Mediaeval Sources in Translation, 48 (Toronto: Pontifical Institute of Mediaeval Studies, 2010).
Mansi	Mansi, *Sacrorum conciliorum nova et amplissima collectio*
MGH	Monumenta Germaniae historica
	Capit. — Capitularia
	Conc. — Concilia
	Const. — Constitutiones
	Epp. — Epistolae (in Quart)
	Epp. sel. — Epistolae selectae
	LL — Leges (in Folio)
	SS — Scriptores
MIC	Monumenta iuris canonici

Pan.	*Panormia*, ed. Bruce Brasington and Martin Brett, available at https://ivo-of-chartres.github.io/panormia.html.
PL	Migne, *Patrologia latina*
Po.	Potthast, *Regesta pontificum romanorum*
q.	*questio,* question contained in the Causae of Gratian's *Decretum* (subdivision of part 2)
RIDC	*Rivista internazionale di diritto comune*
s.v.	*sub verbo*, medieval commentary "on the words"
X	*Liber extra* (*Decretales Gregory IX*), ed. Emil Friedberg, *Corpus iuris canonici*, vol. 2 (Lepizig: Tauchnitz, 1881).
ZRG Kan. Abt.	*Zeitschrift der Savigny-Stiftung für Rechtsgeschichte*, Kanonistische Abteilung

The Proceedings of the International Congresses of Medieval Canon Law will be referred to as, for example, *Proceedings Boston 1965*.

INTRODUCTION

When we consider the relationship between law and theology from the mid-twelfth century forward, two observations come to mind. One is presented by the canonist Stephan of Tournai (d. 1203) in the preface to his *Summa* on Gratian's *Decretum*. There, he comments:

> I invited two men to a banquet, a theologian and a lawyer, whose tastes diverge toward different desires, since this one is delighted by tart things, and that one longs for sweets. Which of these should we offer, which should we withhold? Do you refuse what either one requests?[1]

His caricature presents a portrait of a host thinking about how best to accommodate the tastes of his guests. The other is presented by Stephan's near contemporary Gerard of Wales (d. 1223)—canonist, archdeacon of Brecon, and royal clerk—in a letter to Walter Map, then the archdeacon of Oxford. Despite his renown in the law, his letter extolled the virtues of theology above all other sciences. Likening the disciplines to an edifice, he compared the liberal arts to a foundation and theology to a roof.[2] Extending Gerard's analogy to a logical conclusion, law served as the walls that built upon the foundation and supported the roof.

1 "Preface to the *Summa* of Stephen of Tournai on Gratian's *Decretum*," in *Prefaces to Canon Law Books in Latin Christianity: Selected Translations, 500–1245*, 2nd edn., trans. R. Somerville and B. C. Brasington (Washington D.C., 2021), 194. For an edition of the preface, see H. Kalb, *Studien zur Summa Stephans von Tournai: Em Beitrag zur kanonistischen Wissenschaftsgeschichte des späten 12. Jahrhunderts* (Innsbruck, 1983), 113–120.

2 Giraldi Cambrensis, *Symbolum Electorum*, Epist. 24 in *Opera, Vol. 1*, ed. J. S. Brewer (London, 1861), 271–287. See also J. Baldwin, *Masters, Princes and Merchants: The Social Views of Peter the Chanter and His Circle*, 2 vols. (Princeton, 1970), 1.83.

DOI: 10.4324/9781003465096-1

The observations made by Stephan of Tournai and Gerard of Wales reveal the complex relationship between law and theology. Stephan's caricature is of two men who may have had at least some learning in both disciplines but prefer one over the other. After all, in order to know which one of the two dishes each man preferred—sweet or tart—presumably he had to have tried both first at some point.[3] Gerard of Wales's analogy lends support to this interpretation, implying that a theologian should be intellectually versatile. Liberal arts, law, and theology played an important structural role; the entire building would collapse without each in its proper place. We, therefore, should neither assume that disciplinary specialization meant being walled off from other areas of knowledge nor should we assume that being known for their work in one discipline negated competency in another discipline.[4]

Law in a Culture of Theology: The Use of Canon Law by Parisian Theologians, ca. 1120–ca. 1220 explores some implications of Stephan and Gerard's observation. It argues that, as the schools of Notre Dame, St. Victor, and Ste. Geneviève evolved into the University of Paris; there existed a common intellectual culture that valued porous disciplinary boundaries between theology and Roman-canonical law. Twelfth-century masters known for their work in theology—Hugh of St. Victor, Peter Lombard, Peter the Chanter, Robert of Courçon, Robert of Flamborough, and Thomas of Chobham—serve as the lens through which to view this scholastic environment that fostered such versatility. These theologians found a working knowledge of law useful, and they wove legal thought into their writings. As individual case studies will show, each theologian adapted legal thinking to the environment in which he worked. Thus, the intersectionality of theological and legal thought was fostered by the options available for service in both ecclesiastical and secular administration. With Paris as the center of Capetian administration and with the papacy's vested interest in the university, these *litterati*—theologians who also served as teachers, judges, or administrators—would have had to be comfortable with a corpus of knowledge outside of their area of expertise.

3 John Van Engen presented a different interpretation, stating that Stephan prepared his *Summa* for legists (specialists in Roman law) and theologians. Each had distinct world views, distinct faculties, and, above all, a distinct authoritative text: Justinian's *Corpus* and the Bible. See "From Practical Theology to Divine Law: The Work and Mind of Medieval Canonists," in *Proceedings Munich 1992*, eds. P. Landau and J. Müller (Vatican City, 1997), 873–896, here 873.

4 Scholars have pointed to the intellectual versatility of medieval thinkers and the range of topics on which they publish. Take for example, Robert Grosseteste (d. 1253) whose interests included theology, canon law, Greek philosophy, and the natural sciences (see J. Flood, J. R. Ginther, and J. Goering, eds., *Robert Grosseteste and His Intellectual Milieu* [Toronto, 2013]); the famous canonist Huguccio (d. 1210) also composed works on grammar (see W. P. Müller, *Huguccio: The Life, Works, and Thought of a Twelfth-Century Jurist* [Washington D.C., 1994], chap. 1); and Nicholas Cusanus (d. 1464) whose interests included theology, canon law, cosmology, and mathematics (see J. F Hamburger, *Color in Cusanus* [Stuttgart, 2021]).

A Brief Overview of Secular and Papal Patronage of the Twelfth-Century Schools

As Stephen Ferruolo aptly noted: "The university of Paris grew; it was not founded."[5] Social and political factors—a growth in population, agricultural advancements, increased use of money, urbanization, efforts at reform and renewal within the Church, political and intellectual conflicts that engaged the masters, emergence of communes, and the renaissance of the state—would provide fundamental catalysts. In the end, the growth of the University of Paris owed much to the Capetians and to the papacy as both kings and popes granted privileges to the students and masters.[6]

Kings Louis VI and Louis VII, both of whom had close connections with the Church, connections which they used as a vehicle for extending the power of the French monarchy, laid a foundation for the transformation of the schools in Paris into a university. Louis VI considered his close friends Renaud, archbishop of Reims (1124–1139), and Suger, abbot of St. Denis (1122–1155), key royal advisors.[7] Links between the monarchy and the papacy were strengthened by visits from Popes Urban II (1095–1096), Paschal II (1107), Gelasius II (1119), and Calixtus II (1119–1120). Louis VI supported the candidacy of Innocent II during the schism of 1130 and, at a council at Reims in 1131, Innocent II crowned Prince Louis (VII) the successor of King Louis VI after the unexpected death of Prince Philip.[8] Louis VI saw to it that Louis VII was educated at the cathedral school of Notre Dame in Paris. Louis VI's son and Louis VII's brother, Henri de France, served as bishop of Beauvais from 1149 to 1162 and then as archbishop of Reims, a position which he held until his death in 1175.[9] As Henri de France and Suger exemplify, bishops and abbots

5 S. Ferruolo, *The Origins of the University: The Schools of Paris and Their Critics, 1100–1215* (Stanford, 1985), 206, 223.

6 J. Verger, "A propos de la naissance de l'université de Paris: Contexte social, enjeu politique, portée intellectuelle," in *Schulen und Studium im Sozialen Wandel des Hohen und Späten Mittelalters*, ed. J. Fried (Ostfildern, 1986), 69–96.

7 R. Große, *Saint-Denis zwischen Adel und König: Die Zeit von Suger (1053–1122)* (Ostfildern, 2002); P. Montaubin, "Innocent II and Capetian France," in *Pope Innocent II (1130–43): The World vs. the City*, eds. J. Doran and D. J. Smith (London, 2016), 107–151, here 110.

8 Montaubin, "Innocent II and Capetian France," 107 112, 117–119. Those in Louis VI's circle who supported Innocent II were: Archbishops Renaud of Reims, Henry of Sens (1122–1142), and Hugh of Rouen (1130–1164); Bishops Geoffrey of Chartres (1115–1149), Jocelin of Soissons (1126–1152), Stephen of Paris (1123–40), and Bartholomew of Laon (1113–1151); and Abbots Suger of Saint-Denis, Peter the Venerable of Cluny, Bernard of Clairvaux, Hugh of Saint-Germain-des-Prés, Guigo of Chartreuse, and Norbert of Xanten.

9 P. Montaubin, "Eugenius III and France: The Protected Protector," in *Pope Eugenius III (1145–1153): The First Cistercian Pope*, eds. I. Fonnesberg-Schmidt and A. Jotischky (Amsterdam, 2018), 197–217, here 200; M. Soria, "Alexander III and France: Exile, Diplomacy and the New Order," in *Pope Alexander III (1159–81): The Art of Survival*, eds. P. D. Clarke and A. J. Duggan (Farnham, 2012), 181–201, here 187.

were often recruited from the nobility. The Capetians steadily gained oversight over a number of bishoprics in different dioceses.

While Louis VI had not interfered openly in episcopal elections and had allowed the cathedral chapters and local clerical dignitaries to choose their prelates freely, Louis VII deviated from his father's policy. Between 1137 and 1143, he openly intervened in the elections to the sees of Reims, Poitiers, Langres, Bourges, Châlons, Senlis, and Paris.[10] By the end of Louis VII's reign and into the first decade of Philip II Augustus's reign, the monarchy controlled an impressive list of important archbishoprics and bishoprics. Louis VII ended his reign controlling the archbishoprics of Sens, Reims, Bourges, and Tours. He also controlled the bishoprics of Chartres, Orléans, Paris, Meaux, Troyes, and Auxerre (archdiocese of Sens); Beauvais, Senlis, Soissons, Arras, Noyon-Tournai, Laon, Châlons-sur-Marne, Thérouanne, and Amiens (archdiocese of Reims); Langres, Mâcon, Châlon-sur-Saône, and Autun (archdiocese of Lyon); Le Puy, and Mende (archdiocese of Bourges); Agde (in the archdiocese of Narbonne).[11] The appointment of renowned masters such as Peter Lombard and then Maurice of Sully to the bishopric of Paris and John of Salisbury to the see of Chartres bolstered their reputation as patrons of the schools.[12] The Capetian monarchy continued to expand its reach over the Church. In 1203, King Philip II Augustus added the archdiocese of Rouen and its suffragan bishoprics (Evreux, Lisieux, Bayeux, Avranches, Coutances, and Sées), as well as the bishoprics of Angers, Le Mans, and Poitiers as royal bishoprics. In dioceses such as Paris, Orléans, Senlis, and Sens, the king exercised seigneurial authority over the episcopal cities, leaving the bishops little authority beyond the spiritual. The conversion of dioceses such as Tournai in Flanders, and Reims, Troyes, and Chartres in Champagne into regalian dioceses afforded the king the opportunity to extend his influence.[13]

The Capetians' transformation of Paris into the administrative center of the monarchy brought more prestige to the schools in the city: the cathedral school of Notre Dame on the Île de Cité; and the abbeys of Ste. Geneviève and St. Victor, both on the Left Bank and both exempt from episcopal jurisdiction.[14] These schools organically grew into the University of Paris and attracted students from an increasingly wider geographical range. Having become a stable

10 Moutaubin, "Innocent II and Capetian France," 145–146.

11 R. Fawtier, *The Capetian Kings of France: Monarchy & Nation (987–1328)*, trans. L. Butler and R. J. Adam (New York, 1966), 71; J. Baldwin, *The Government of Philip Augustus: Foundations of French Royal Power in the Middle Ages* (Berkeley, 1986), 67–68, 304–305; Elizabeth M. Hallam and J. Everard, *Capetian France 987–1328*, 2nd edn. (New York, 2001), 112.

12 Ferruolo, *The Origins of the University*, 283.

13 Fawtier, *The Capetian Kings of France*, 71; Baldwin, *The Government of Philip Augustus*, 67–68, 304–305; Hallam and Everard, *Capetian France 987–1328*, 112.

14 P. Bermon, *La fondation de l'Université de Paris (1200–1260)* (Paris, 2017), 25.

and consistent force, the king could take a more active role in the execution of justice. It was toward the end of King Louis VII's reign that records of men referred to as *viri pruduentes*, *jurisperiti*, or *sapienti* appeared in the records. These learned experts consisted of the bishop, dean, chanter, or chancellor of Paris. They were not necessarily permanently appointed counselors but more likely advisors whom the king occasionally consulted.[15] Louis VII essentially appointed *familiares*, who had some expertise in the law, to oversee a judicial tribunal. The University of Paris prepared students for careers in church, government, and society. Many of the students who studied theology and canon law became secular administrators, diocesan administrators, and bishops.[16] Under Louis VII (1137–1180) only 3% of the bishops in royal bishoprics employed held the title of *magister* (master). Under Philip Augustus, this number rose to 20%. By comparison, 30% of those employed by the kings of England during this same time held the title of *magister*. The percentages would not compare favorably for the French until the reign of Louis IX (1226–1270) when the number of masters reached 41%.[17]

With Philip II Augustus's consolidation of Capetian power, he was in a position to grant the students of Paris certain rights in order to ensure their safety. He mandated that citizens of Paris swear to testify if he witnessed a layman causing injury to any student. If anyone witnessed a layman striking a student with a weapon, club, or stone—unless it was in self-defense—that witness should seize the assailant and deliver him to a judge. He may not flee the scene to avoid getting involved. Whether the assailant was seized at the time of the attack or later, clerks, laymen, or certain lawful persons, along with the king's count and judges, would conduct a full investigation. Furthermore, neither the count nor judges could lay hands on any student. If a student committed a crime, he should be arrested without harm and handed over to the ecclesiastical judge, who ought to guard him. These privileges essentially established a *privilegium fori* by which students held the status of clergy and were subjected solely to ecclesiastical jurisdiction.[18] King Louis IX would reissue this privilege virtually verbatim in 1229.[19] When King Philip III reissued it in 1276, he did not repeat the text but simply referred back to the privilege issued by Louis IX without referring to Philip II Augustus as the original issuer.[20] In

15 Baldwin, *The Government of Philip Augustus*, 38, 41. Baldwin, nevertheless, asserts that there is no evidence to support a body of trained legal experts.

16 Fawtier, *The Capetian Kings of France*, 221.

17 P. Moraw, "Careers of Graduates," in *A History of the University in Europe, Vol. 1: Universities in the Middle Ages*, ed. Hilde de Ridder-Symoens (Cambridge, 1992), 244–279, here 249; Ferruolo, *The Origins of the University*, 283.

18 H. Denifle, ed., *Chartularium Universitatis Parisiensis*, 4 vols (Bruxelles, 1964), 1.1, pp. 59–61; D. C. Munro, ed., *Translations and Reprints from the Original Sources of European History, Vol. 2: The Medieval Student* (Philadelphia, 1895), 5–6.

19 Denifle, ed., *Chartularium Universitatis Parisiensis*, 1.66, pp. 120–122.

20 Denifle, ed., *Chartularium Universitatis Parisiensis*, 1.466, p. 538.

1297, King Philip IV, in turn, referenced the privilege granted by Philip III without reference to either Louis IX or Philip II Augustus.[21]

Because Roman families sent their sons to study in Paris with the hopes they would obtain a lucrative position within the Church,[22] the papacy likewise took a keen interest in the university by issuing privileges that echoed those issued by the monarchy. At the end of the twelfth century, Pope Celestine III also issued a *privilegium fori* subjecting clergy solely to ecclesiastical jurisdiction. He stated that neither bishops nor clerics were to be brought before secular judgment. Irrespective of the nature of the case, they were subject to canon law.[23] Pope Innocent IV would reiterate this privilege in 1245. It did not matter whether the supposed transgression occurred inside or outside of Paris.[24] In 1259, Pope Alexander IV echoed Innocent IV, noting that the privileges the masters and students enjoyed while performing their duties or attending their studies in Paris followed them on their travels outside of the city.[25] He also would extend the privileges and immunities granted to masters and scholars to their servants.[26] In 1263, Pope Urban IV declared that the masters or scholars of Paris could be seized outside of Paris only by a letter from the pope or his legate. While in the city, they must be given formal notice of the offense if accused.[27] This *libertas scholarium*, which both secular and ecclesiastical authorities granted, can be regarded as essentially placing those affiliated with the university under the domain of canon law. The quest for internal jurisdiction—a desire for more autonomy and liberty—resulted in the masters and scholars being placed under the protection of the papacy.[28]

Papal protection brought papal influence into the schools. First, the papacy sought to strengthen its power to counter feudal interests and the growing power of the monarchy. As discussed above, Kings Louis VII and Philip II Augustus made tremendous inroads in gaining control over churches. Second, and by extension, the papacy sought a well-trained and ready pool of administrators to staff ecclesiastical offices. Between the years 1075 and 1215, approximately 38–46% of the Parisian master became prelates, that is, cardinals, archbishops, bishops, abbots, or priors. Approximately 35–36% became dignitaries of collegiate chapters, be it dean, chanter, archdeacon, *officialis*, or chancellor. From the 1140s onward, former students of Paris achieved preeminence at the papal court and in the College of Cardinals. One in six cardinals appointed by Pope Innocent III and one in two appointed by Pope Gregory IX had studied or

21 Denifle, ed., *Chartularium Universitatis Parisiensis*, 2.603, p. 77.
22 Montaubin, "Innocent II and Capetian France," 108.
23 Denifle, ed., *Chartularium Universitatis Parisiensis*, 1.15 (Pars Introductoria), p. 12.
24 Denifle, ed., *Chartularium Universitatis Parisiensis*, 1.142, p. 181.
25 Denifle, ed., *Chartularium Universitatis Parisiensis*, 1.351, p. 400.
26 Denifle, ed., *Chartularium Universitatis Parisiensis*, 1.349, p. 399.
27 Denifle, ed., *Chartularium Universitatis Parisiensis*, 1.382, pp. 426–427.
28 Verger, "A Propos de La Naissance de l'université de Paris," 79, 81.

taught in Paris. Third, the papacy sought to institutionalize the study of theology as the threat of heresy grew.[29] Jean LeClerq has pointed to a theological renewal taking place between the years 1075 and 1224. Theologians associated with the reform of the Church were Peter Damian (d. 1072), Anselm of Laon (d. 1117), Bruno of Segni (d. 1123), and Rupert of Deutz (d. 1129). The renewal reached its height between 1125 and 1150 with the works of Hugh of St. Victor (d. 1141), Abelard (d. 1141), William of St. Thierry (d. 1148), St. Bernard of Clairvaux (d. 1153), Gilbert of Poitiers (d. 1154), Peter the Venerable (d. 1156), and Peter Lombard (d. 1160).[30] Popes Celestine II (1143–1144), Alexander III (1159–1181), and Celestine III (1191–1198) were pupils of Abelard.

The schools of Paris were known for their focus on theology, with engaging personalities that drew students to the city. William of Champeaux, the first known master of the cathedral school of Notre Dame, set Paris on the path to rivaling the schools at Bec, Chartres, and Reims.[31] Abelard, whose name no doubt lured students to Paris, could be seen as an initial figure helping to hone the focus. At Paris, dialectic and grammar were highly regarded as necessary prerequisites for the study of the arts and theology. Rhetoric, a necessary element in law, would be subsumed under grammar.[32] The liberal arts were thus considered as preparation for the study of theology, law, and medicine.[33] Alex Novikoff has argued that dialectic, rhetoric, and disputation played a critical role in the broader cultural phenomenon between 1050 and 1300, stressing the verbal and dramatic conflict of ideas as vehicles to public persuasion and a path toward a deeper understanding of Christian truth.[34]

Liberal arts and theology were the cornerstones of the schools of Paris, but a knowledge of law would be equally important. Priests needed a practical education in order to exercise the pastoral care of souls. Bishops and their advisors had a practical need to access the canonical tradition, systematically organized ecclesiastical canons that influenced the systematization of theological

29 W. Rüegg, "Themes," in *A History of the University in Europe, Vol. 1: Universities in the Middle Ages*, ed. H. de Ridder-Symoens (Cambridge, 1992), 3–34, here 15–16, 21; Moraw, "Careers of Graduates," 249; S. E. Young, *Scholarly Community at the Early University of Paris: Theologians, Education and Society, 1215–1248* (Cambridge, 2014), 26; Baldwin, *Masters, Princes, and Merchants*, 149, 151; Verger, "A Propos de La Naissance de l'université de Paris," 89. Jacques Verger also noted that between 1180 and 1210 the position of *officiales* was entrusted to *magistri*.

30 J. Leclerq, "The Renewal of Theology," in *Renaissance and Renewal in the Twelfth Century*, eds. R. Benson and G. Constable with C. D. Lanham (Toronto, 1991), 68–87, here 70.

31 H. Rashdall, *The Universities of Europe in the Middle Ages*, new edn. in 3 vols, eds. F. M. Powicke and A. B. Emden (Oxford, 1936), 1.43–58, 1.276.

32 G. Leff, "The *Trivium* and the Three Philosophies," in *A History of the University in Europe, Vol. 1: Universities in the Middle Ages*, ed. H. de Ridder-Symoens (Cambridge, 1992), 307–336, here 312, 316.

33 Young, *Scholarly Community at the Early University of Paris*, 24.

34 A. J. Novikoff, *The Medieval Culture of Disputation: Pedagogy, Practice, and Performance* (Philadelphia, 2013).

teaching. The works of the masters at Paris allowed for the fruits of doctrinal developments in the schools to be applied to a world of rapid social and intellectual change. Law and theology served societal needs, and thus masters (be it of law or theology) were well-versed in the Bible, the writings of the Church Fathers, and the canons.[35] Potentially from Germany, Hugh of St. Victor would teach at the abbey. Peter the Chanter and his circle drew students for their expertise in pastoral theology and penitential manuals. Peter Lombard solidified Paris as a center of theology as his *Sententiae in IV libris distinctae* (hereafter *Sentences*) became the textbook for study.[36] Robert of Courçon noted what texts could and could not be studied. For example, Aristotle's treatises on logic, both old and new, were to be read in the regular, not in the extraordinary, courses. Priscian's *Institutiones Grammaticae* was also to be read in the regular courses. On feast days, nothing was to be read except for philosophy, rhetoric, works on the *quadrivium*, the third book of Donatus's *Ars maior*, Aristotle's *Nichomachean Ethics*, and, if they desired, Boethius. The books of Aristotle on metaphysics or natural philosophy—or the abridgments of these works—were not to be read, nor were the writings of Master David of Dinant, the heretic Amauri, and the Spaniard Mauricius to be read.[37] Pope Gregory IX would reiterate these guidelines, noting that books on natural philosophy were prohibited from being used at Paris until they had been examined and purged of all suspicion of error. In an effort to avoid the spread of heresy, theologians should confine themselves to disputing only such questions as could be determined by theological books and the writings of the Holy Fathers; they should not show themselves to be philosophers.[38]

The papacy's interest in the schools led it to steer the focus of the university. In the first half of the twelfth century, the chancellor of Notre Dame licensed masters to teach on the Île-de-la-Cité while the abbot of Ste. Geneviève would license masters for the schools of the Left Bank.[39] In 1179, Pope Alexander III (1159–1181) established a general system of *licentia docendi* and placed the

35 J. Goering, "The *Summa* of Master Serlo and Thirteenth-Century Penitential Literature," *Mediaeval Studies* 40 (1978): 290–311, here 290; C. J. Mews, "Law, Theology, and Praxis ca. 1140–1380: New Approaches to the Study of Law and Theology in Medieval Europe," *Journal of Religious History* 37, no. 4 (2013): 435–440, here 437–439; A. Larson, "The Reception of Gratian's *Tractatus de penitentia* and the Relationship between Canon Law and Theology in the Second Half of the Twelfth Century," *Journal of Religious History* 37, no. 4 (2013): 457–473, here 460–461.

36 Denifle, ed., *Chartularium Universitatis Parisiensis*, 1.5, p. 65.

37 Denifle, ed., *Chartularium Universitatis Parisiensis*, 1.20, pp. 78–79; Munro, ed., *Translations and Reprints from the Original Sources of European History, Vol. 2*, 12.

38 Denifle, ed., *Chartularium Universitatis Parisiensis*, 1.79, p. 138; Munro, ed., *Translations and Reprints from the Original Sources of European History, Vol. 2*, 9.

39 J. W. Baldwin, *Paris, 1200* (Stanford, 2010), 177–178.

écolâtre, or his equivalent, at Paris, the chancellor in charge of issuing it.[40] During his pontificate, he also permitted scholars and would-be students to be supported by their benefices while they studied. Furthermore, he authorized the schools to hold primary jurisdiction over the students. Further papal intervention came in 1207 when Innocent III instructed Odo of Sully, bishop of Paris, to limit the number of masters teaching theology to eight.[41] With the coalescing of the schools of Paris into the University of Paris in the early thirteenth century, the chancellor of Notre Dame appears as the primary figure charged with licensing masters; although, as John Baldwin notes, it cannot be assumed that the abbot of Ste. Geneviève had relinquished his rights to issue licenses on the Left Bank.[42] Robert of Courçon, cardinal, legate, and chancellor of Paris, was tasked with codifying the program of educational reform in 1215. He provided official papal recognition of the corporate rights of the university. He set forth the age and criteria that had to be met in order for a master to teach in the faculty of arts and theology. To teach in the faculty of arts, one must be at least 21 years old, have completed at least six years of study, and not stained with infamy. He must be examined by the chancellor according to the guidelines which Peter, bishop of Paris, brokered in 1213 between the chancellor and the masters and scholars. As noted above, he must be 21-years old to lecture in the arts, have studied in the arts for at least six years before he began to lecture, and he must not be besmirched by any infamy. When he began his position, he had to promise to hold it for at least two years unless he was prevented by some good reason that had been verified publicly or before examiners. To lecture in theology, one had to be at least 35 years old and must have had formal training, that is, having studied for at least eight years, five of which must have been focused on theology. No one was to lecture in theology before the third hour on days when the masters lecture. No one was to be received at Paris for important lectures or sermons unless his character and learning were preapproved. Robert also commented on the attire of masters. No master lecturing in arts was to wear anything except a round and black cope that reached

40 N. Gorochov, "L'évêque de Paris, le chapitre cathedral de Notre-Dame et l'université Moyen Âge," in *Notre-Dame de Paris, 1163–2013: Actes du colloque scientifique tenu au Collège des Bernardins, à Paris, du 12 au 15 décembre 2012*, ed. C. Giraud (Turnhout, 2013): 113–124, here 113;

41 Ferruolo, *The Origins of the University*, 291–294; N. Gorochov, *Naissance de l'université: Les écoles de Paris d'Innocent III à Thomas d'Aquin (v. 1200–v. 1245)* (Paris, 2016), 218–222. The connection between Odo of Sully as bishop of Paris and Innocent III would give rise to greater papal intervention in university affairs.

42 Young, *Scholarly Community at the Early University of Paris*, 20; Baldwin, *Masters, Princes, and Merchants*, 1.74.

to the heels. He also may wear a pallium, though not under the round cope and never any with long bands.[43]

One of the most explicit examples of the papacy's steering of the university's direction came with Pope Honorius III's 1219 *Super speculam*.[44] Bemoaning the worldliness of secular law and medicine, he renewed c.8 of the Council of Tours (1163) at which Pope Alexander III prohibited anyone who had professed religious vows from studying secular law or medicine. If he had left to study law, he would have had two months to return to his cloister before being excommunicated. Furthermore, he was not to be heard in any case in which he served as an advocate. If he returned to the monastery, he was to be last in rank and lose hope of promotion except by papal dispensation.[45] Honorius III extended this prohibition to archdeacons, deans, provosts, and all those of clerical status, including parish priests. While not rejecting the authority of secular law, Honorius III noted that rarely could ecclesiastical matters not be resolved with canonical texts. Thus, he strictly prohibited anyone from teaching or studying Roman secular law (*ius civile*) in Paris or nearby cities. Whoever did so not only would be excluded from participating as an advocate in the (ecclesiastical) courts for a period of time but also would be excommunicated by the local bishop.[46] Honorius intended not to ban the study of Roman law in general but to prevent students, financially supported by the Church, from giving their attention to studies other than those they were sent to undertake. Clerics had to be trained in theology and canon law, and the government of the Church envisioned that the graduates stay in ecclesiastical service after their return home instead of eyeing a secular career. The prohibition would lead to the rise of a school of law at Orléans in 1235,[47] and, as Lydia

43 Denifle, ed., *Chartularium Universitatis Parisiensis*, 1.20, pp. 78–80; Munro, ed., *Translations and Reprints from the Original Sources of European History, Vol. 2*, 11–14; Ferruolo, *The Origins of the University*, 306–310; Bermon, *La Fondation de l'Université de Paris (1200–1260)*, no. 10, pp. 115–138. For the agreement reached by Peter, bishop of Paris, to settle matters between the chancellor and the masters and scholars of Paris, see Denifle, ed., *Chartularium Universitatis Parisiensis*, 1.16, pp. 75–76.

44 Denifle, ed., *Chartularium Universitatis Parisiensis*, 1.32, pp. 90–93.

45 R. Somerville, *Pope Alexander III and the Council of Tours* (Berkeley, 1977), 50.

46 Denifle, ed., *Chartularium Universitatis Parisiensis*, 1.32, pp. 91–92.

47 C. Coppens, "Teaching of Law in the University of Paris in the First Quarter of the 13th Century," RDIC 10 (1999): 139–173, here 168–169; Stephan Kuttner, "Papst Honorius III. und das Studium des Zivilrechts," in *Festschrift für Martin Wolff: Beiträge zum Zivilrecht und internationalen Privatrecht*, eds. E. von Caemmerer et al. (Tübingen 1952), 79–101; reprinted in Kuttner, *Gratian and the Schools of Law, 1140–1234*, 2nd edn., ed. P. Landau (London, 2018), no. X.

Schumacher and David d'Avray have argued, an antipathy between theologians and canon lawyers.[48]

Historiographical Threads: The Growth of the University of Paris and Disciplinary Boundaries

Scholars have devoted significant attention to the intellectual culture of northern France. Much of this attention has focused on two key areas. The first is the evolution of the University of Paris. The second is the importance of theology and theological works to the school's fame. Much of this work has been done, however, in isolation from those studying the intersection of law and penitential theology.

The growth of the university has served as one historiographical thread. In his lengthy chapter, approximately 275 pages, Hasting Rashdall traced the institutional evolution of the *universitas* from the *studium generale* beginning with the monastic and palace schools in the ninth century, then moving to the cathedral schools, and then to the twelfth-century Parisian schools of Notre Dame, St. Victor, and Ste. Geneviève. As the influence of these masters grew and privileges were granted to them, conflicts arose with the chancellor and with the laity, which, in turn, shaped the structure of the university. He focused keenly on the influence of the mendicant orders over the university and their conflict with the secular masters between 1250 and 1260. The mendicants had claimed to be entitled to the privileges afforded to those affiliated with the university, while at the same time remaining exempt from the authority of the university guild. He devoted space to the relationship between the papacy and the government as it relates to the university in the fourteenth century. He also treated the individual disciplines, their curriculum structure, and the standards for completion. Rashdall seemed to have little interest in canon law, including the two-page discussion on it in the sub-section labeled "abuses." This contrasts with the thirteen pages devoted to theology. He ended the chapter with a description of the various colleges and the university's place within the wider European context.[49]

48 L. Schumacher and D. d'Avray, "Aquinas and the Place of Canon Law in Legal History," *Archivum Fratrum Prædicatorum*, n.s. 5 (2020): 29–44. They note the thirteenth-century theologians' view of canon law as having almost no place in legal history. Aquinas, for example, passes over it in his typology of laws despite citing Gratian's *Decretum* 81 times in the *Summa Theologiae*. They posit two explanations for this apathy: (1) by Aquinas's day, theologians tended to regard canon law as, in some sense, a rival social system, sharing the same basic beliefs but attracting a different, more worldly, kind of person; (2) perhaps Aquinas thought of canon law as theology, rather than as law. This second suggestion is worth a deeper look because it provides some continuity with twelfth-century theologians as opposed to a stark break from them.

49 Rashdall, *The Universities of Europe in the Middle Ages*, 1. 271–557. He treats canon law on pp. 431–432 and treats theology on pp. 464–477.

Alan Cobban paid particular attention to organizational influences: the power of students, the power of masters, and the turbulence engulfing masters and scholars and the surrounding communities. He argued that the commonly espoused characteristics of a *studium generale*—the ability to attract students from a wide area beyond its region; the ability to offer instruction both in arts and in at least law, theology, or medicine; and the two associated privileges of beneficed clergy being able to receive the fruits of their benefices while studying and the *ius docendi*, that is, the right of the degree holder from one *studium generale* to teach at another *studium generale* without undergoing further examination—were not as binding as Rashdall presented and, based on his study of the development of individual institutions, there was no final contemporary agreement to what exactly constituted a *studium generale*. That there was no hard-and-fast definition paved the way for Cobban to analyze the foundation of individual universities based on when their particular characteristics developed. He categorized Salerno as the prototype of a university. While it did not possess all of the characteristics of the university until the late thirteenth century, it was a center for the arts and the dissemination of Greek and Arabic science and philosophy in the twelfth and into the thirteenth century. Bologna served as a model of a school growing from the power of students with conflict, serving as the principal agent of its constitutional development. In Paris, it was masters who possessed the power, and they were the principal agents of its constitutional development. Cobban disagreed with Rashdall's assessment that Oxford grew out of the migration of masters and students from Paris in 1167 on account of the Becket Controversy. Oxford had already possessed a scientific tradition in the twelfth century. Furthermore, it was unaffected both by the papal ban on the teaching of Aristotle's works on natural science and by the political and theological controversies that followed.[50]

Jacques Verger's volume surveyed the history of the universities in France over the *longue durée*: from their antecedents as cathedral and monastic schools in the Middle Ages, to their advancement in the sixteenth and eighteenth century, to the Napoleonic Era and the Third Republic, and ending with the period between 1950 and 1980. With respect to the Middle Ages, Verger and Charles Vulliez noted the particular ecclesiastical character of the schools in northern France and they traced this evolution beginning with the traditional cathedral and monastic sites of Reims, Chartres, Laon, Bec, and Fécamp. The "renaissance of the twelfth century" and contacts with Byzantium and Islam paved the way for the rise of the schools of Paris. Collectively, these factors resulted in an enlarged knowledge base for teaching and reconstructed scholarly networks with the decline of the traditional sites after 1150. The school at Angers was known for its teaching of the *trivium* and while the school at Orléans was known for its teaching of grammar, rhetoric, and the *ars*

50 A. B. Cobban, *The Medieval Universities: Their Development and Organization* (London, 1975).

dictaminis. The University of Paris, in particular, can be marked by two phases. The first, to 1231, marked the establishment of the University of Paris's constitution: the need for an association for mutual defense and support and the formation of a professional organization like other urban organizations. The second phase, that is, from 1231 to the end of the thirteenth century, was seen as the blossoming of the university and marked by the rise of the mendicants and the foundation of the colleges. In the thirteenth century, both Angers and Orléans benefited from Honorius III's issuance of *Super speculam* (1219), which banned the teaching of Roman law at Paris. Orléans would become a center for civil and customary law. The schools of the Midi—Montpellier and Toulouse—would be known for medicine as well as law.[51]

Stephen Ferrulo similarly devoted his attention to the early history of the university, focused specifically on the period 1100 to 1215 when the "University of Masters" formed as a result of prevailing influences on educational principles and values within the schools. There was a unified belief among the masters and scholars that they were pursuing knowledge and truth, which stood in opposition to specialized and professionalized training that served personal ambitions.[52] A key focus for Ferruolo was the critics of the schools who expressed alarm about the comportment and behavior of those who flocked to the schools in Paris and the end goals for which they wanted to receive an education. Monastic orders, such as the Cistercians led by St. Bernard of Clairvaux, vocally expressed concern with the reliance on scholastic disputation, the morals of scholars, and the growing influence education had on acquiring ecclesiastical positions.[53] Satirists, such as Walter of Châtillon (ca. 1135–1203), bemoaned the decline in the substance of learning as seen by the lessened regard for the *trivium* while the corruption of wealth through the prelacy, legal system, or medicine was on the rise and undermined the value of education.[54] Humanists, such as John of Salisbury, had received an education that was primarily literary and philosophical. They too bemoaned specialization and professionalization as they cut away at the value of a proper liberal arts education.[55] Moralists—such as Peter Lombard and Maurice of Sully, both of whom served as bishop of Paris from 1159 to 1160 and from 1160 to 1196, respectively, along with successive chancellors of Notre Dame Odo of Soissons (ca. 1153 or 1160–ca. 1167), Peter Comestor (1168–1178), Hilduin (ca. 1178–1193), Peter of Poitiers (1193–1205), and

51 J. Verger and C. Vulliez, "Naissance de l'Université," and "Enseignement et culture universtiaires (jusque vers 1350)," in *Les Universités Au Moyen Age*, ed. J. Verger (Paris, 1973), 17–75. See also Verger, "The First French Universities and the Institutionalization of Learning: Faculties, Curricula, Degrees," in *Learning Institutionalized: Teaching in the Medieval University*, ed. J. Van Engen (Notre Dame, 2000), 5–19.

52 Ferruolo, *The Origins of the University*, 5.

53 Ferruolo, *The Origins of the University*, 48.

54 Ferruolo, *The Origins of the University*, 98–103, 128.

55 Ferruolo, *The Origins of the University*, 131.

Prévostin of Cremona (1206–1209)—gave sermons exhorting the scholars of Paris to clean up their behavior and to train men for active ministry.[56]

Pascale Bermon's work provides a collection of statutes, letters, and sermons, translated into French along with commentary, from 1200 to 1260—the period which bears witness to the transformation of the twelfth-century schools of Paris into the University of Paris in the thirteenth century. Collectively, the documents center on the corporate nature of the university and the increasing complexity of its organization. Bermon noted that the formation of an *universitas* owed much to the diffusion of Roman law, particularly to Book 3 title 4 of the *Digest* which deals with the organization of groups of people in a corporate body for the management of their affairs in common.[57] Included are documents—such as c.18 of the Third Lateran Council, c.11 of the Fourth Lateran Council, the privileges of Philip II Augustus, and the statutes presented by Robert of Courçon—that fixed the corporate identity of the university. Bermon includes documents that reflect direct papal involvement in the university, such as Pope Innocent III's limiting of the number of masters who could teach theology to eight, Pope Gregory IX's ending of the Great Dispersion, and those that address courses and exams. Also included are documents related to crises that engulfed the university, such as the heresies of David de Dinant and Amaury de Bène, urban violence that led to the Great Dispersion, and rivalries between the masters and scholars and the chancellor, especially Jean de Candeilles, and between the secular masters and the mendicants between 1250 and 1260.[58]

Nathalie Gorochov asked the central question: Who were the inventors of the University of Paris, and what were the institutional, political, social, and religious milieux in which they worked? Stated another way, her interest lay with the actors at the heart of the creation, transformation, and structuring of the University of Paris. She began with Pope Innocent III, whose engagement in the nascent university was critical to its development. She ended with the entrance of Thomas Aquinas, who would personify the dominance of the mendicants over the university. Progressing chronologically, Gorochov covered much of the same terrain as Bermon, addressing the corporate nature of the university, heresies, conflicts, and the Great Dispersion. Her work, however, is very much rooted in prosopography, focused on the masters and students, those who traveled to Paris to study or to teach, and those who discussed and legislated on matters related to the direction the university would take. Gorochov grouped

56 Ferruolo, *The Origins of the University*, 282.

57 Bermon, *La Fondation de l'Université de Paris (1200–1260)*, 27; Dig. 3.4.1.1:

> Those permitted to form a corporate body consisting of a collegium or partnership or specifically one or the other of these have the right on the pattern of the state to have common property, a common treasury, and an attorney or syndic through whom, as in a state, what should be transacted and done in common is transacted and done.

58 Bermon, *La Fondation de l'Université de Paris (1200–1260)*.

these masters and scholars into their disciplines of liberal arts, theology, and law and placed the masters into the broader climate in England and Italy. She concluded that the period between 1216 and 1229, during the pontificate of Honorius III and the chancellorship under Philip (1217–1236), marked a critical period in the university's structural development.[59]

The growth of the University of Paris shined a light on the second historiographical thread: Paris's intellectual history and the importance of theology and theological works. Hastings Rashdall focused on the impact that the "New Aristotle"—translations of Aristotle's works on physics and metaphysics—had on theological thought at Paris. Jacques Verger and Charles Vulliez's analysis of the second phase of the University of Paris's institutional development pointed to the intellectual turn of the faculty of arts and theology at Paris beginning in 1277 when Stephen Tempier, bishop of Paris from 1268 to 1279 and previously chancellor of the Sorbonne from 1263 to 1268, condemned and prohibited the teaching of 219 theses that had been debated among the philosophical and theological faculty at the university. Helene Wieruszowski keenly aligned theology with the University of Paris. The first part of her work is a study of liberal arts at the cathedral schools, and then she moves to the individual universities. She devotes two chapters to theology at Paris, then moves to discuss theology and philosophy at Oxford—which suggests a dependence of philosophy upon theology, which Cobban cautioned against—followed by law at Bologna and medicine at Salerno and Montpellier. She concluded with an overview of the expanding number of universities in the thirteenth century. The second part consists of abridged versions of translated sources that correspond to the first part.[60] The volume edited by Hilde de Ridder-Symoens focused on the concept of a university. The contributions do not address a specific university per se but rather take a comparative approach by drawing upon the various universities to explore particular themes, such as a university's relationship to authority, the resources available and how they were managed; teachers; admissions; students; careers; and mobility. With that said, Monika Asztalos's essay on the faculty of theology does feature the University of Paris prominently.[61] Theology held the first—and the only—position at the university.

Jean Longère synthesized the teachings of twelfth-century Parisian masters found in their sermons. His work provides a resource for the thought of a wide swath of writers on a wide swath of topics. He divided the featured preachers into bishops (Peter Lombard and Maurice de Sully), chancellors of Paris (Odo of Soissons, Peter Comestor, Hilduin, Peter of Poitiers, Prévostin of Crémona), masters of Paris (Alain of Lille and Stephen Langton), and finally non-Parisian

59 Gorochov, *Naissance de l'université.*

60 H. Wieruszowski, *The Medieval University: Masters, Students, Learning* (Princeton, 1966).

61 H. de Ridder-Symoens, ed., *History of the University in Europe, Vol. 1: Universities in the Middle Ages* (Cambridge, 1992). For Asztalos's essay, see pp. 409–441.

preachers (Honorius Augustodunensis, Raoul Arden, and Jacques de Vitry). On occasion, Longère wove in the sermons of Bernard of Clairvaux and the Victorines Hugh (d. 1141) and Richard (d. 1173). Their sermons covered a lot of ground. Topics included the nature and imitation of Christ, ecclesiology, the liturgical year, death and purgatory, heaven and resurrection, and hell. Religious figures, such as angels, demons, saints, martyrs, confessors, Mary Magdalene, and the Virgin Mary and Immaculate Conception, were also popular topics. Naturally, one's spiritual health was of interest: the sacraments of baptism, confirmation, Eucharist and the mass, marriage, and penance, as well as the virtues and vices. Also popular were sermons tailored to particular groups of people: monks, canons, prelates, the hierarchy of the priesthood; students and the hierarchy of knowledge; family as it pertained to the education of children and the place of women; the different professions found among the laity, specifically judges and advocates, princes and the powerful, merchants, agriculture and workers, knights and pilgrims; Jews, pagans, and heretics. The treatment of these topics reveals the deeply thoughtful nature of the sermons and the importance of using examples to avoid monotony. Longère highlighted the importance of the Bible. The Old Testament, in particular, was central to sermons treating the nature of Christ, ecclesiology, and the Virgin Mary. Patristic commentary, particularly those of Origen, Jerome, Augustine, and Gregory the Great, were also important sources. Longère noted, however, that these commentaries were not unique to sermons. Canonical texts also drew on similar sources.[62]

Ian Wei explored the intellectual culture of Paris between 1100 and 1300. He began by exploring the shift from poetry and myth to logic as a way to understand the physical world. Here, the thought of Peter Abelard played a central role. Wei then turned to Anselm of Canterbury, Bernard of Clairvaux, William of St. Thierry, Hildegard of Bingen, and Hugh of St. Victor in the twelfth century, with Bonaventure and Aquinas taking center stage in the thirteenth century. The statutes of 1215 and Pope Gregory IX's bull *Parens scientiarum* (1231), which ended the Great Dispersion, institutionalized the university and shaped it according to the monastic ideals of virtuous behavior needed to obtain knowledge and the responsibility of masters to properly guide that endeavor. Theologians also thought deeply about how they should conceive of their authority within society and their duty to engage with it, a point which Wei illustrated by analyzing writings of university masters on sex and marriage, and usury.[63]

62 J. Longère, *Oeuvres Oratoires de Maitres Parisiens au XIIe Siècle: Études Historique et Doctrinale*, 2 vols. (Paris, 1975). Vol. 1 consists of the texts while Vol. 2 includes the notes.

63 I. Wei, *Intellectual Culture in Medieval Paris: Theologians and the University c.1100–1330* (Cambridge, 2014).

Akin to Ian Wei, Spencer Young devoted his attention to the faculty of theology, though with a shorter chronological spread, covering what he dubbed the "*Parens scientiarum* generation." Whereas the preceding period, up to 1215, was the age of Peter the Chanter and the biblical-moral school, this generation began in 1215 with the statutes of Robert of Courçon and ended, similar to Natalie Gorochov who ended her work in 1245, in 1248, that is with the rise of the mendicants' influence at the university and the ensuing secular-mendicant controversy of the 1250s. Impacting the course of studies during this "*Parens scientiarum* generation" were the decrees stemming from the Fourth Lateran Council and interpretations of Aristotle's works, especially the *libri naturales*. The "*Parens scientiarum* generation" would resolve internal debates about what the university could and should become, a resolution that the papacy validated. The masters of the University of Paris lectured, debated, and preached with the end goal of serving the intellectual objectives of the Church and providing urban pastoral care. Also like Wei, Young focused on particular theologians, in this case William of Auxerre, and how theologians at the university viewed their authority in secular society. Rather than usury and sex and marriage, which Wei examined, Young used almsgiving and the seven deadly sins as case studies. The university theologians had destigmatized money and thus broadened the categories of people who had the duty to contribute alms. Sermons on the seven deadly sins fit nicely into both their social goals and disciplinary objectives for the university community.[64]

Examinations of the schools in and around Paris are often done so within the context of the theologians who taught there. As such, the history of the internal organization of the University of Paris has been a dominant voice, with its theology faculty as the principal area of inquiry. While Natalie Gorochov's recent work on the history of the university has paid some direct attention to the law faculty,[65] a more typical approach has been to focus solely on theological thought without noting any connection to the law. Such can be seen in the approaches of Hastings Rashdall, Helene Wieruszowski, Stephen Ferruolo, Ian Wei, and Spencer Young, for example.[66] Of central importance are the dual influences of Pope Honorius III's ban on the teaching of Roman law (1219), which forced students to go elsewhere to study Roman law before pursuing the study of canon law at Paris, and the Great Dispersion (1229–1231), when lectures largely ceased at Paris over the punishing of students in secular court after a bar brawl, which opened the door for mendicants to assert their influence over the university. As legal scholars shifted their

64 Young, *Scholarly Community at the Early University of Paris*, 27, 50–51, 95–99.

65 Gorochov, *Naissance de l'université*.

66 Rashdall, *The Universities of Europe in the Middle Ages, Vol. 1*; Wieruszowski, *The Medieval University*; Ferruolo, *The Origins of the University*; Wei, *Intellectual Culture in Medieval Paris*; Young, *Scholarly Community at the Early University of Paris*.

attention to the importance of Orléans as the school of civil law and Bologna as *the* school for legal training, theological inquiry dominated the conversation at Paris with an interplay of law and theology not explored.

The University of Paris's preeminence in theology has traditionally not fostered an interest in the interdisciplinarity taking place there. John Baldwin made the important observation that the Parisian masters divided themselves into theology (*theologia*), canon and Roman law (*decreta et leges*), medicine (*phisica*), and arts (*artes*) in 1213. These groups would evolve into the four faculties in the thirteenth century.[67] Thus, a firm line seems to be drawn between theology and law beginning in the late twelfth century. Theology and law were two distinct disciplines, particularly as teaching licenses evolved with the foundation of the university. The academic discipline of law at Paris was relegated to a seat behind theology, while Bologna was the center of legal studies. In its very organization, *Renaissance and Renewal in the Twelfth Century* repeated this standard disconnect between theology and law. Theology was addressed in Part 1 devoted to "Religion," and applied in Part 2 on "Education." Law was dealt with in an entirely different section, Part 4 on "Law, Politics, and History." Law and theology were in distinct sections, in distinct silos. Jean LeClercq reinforced these silos in his essay on theology in the volume. Distinguishing between the contemplative monastic theology of cloister and the theology of the schools, he noted that the "new pastoral theology…was the work neither of men of action nor of canonists, but of schoolmasters; and so it included both questions of Christian morality and the doctrine which underlay and justified it." LeClercq's words disentangled law from [pastoral] theology, attributed the designation of "school masters" to pastoral theologians a designation which in turn does not connect masters of law to masters of theology, and does not readily hint that law was one the sources that helped to underlay and justify questions of Christian morality. His observation that while monks, who preferred contemplative texts, did refer to the law, they did so much less than pastoral school masters who used texts with immediate applications to human action was LeClercq's only recognition that a link existed between law and theology.[68] G. R. Evan's work *Law and Theology in the Middle Ages*, as another example, contrasted twelfth- and thirteenth-century theologians' conception of virtue and sin in opposition to the lawyers' conception of keeping and breaking the law.[69] One again is left with the impression that the concepts, and thus the disciplines, paralleled but remained separate from one another.

67 Baldwin, *Masters, Princes, and Merchants*, 1.143. See also Denifle, ed., *Chartularium Universitatis Parisiensis*, 1.76, pp. 134–135.

68 LeClercq, "Renewal of Theology," 68–87, esp. 83; quote on p. 79.

69 G. R. Evans, *Law and Theology in the Middle Ages* (London, 2002). See also Kenneth Pennington's review in the *Journal of Ecclesiastical History*, 54 no. 2 (2003): 339–340.

The corollary to John Baldwin's observation of the disciplinary division in 1213 is that prior to 1213 the schools of Paris did not necessarily have stark formal divisions. Teachers may have been known for their writing in one field of study, but the porous disciplinary walls meant that their knowledge was broad and versatile. The canons of Paris, for example, taught both theology and canon law.[70] Baldwin focused on the intellectual climate, homing in more directly on the secular masters of the Parisian schools who dominated the university from approximately the mid-1170s through 1219 and compiled pastoral penitential manuals for their work in society. These secular masters included Peter the Chanter and his circle, comprising Robert of Courçon, Robert of Flamborough, Peter of Poitiers, and Thomas of Chobham. Baldwin placed these theologians within the fervent intellectual tradition of Paris as they corresponded to the growth of the schools' renown. He then placed their *libri penitentiales* within the context of the theological climate and the renewed emphasis on pastoral care. Baldwin keenly noted that these figures did not confine themselves to the theological arena. They served as a papal judge-delegate and engaged in the debates between *regnum* and *sacerdotium* regarding jurisdictional disputes over criminous clerics. They also were at the forefront of the changing views toward commercial activities as the city was becoming more urbanized and the use of money more pronounced.[71] Baldwin, like LeClercq, noted in passing the use of Gratian's *Decretum* and Roman law as sources, yet his focus was not the interplay of theology and law.

Scholars more frequently tend to study the intersections between law and theology from the perspective of those traditionally known for their legal, not their theological, thinking. Early studies examined sacramental matters and then moved into matters of ecclesiology.[72] Theological thought permeated legal collections. For example, Causa 33 q.3 of Gratian's *Decretum* constitutes a tract on penance while Part 3 of the *Decretum*, compiled by someone other than Gratian, is entitled *De consecratione*. Book 1 of Pope Gregory IX's *Liber extra* treats the Trinity, while Book 3 titles 42 and 43 deal with baptism. Paul Fournier and Gabriel LeBras noted that the same men often cultivated legal and

70 See Baldwin, *Masters, Princes, and Merchants*, 1.143. See also Denifle, ed., *Chartularium Universitatis Parisiensis*, 1.76, pp. 134–135. Rashdall, *The Universities of Europe in the Middle Ages*, 1.333.

71 Baldwin, *Masters, Princes, and Merchants*.

72 J. de Ghellinck, *Le mouvement théologique du XIIe siècle: Études, recherceħs et documents*, 2nd. edn. (Bruges, 1948); S. Kuttner, "Zur Frage der theologischen Vorlagen Gratians," ZRG Kan. Abt. 23 (1934): 243–268 and *Kanonistische Schuldlehre von Gratian bis auf die Dekretalen Gregors IX*, Studi e testi 64 (Vatican City, 1935); A. M. Landgraf, "Diritto canonico e teologia nel secolo XII," *Studia Gratiana* 1 (1953): 373–413; N. M. Häring, "The Interaction between Canon Law and Sacramental Theology in the Twelfth Century," in *Proceedings Toronto 1972*, ed. S. Kuttner (Vatican City, 1976), 483–493; F. Gillmann, *Die Notwendigkeit der Intention auf Seiten des Spenders und des Empfängers der Sakramente nach der Anschauung du Frühscholastik* (Mainz, 1916). For discussion see Van Engen, "From Practical Theology to Divine Law," 875.

theological sciences because of their training in the dialectical method. There was, for example, significant overlap between the two with respect to marriage and simonical priests. While Fournier and LeBras point to the heyday of interplay as being from the end of the eleventh century to the beginning of the twelfth century,[73] most scholars seem to include the period ca. 1150 to ca. 1219, between Ivo of Chartres and Gratian, within that heyday as well. Roger E. Reynolds, as a case in point, provided a robust list of canon law manuscripts compiled in central and southern Italy between the tenth and twelfth centuries that included penitential texts.[74] Joseph Goering has focused on the interconnections between law and pastoral care.[75] Kathleen G. Cushing has likewise made the point that "[i]f the boundaries of law and theology were still not clear cut after 1140 (as they were before 1140), we need to think about how compilers come to their collections trained in theology as much as law."[76] Along those lines, Jason Taliadoros's study of Master Vacarius as a lawyer-theologian showed how he was informed by a practical and pastorally oriented scholasticism. Vacarius was tremendously important as the first known teacher of Roman law in England. Taliadoros argued that Vacarius was a typical *litteratus* of the twelfth century, trained and able to use both legal and theological thought as opposed to being confined to one or the other.[77] Both Atria Larson and John Wei have used C.33 q.3 of Gratian's *Decretum*, known as the *De penitentia*, to re-evaluate the renowned canonist as a pastoral theologian influenced by the school of Laon.[78]

73 P. Fournier and G. LeBras, *Histoire des Collections Canonique en Occident: Depuis les Fausses Décrétales jusqu'au Décret de Gratien*, 2 vols. (Paris, 1932), 2.316–322, 2.351.

74 R. E. Reynolds, "Penitentials in South and Central Italian Canon Law Manuscripts of the Tenth and Eleventh Centuries," *Early Medieval Europe* 14, no. 1 (2006): 65–84 with the list of manuscripts on pp. 84–84.

75 See, for example, J. Goering, "The Internal Forum and the Literature of Penance and Confession," in HMCL 2, 379–428.

76 K. G. Cushing, "Law and Reform: The Transmission of Burchard of Worms' *Liber decretorum*," in *New Discourses in Medieval Canon Law Research: Challenging the Master Narrative*, ed. C. Rolker (Leiden, 2019), 33–43, here 43.

77 J. Taliadoros, *Law and Theology in Twelfth-Century England: The Works of Master Vacarius (c.1115/20-c.1200)* (Turnhout, 2006). Vacarius compiled a number of works: the legal textbook *Liber pauperum*; the *Summa de matrimonio* that offered a "third way" to either the consensual theory advocated by Peter Lombard or the consummation theory posted by Gratian and Rufinus; the *Tractatus de assumpto homine* which was a christological work engaging in the conciliar scholastic debates on the hypostatic union in the mid-to later-twelfth century; the *Liber contra* which was the final section of the *Tractatus de assumpto homine* and responded to Speroni's polemical anti-sacerdotal and anti-sacramental piece.

78 A. Larson, *Master of Penance: Gratian and the Development of Penitential Thought and Law in the Twelfth Century* (Washington, D.C., 2014); Wei, *Gratian the Theologian* (Washington, DC., 2016). See the earlier efforts of On the *Sentences* and Anselm's school at Laon see L. Hödl, *Die Geschichte der Scholastischen Literatur und der Theologie der Schlüsselewalt, Teil I* (Münster, 1960), 155–186.

A few scholars have looked at the use of legal sources by theologians. Adriaan Gaastra has demonstrated the close relationship between eleventh-century penitentials compiled in central and southern Italy and the *Collectio IX librorum* (*9L*) and the *Collectio V librorum* (*5L*). Though having a "legal" context, he argued that the penitentials were neither fully legal nor purely liturgical. They, like the *9L* and *5L*, pay particular attention to sins related to sex and marriage—fornication, adultery, remarriage, and incest—as such sins would cause scandal. They also sought to counter crimes, such as violence and treason, that could cause disruption in society. They were vehicles for clergy to reinforce their authority and social control over the laity. It is thus possible to speak of a "fusion" of the penitentials and canonical genres as both showed an interest in normative texts.[79] Atria Larson devoted some pages to the use of Gratian's *De penitentia* by theologians such as Peter Lombard, the compiler of the *Sententiae divinitatis* (ca. 1140s), and by Peter the Chanter. She showed, for example, how Peter Lombard sometimes drew upon Gratian's text verbatim, while other times he paraphrased or adapted to suit his needs both the sources found in Gratian's tract as well as Gratian's own thoughts.[80] A few individual essays have delved into Thomas Aquinas's use of natural law within the context of scholastic theology.[81] John Lorenc's dissertation demonstrated that Dominican John of Freiburg (d. 1314) had a deep understanding of the law, which he most likely acquired by attending lectures while formally studying theology at Paris.[82] Thomas Turley has shown how the Dominican Peter of Palude (d. 1342) drew upon canon law, ecclesiastical practice, and church history to defend papal primacy against the John of Pouilly and other episcopalists who fought for the rights of bishops.[83] Such studies bring an important

79 A. H. Gaastra, "Between Liturgy and Canon Law: A Study of Books of Confession and Penance in Eleventh and Twelfth Century Italy" (PhD diss., Universiteit Utrecht, 2007).

80 Larson, *Master of Penance*, 315–342 (Peter Lombard's use of the *De penitentia*), 365–381 (influence of *De penitentia* on *Sententiae*), and 382–391 (Peter the Chanter's use of the *De penitentia*).

81 See, for example, W. Zemler-Cizewski, "*Lex* and *ius* in the *Summa Theologiae* of Thomas Aquinas: A Review of the Nuances," in *Proceedings of the PMR Conference, 19–20*, eds. K. A. Gersbach, F. Van Fleteren, and J. C. Schnaubelt (Villanova, 1997), 215–224; S. Theron, "Justice: Legal and Moral Debt in Aquinas," *American Catholic Philosophical Quarterly* 78, no. 4 (2004): 559–571; J. Porter, "Right Reason and the Love of God: The Parameters of Aquinas' Moral Theology," in *The Theology of Thomas Aquinas*, eds. R. Van Nieuwenhove and J. Wawrykow (Notre Dame, 2005), 167–191; J. P. Reilly, Jr., "Saint Thomas on Law," in *The Gilson Lectures on Thomas Aquinas*, eds. J. P. Reilly and E. Gilson (Toronto, 2008), 163–178; E. Marmursztejn, "Loi ancienne, loi nouvelle et normes chrétiennes dans la théologie scolastique du XIIIe siècle," *Revue de l'histoire des religions* 228, no. 4 (2011): 509–539.

82 J. Lorenc, "John of Freiburg and the Usury Prohibition in the Late Middle Ages: A Study in the Popularization of Medieval Canon Law" (PhD diss., University of Toronto, 2013).

83 T. Turley, "History and Legitimacy in the Dominican Responses to John of Pouilly," in *Inventing Modernity in Medieval European Thought ca. 1100–ca. 1550*, eds. C. J. Nederman and B. Koch (Kalamazoo, 2019): 53–70.

observation to the foreground, an observation upon which this work builds: theologians were well-rounded and did not necessarily make hard and fast distinctions between their sources. Law and theology informed each other.

As has been suggested though, the academic discipline of law at Paris has traditionally been viewed as secondary to that of theology. The dominance of Bologna as the center of legal studies and papal promotion of the study of theology at Paris leaves little room to dispute the traditional view, though Stephan Kuttner, Anne Lefebvre-Teillard, and Rudolf Weigand have done much to highlight the French school of canon law at Paris.[84] This school began with Stephan of Tournai in the mid-1160s, who studied canon and Roman law at Bologna and then returned to Orléans, compiling his *summa* to Gratian's *Decretum* ca. 1166 and becoming the abbot of St. Euverte, a Victorine house of canons regular, from 1168 to 1176. He then became the abbot of Ste. Geneviève in Paris, also a Victorine abbey of canons regular, from 1176 to 1192. He ended his career as bishop of Tournai from 1192 until his death in 1203.[85] Following on Stephan's heels were a number of anonymous commentaries on Gratian's *Decretum*. Following those were a series of decretal collections, collections that updated Gratian's *Decretum* that had brought together the *ius vetus* with the *ius novum* of the most recent papal decretals. The compilation of such collections, and with it the French school of canon law, declined with the statutes of Robert of Courçon for the masters and students of Paris and the Fourth Lateran Council (1215), both of which emphasized the importance of the study of theology. The activity of the French school of canon law is thought to have slowed with Honorius III's decretal *Super speculam* (ca. 1219), which banned the study of Roman law at Paris, though Gorochov recognizes a short-lived rebirth of canon law between 1230 and 1250. This brief revival owed much to the issuance of Pope Gregory IX's *Liber extra*, the teaching careers of well-known clerics such as the Hostiensis, and finally the

84 S. Kuttner, "Les débuts de l'école canoniste française," *Studia et documenta historiae et iuris* 4 (1938): 193–204; S. Kuttner and E. Rathbone, "Anglo-Norman Canonists of the Twelfth Century," *Traditio* 7 (1951): 279–358; S. Kuttner, *Gratian and the Schools of Law 1140–1234*, 2nd edn.; A. Lefebvre-Teillard, "Un maître parisien: Pierre Peverel. In memoriam alii magistri Petri," BMCL 36 (2019): 209–242; A. Lefebvre-Teillard, "L'école de droit parisienne (fin XIIe-début XIIIe siècle)," ZRG Kan. Abt. 136 (2019): 45–54; A. Lefebvre-Teillard, "Un précieux témoin de l'École de droit canonique parisienne à l'aube du XIIIe siècle: Le manuscrit 649 de la bibliothèque municipale de Douai," *Revue historique de droit français et étranger* 95 (2017): 1–57; R. Weigand, "The Transmontaine Decretists," in HMCL 2, 174–210; R. Weigand, *Glossatoren des Dekrets Gratians* (Keip, 1997); R. Weigand, "Die Dekretabbreviatio 'Exceptiones ecclesiasticarum regularum' und ihre Glossen," in *Christianità ed Europa: Miscellanea di studi in onore di Luigi Prosdocimi*, ed. C. Alzati (Rome, 1992), 1.511–529. A. Gouron has shed tremendous light on the teaching of law in southern France, see *La science du droit dans le Midi de la France au Moyen Age* (London, 1984).

85 Kalb, *Studien zur Summa Stephans von Tournai;* R. Weigand, "Studien Zum Kanonistischen Werk Stephans von Tournai," ZRG Kan. Abt. 72 (1986): 349–361.

high-profile condemnation of the Talmud that involved 14 doctor regents in canon law.[86]

Despite both the subordination of canon law to theology and Honorius III's ban on teaching Roman law at Paris in 1219, legal studies at Paris continued to retain some relevance at the turn of the fourteenth century, as evidenced by a list of textbooks and associated prices. The *Decretum* of Gratian and the *Liber extra* of Gregory IX were the two principal canonical collections studied. In addition to these collections, a student should also own the *summae* and the apparatuses: the ordinary gloss of Bartholomew of Brescia, the *summa* of Huguccio, and the commentaries on the *De penitentia* and the *De consecratione* of Petrus de Salinis (canonist from Besançon). Supplementing the *Liber extra* were the ordinary gloss of Bernard of Pavia, the *summa* of Geoffrey of Trani, the apparatus of Innocent IV, and the *summa* of Hostiensis and its apparatus. Students should also have the *Summa de casibus* of Raymond of Peñafort and its apparatus written by the Dominican William of Rennes. Treatises such as Bartholomew of Brescia's *Casus decretorum*; Bernard of Pavia's *Casus decretalium*; Roffredus Beneventanus's *Libelli de iure canonico*, which he wrote for civilians with little or no training in canon law, and as a useful introduction to procedure for canonists; William of Durantis's *Repertorium iuris canonici* (often published with his *Speculum iudiciale*); and Bernardus Compostellanus (junior)'s *Margarita ipsius* (i.e., *Summarium sive Margarita ad apparatum in Decretales Innocentii IV*) were expected to be owned. In the area of Roman law, students were expected to have the *Digest vetus* (Bk. 1–24.2) and its apparatus; the *Infortatium* (Bk. 24.3–38.17) and its apparatus; the *Digest novum* (Bk. 39.1–50.17) and its apparatus; the *Codex* and its apparatus; and the *Parvum volumen*—which contains the *Instituta*, *Authenticum*, *Usus feudoroum*, and the *Tres libri* of the *Codex* (the last three books, Bk. 10–12)—and its apparatus. This list of texts expected to be readily copied further reinforces that legal studies at Paris remained important.[87]

Whether as teachers, judge-delegates, or administrators, theologians would have benefited from a corpus of knowledge outside of their area of expertise. Twelfth-century theologians oriented toward matters of practice turned to Scripture and the canons to help in the work. John Van Engen dubbed them "practical theologians-canon lawyers." They, Van Engen went on to note, drew upon canons as they suited their purposes, and they did so without a strong sense of having crossed into another discipline (*scientia*) or body of learning. Law, in a sense, could be viewed as "applied" or "practical" theology.[88] Thus,

86 Gorochov, *Naissance de l'université*, 540–548.

87 Denifle, ed., *Chartularium Universitatis Parisiensis*, 1.530, pp. 648–649 with nn. 33–58. See the charter for the prices. For Honorius III's ban on the teaching of Roman law at Paris in his bull *Super speculam*, see Denifle, ed., *Chartularium Universitatis Parisiensis*, 1.32, pp. 90–93.

88 Van Engen, "From Practical Theology to Divine Law," 874–886, esp. 877.

the agency shown by theologians associated with the twelfth-century schools of Paris in their use of legal sources is an area ripe for further exploration. Though acknowledging the merit of the traditional view of theology's preeminence at Paris, this work argues that the *ius commune*—those principles of substantive law (the body of rules setting forth rights and obligations) and procedure that were in common use throughout Christendom found in canon law, Roman law, and the glosses—were woven into the fabric of a common intellectual tradition of Paris. While not denying that disciplines existed, this work looks past disciplinary silos that have played such a large role in the scholarship to focus on a climate that valued, and would have necessitated, intellectual permeability. Medieval thinkers did not necessarily see the disciplines as airtight but drew upon theology and law as needed to make the desired argument. Teachers of law and those of theology both presented contrary viewpoints in order to explore their implications and provide their students with the tools essential for their future careers. The scholastic culture in which each engaged necessitated both a knowledge of Gratian's *Decretum*, recent conciliar legislation, and contemporary papal decretals, as well as a knowledge of Peter Lombard. They complimented each other.[89] Teachers had overlapping responsibilities as Thierry Kouamé has shown. In addition to teaching, William of Champeaux also served as archdeacon of Paris, and Anselm was dean of the cathedral at Laon. Similar situations can be found in the dioceses of Châlons-en-Champagne, Bourges, Chartres, Paris, Tours, and Rouen, and in England where the chancellors also fulfilled the role traditionally assigned to scholasters which was to oversee the pedagogical functions of cathedral episcopal schools.[90] This work builds upon previous scholarship on the connections between Gratian and theologians such as Abelard,[91] Peter Lombard,[92]

89 J. Goering, "The Scholastic Turn (1100–1500): Penitential Theology and Law in the Schools," in *A New History of Penance*, ed. A. Firey (Leiden, 2008), 219–237.

90 T. Kouamé, "The Institutional Organization of the Schools," in *A Companion to Twelfth-Century Schools*, ed. C. Giraud (Leiden, 2020), 30–48.

91 For an introduction to Gratian and his theological models, see S. Kuttner, "Zur Frage der theologischen Vorlagen Gratians," rpt. idem *Gratian and the Schools of Law 1140–1234*, 2nd edn., no. v. The current thread of scholarship maintains that similarities between Gratian and Abelard lie not in their use of each other's works but rather in the intellectual climate. See D. E. Luscombe, *The School of Peter Abelard: The Influence of Abelard's Thought in the Early Scholastic Period* (Cambridge, 1969), 217; J. Wei, "Of Scholasticism and Canon Law: Narratives Old and New," in *New Discourses in Medieval Canon Law Research*, ed. C. Rolker (Leiden, 2019), 105–126.

92 See, for example, Larson, *Master of Penance*, 315–342. See also Kuttner, "Zur Frage der theologischen Vorlagen Gratians," 246–268; rpt. *Gratian and the Schools of Law, 1140–1234*, 2nd edn., no. iii. Kuttner examined, for example, the "Sententiae Magistri A," Anselm of Laon, Peter Lombard's *Sentences*, Hugh of St. Victor's *De Sacramentis*, and Abelard's *Sic et Non* as theological models for Gratian's *De penitentia* (C.33 q.3).

and Alger of Liège[93] by providing a study focused specifically on the law used by theology masters and how they used it within the context of contemporary thought and practice. It keeps at the fore the observation made by Joseph Goering who, within the context of cultivating a new history of penance, noted that it is important "to unravel the threads of [the] late medieval 'conflict of the faculties.'"[94] Rather than emphasizing the divisions, this work seeks to understand how theologians adapted canon law and for what ends.

Methodology of This Work

While recognizing that masters teaching at Paris in the twelfth century specialized in theology, this work stresses that theology was not an exclusive area of knowledge. Pivotal theologians, such as Hugh of St. Victor, Peter Lombard, Peter the Chanter, Robert of Courçon, Robert of Flamborough, and Thomas of Chobham, valued a working knowledge of Roman-canonical law, which had proliferated in circulation at the turn of the twelfth century in northern France. Furthermore, they tailored this knowledge to fit the environment in which they worked: teaching, administration on behalf of the papacy, hearing the confessions of the students of Paris, and as an *officialis* and subdean. This work thus focuses on a common intellectual climate that valued, and would have necessitated, intellectual permeability. It asks three central questions: what legal sources did these theologians find helpful; how did they adapt and use that legal knowledge; and how did that adaption and use correspond to contemporary legal thought?

Northern France was an area steeped in legal knowledge. Chapter 1, "Setting the Stage: Sharing and Producing Legal Collections in Northern France, ca. 1050–ca. 1130," shines a light on the proliferation in the production of law in the region, which, in turn, made it an area with a robust culture of law in the late eleventh and early twelfth century. The chapter lays the foundation for the chapters that follow by placing law into a wider cultural context of intellectual versatility. While there was no formal course of training in law—no formal curriculum per se—the proliferation of Roman-canonical thought at the turn of the twelfth century suggests that a working knowledge of it was valued as part of a wider liberal arts training designed to prepare individuals for administrative careers, careers that would require service in both the secular and ecclesiastical arenas. Networks of administrators, many of whom circled the orbit of the canonist-bishop Ivo of Chartres, worked and debated with one another, which, in turn, led to compilers and copiers sharing legal texts and adapting them to suit the needs of the users. Administrators, renowned in

93 G. LeBras, "Alger of Liège et Gratien," *Revue des Sciences Philosophiques et Théologiques* 20 (1931): 5–26.
94 Goering, "The Scholastic Turn (1100–1500)," 236–237.

theology, likewise would have engaged in this same environment, being exposed to the proliferation of legal texts. When relevant to their purpose, these theologians comfortably wove legal principles into their works.

Chapter 2, "Theologians and Their Engagement with Legal Knowledge," explores what legal sources the theologians discussed in subsequent chapters used and how they incorporated them. Hugh of St. Victor, Peter Lombard, Peter the Chanter, Robert of Courçon, Robert of Flamborough, and Thomas of Chobham engaged in a common intellectual tradition, a tradition in which tehology and law occupied the same academic space. The disciplinary boundaries between theology and law were porous. Our tehologians drew from the swath of legal knowledge available and used different techinquest to cite those sources. Some, such as Hugh of St. Victor and Peter Lombard, drew upon legal sources sparingly, while others, such as Peter the Chanter and his circle, were more robust in their usage. Nevertheless, they all drew upon those sources when they saw fit to do so, and they were familiar enough with the legal tradition that they could be versatile in their usage.

Chapter 3, "Hugh of St. Victor, Peter Lombard, and Northern French Canonical Collections: Intellectual Interplay on Marriage," uses marriage as a lens through which to understand the intellectual interplay and porous boundaries between theology and law on the cusp of the growth of the University of Paris. Hugh of St. Victor and Peter Lombard were very much a part of the dialogue surrounding marriage as a sacrament. They—along with Ivo of Chartres, the compiler of the *Collectio St. Victor*, Walter of Thérouanne, who possibly compiled the *Collectio decem partium*, and Gratian—thought and taught at a time questions about the formation of and ability to dissolve a marriage were bubbling to the forefront of conversations among and between theologians and canonists.

Within each of the central themes and connected subthemes, Hugh of St. Victor and Peter Lombard, on the whole, echoed one another, which, to some extent, makes sense as the latter drew on the former. How the topics were treated, however, differed, which, again, makes sense considering each's primary duties. A similar observation could be made of Ivo of Chartres, the author of the *Collectio canonum* of St. Victor, and Walter of Thérouanne. As a canon regular at St. Victor, Hugh approached marriage from the standpoint of monastic theology as the *De Sacramentis* both served as an exegetical treatise and provided spiritual instruction. A monastic framework offers a backdrop to the *Collectio canonum* of St. Victor which covers the high points of marital law quickly and efficiently. While both Hugh of St. Victor and Peter Lombard were teachers and committed to pastoral care, Peter approached the topics from the vantage point of a secular cleric and his role as archdeacon of Reims. Often using legal sources to do so, he tended to discuss specific situations that a cleric might come across ministering to the laity or in adjudicating a case. Similarly, the compiler of the *Collectio decem partium*, possibly Walter, archdeacon of Thérouanne, drilled into specific situations that could be missed in a detailed corpus of canon law such as Ivo's *Decretum*. The implicit and explicit back and forth reveals a complex interplay between theology, law, and the respective vantage point of the author.

With an established legal culture and a comfortability of theologians using the Roman-canonical tradition set forth, the work turns to focus on the *Libri penitentiales* and *Summae confessorum* that further facilitated the *cura animarum*. By making Paris the center of administration and commerce and by granting privileges to scholars, the Capetian dynasty created a city conducive for masters and students. Education both provided the pathway into ecclesiastical administrative positions in addition to thinking about the pastoral theologian's role in engaging with society. Extending the work of John Baldwin, the remaining chapters explore the manner in which secular masters—Peter the Chanter (Chapter 4); and his circle comprising Robert of Courçon (Chapter 5), Robert of Flamborough (Chapter 6), and Thomas of Chobham (Chapter 7)—used law in service of theology; they adapted Roman-canonical thought for their needs. The particular themes explored—excommunication in Peter the Chanter's *Summa de sacramentis et animae consiliis*, crusade activity and heresy in Robert of Courçon's *Summa penitentiae*, homicide in Robert of Flamborough's *Liber penitentialis*, and the sins associated with greed in Thomas of Chobham's *Summa confessorum*—can be seen as having a pragmatic element. The treatment of these particular issues suggests that their authors were thinking about the human context of the law: law serviced the on-the-ground needs of pastoral theology. Furthermore, this human context of the law reflected the environment in which each master worked: Peter the Chanter as a master at the school of Notre Dame teaching his students how to analytically navigate complex questions of pastoral care; Robert of Courçon as a papal judge-delegate, on the cusp of full-time administration on behalf of the papacy; Robert of Flamborough as the *penitentiarius* of St. Victor and the students at the University of Paris; and Thomas of Chobham as an *officialis* and subdean of Salisbury. Collectively they addressed jurisdictional and procedural questions, urban pastoral care, and diocesan management.

As Marcia Colish noted, scholastic thought from the eleventh to the fourteenth century encompassed thinkers in areas such as mathematics, logic, theology, and law.[95] An interesting feature of scholastic thought is how knowledge permeated disciplinary boundaries: theologians knew law, and lawyers knew theology. Scholar-administrators shared the same intellectual milieu. John Wei brought attention to this point in this challenge of the traditional narrative that linked Abelard's *Sic et Non* to Gratian's *Decretum*, arguing rather that there was no evidence to suggest Gratian used Abelard or that Gratian could

95 Marcia Colish, *Remapping Scholasticism* (Toronto, 2000), 1–21.

be attached to a particular school.[96] The climate of the schools framed their thought and influenced their practice. For example, Richard Southern pointed to how scholastics, such as the elder Peter of Blois, the younger Peter of Blois, John of Salisbury, and Vacarius, applied their learning to governmental service. They applied the knowledge they learned in the schools to practical use by adapting it to various needs.[97] The same applies to the pastoral theologians and penitential manuals. The intellectual milieu of the schools framed their thought and influenced their practice as they applied their learning to active ministry and the care of souls.

Law in a Culture of Theology: The Use of Canon Law by Parisian Theologians, ca. 1120–ca. 1220 neither seeks to diminish nor to deny the importance of theology at the University of Paris. At the core, I am interested in how theologians associated with the schools of Paris in the twelfth century drew upon legal thought, that is, the law they were drawing upon, for what end they were using it, and how their use of law fit into contemporary legal thought. This work argues that we need to consider the study of law within its intellectual environment and thus need to delve more deeply into how it engaged with and crossed disciplinary boundaries. And, while no one work can consider every angle and every facet (e.g., Stephen Langton, Geoffrey of Poitiers, and John of Kent are not discussed), I hope that this work widens the discussion. Theologians worked in an environment where lay and ecclesiastical jurisdictions would overlap. The audience their works served differed, and with that, so too did their need for and use of the law. Theologians needed to be intellectually versatile, and being known for their work in one discipline did not negate competency in another discipline. Law was woven into the fabric of the schools of Paris and their works betray at least a working knowledge of canon law and Roman law of the *ius commune*. We thus should not assume that disciplinary specialization means being walled off from other areas of knowledge. The secular masters at the University of Paris—at least the ones studied here—had a knowledge of law and they clearly studied it and used it, even if it was not their primary area of expertise. They saw law as serving theology and the needs of urban pastoral care, as well as being important for answering jurisdictional, procedural, and administrative questions.

96 Wei, "Of Scholasticism and Canon Law," 105–126. Heinrich Denifle first espoused, and Friedrich Thaner set out to prove, the traditional narrative with which Wei engages. Paul Fournier expanded the narrative to incorporate Ivo of Chartres. According to Fournier, Gratian took his method from Abelard and other theologians, but both Gratian and Abelard drew upon Ivo, and Ivo was inspired by Pope Urban II to develop his hermeneutics.

97 R. W. Southern, *Scholastic Humanism and the Unification of Europe, Vol. II: The Heroic Age* (Oxford, 1997), 4–5.

1

SETTING THE STAGE

Sharing and Producing Legal Collections in Northern France, ca. 1050–ca. 1130

Introduction

The working knowledge of legal principles woven into twelfth-century theological works was not done so in a vacuum. Networks of administrators, many of whom circled the orbit of the canonist-bishop Ivo of Chartres, worked and debated with one another, which, in turn, led to compilers and copiers sharing legal texts and adapting them to suit the needs of the users. Administrators, renowned in theology, would have engaged in this same environment, being exposed to the proliferation of legal texts.

A Region's Legal Culture

Quite literally paving the way for the spread of intellectual activity from England to Rome was the *Via Francigena*, which served as the main pilgrimage route from Canterbury to Rome beginning in the tenth century. It facilitated the dissemination of legal knowledge. Canonical collections, *farragines* (collections without a particular internal order), legal texts, and people steeped in legal learning easily traveled along this route which included, for example, Canterbury, Arras, Laon, Reims, and Pavia. In particular, the route between Châlons-sur-Marne (69th station) and Thérouanne (77th station) was of considerable significance for the development of canon law in northern Europe in the late eleventh and early twelfth centuries, with Reims as a central hub (70th station). Clerics accessed different libraries—be it cathedral or monastic—and copied legal texts of particular interest to them. As Christof Rolker has noted, teachers and students traveled between centers of learning such as Reims, Liège, Chartres,

DOI: 10.4324/9781003465096-2

Beauvais, Laon, Paris, and Orléans.[1] Drawing upon one another, a number of collections would be compiled along the *Via Francigena*. *Collectio Sinemuriensis* was compiled at Reims. Bernold of Constance, the compiler of *Collectio Atrebatensis*, possibly the collection in Cambridge, Corpus Christi College, MS 442, the second version of *Liber Tarraconensis*, and the *Collectio II librorum* all drew upon this collection. The *Collectio Atrebatensis* was probably compiled at Arras and employed Burchard of Worms' *Decretum*, the *Collectio Sinemuriensis*, and the *Collectio Hibernensis*. The collection in Cambridge, Corpus Christi College 442, which drew from the *Collectio Atrebatensis*, was compiled at or near Thérouanne. The chronologically arranged pseudo-Isidorian *Collectio canonum Brugensisis* was compiled in Flanders. The *Collectio IX librorum* (aka *Collectio de Thérouanne* or *Collectio Sangermanensis IX voluminum*), which also drew from the *Collectio Atrebatensis*, is often credited to John of Warneton, bishop of Thérouanne (d. 1130). The *Collectio decem partium* was also compiled along the *Via Francigena*. This collection relied heavily on the *Collectio IX librorum* and the *Panormia*, in addition to drawing from the *Collectiones Catalaunenses* (i.e., the *Catalaunensis I* and *II*). The appendices to the *Panormia*, which contained the canons unique in the *Collectio decem partium*, also spread along the *Via Francigena*.[2]

The *Collectio Britannica* and the *Collectio canonum* in Paris, Bibliothèque de l'Arsenal, MS 713 (fol. 117r–192v) were important sources for legal texts included in other collections. The *Collectio Britannica*, compiled shortly after 1090, survives in one manuscript London, British Library, Additional 8873. Though compiled in northern France and perhaps specifically for use at Chartres, the canonist Ivo of Chartres, who will be discussed below, was not known to have used this manuscript.[3] The Roman law texts found in the two

1 C. Rolker, *Canon Law in the Age of Reforms (c. 1000 to c. 1150)* (Washington D.C., 2024), 287. For an analysis of canonical collections in northern France at the dawn of the French schools—*Collectio Lanfranci*, *Collectio Britannica*, *Tripartita*, Ivo's *Decretum*, Alger of Liège, *Panormia*, and *Caesaraugustana*—see pages 287–420. Rolker delves into biography, overview of the collection, date and structure, formal sources, uses, overall themes with case studies of specific themes, and influence.

2 L. Fowler-Magerl, "The Collection and Transmission of Canon Law along the Northern Section of the *Via Francigena* in the Eleventh and Twelfth Centuries," in *Bishops, Texts and the Use of canon Law Around 1100: Essays in Honour of Martin Brett*, eds. B. C. Brasington and K. G. Cushing (Farnham, 2008), 129–139; C. Rolker, *Canon Law and the Letters of Ivo of Chartres* (Cambridge, 2010), 70–71, 82.

3 P. Fournier and G. Le Bras, *Histoire des Collections Canonique en Occident: Depuis les Fausses Décrétales jusqu'au Décret de Gratien, Vol. 2: De la réforme grégorienne au Décret de Gratien* (Paris, 1932), 155–163; L. Fowler-Magerl, *Clavis Canonum Clavis Canonum: Selected Canon Law Collections Before 1140* (Hannover, 2005), 184–187; L. Kéry, *Canonical Collections in the Early Middle Ages, ca. 400–1140: A Bibliographic Guide to the Manuscripts and Literature* (Washington D.C., 1999), 237–238. For the *Collectio Britannica*'s inclusion of decretals from Urban II's early pontificate, see R. Somerville, "The Letters of Pope Urban II in the *Collectio Britannica*," in *Proceedings Cambridge 1984*, ed. P. Linehan (Vatican City, 1998), 103–114.

Varia sections of the *Collectio Britannica* include substantial fragments from the *Digest vetus* placed at the end of the collection after the decretals of Pope Alexander II.[4] Jean Gaudemet has noted that the *Collectio Britannica* exemplifies the triumph of Justinianic law and may very well be the earliest example of the use of the *Digest* in a canonical collection.[5] The *Collectio canonum* in Arsenal 713, oftentimes referred to as *Arsenal 713B*, dates from the early twelfth century and was possessed by the library of St. Victor in Paris by 1200, a library known to have had a number of Chartrain manuscripts.[6] The *Collectio Britannica* and *Arsenal 713B* share a close relationship, as the latter includes texts known only from the former. Not only did *Arsenal 713B* exploit and thus resemble the *Collectio Britannica*, but it also served as a preparatory work for the earliest stages of two tremendously important northern French canonical collections: the *Decretum* of Bishop Ivo of Chartres and the *Panormia*.[7] Ivo most likely used an unknown intermediary collection, though one similar but in an incomplete form, to that found in *Arsenal 713B*, for his texts from

4 C. Rolker, "History and Canon Law in the *Collectio Britannica*: A New Date for London, BL Add. 8873," in *Bishops, Texts and the Use of Canon Law around 1100: Essays in Honour of Martin Brett*, eds. B. C. Brasington and K. G. Cushing (Aldershot, 2008), 141–152, here 141–142. In addition to Roman law, the *Varia* sections include decretals and patristic texts. Rolker maintained (pp. 143–145) that the London manuscript was compiled sometime after 1108 on account of the parallels between *Variae II*, 14 and letter 189 of Ivo of Chartres defending the coronation of King Louis VI, a ceremony performed by the Archbishop of Sens as opposed to the Archbishop of Reims who had traditionally coronated the Capetians kings. Pope Urban II had likewise affirmed the Archbishop of Reims' right to conduct the coronation.

5 J. Gaudemet, "Le droit romain dans la pratique et chez les docteurs aux XIe et XIIe siècles," *Cahiers de civilization médiévale* 8, no. 31–32 (1965): 365–380, here 377.

6 On *Arsenal 713A* as a copy of the *Panormia*, see Fowler-Magerl, *Clavis canonum*, 192–193. Greta Austin has confirmed ideas posited by Martin Brett and Christof Rolker that *Arsenal 713B* may, in fact, represent two separate collections—*Arsenal I* and *Arsenal II*—that may have been compiled on loose pages or quires. The meshing of the two collections into one, as represented in Arsenal 713B, suggests that the pages or quires had become disorganized. *Arsenal I* omitted texts from Burchard of Worm's *Decretum*, and *Arsenal II* only occasionally included such texts. Both Ivo's *Decretum* and the *Collectio Britannica* drew upon the collection. See G. Austin, "Were There Two Arsenal Collections? Arsenal 713B and the Ivonian Panormia," in *Canon Law, Religion, and Politics: Liber Amicorum Robert Somerville*, eds. U-R Blumenthal, A. Winroth, and P. Landau (Washington D.C., 2012), 3–14; M. Brett, "The Sources and Influence of Paris, Bibliothèque de l'Arsenal MS 713," in *Proceedings Munich 1992*, eds. P. Landau and J. Müller (Vatican City, 1997), 149–167, here 149–150; R. Somerville, "Papal Excerpts in Arsenal MS 713B: Alexander II and Urban II," in *Proceedings Munich 1992*, 169–184, here 170.

7 M. Brett, "The Sources and Influence of Paris, Bibliothèque de l'Arsenal MS 713," 150–159, 167. Virtually all of the canons in the *Panormia* that are found in the *Collectio Britannica* but not found in Ivo's *Decretum* are found in *Arsenal 713B*. Brett did note that while the greater part of the canons in *Arsenal 713B* were included in Ivo's *Decretum*, there are no significant contributions to ID Books 2–3, 6, and 15 and none at all to Bk. 17 (p. 151).

Roman law.[8] The connections between the four collections—*Collectio Britannica*, *Arsenal 713B*, Ivo of Chartres' *Decretum*, and the *Panormia*—in addition to the compilation of the *Tripartita A*, suggested to Martin Brett that there very well may have been a "school" of northern French canonists, possibly at Chartres, around the year 1100.[9]

As the *Collectio Britannica* bears witness, Roman law in the late eleventh and early twelfth century was not unknown in northern France. It had been preserved in the early Middle Ages in different forms: extracts and *florilegia* recounting the juridical debate involving Hincmar of Reims, as well as the councils of Hincmar and his canonical collection *Opusculum LV capitulorum*;[10] formularies; charters; cartularies; and the *Pseudo-Isidorian Decretals*, for example.[11] There were also a number of sources used directly. The *Epitome Juliani* represents a lecture course given by Julian, the best-known law professor at Constantinople, on—and provides a summary of—the 124 Greek *Novellae* of Justinian (d. 565). As Simon Corcoran has noted, its use in teaching at Constantinople may not have extended far past Justinian's death as Justin II (d. 578) closed the law school. The *Epitome Juliani* lived on, however, as it was very well known in Italy and Gaul until the twelfth century when the *Authenticum*, Justinian's official Latin compilation promised for Italy, was rediscovered.[12] The *Breviarium Alarici*, also known as the *Lex Romana Visigothorum*, was compiled at the request of Alaric II in 506 and comprises of: the *Theodosian Code* (16 bks) compiled in 438; the *Novels* of Theodosius II, Valentinian III, Marcian, Majorian, and Libius Severus; the *Institutes* of Gaius; the *Sententiae Receptae* of Julius Paulus (5 bks); the *Gregorian Code* (13 titles); *Hermogenian Code* (2 titles); and the *Responsa Papiniani* (fragment of the first book). Justinian's *Corpus iuris civilis* was also used, though less so. The *Institutes* remained known throughout the early medieval period. There is some evidence that the *Digestum vetus* (Books 1–24.2) and the *Infortatium* (Books 24.3–38.17) were used, as were Books 1–9 of the *Codex*.[13] As

8 Antonia Fiori has examined the Roman law texts found in the *Collectio Britannica*. She rightly argued that Ivo did not draw the texts he incorporated into his collections from the version of the *Collectio Britannica* contained in the London manuscript. With her focus on the *Collectio Britannica* and not *Arsenal 713B*, Fiori posited that Ivo could have taken the Roman law texts from another, no longer extant, version of the *Collectio Britannica* or, more interestingly, he would have consulted sources similar to the compiler of the *Collectio Britannica* —the libraries and archives of the papal curia. Ivo was in Rome between November 1093 and January 1094. See A. Fiori, "La 'Collectio Britannica' e la riemersione del Digesto," RIDC 9 (1998): 81–121, here 109–110.

9 Brett, "The Sources and Influence of Paris, Bibliothèque de l'Arsenal MS 713," 159–160.

10 Cdp 2.23.3.2 and 2.28.1.1 are also found in Pan. 2.43 and 2.50. They are also found in Reg. I of Hincmar of Reims. For example, 2.28.1.1 is found in Reg. I, 222. Cdp 6.20.1 is found in Pan. 1.224 and Hincmar's *Opusculum LV* c.28 and c.30.

11 Gaudemet, "Le droit romain dans la pratique et chez les docteurs aux XIe et XIIe siècles," 367–369.

12 S. Corcoran, "UCL Volterra Project," https://www.ucl.ac.uk/volterra/texts/epitome-iuliani.

13 S. Kuttner, "Harmony from Dissonance: An Interpretation of Medieval Canon Law," in *Wimmer Lecugre X, 1956, St. Vincent College* (Latrobe, 1960), 6. J. Gaudemet, however, has

with the *Authenticum* (the *Novellae Constitutiones*), however, the *Digestum novum* (Books 39.1–50.17) and Books 10–12 of the *Codex* (the *Tres libri*) were not rediscovered until the twelfth century.[14] The *Digest novum* was not taught until the middle of the twelfth century when it was done so by the four doctors (Bulgarus de Bulgarinis, Martinus Gosia, Hugo da Porta Ravennate, and Jacobus de Porta Ravennate) at Bologna.[15]

Law was also critical to monastic prerogatives.[16] The *Diversorum partum sententiae* (*Collection in Seventy-Four Titles*; *74T*), now thought to have been compiled around Reims,[17] emphasized papal primacy to protect monastic liberties. The collection, which drew heavily upon the *Pseudo-Isidorian Decretals*, is, yes, concerned principally with the primacy of the Roman church, but also with criminal and other legal procedures affecting the clergy, the quality of a candidate put forth for clerical office and whether simony was involved, and the powers of ministers in the church.[18] It is this emphasis on papal primacy, an emphasis characteristic of Italian collections but not of collections of northern France, that led scholars to see the *74T* as a collection with a monastic agenda, one using papal primacy to formulate an argument in support of the freedom of a monastery from outside interference. The choice of texts in titles two and three show a clear concern with the privileges of religious communities, thus linking the theme of papal authority, found in the first title, with monastic rights. The compiler either purposefully chose texts that favored monastic houses or adapted Pseudo-Isidorian texts to favor monasteries. The compiler thus intended to circumscribe the authority of bishops. For example, the compiler altered the Pseudo-Gregory I canon "Quam sit necessarium"

---

argued that the *Digest* was not used, and the *Codex* was unknown in Gaul and quickly forgotten in Italy, although it initially had a little more success there because of the *Sententiae Pauli*. The *Institutes* were studied and glossed, but they too did not cross the Alps. See "Le droit romain dans la pratique et chez les docteurs aux XIe et XIIe siècles," 366–367.

14 M. Bellomo, *The Common Legal Past of Europe, 1000–1800*, 2nd edn., trans. L. G. Cochrane (Washington D.C., 1995), 61.

15 W. P. Müller, "The Rediscovery of Justinian's Digest in the Middle Ages," BMCL 20 (1990): 3.

16 For a fresh analysis of monastic engagement with the law, see C. Rolker, *Canon Law in the Age of Reforms*, 84–185.

17 Because of the emphasis on papal primacy, Gilchrist had attributed an Italian origin to the collection; see *Diversorum patrum sententie sive Collectio in LXXIV titulos digesta*, ed. J. Gilchrist (Vatican City, 1973), xxii; J. Gilchrist, trans., *The Collection in Seventy-Four Titles: A Canon Law Manual of the Gregorian Reform* (Toronto, 1980); 2. J. Gilchrist, "Changing the Structure of a Canonical Collection: The *Collection in Seventy-Four Titles*, Four Books, and the Pseudo- Isidorian Decretals," in *Iure Veritas: Studies in Canon Law in Memory of Schafer Williams*, eds. S. B. Bowman and B. E. Cody (Cincinnati, 1991), 93–117, here 93–94. For additional historiography on its Italian origin, see C. Rolker, "The *Collection in Seventy-Four Titles*: A Monastic Canon Law Collection from Eleventh-Century France," in *Readers, Texts and Compilers in the Earlier Middle Ages: Studies in Medieval Canon Law in Honour of Linda Fowler-Magerl*, eds. M. Brett and K. G. Cushing (Aldershot, 2009), 59–72, here 60–62.

18 Gilchrist, trans., *The Collection in Seventy-Four Titles*, 17, 23–26; Rolker, "The *Collection in Seventy-Four Titles*," 60.

(JE †1366) so that the text would authorize abbots—not bishops—to solve internal conflicts and conflicts over monastic property. The alterations to Pseudo-Isidorian texts and the compilation date of the late eleventh century correspond to the trend toward monastic liberties and exemptions from episcopal control. The *74T* was a popular collection in monastic houses. Monastic libraries either copied or owned a large portion of the existing manuscripts, such as the copy in the cartulary at St. Denis.[19]

At the abbey of St. Victor, William of Champeaux, who had studied at the renowned theological school at Laon,[20] possibly inspired the collection *Collectio canonum* (Paris, Bibliothèque de l'Arsenal, MS 721, fol. 165ra–250vb) where it may have been copied around 1125.[21] The collection drew from the books of Burchard of Worm's *Decretum* but omitted those books that did not suit the compiler's needs: Books 4–6 (sacraments, homicide), Book 8 (men and women), Book 10 (divination and magic), Books 13–14 (fasting and drunkenness), Book 18 (visitation and last rights), and Book 20 (penance). The compiler then supplemented the collection with texts drawn from *Pseudo-Isidorian Decretals*; from a version of the *74T* with an appendix compiled at the abbey of St. Blasien in the south of Hirasu (known as the "Swabian Appendix"); from Martin of Braga's "Ex decretis Orientalium Patrum"; and possibly from the *Codex Udalrici*, a pro-German collection of poems, official records, and documents dedicated Bishop Gebhard of Würzburg in 1125. It begins with two *ordines*, one for a provincial synod and one for a diocesan synod. The nine books are devoted to (1) the authority and privileges of the Roman Church, archbishops, and bishops; (2) ordinations and regulations for other clergy, including canons prohibiting simony and, in particular, nicolaitism; (3) churches, liturgy, ecclesiastical properties and possessions; (4) excommunications and consequences; (5) oaths, perjury, penance; (6) emperors, kings, princes, and laity; (7) juridical procedures and problems; (8) incest and fornication; and (9) marriage.[22] In addition to the liturgical and theological material seamlessly woven into canonical texts, the excerpts taken from the *Codex Udalrici* demonstrate

19 Fowler-Magerl, *Clavis Canonum Clavis Canonum*, 116; Rolker, "The *Collection in Seventy-Four Titles*," 65–70. No copy can be shown to have come from an episcopal library.

20 On the Laon's library, see J. Contreni, "The Formation of Laon's Cathedral Library in the Ninth Century," in *Carolingian Learning, Masters and Manuscripts* (London, 1992), no. XIII.

21 U-R Blumenthal, "The Collection of S. Victor (=V), Paris: Liturgy, Canon Law, and Polemical Literature," in *Ritual, Text and Law: Studies in Medieval Canon Law and Liturgy Presented to Roger E. Reynolds*, eds. K. G. Cushing and R. F. Gyug (Aldershot, 2004), 293–307, here 294; Paris, Bibliothèque de l'Arsenal, lat. 721, fol. 165r–250v.

22 Blumenthal, "The Collection of S. Victor (=V), Paris," 294–295, 297. Book 1 (fols. 170r–175ra); Book 2 (fols. 175ra–192rb); Book 3 (fols. 193ra–207r); Book 4 (fols. 207ra–222va); Book 5 (fols. 222vb–228ra); Book 6 (fols. 229ra–239rb); Book 7 (fols. 239rb–244ra); Book 8 (fols. 244rb–251vb); Book 9 (fols. 252vb–257r).

an interest in the affairs between *regnum* and *sacerdotium* that took place in Germany between 1060 and 1125.[23]

Ivo of Chartres and the Proliferation of the Legal Culture

Ivo of Chartres has traditionally been associated with Bec as a student of Lanfranc and a contemporary of Anselm of Canterbury. Though writing in the 1150s, Robert of Torigni spent much of his career at Bec, and both he and Hugh the Chanter attest to Ivo's presence there.[24] Ivo received the same type of training as was common for the time: a thorough grounding in the *trivium* and the *artes liberales*, which in turn prepared students to serve in their administrative function as either abbots or bishops.[25] They used the skills They learned to select the sources relevant to their needs in order to compile the collections that suited them, whatever that may have been. While at Chartres, Ivo had access to a number of legal texts, though Brett and Brasington have excluded the *Collectio Lanfranci* as a formal source for Ivo's canonical collections. The cathedral had access to or possessed copies of: the *Pseudo-Isidore Decretales*,[26] the *Collectio Abbreviatio Anegisi et Benedicti Levitae*,[27] a copy of Pope Gregory I's register,[28] an abbreviation of the *Collectio Hibernensis*,[29] the *Breviarium*

23 P. Fournier, "Collections Issues du Décret de Burchard," in *Mélanges Paul Fabre: Études d'histoire du Moyen Age* (Paris, 1902), 199–203; Fournier and Le Bras, *Histoire des Collections Canonique en Occident*, 2.261–265; Fowler-Magerl, *Clavis Canonum*, 237–238; Kéry, *Canonical Collections in the Early Middle Ages*, 288; Blumenthal, "The Collection of St. Victor (=V), Paris," 293–308.

24 S. Vaughn, "Lanfranc at Bec: A Reinterpretation," *Albion* 17, no. 2 (1985): 135–148, here 136; Robert of Torigni, *Chronicle*, in *Chronicles of the Reigns of Stephen, Henry II, and Richard II*, ed. R. Howlett, 4 vols (London, 1884–1889; rpt. Wiesbaden, 1964.), 4.100; Hugh the Chanter, *The History of the Church of York, 1066–1127*, ed. and trans. C. Johnson (London, 1961), 2; Rolker, *Canon Law and the Letters of Ivo of Chartres*, 7 has maintained that claims for Ivo being a student of Lanfranc of Bec are not decisive, and there is no evidence for him studying at Paris or at Laon.

25 B. Brasington, "Lessons of Love: Bishop Ivo of Chartres as Teacher," in *Teaching and Learning in Northern Europe, 1000–1200*, eds. S. N. Vaughn and J. Rubenstein (Turnhout, 2006), 129–147, here 131–133, 136. In noting the importance that the teaching of canon law played in the development of universities, James Brundage pointed to the often-repeated trope of the University of Paris: the liberal arts were taught first, then theology, and finally, a bit later canon law, civil, law, and medicine. See J. Brundage, "Teaching Canon Law," in *Learning Institutionalized: Teaching in the Medieval University*, ed. J. Van Engen (Notre Dame, 2000), 177–196, here 177–178.

26 Vat. Ottob. lat. 93; Ministere de l'Instruction Publique et des Beaux-Arts, *Catalogue Général des Manuscrits des Bibliothéques de France, XI Chartres* (Paris, 1890), Chartres BM 26, 193, and 376.

27 See Rolker, *Canon Law and the Letters of Ivo of Chartres*, 57–58 for a discussion of Fulbert of Chartres's use of the collection.

28 Ministere de l'Instruction Publique et des Beaux-Arts, *Catalogue Général des Manuscrits des Bibliothéques de France, XI Chartres* (Paris, 1890), Chartres BM 50.

29 Ministere de l'Instruction Publique et des Beaux-Arts, *Catalogue Général des Manuscrits des Bibliothéques de France, XI Chartres*, Chartres BM 124.

Alarici,[30] a collection of capitulary canons, the letter collection of canonist-bishop Fulbert of Chartres (d. 1028),[31] and numerous manuscripts of Saint Augustine's writings.[32] As noted above, Ivo may have also known of the *Collectio Britannica* (London, BL Add. 8873), which contains decretal and Roman law (*Digestum vetus* with one from *Digestum novum*) material through an intermediary source.[33]

Ivo, like Lanfranc, demonstrated a concern for good administration. Ivo's *Prologue* addressed the importance of *caritas* and *misericordia*, both of which the judge was to keep at the forefront of his mind as he used dispensations as a way to restore order and harmony. Ivo identified *preceptiones immobiles* (invoked the unchanging *lex eterna*), *preceptiones mobiles* (an historical tradition that was authoritative based on necessity and utility), *prohibitiones immobiles* (pertained to matters of discipline and practice, and to the tenets of faith), and *prohibitiones mobiles* (deliberation of the historical context). Judges could use dispensations as a way to navigate *prohibitiones mobiles* and, as such, enact legal change.[34] Having been trained for administration, Ivo was not concerned with the source and agent of patristic texts, unlike polemists such as Peter Crassus, Bonizo of Sutri, and Peter Damian. Ivo saw dispensation as a medicine to heal and thus was concerned with the nature and limits of dispensation, a right that he felt belonged to the episcopacy. He focused not on papal primacy but on how the law applied to the Church and, to that end, on the systemization and defining of legal norms in order to balance rigor and mercy.[35]

Ivo of Chartres has often been associated as the compiler of the *Tripartita A*, *Decretum*, *Tripartita B*, and the *Panormia*. Christof Rolker, however, most recently has shown that he did not compile the *Panormia*. The collection drew upon different sources than those used to compile the *Tripartita A* and the

30 See Rolker, *Canon Law and the Letters of Ivo of Chartres*, 55–57 for a discussion of Fulbert of Chartres use of the collection.

31 See Rolker, *Canon Law and the Letters of Ivo of Chartres*, 57–58.

32 Ministere de l'Instruction Publique et des Beaux-Arts, *Catalogue Général des Manuscrits des Bibliothéques de France, XI Chartres*, for example Chartres BM 65, 86–88, 93, and 104.

33 Rolker, *Canon Law and the Letters of Ivo of Chartres*, 55 n.23, 57, 92–93, 95, 97, 99. While Fournier argued that the compiler of the *Collectio Britannica* drew on the *Tripartita* and *Decretum*, Kuttner has contested this point and argued that, in fact, Ivo used the *Collectio Britannica*. The *Prologus* took a quote from the *Institutes* (Inst. 1.1.2.6) either from the *Collectio Britannica* directly or the *Collectio Britannica* via the *Decretum* (97). JE 3180, a decretal of Pope John VIII, is found in a very similar version both in *Decretum* and in *Collectio Britannica*, but there is no evidence for where it was taken.

34 B. Brasington, *Ways of Mercy: The Prologue of Ivo of Chartres, Edition and Analysis* (Münster, 2004), 34–36, 40.

35 Brasington, *Ways of Mercy: The Prologue of Ivo of Chartres, Edition and Analysis*, 11, 30–31, 42–43, 74, 77.

Decretum.[36] Though the compiler of the *Panormia* did take nine-tenths of the canons from Ivo's *Decretum*, he reworked them.[37] While Ivo may not have compiled the *Panormia*, it was influenced by Chartres and compiled north of the Loire between ca. 1095 and ca. 1118, probably around 1115. It remains possible that the *Panormia* originated at Chartres and that Hildebert of Lavardin could have compiled it. He was in close contact with Ivo and is often called his pupil. He knew the *Decretum* and *Prologue*. However, nothing in his correspondence suggests a connection between him and the *Panormia*. Paris has been suggested as another option for the compilation of the *Panormia*. In 1095, Ivo supported William of Montfort (d. 1101), apparently his pupil, as bishop of Paris. He also supported his pupil Galo in 1104 when he transferred to the see of Paris. In 1116, Galo was succeeded by Gilbert (d. 1123) as bishop of Paris; he, too, was Ivo's student.[38] On account of Ivo's *Prologue* being attached, other collections have often been associated with him as well: the *Collectio decem partium* and the *Collectio Catalaunensis II*, which is dependent on the *Collectio decem partium*.[39]

Circling the Orbit of Ivo

After his departure from Bec in 1067 to become the first abbot of the Augustinian house of St. Quentin in Beauvais, a position he held for almost 20 years before becoming bishop of Chartres in 1090, Ivo sat at the heart of the archdiocese of Reims and thus exposed to the circulation of legal texts.[40] While abbot, he taught John of Warneton (future bishop of Thérouanne), Lambert (future bishop of Arras), and Ernulf (future abbot of Christ Church in Canterbury and eventually bishop of Rochester).[41] Lambert of Arras, John of Thérouanne, and Ivo of Chartres—along with Baudry of Noyon-Tournai, Manasses of Cambrai and his uncle Archbishop Manasses II of Reims—would be dubbed the "Band of Brothers" by John Ott. This group, along with their wider circle, engaged with one another throughout their careers at provincial councils and in the course of administrative challenges. Collectively, they exemplify the level of learnedness of the episcopate in the *trivium* with

36 The compiler of the *Panormia* did not draw upon Burchard's *Decretum*; the *Collectio Britannica*; *Tripartita A*; or minor sources such as part four of the *Quadripartitus*, the *Collectio Sinemuriensis*, or *TC* (Paris, BnF, lat. 13368, fol 9r–20v). These collections would have been at Ivo's disposal.

37 Rolker, *Canon Law and the Letters of Ivo of Chartres*, 59, 124–125.

38 Rolker, *Canon Law and the Letters of Ivo of Chartres*, 59, 285–288.

39 Rolker, *Canon Law and the Letters of Ivo of Chartres*, 29–30, 134.

40 Brasington, "Lessons of Love: Bishop Ivo of Chartres as Teacher," 133; Rolker, *Canon Law and the Letters of Ivo of Chartres*, 91. Both Brasington and Rolker believe that Ivo's time at St. Quentin may have been formative to his engagement with canon law.

41 Rolker, *Canon Law and the Letters of Ivo of Chartres*, 89.

extensive expertise in theology and canon law.[42] Lambert of Arras was close personal friends with Ivo of Chartres and Archbishop Anselm of Canterbury.[43] Both Ivo and Lambert were opponents of King Philip I's adulterous marriage to Bertrada of Montfort. Ivo also scuffled with the papal legal Hugh of Lyon over his deposition or suspension of 34 bishops, including Manasses of Reims, and 18 prelates.[44] Lambert was connected to Archbishop Manassas of Reims, as the latter wrote the former asking for his participation in the ordination of the bishop-elect of Cambrai, his nephew Manassas who was an archdeacon of Reims.[45] Lambert also assisted in securing the elevation of John of Warneton to the see of Thérouanne.[46] John had been a regular canon at Mont-Saint-Eloi, which was a few kilometers from Arras. As noted above, John Warneton may have compiled the *Collectio IX librorum* (ca. 1100) while serving as bishop of Thérouanne. Hugh of Châlons may have compiled the *Collectio Catalunensis I* (Châlons-en-Champagne, BM 47, fols. 1–57). While serving as bishop of Châlon (1113–1121), William of Champeaux would teach both Peter Abelard and Josselin of Vierzy. As bishop of Soissons (1126–1152), Josselin would become Peter Abelard's antagonist. Archbishop Manasses I of Reims (ca. 1069–1080) was a student of Lanfranc of Bec and Herimann of Reims. Both Enguerran, bishop of Laon (1098–1104), and Walter II, bishop of Laon (1155–1174), may have studied under Godfrey, the schoolmaster at Reims from ca. 1076/77–1094/95. Alberic, bishop-elect of Châlons (1126–1127) and later archbishop of Bourges (1136–1141), was schoolmaster at Reims from 1117 to 1136 and had been a student of Anselm of Laon.[47]

As with those known for theology, legal knowledge spreads from master to student even if there is no record of a formal curriculum. Lambert, having studied under Ivo, earned a reputation for his legal knowledge and his letters state he possessed a background in canon law.[48] He preserved canons issued by Pope Urban II at Clermont in 1095 and at Rome in April 1099 in his *Codex* or

42 J. Ott, *Bishops, Bishops, Authority, and Community in Northwestern Europe c.1050–1150* (Cambridge, 2015), 47 nn. 85–86, 112–123.

43 Ivo and Anselm correspondence in PL 162, cols. 46–47 (no. 33) and 117 (no. 97).

44 Rolker, *Canon Law and the Letters of Ivo of Chartres*, 2–3. See also K. R Rennie, *Law and Practice in the Age of Reform: The Legatine Work of Hugh of Die (1073–1106)* (Turnhout, 2010), esp. Chapter 6 on reform efforts in France.

45 *Le register de Lambert, évêque d'Arras (1093–1115)*, ed. and trans. C. Giordangengo (Paris, 2007), no. 10, 342–343.

46 Walter of Thérouanne, *Vita domini oannis Morinensis episcopi*, ed. J. Rider (Turnhout, 2006); L. Kéry, *Die Errichtung des Bistums Arras 1093/1094* (Ostfildern, 1994), 356; *Le register de Lambert*, 25–27. Rolker is a bit more skeptical of John of Warneton as a student of Ivo, see *Canon Law and the Letters of Ivo of Chartres*, 241 n. 184.

47 Ott, *Bishops, Bishops, Authority, and Community in Northwestern Europe c.1050–1150*, 47 nn. 85–86, 112–123; J. R. Williams, "Cathedral School of Reims in the Time of Master Alberic, 1118–1136," *Traditio* 20 (1964): 93–114.

48 *Le register de Lambert*, 27–30.

Liber Lamberti.[49] The canons, if not recorded by Lambert personally, may have been recorded by his archdeacon, John Warneton, at his request as a way to expand the law library for the diocese.[50] Both lay and ecclesiastics from Soisson, Beauvais, Chartres, Reims, Nantes, and as far away as Metz consulted him for legal advice.[51] As Lambert's archdeacon, John Warneton, a former student of Ivo, was likewise known for his legal acumen. He signed charters drawn up under Lambert's episcopal tenure.[52] John served as bishop of Thérouanne from 1099 to 1130, and he maintained relationships with both Ivo and Lambert.[53] John was present at the Councils of Clermont (1095), Troyes (1107), Beauvais (1114), and Reims (1119); as well as at the provincial synods Saint-Omer (1100), Reims (1103, 1115), and Beauvais (1120).[54]

The connection between Lambert and John, and thus between Arras and Thérouanne, gave rise to numerous canonical collections aside from the *Liber Lamberti*. The *Collectio Atrebatensis* was compiled before 1100 either at the cathedral library or in the vicinity of Arras. Both Alphons Van Hove and Joseph Marie De Smet credited John for its compilation either during his time as a canon regular at Mont-Saint-Éloi or as archdeacon at Arras. The collection drew upon Burchard of Worms' *Decretum*, the *Collectio Sinemuriensis*, which was compiled at Reims, and the *Collectio Hibernensis*. According to Van Hove and De Smet, the *Collectio Atrebatensis* would serve as a preparatory piece for the *Collectio IX librorum* (aka *Collectio de Thérouanne* or *Collectio Sangermanensis IX voluminum*) (ca. 1100). Irrespective of whether or not John compiled the *Collectio Atrebatensis* or whether it served as a preparatory work, the *Collectio IX librorum* did draw texts from the *Collectio Atrebatensis* and from a collection of canons (fol. 9r–20v) contained in the composite manuscript Paris, BnF, lat. 13368 originating around Paris.[55] Known to exist in two manuscripts, John most

49 R. Somerville, *Councils of Urban II, Vol. I: Decreta Claromontensia* (Amsterdam, 1972), 6–7, 46–56; for a hypothetical reconstruction of the *Liber's* contents taken from seventeenth century copies formerly of St. Vaast (now Arras, BM 1051 and 1062), see Kéry, *Die Errichtung des Bistums Arras*, 61–66 and 80–88.

50 L. Waelkens and D. Van den Auweele, "La collection de Thérouanne ex IX livres à l'abbaye de Saint-Pierre-au-Mont-Blandin: Le codex Gandavensis 235," *Sacris erudiri: Jaarboek voor Godsdienstwetenschappen* 24 (1980): 115–153.

51 *Le register de Lambert*.

52 B-M. Tock, ed., *Les Chartres des Évêques d'Arras (1093–1203)* (Paris, 1991), nos. 1–7.

53 B-M. Tock, "Jean de Warneton, Évêque de Thérouanne (1099–1130): Un Grégorien," in *Le diocese de Thérouanne au Moyen Age: Actes de la journée d'études tenue à Lille, 3 mai 2007* (Arras, 2010), 107–118, here 107.

54 W. Simons, "Jean de Warneton et la Réforme Grégorienne," *Mémoires de la Société d'histoire de Comines-Warneton et de la region* 17 (1987): 35–54, here 51.

55 Arras, Bibliothèque municipale 425, fol. 1v–67v; Rolker, *Canon Law and the Letters of Ivo of Chartres*, 71; L. Waelkens and D. Van den Auwelle, "La collection de Thérouanne en IX livres à l'abbaye de Sainte-Pierre-au-Mont-Blandin: Le codex Gandavensis 235," 139–151; Fournier and Le Bras, *Histoire des Collections Canonique en Occident*, 2.259–260; Fowler-Magerl, *Clavis canonum*, 136–137, 206–207; Kéry, *Canonical Collections of the Early Middle Ages*, 279;

often receives credit for compiling the *Collectio IX librorum* around 1100.[56] Pointing further to the close relationship between Arras and Thérouanne—and between Lambert and John—are the common synopses to the decrees of the

M. Brett, "The Collectio Lanfranci and its Competitors," in *Intellectual Life in the Middle Ages: Essays Presented to Margaret Gibson*, eds. L. Smith and B. Ward (London, 1992), 157–174, esp. 169. For Van Hove and De Smet, see Fowler-Magerl, "The Collection and Transmission of Canon Law along the Northern Section of the *Via Francigena* in the Eleventh and Twelfth Centuries," 131–132. Paris, BnF, lat. 13368 includes the rule of St. Augustine (fol. 5), *Decreta* (fol. 9), Augustine's *De natura animae* (fol. 21), extracts of the fathers (fol. 40), dialectica of Peter of Abelard (fol. 128), Rabanus's *Super Terentium* (fol. 225) and *In pslamos* (fol. 232).

56 John of Warenton's authorship of the *Collectio IX librorum* remains an open question. Max Sdralek first linked him to the collection based on his examination of the Wolfenbüttel, Herzog-August-Bibliothek Gud. lat. 212 manuscript in 1891. The manuscript was likely compiled in the archdiocese of Reims, probably the area of Thérouanne. From the end of the Middle Ages, the abbey of St. Germain-des-Prés held the manuscript and thus it is also known as the "Collection of St. Germain-des-Prés." In 1710, a Danish diplomat, Marquard Gude, who had acquired the manuscript from St. Germain, gave it to Wolfenbüttel. Sdralek noticed an obvious link between the canonical collection found in the first part of the manuscript and the epistolary collection in the fifth part of the manuscript. The epistolary recounted events in the diocese of Thérouanne and in those letters John was a central figure. In 1943, De Smet would echo Sdralek's conclusions and expand them to argue that Walter of Thérouanne revised the *Collectio IX librorum* into a new collection, the *Collectio decem partium*. The attribution of the *Collectio decem partium* to Walter flew in the face of Augustin Theiner's work, which had attributed the collection to Hildebert of Lavardin. At the time, the Wolfenbüttel manuscript was the only known copy of the collection. To this day, scholars cite Sdralek and De Smet when crediting John with the compilation of the *Collectio IX librorum*. Then, in 1980, Waelken and Van den Auwelle challenged this conclusion based on their discovery of a second copy of the *Collectio IX librorum* contained in Ghent, Bibliothèque Universitaire, MS 235. The provenance of the manuscript is the Benedictine abbey of Saint-Pierre-au-Mont-Blandin in Ghent. They considered this copy to be the original version of the collection—the ninth book is missing—and dated it to shortly before 1095. John could not have been the compiler as he had just arrived at Arras in 1094 and would not have had time to compile the first eight books. Following Waelken and Van den Auwelle, Joaquín Sedano has expressed caution about attributing the *Collectio IX librorum* to John despite strong clues to do so. Though writing before Sedano, Linda Fowler-Magerl, in her magisterial fashion, seemed to provide a middle ground. She suspected that John would have had access to the *Collectio of Arras* while he was a canon regular at the abbey of Mont-Saint-Éloi near Arras, before becoming archdeacon. He could have completed the first eight volumes (as found in Ghent 235) while there and then completed the collection with the ninth volume (as found in Wolfenbüttel 212) at a later point. What does this leave us? While it is not for certain that John of Warneton compiled the *Collectio IX librorum*, it is well within the realm of possibility that he did. For the literature review see: M. Sdralek, *Wolfenbüttler Fragmente: Analekten zur Kirchengeschichte des Mittelalters aus Wolfenbüttler Handschriften* (Münster, 1891), 3–86; J. M. De Smet, *De heilige Jan van Waasten en de Gregoriaansche hervorming in het bisdom Terwaan* (Université de Louvain, 1943), 125–138; L. Waelkens and D. Van den Auwelle, "La collection de Thérouanne en IX livres à l'abbaye de Sainte-Pierre-au-Mont-Blandin: Le codex Gandavensis 235," 115–153; J. Sedano, "The Manuscript Tradition of the *Collection in Ten Parts*," in *Proceedings Esztergom 2008*, eds. P. Erdő and S. A. Szuromi (Vatican City, 2010), 262–263, 268–269; Fowler-Magerl, "The Collection and Transmission of Canon Law along the Northern Section of the *Via Francigena* in the Eleventh and Twelfth Centuries," 133–134; Somerville, *The Councils of Urban II, Vol. 1*, 57–58; Rolker, *Canon Law and the Letters of Ivo of Chartres*, 71; Fournier and Le Bras, *Histoire des Collections Canonique en Occident*, 2:285–296; Fowler-Magerl, *Clavis canonum*, 207–209; Kéry, *Canonical Collections of the Early Middle Ages*, 262–263.

Council of Clermont (1095). Somerville posited that John, as part of the Arras delegation to Clermont, may have had access to the notes and documents.[57] The *Collectio IX librorum*, however, reveals the interest of its compiler with fuller expositions of matters that the *Liber Lamberti* only summarized. The *Collectio IX librorum* contains extended discussions on the Peace of God and on those below the order of subdeacon not being chosen as bishop.[58] The *Collectio IX librorum* includes a few decrees not found in the *Liber Lamberti*, such as regulations for autumn and winter Ember Days and that the local bishop, in consultation with the monks, should install chaplains in parish churches under monastic control.[59]

The *Collectiones Catalunenses* reveal a vibrant study and use of canon law based on collections from Chartres and Thérouanne. The *Collectio Catalunensis I* and *Collectio Catalunensis II* were compiled at the monastery of St. Peter in Châlons-sur-Marne between 1130 and 1140.[60] The former drew upon the *Tripartita B* with fragments also drawn from the *Collectio decem partium*. The compiler followed the structure and content of the third part of Collection B through title 1 to title 10, focusing on discipline and behavior.[61] The second part of the collection, title 11 through title 18, is in a different hand and does not follow the structure of the *Tripartita*, focusing rather on judgment, though it does continue to take the content from its source.[62] The *Collectio Catalunesis I* shows the preoccupation of canons at the beginning of the twelfth century with pastoral care and correction.[63] The *Collectio Catalunesnsis II* drew upon the *Tripartita B* with fragments also from the

57 Somerville, *The Councils of Urban II, Vol. 1*, 59.

58 Somerville, *The Councils of Urban II, Vol. 1*, 143 (Appendix III). On the Peace of God: c.1 in the *Liber Lamberti*, and c. 5 and c.6 in the Wolfenbüttel manuscript of the *Collectio IX librorum* (which was the only manuscript known to Somerville at the time). On those below the subdeaconate not being chosen as bishop: c.3 in the *Liber Lamberti*, and c.10 and c.4 in the *Collectio IX librorum*.

59 Somerville, *The Councils of Urban II, Vol. 1*, 146, 147 (Appendix III). Regarding the regulation of Ember days, c.25 in the *Liber Lamberti* and c.1 in the *Collectio IX librorum* both address the regulations for spring and summer Ember Days. It is only the *Collectio IX librorum*, however, that addresses regulations for autumn and winter Ember Days. On installing chaplains in parish churches under monastic control, see c.30 in the *Collectio IX librorum*.

60 Châlons-sur-Marne, Bibliothèque municipale, MS 47 and MS 75. See P. Fournier, *Les collections canoniques attribuées a Yves de Chartres* (Paris, 1897), 158, 172.

61 I. De baptism; II. De sacramentis ecclesiasticis; III. De rebus ecclesiasticis et fugientibus ad ecclesiam; IV. De observatione dierum; V. De ieiunio; VI. De consuetudinibus ecclesiasticis; VII. De consuetudine; VIII. De primatu Romanae Ecclesiae; IX. De episcopis; X. De clericis.

62 XI. De accusatione; XII. De appellatione; XIII. De iudiciis; XIV. De testibus; XV. De purgatione; XVI. De juramentis; XVII. De superstitionibus de-monum; XVIII. De penitentia.

63 Fowler-Magerl, *Clavis canonum*, 238–239; Kéry, *Canonical Collections of the Early Middle Ages*, 290–291; Fournier, *Les collections canoniques attribuées a Yves de Chartres*, 158–172; Fowler-Magerl, "The Collection and Transmission of Canon Law along the Northern Section of the *Via Francigena* in the Eleventh and Twelfth Centuries," 135.

Collectio decem partium and the *Collectio Catalunensis I*. As a collection, it echoes the first, drawing upon the same sources, but brings it to a more complete state. It begins with matters relating to ecclesiastical persons and, echoing Italian collections, addresses papal primacy first, followed by bishops, clerics, and monks. It then focuses on the sacraments, followed by ecclesiastical goods, worship, crimes and procedure, penance, and, akin to the *Tripartita*, it ends with a book on *causis laicorum*.[64] Unlike *Catalunesis I*, *Catalunesis II* addresses marriage.[65] The *Collectiones Catalunenses*, along with Haimo's *Summa decretorum*, demonstrate the connections of Châlons-sur-Marne in the early twelfth century to the legal culture of the Paris region.

Also compiled around Thérouanne, the *Collectio decem partium* demonstrates how northern French compilers borrowed and adapted the legal texts in circulation to suit their particular needs. Traditionally attributed to Walter of Thérouanne, the collection was compiled between 1125 and 1130.[66] At its core,

64 Fowler-Magerl, *Clavis canonum*, 238–239; Kéry, *Canonical Collections of the Early Middle Ages*, 290–291; Fournier, *Les collections canoniques attribuées a Yves de Chartres*, 172–182; Fowler-Magerl, "The Collection and Transmission of Canon Law along the Northern Section of the *Via Francigena* in the Eleventh and Twelfth Centuries," 135.

65 I. De primatu Romane Ecclesie; II. De episcopis; III. De clericis; IV. De monachis, De sanctimonialibus, De canonicis regularibus; V. De baptismo, De sacramentis; VI. De rebus ecclesiasticis; De fugientibus ad ecclesiam; De observatione dierum; De jejunio; De consuetudinibus ecclesiasticis; De consuetudine; VII. De conjugiis; VIII. De homicidiis, De incesta copulatione; IX. De excommunicatione, De septem gradibus consanguinitatis; De nocturna illusione; De venatoribus; De usurariis; X. De accusatione, De conciliis vel synodis; De appellatione; XI. De judiciis, De testibus, De purgatione, De juramentis, De superstitionibus demonum; XII. De penitentia; XIII. De causis laicorum.

66 Fournier, *Les collections canoniques attribuées a Yves de Chartres*, 156–158; J. Sedano, "The Manuscript Tradition of the *Collection in Ten Parts*," 268–269. Fournier noted that Theiner attributed work to Hildebert of Lavardin, bishop of LeMans and then archbishop of Tours. But he did not necessarily agree with that attribution. Sedano's wariness towards the conclusions of Sdralek and De Smet regarding John of Thérouanne's authorship of the *Collectio IX librorum* leads him to be equally wary of attributing the *Collectio decem partium* to Walter, just as Van den Auweele and Waelkens were wary. While Somerville and Brasington noted in their own commentary that the author of the preface and the patron remained unknown, the preface of the *Collectio decem partium* that accompanied Ivo's *Prologue* is often attributed to Walter of Thérouanne and presumably dedicated to John of Warenton. Walter notes that he obeyed his patron's will and diligently surveyed the libraries of many churches to gather what would be useful. See "Preface to the Collection in Ten Parts," in *Prefaces to Canon Law Books in Latin Christianity: Selected Translations, 500–1245*, 2nd edn., trans. R. Somerville and B. C. Brasington (Washington D.C., 2021), 116, 158. See M. H. Eichbauer, "A Desire for the Latest and the Greatest: Papal Decretals and Roman Law in the *Collectio decem paritum*," BMCL 36 (2019): 195–208, where I analyze the inclusion of recent papal decrees and conciliar canons in the *Collectio decem partium* to situate the collection a bit closer with Walter, Thèrouanne, and the social and professional network that included Pope Urban II, Pope Paschal II, Pope Calixtus II, Lambert of Guines (bishop of Arras), and John of Warneton (archdeacon of Arras) under Lambert and then confirmed by Urban II as bishop of Thèrouanne.

it is essentially a revised, updated, and enlarged version of the *Panormia*.[67] Parts 1–3 and 5–9 of the *Collectio decem partium* correspond to Books 1–3 and 4–8 of the *Panormia*, respectively. Each of the parts retains the vast majority of the canons found in the respective book of the *Panormia* and, for the most part, follows the sequence laid out there.[68] Though the *Collectio decem partium* drew its structure from the *Panormia*, the compiler did tailor the presentation of some of the contents to cater more effectively to the practical needs of diocesan administration.[69] Part 1 of the *Collectio decem partium* specified a section on the preparation and distribution of the chrism not specified in Book 1 of the *Panormia*. Part 2 of the *Collectio decem partium* more broadly addressed the relocation of those ordained, while Book 2 of the *Panormia* specifically addressed the relocation of bishops. Book 3 of the *Panormia* included texts related to child oblates—*De etate qua possint parentes contradicere religioni filiorum et qua non possunt*. Part 3 of the *Collectio decem partium* omitted this section as it would be more concerned with the canons regular (i.e., Part 4), that is, those who observe the rule of St. Augustine, as opposed to the traditional Benedictine monasticism. Here, the possible influence of John of Thérouanne comes forth. John was devoted to the reform of religious houses in his diocese, and, as a tremendous advocate of the canons regular, he oversaw the transformation of a number of houses of secular canons to houses of canons regular.[70]

As judgment and correction were essential elements of a diocesan administrator's duties, the *Collectio decem partium* specified particular titles that the corresponding book of the *Panormia* did not specify. Part 5 included topics concerning the choosing of judges, the condemning of bishops and clerics, and

67 Fournier, *Les collections canoniques attribuées a Yves de Chartres*, 147–156, esp. 147–148, 154; Fowler-Magerl, "The Collection and Transmission of Canon Law along the Northern Section of the *Via Francigena* in the Eleventh and Twelfth Centuries," 134; Sedano, "The Manuscript Tradition of the *Collection in Ten Parts*," 262–263. An early plan for the collection is preserved in Paris, BnF, lat. 14145 and has a provenance of Saint-Germain-des-Prés. Dating to approximately 1116, it contains the capitulation for the canons of the first part, Ivo's *Prologue*, and the texts for canons Part 1, title 1, canon 1 to Part 1, title 5, canon 1. The most recent version of the text was found in Paris, BnF, lat. 10743 and has a provenance of the cathedral of Évreaux, including decrees from the Council of Reims in 1131. However, all other copies of the collection contain no texts later than the First Lateran Council in 1123.

68 Fournier, *Les collections canoniques attribuées a Yves de Chartres*, 149–150, 154. For a complete list of canons not included from the *Panormia* for each part of the *Collectio decem partium*, see J. Sedano, "A Comparative Analysis of the *Panormia* and the *Collectio X partium*," ZRG Kan. Abt. 96 (2010): 80–110, here 81–94; idem, "The Manuscript Tradition of the Collection in Ten Parts," 263–264.

69 A detailed comparison of the contents listed in each section of the *Collectio decem partium* against the *Panormia* is available at https://ivo-of-chartres.github.io. See also "Preface to the Collection in Ten Parts," in *Prefaces to Canon Law Books in Latin Christianity*, 162–164.

70 Tock, "Jean de Warneton, Évêque de Thérouanne," 111, 118.

sentences. Part 6 specified a section on the power of binding and loosing. Part 9 specified a title concerning parricides and killers of spouses and penitents. It would include a number of additionally specified titles related to the oath: concerning oaths which should or should not be observed as well as legitimate oaths, concerning the requiring of an oath and deceitful oaths, and concerning the eight types of lies. Finally, there is the addition of Part 10 on penance.

Some of the most interesting adaptations of the *Panormia* appear in Part 7 on marriage. The *Collectio decem partium* specified topics on adultery, the marriage and divorce of Lothar and Theutberga, who should be prohibited from being or ordered to marry and why, and that marriages should not be dissolved except for fornication. By contrast, the corresponding book of the *Panormia*, Book 7, specified that marriages should be between men and women; that marriage should not happen between co-parents; that a man is not able to lead two godmothers (*commatres*), one after another, into marriage; and inquests for parental divorce and incest. Particularly as it pertains to marriage, the compiler of the *Collectio decem partium* highlighted specified topics of particular everyday concern to the practitioner. If Walter were indeed the compiler, the adjustments would make a lot of sense. As archdeacon of Thérouanne, the topics omitted and added would assist the administrator more readily in fulfilling his requisite duties related to the *cura animarum*.

The compiler further supplemented *Collectio decem partium* with two parts not corresponding to the *Panormia*, Parts 4 and 10. For Part 4, the compiler takes the majority of canons from the *Collectio IX librorum* (approximately 110 canons) and from Burchard of Worm's *Decretum* (130 canons). The section deals with canons regular; bishop- and archbishop-elects, clerical discipline and correction, the duties of the bishop, their goods, their behavior, their liberty, and with respect to secular rulers; and the goods of deceased clerics. Part 10 is likewise drawn primarily from the *Collectio IX librorum* and addresses confession, penance, and reconciliation as it pertains to both the laity and clerics alike.[71] In terms of diocesan administration, both Part 4 and Part 10 would have served critical functions.

The compiler of the *Collectio decem partium* (possibly Walter of Thérouanne) and the compilers of the collection from which he drew—the *Panormia* and the *Collectio IX librorum* (possibly of John of Thérouanne)—were eager to incorporate the most recent papal decretals and Roman law.[72] They incorporated papal

71 J. Sedano, "The *Collectio decem partium*'s Distinctive Sections: Parts 4 and 10," in *Proceedings Toronto 2012*, eds. J. Goering, S. Dusil, and A. Thier (Vatican City, 2016), 31–60, here 31–33, 38–39; "Preface to the Collection in Ten Parts," in *Prefaces to Canon Law Books in Latin Christianity*, 162, 164.

72 Joaquín Sedano has argued that Part 2 drew 49 canons from the *Collectio IX librorum*, Part 3 drew 60 canons from the *Collectio IX librorum*, and Part 4 drew more than 100 canons from the *Collectio IX librorum*. See Sedano, "The Manuscript Tradition of the *Collection in Ten Parts*," 263.

decretals of Pope Urban II in particular, along with those of Popes Paschal II and Calixtus II most heavily in areas of strategic emphasis: Part 2, Part 3, and Part 4. Joaquín Sedano has nicely summarized the contents. Part 2 deals with the constitution of the Church, construction and blessing of the temples, tithes and Church property, fasting and customs, books of Sacred Scripture, as well as authentic and apocryphal councils. Part 3 represents the most deliberate and concerted effort to incorporate the new law of Pope Urban II and, to a lesser extent, that of Pope Calixtus II and Pope Paschal II. This law focused quite poignantly on the issues most central to the reform movement in the eleventh and early twelfth centuries. Broadly speaking, it focused on the ecclesiastical orders and their conduct. It addresses issues related to the election and consecration of the pope and the bishops; of various crimes and sins of the clergy; and of the abbots and abbesses, monks, virgins, and widows. Complementing Part 2 and Part 3, Part 4 reveals the collection's "unique personality" beginning with the Augustinian Rule and dealing with the life of canons regular, the conduct and responsibilities of bishops and clergy as well as pastoral care in the diocese, and finally the place of the laity within the ecclesiastical.[73]

The *Collectio decem partium* liberally incorporated Roman law in Part 6 treating judicial organization involving the accuser, the accused, the judge, and the witnesses; along with the rights of children, debts, loans, and moveable and immovable property. Though not used as extensively as in Part 6, Roman law was also important in Part 7, which treated marriage. Roman law was key to clarifying key issues of concern: the legitimacy of the betrothal and marriage, the ability to contract a second marriage, and the care of minor children. Betrothal, like marriage, requires the consent of both parties.[74] Collectively, the collection's use of Roman law reveals much about the eleventh and early twelfth centuries. First, while the complete Justinianic corpus may not have been available to legal thinkers, that does not mean they were ignorant of Roman law. Efforts were being made to uncover it from the archives and libraries of the Roman curia. The *Digest*, *Codex*, and *Institutes* were incorporated alongside the *Theodosian Code* and the *Sententiae Pauli*—both preserved in the *Breviarium Alarici*—and the work of *Benedictus Levita*. Second, the Roman law available was used extensively to formalize the trial process, particularly that of witnesses and testimony, and, with-it, people's legal rights. With the *Collectio decem partium*, particular attention was given to the legal rights of children. The normalization of the legal process in canonical collections highlights the Church's role in judicial matters. As diocesan courts became more formalized, understanding and following proper procedure became more important. Third,

73 Sedano, "The Manuscript Tradition of the *Collection in Ten Parts*," 263–264; idem, "A Comparative Analysis of the *Panormia* and the *Collectio X partium*," 80–81; idem, "The *Collectio decem partium*'s Distinctive Sections," 32–33.

74 Berlin, Staatsbibliothek Preußischer Kulturbesitz, Phill. 1746.

Roman law played a central role in regulating economic transactions. As the twelfth-century economy began to change, becoming more urbanized and with the increased circulation of money, legal issues pertaining to sales and loans came to the fore. As agriculture remained a central premise of the medieval economy, legislation regarding property rights and animals likewise remained important. Fourth, while not reaching its fullest fruition until the pontificate of Alexander III in the later twelfth century, ecclesiastical administrators were turning to Roman law for its understanding of marriage. Though by no means fully fleshed out, they were thinking deeply about the legal ramifications of unions.

Conclusion

Legal knowledge spread in much the same way as theological knowledge: between master and student and among colleagues. Ivo of Chartres was central to the proliferation of legal thought in northern France. His most obvious influence is the compilation of his own legal texts, the *Decretum*. But of equal importance was his influence on the proliferation of legal texts through his role as teacher at St. Quentin at Beauvais. There he taught Lambert, the future bishop of Arras, and John, the future bishop of Thérouanne. Ivo's influence must be traced back to the abbey of Bec and Lanfranc. Steeped in legal knowledge, Lanfranc sought to impart it to his students by infusing law into training in rhetoric and dialectic. It should not come as a surprise that Lanfranc taught legal principles while at Bec, as his *Liber Lanfranci*, compiled while serving as Archbishop of Canterbury, distilled the *Pseudo-Isidorian Decretals* into a teachable and usable form.

Lambert and John thus followed in the footsteps of their master, Ivo. The bonds formed in the classroom extended throughout their professional careers as Lambert helped John obtain his bishopric, and both were charged with adjudicating matters on behalf of the papacy. Under their administrative oversight, the dioceses of Arras and Thérouanne were actively engaged in the use and production of law: *Liber Lamberti*, *Collectio Atrebatensis*, the *Collectio IX librorum*, and the *Collectio decem partium*. These collections drew upon each other, such as the *Collectio IX librorum* drawing upon the *Collectio Atrebatensis*, and from other collections compiled in the region such as the *Collectio Sinemuriensis* compiled at Reims.

Vital to the spread of legal knowledge and the proliferation of legal texts was the *Via Francigena*. The pilgrimage route between Canterbury and Rome also facilitated the spread of people and texts. It, as much as the classroom, laid the path for networks to form. As networks formed, texts could move from one location to another. These texts were not simply copied but rather were adapted and transformed into new collections that suited the needs of the compiler. The inclusion of Ivo of Chartres's *Prologue* with other collections, leading earlier generations of scholars to attribute those collections to him, exemplifies this spread of legal texts. The *Diversorum partum sententiae* (*74T*), *Collectio canonum* of St. Victor, *Decretum* and *Tripartita* of Ivo of Chartres, *Panormia*, *Collectio decem partium*, *Summa decretorum* of Haimo, and *Collectiones Catalaunensis* all exemplify adaptation. Each of these collections was compiled in the region and, in many cases, the collections drew from each other but tailored those contents to suit a particular purpose, be it the protection of monastic rights or to better fulfill the ecclesiastical and judicial duties associated with one's office.

Bruce Brasington has noted:

> For centuries, there had been reflection on how the canons were to be organized, interpreted, and applied. *Iuris periti*, men learned, if not yet formally trained, in canon law had labored to establish what Peter Landau has judged the elements essential for canon law to become a coherent legal system: unity, logical order and consistency, ability to change to meet new circumstances.[75]

The proliferation and intersection of canonical collections in northern France and the manner in which collections reflected upon contemporary ecclesiological questions can be attributed to the particular need of the compiler and user. Compiled to help diocesan functionaries, especially archdeacons, fulfill their duties, the *Collectio decem partium*, possibly of Walter of Thérouanne, reflected both the climate of reform and a climate of change. Compiled in a territory where men were on the move and actively engaged in reform efforts, the *Collectio decem partium* reflects an interest in the canons regular as well as an interest in stemming the tide of investiture, simony, the plundering of ecclesiastical property and goods, and the poor moral character of those who occupy ecclesiastical offices. Society was likewise changing and thus required a law that could change with it. In this case, change meant going back to Roman law to find texts that could assist in adjudicating what came before ecclesiastical judges. It is precisely because it was not unique, which is why the *Collectio decem partium* makes an excellent case study. Networks facilitate the spread of men, manuscripts, and knowledge. Compilers, as users, took from the texts available to create a work that suited their purposes and filled their needs. Producers, after all, were also consumers. Theologians studied, wrote, worked, and collaborated within this vibrant climate. They were not walled off from, but rather immersed in, this exciting time in legal activity.

75 Brasington, *Ways of Mercy*, 101; P. Landau, "Kanonisches Recht und römische Form: Rechtsprinzipien im ältesten römischen Kirchenrecht," *Der Staat* 32, no. 4 (1993): 553–568, here 564–566.

2

THEOLOGIANS AND THEIR ENGAGEMENT WITH LEGAL KNOWLEDGE

Introduction

As Chapter 1 set forth, the *Via Francigena* had, quite literally, created a road for the dissemination of legal thought and canonical collections. This proliferation of legal thought in northern France coincided with a climate interested in the reconciliation of disputes and methodical harmonization of authoritative texts. John Wei has acutely noted that "…theology and canon law…encompassed habits of thought and intellectual practice cultivated and formed in the medieval schools."[1] The interweaving of authorities and commentary, the compiling of a *Glossa ordinaria* as an authoritative text, and the utilization of *questiones* as new literary genres represent examples of the influence of the schools.[2] Lanfranc had laid a foundation in the late eleventh century when he used reason (*ratio*) to prove the point through debate (*disputatio*) as a teaching technique at Bec. His commentary on Paul was organized in a question-and-answer format between those asking the questions and Paul answering them. Lanfranc repeatedly interjected phrases such as "it is as if someone said said" ("quasi quis diceret)" to help the reader reconstruct the debate between Paul and the other party.[3] Glosses, such as those on Paul's letter to the Galatians (Gal. 4:1–3), would then explain the text; elaborate or restate various words and phrases;

1 J. Wei, "Of Scholasticism and Canon Law: Narratives Old and New," in *New Discourses in Medieval Canon Law Research: Challenging the Master Narrative*, ed. C. Rolker (Leiden, 2019), 105–126, here 116.

2 Wei, "Of Scholasticism and Canon Law," 116–117.

3 A. Novikoff, "Anselm, Dialogue, and the Rise of Scholastic Disputation," *Speculum* 86, no. 2 (2011): 387–418, here 395. Novikoff has argued that applying dialectical disputation to Scripture was uncommon prior to 1050.

DOI: 10.4324/9781003465096-3

separate the arguments into the categories of *per similitudinem*, *pro diversitate causarum*, and *totum pro parte*; and reorder the words to remove obscurities.[4] Lanfranc's successor, Anselm of Canterbury, likewise employed the dialectical method of question-answer in his *Cur Deus Homo*. His use of the *lectio* was an important pedagogical development as this narrative explanation interprets texts and distills the exegesis of past authorities.[5] The *Prologue* that circulated with the canonical collections *Tripartita A*, *Decretum*, *Tripartita B*, *Panormia*, the *Collectio decem partium*, and the *Catalaunensis II* reveals Ivo of Chartres's methodology of reconciliation.[6] Authorities (*auctoritates*) who hold seemingly contradictory views should be considered through the lens of whether strict judgment was warranted or whether compassion and leniency were the better path. Ivo identified *preceptiones immobiles* (invoking the unchanging *lex eterna*), *preceptiones mobiles* (historical tradition that was authoritative based on necessity and utility), *prohibitiones immobiles* (pertaining to matters of discipline and practice, and to tenets of faith), and *prohibitiones mobiles* (deliberation of the historical context) as considerations for balancing rigor and mercy.[7]

The above examples of Lanfranc, Anselm of Canterbury, and Ivo of Chartres highlight a culture in which *litterati* drew upon sources and techniques important to both theology and law, and they sought to bring attention to discordant sources. In this intellectual climate, theologians would have had some comfortability with the canonical tradition and seem to have found such sources useful. Theologians such as Hugh of St. Victor, Peter Lombard, Peter the Chanter, Robert of Courçon, Robert of Flamborough, and Thomas of Chobham serve as such examples. Engaging in an intellectual culture in which the disciplinary boundaries between theology and law were porous, their works bear witness to legal principles filtering into the thinking of those associated with theology at the schools in Paris.[8] This chapter explores what legal sources these theologians used and how they incorporated them. Some, such as Hugh of St. Victor and Peter Lombard, drew upon legal sources sparingly, while others, such as Peter the Chanter and his circle, were more robust in their usage. Yet, they all drew upon those sources when they saw fit to do so. As we will see,

4 C. Radding, "The Geography of Learning in Early Eleventh-Century Europe: Lanfranc of Bec and Berengar of Tours Revisited," *Bullettino dell'Istituto storico italiano per il Medio Evo e archvio muratoriano* 98 (1992): 145–172, esp. 149–160.

5 M. Clanchy and L. Smith, "Abelard's Description of the School of Laon: What Might it Tell Us about Early Scholastic Teaching?," *Nottingham Medieval Studies* 54 (2010): 1–34.

6 C. Rolker, *Canon Law and the Letters of Ivo of Chartres* (Cambridge, 2010), 29–30, 134.

7 B. Brasington, *Ways of Mercy: The Prologue of Ivo of Chartres, Edition and Analysis* (Münster, 2004), 11, 30–43, 74, 77.

8 From the charter evidence, Nicholas Vincent has reconstructed the active engagement of English *litterati* in and around the schools of Paris at the turn of the thirteenth century. See "Albion Adrift: The English Presence in Paris and its Environs after 1204," in *Thirteenth Century England XVIII: Proceedings of the Cambridge Conference, 2019*, eds. A. Spencer and C. Watkin (Woodbridge, 2023), 209–246.

these theologians were familiar enough with the legal tradition that they could be versatile in their usage.

A Common Intellectual Tradition

In his introduction to the critical edition of Thomas of Chobham's *Summa confessorum*, Rev. Bloomfield grappled with the extent of Thomas's legal knowledge. According to him, Thomas regarded himself a theologian and his work as a theological treatise. Confessors' manuals, he noted, originated out of the Parisian theological tradition... not its legal tradition.[9] Though Thomas composed his manual working in England, he was trained at Paris, studying under Peter the Chanter. Yet, Bloomfield also pointed to the Prologue where Thomas stated that since canon law had much to say on penance it would sometimes be necessary to refer to it; such a comment, he held, could only be made by an author who regarded his book as a predominantly theological manual. The *Summa confessorum*, after all, lacked a scholarly apparatus: Thomas told the readers that a canon stated such-and-such, but he did not tell them where to find the canon; there is, for example, no reference to Gratian's *Decretum* but its presence is felt.[10] Bloomfield's observations, I would maintain, point to a common intellectual tradition with porous disciplinary boundaries. Like Peter the Chanter and Robert of Courçon, Thomas mixed theology and law. Seen through this lens, Thomas's comment in the Prologue was made by someone steeped in the northern French intellectual tradition of comfortably navigating sources and ideas found in theology and law. Yet, those for whom he was writing his manual may not be so comfortable thus he needed to distill the material for his readers. Confessors needed to know what the law held, not where to find the law or its minute details.

At the heart of theologians' use of legal sources was a common intellectual tradition in which they engaged, a tradition in which the lines between theology and law blurred as they occupied the same academic space. Gregory the I's categorization of the seven deadly sins, for example, can be found in Burchard of Worms' *Decretum*, the penitentials of Bartholomew of Exeter and Robert of Flamborough, and Thomas of Chobham's *Summa confessorum*.[11] Gregory's thoughts on the qualities a man who oversees others, such as a priest, should have are found in his *Pastoral Rule*, which both Gratian and Thomas of Chobham included in their respective works.[12] Thomas's

9 *Thomae de Chombham Summa Confessorum*, ed. Revd. F. Broomfield (Louvain, 1968), xxi.

10 *Thomae de Chombham Summa Confessorum*, xxi–xxiii. "Et quia circa penitentiam multa a iure canonico statuta sunt, in omnibus predictis canonicas institutiones quandoque interserere oportet" (p. 4).

11 Gregory I, *Moralia in Job*, Bk. 31 c.45; BD 19.6; Bartholomew c.38; Chobham 3.1.1 (Art. 3, dist. 1, qu. 1). Burchard changed the attribution to the Penitential of Theodore. While Bartholomew of Exeter attributed the text to Gregory, he abbreviated it.

12 Gregory I, *Pastoral Rule*, Bk. 1 c.11; GD D.49 c.1; Chobham 3.3.6, 7.

discussion of the penance for killing one's wife includes papal decretals and conciliar canons found in Gratian, Peter Lombard's *Sententiae in IV libris distinctae* (*Sentences*), and Bartholomew of Exeter.[13] Jacques Verger, in fact, noted that "[o]n the whole, the distinction of faculties [in the thirteenth century] was conceived as a means to fight against the confusion and reciprocal overlapping of disciplines strongly denounced in the previous century."[14] The intertwining of law and theology was a feature of the twelfth century. Examples from Hugh of St. Victor, Peter Lombard, and Peter the Chanter demonstrate that times arose in which a particular text could be found in both the legal and the theological tradition. It can raise the question of whether the text came from the other tradition or from the original material source.

Hugh of St. Victor engaged in the intellectual climate orbiting Ivo of Chartres, drawing on occasion from his sermons. Hugh's chapter "De sacramentis neophytorum" in Part 6 dealing with baptism of his *De Sacramentis Christianae Fidei* (*On the Sacraments of the Christian Faith*) echoes Ivo's sermon on the same title. In instructing those new to the faith that both the faith and the sacraments are old, both Ivo and Hugh divide history into six points of restoration denoted by the sacrament it foreshadows. Ivo's first age was man, Adam originated from virgin land but without an earthly father. Such was similar to Christ who was formed from an earthly mother but without an earthly father, and would usher in a new age. In this first stage, Hugh would differ a bit, using Abel to denote the first age as he killed the lamb in sacrifice, an image of the death of Christ. In the second age, Noah guided the ark in the flood, just as Christ guided the Church in the midst of floods of temptations, keeping it from being submerged. In the third age, the people of Israel were led out of Egypt through the Red Sea by Moses, just as the faithful of God are freed from sin, renewed through the sacrament of baptism, consecrated by the blood of Christ. Jerusalem and King David marked the fourth age; they prefigured the kingdom of the Church and Christ. The Babylonian captivity marked the fifth age, a 70-year captivity resulting from Israel's sins. Despite this dark time the sacraments remained, and their sins would be forgiven. The sixth age was that of Christ, born of the virgin just as on the sixth day the first man was molded from virgin land.[15] Collectively, the sacraments of the Christian faith were present from the beginning, and their benefit has no end. Hugh likewise may have drawn from Ivo's sermon "De significationibus indumentorum sacerdotalium", which describes each piece of clerical attire and its significance. A difference

13 Chobham 7.4.9.9; GD C.33 q.2; Lombard 4.37; Bartholomew c.50.

14 J. Verger, "The First French Universities and the Institutionalization of Learning: Faculties, Curricula, Degrees," in *Learning Institutionalized: Teaching in the Medieval University*, ed. J. Van Engen (Notre Dame, 2000), 10.

15 De Sacr. 2.6.8 (PL 176: 454–455); Deferrari, trans. 295–297; Ivo of Chartres, Sermon 1 (PL 162, col. 506–508); Paul Rorem, *Hugh of Saint Victor* (Oxford, 2009), 98–99.

between the two treatments is that Ivo does not appear to treat the bishop's ring and staff, the archbishop's pallium, and sacred vessels, though Hugh does.[16]

Theologians and canonists engaged in similar topics using similar techniques. Hugh of St. Victor and Peter Lombard, as a case in point, looked to define what a marriage was, when it began, clandestine marriages, whether marriages could be dissolved, who legitimately could enter into a marriage, the marriage of unbelievers, and consanguinity and affinity. Hugh of St. Victor embraced the wider scholastic climate of posing hypotheticals and facets to consider, analyzing the individual elements from a *sic et non* perspective, and finally offering a solution to the matter at hand. Take, for example, situations in which two people marry in secret only to have one or both of them deny the marriage and marry another. Hugh presented the situation in this way:

> A certain man took a wife secretly without the presence of witnesses, marital consent alone being confirmed between the two, as customarily happens sometimes, avoiding for some reason another's notice; afterwards, when a short time has intervened, before he has proven the secret consent by manifest deed, he repented of the deed and dismissed her whom he had taken as his wife in this way; he married another with distinguished pomp openly in the church, perhaps with parents giving her away; he accomplished the marriage with the blessing of the priest; he begot children. The former wife comes to the church, interrupts the judgment, demands justice, explaining that an injury was done her secretly. He denies it, and there are no witnesses who can prove what is hidden.
>
> Here you ask what should the Church do, since on both sides something improper seems to be occurring. For in that woman who tells the truth indeed, credence is placed without legitimate testimony, but yet it is hidden and what she says is not proven on account of her word alone; and on account of what is uncertain and hidden what is certain and manifest is destroyed; then any man or woman will be able to trump up whatever he or she should wish against any man or any woman that credence may be placed in them in a similar way. ... But if to preserve the authority of the Church the marriage which was made first is broken and the adultery which was assumed in the second is confirmed, ...[17]

16 De Sacr. 2.4 (PL 176: 443–456); Deferrari, trans. 273–278; Ivo of Chartres, Sermon 3 (PL 162: 519–527); Rorem, *Hugh of Saint Victor*, 95–96. See cap. 15 for Hugh's treatment of the bishop's ring and staff, cap. 16 for the archiepiscopal pallium, and cap. 16 for sacred vessels.

17 De Sacr. 2.11.6 (PL 176:487–489):

> Quidam uxorem duxit clanculo sine praesentia testium solo ad invicem maritali consensu firmato, devitans ut nonnunquam fieri solet aliqua de causa conscientiam alienam, postea brevi tempore interiecto, priusquam consensum occultum facto manifesto probasset de facto poenituit, eam quam in hunc modum uxorem duxerat dimisit: aliam duxit celebri apparatu manifeste coram Ecclesia fortassis cum parentum traditione, cum sacerdotis

Hugh provided a very plausible scenario of two people who wed in secret only to have the man deny the union and marry another. When the aggrieved woman made her claim of their union known in public, the issue became which of the two unions was valid: the clandestine marriage or the public marriage that had resulted in children. Throughout his analysis, Hugh used phrases such as "some think" and "but you say" to put forth different views. He concluded that because she could not provide proof of her assertion, the Church could not support her claim. The second union could be validated as it was legitimately performed in the judgment of the Church. In the end, what was hidden could not be proven and what was evident could not be undermined.[18]

This common intellectual tradition sometimes results in difficulty knowing which source—legal collection or the original material source—a theologian turned. For example, in Book 3 Dist. 38 and Dist. 39 of Peter Lombard's *Sentences* deal with the oath and perjury. With Augustine's *Enchiridion* as a material source, Lombard questioned what was and was not dangerous to error. He began by noting "in some things, it is a great evil to be deceived; in some it is a small evil, and in others none at all."[19] Gratian expressed a similar concept in a *dictum*: "at one time it stands that to be deceived is the littlest or not sin, at another time from the various consideration of things to deceive is less [a sin] than to be deceived."[20] From that, Lombard followed another text from Augustine stating that

> some matters are of no relevance to our obtaining the kingdom of God, whether we believe them or not, and whether they are held to be true or false, and whether they are as we hold them to be: to err with regard to these, that is, to believe one of them instead of another is not to be a thought to be a sin; or if it is one, then it is very small and trifling sin.[21]

---

benedictione nuptias fecit, filio genuit. Venit prior illa ad Ecclesiam, iudicium interpellat, iustitiam postulet. Iniuriam aibi illatam palam exponens. Negat ille, nec sunt testes qui possunt probare quod occuitum est. Hic quaeris quid facere debet Ecclesia, quia utrinque inconveniens aliquid incurrere videtur. Si enim illi mulieri quae quidem verum dicit, sed tamen occultum est, nec probatum quod dicitur, sine legitimo testimonio propter solum dictum eius creditur, et pro eo quod incertum est et occultum, id quod certum et manifestum est dissolvitur, poteterit deinceps quilibet sive quaelibet in alium vel in aliam quodcumque voluerit fingere, ut sibi simili ratione credatur. .... Si vero propter auctoritatem Ecclesiae connervandum coniugium, quod primum factum est, scinditur, et adulterium, quod secondo praesumptum est, confirmatur, ...;

Deferrari, trans. 333.

18 De Sacr. 2.11.6 (PL 176: 493–494); Deferrari, trans. 334.

19 Lombard 3.38.6.1: "in quibusdam rebus magno malo, in quibusdam parvo, in quibusdam nullo fallimur."

20 GD C.22 q.2 d.p.c.5: "...aliquando contingit falli uel nullum, uel minimum esse peccatum, aliquando ex ipsa rerum varia consideratione minus esse fallere quam falli."

21 Lombard 3.38.6.1.

This same text directly follows the *dictum* in the *Decretum*,[22] and the text from Augustine's *Enchiridion* also appears in popular collections such as Ivo of Chartres' *Decretum* and the *Panormia*.[23] Yet, following the Augustinian point on matters that are of no relevance to our obtaining the kingdom of God, Lombard followed with another sentence from the text: "But there are truths which, although they cannot be seen, must be believed, or it is impossible to come to eternal life." It seems that it came from neither Gratian, Ivo, nor the *Panormia*, but maybe from Augustine himself.[24]

Peter the Chanter's *De sacramentis legalibus et de effectu sacramentorum*, contained in his *Summa de sacramentis et animae conciliis*, drew upon texts found both in Gratian's *Decretum* and Peter Lombard's *Sentences*. For example, the Chanter asked about the idea that exterior satisfaction (*exterior penitentia*) was relaxed with baptism. He drew attention to the Apostle Paul who supposedly stated that the gifts and calling of Holy Spirit are without penance, but in the end concluded that the source for such a position was Ambrose.[25] Found in his *Commentary on the Letter to the Romans*, both the theologically based tract in Gratian's *Decretum*, the *De consecratione* (D.4 c.99),[26] and Book 4 of Peter Lombard's *Sentences* (Dist. 4 c.6) included Ambrose's words. Both note the phrase "Sine penitencia sunt dona et vocatio Dei" and both go on to state that the grace of God in baptism does not require crying or sighing, or any work, but only faith, and it all things freely.[27] In noting the efficacy of baptism for children, Peter the Chanter included the text, attributed to Gregory I, "What the water of baptism achieves in us, in the people of old faith alone accomplished for children, or the power of sacrifice for adults; or the mystery of circumcision for those who issued from the stoic of Abraham." It is both

In quibus rebus nihil interest ad capessendum Dei regnum, utrum credatur, an non vel utrum vera putentur, an falsa, sive sint; in his errare, id est aliud pro alio putare, non arbitrandum est esse peccatum; vel si est, minimum atque levissimum.

22 Lombard's use of Gratian's *Decretum* has been noted. See J. de Ghellinck, *Le Mouvement Thèlogique du XIIe Siècle*, 2nd edn. (Paris, 1948), 142; M. Colish, *Peter Lombard*, 2 vols (Leiden, 1994), 1.82; P. Rosemann, *Peter Lombard* (Oxford, 2004), 56; A. Larson, *Master of Penance: Gratian and the Development of Penitential Thought and Law in the Twelfth Century* (Washington, D.C., 2014), 319–332.

23 GD C.22 q.2 c.6; ID 12.48; Pan. 8.132.

24 Lombard 3.38.6.1: "Et sunt vera, quamvis non videantur, quae nisi credantur, ad vitam aeternam non potest perveniri."

25 Chanter 1 §4, p. 24, ln. 34–37, here ln. 34: "Sine penitentia sunt dona et vocatio Spiritus Sancti…"

26 The *De conscecratione* is a later addition to the *Decretum* tradition and was not compiled by Gratian. See J. Van Engen, "Observations on *De consecratione*," in *Proceedings Berkeley 1980*, eds. S. Kuttner and K. Pennington (Vatican City, 1985), 309–320.

27 Chanter I §4, p. 24; GD De. con. D.4 c.5: "Sine penitencia sunt dona et vocatio Dei, quia gratia Dei in baptismate non requirit gemitum, non requirit planctum, vel opus aliquod, sed solam fidem, et omnia gratis condonat." See also Lombard 4.4.6.

found in its entirety in the *De consecratione* (Dist.4 c.99) and is quoted in Peter Lombard (Bk. 4, Dist. 1, c.8).[28] Finally, in his discussion of what makes baptism effective, Peter the Chanter noted Augustine's words that baptism is made sacred by the word, but the efficacy comes not from the speaking but from belief, words found in the *Decretum* C.1 q.1 c.54 and the *Sentences* Book 4, Dist. 3, c.1. Peter would elaborate on this viewpoint, noting that authority is seen in the words because the form of the sacrament is in the words.[29] While it may not be certain which source Peter the Chanter used in the examples noted above, it is plausible that he could have turned to either a theological text or to a legal text that included a theologically-rooted tract on the sacraments.

The few examples noted above illustrate how similar texts were used to reach similar ends by both traditions. Thomas of Chobham, who likely studied under Peter the Chanter, drew upon an intellectual tradition represented in Gratian's *Decretum* and Peter Lombard's *Sentences*, particularly as it concerned marriage. For example, he repeated the common definition of lawful marriage as one between a man and a woman consenting to live an undivided way of life.[30] He reaffirmed the three-fold distinction of marriage: the beginning of a marriage through consent in the present tense, consummation through carnal copulation, and established when both of are the catholic faith.[31] He also reaffirmed the three goods of marriage as: fidelity, offspring, and the sacrament.[32] Thomas's discussion on the diriments to contracting a marriage—vows, consanguinity, affinity, spiritual affinity, error of person, error of condition, differences of faith, and adultery—pulls together an intellectual tradition that wrestled with such topics.[33] Regarding the impediment of adultery, he quoted that "no woman should be led into marriage when polluted

28 Chanter I §10, p. 39; GD De. con. D.4 c.99: "Quod apud nos valet aqua baptismatis, hoc egit apud veteres vel pro paruulis sola fides, vel pro maioribus virtus sacrificii, vel pro his, qui de stirpe Abrahae prodierunt, misterium circumcisionis." See Lombard 4.1.8.

29 Chanter I §35, p. 101; GD C.1 q.1 c.54:

> Detrahe verbum, quid est aqua nisi aqua? Accedit verbum ad elementum, et fit sacramentum. Unde ista tanta virtus aquae, ut corpus tangat et cor abluat, nisi faciente verbo? Non quia dicitur, sed quia creditur. Nam et in ipso verbo aliud est sonus transiens, aliud virtus manens.

See Lombard 4.3.1.

30 Chobham 4.2.7.1, p. 145: "matrimonium coniunctio maris et femine legitima indissolubilem vite consuetudinem retinens."; GD C.27 q.2 d.a.c.1; Lombard 4.27.2.

31 Chobham 4.2.7.6, pp. 149–150: "quoddam matrimonium est initiatum, ut quando fit consensus per verba de presenti; et quoddam est consummatum, ut quando intervenit carnalis copula; quoddam est ratum, ut quando ambo sunt in fide catholica."; GD C.28 q.1 d.p.c.17; Lombard 4.39.5, 7. As will be discussed in the next chapter, Lombard recognized consummation as important but maintained that a true marriage began with consent.

32 Chobham 4.2.7.9, pp. 153–154: "…fides, proles, et saramentum."; C.27 q.2 c.10, Lombard 4.31.1.

33 Chobham 7.2.7.10–18. See the next chapter for a more detailed discussion of marriage in the theological and canonical tradition.

beforehand by adultery," a text found both in Gratian and Peter Lombard.[34] Thomas of Chobham again illustrates a culture in which ideas and texts floated between *litterati*, between those whose knowledge was versatile enough to work between disciplines.

Familiarity Led to Versatility

Hugh of St. Victor, Peter Lombard, and Peter the Chanter and his circle were all familiar enough with the legal tradition that they could be versatile in their usage of it. With that, a few trends come to the fore. First, theologians drew from the swath of legal knowledge available. Second, they used different techniques to cite those sources.

Hugh of St. Victor drew upon canonical thought sparingly, though when he did, he looked to works that originated and circulated widely in northern France. Part 3 of the *De Sacramentis Christianae Fidei* on spiritual powers and the ecclesiastical orders (Bk. 2) demonstrates that Hugh drew both upon Ivo's sermon *De excellentia ordinum* and a canonical collection, such as Ivo's *Decretum* or the *Panormia*. The chapter on door-keepers (Table 2.1) serves as an excellent example.[35]

Hugh crafted the chapter on the office of the door-keeper from both Ivo's sermon, and either the *Decretum* or the *Panormia*. A similar trend can be seen in the chapters on deacons (cap. 11) and presbyters (cap. 12). Hugh relied exclusively on a legal collection for other chapters, drafting chapter 13 on bishops from a series of canons included in both Ivo's *Decretum* (5.72b, 6.20, 5.138, 5.124, 5.69a, 5.109med., 5.338) and in the *Panormia* (3.5, 3.41, 3.15, 3.18, 3.12, 3.14, 3.19). He likewise drew on canonical texts for the chapters on archbishops (cap. 14)[36]; the pope (cap. 15)[37]; other ecclesiastical offices such as archdeacons, head-chamberlain, and treasurer (cap. 16–19)[38]; the age for ordination (cap. 21)[39]; when and how ordinations should be performed (cap. 20)[40]; that priests should not be ordained without a title (cap. 22)[41]; nature of those to be

34 Chobham 4.2.7.18, p. 180: "nemo illam ducat in matrimonium quam prius polluit per adulterium."; GD C.31 q.1 c.1; Lombard 4.35.4.

35 De Sacr. 2.3.6 (PL 176: 423–424); Pan. 3.29, 41; Ivo of Chartres, Sermon 2 (PL 162: 514); Isidore of Seville, *De officiis ecclsiasticis*, Bk. 2 (PL 83: 794); H. Weisweiler, "Die Arbeitsmethode Hugos von St. Viktor: Ein Beitrag zum Entstehen seines," *Scholastik* 20, no. 24 (1949): 59–87, 232–267, here 77–78.

36 ID 5.139b, 5.136; Pan. 3.10–11.

37 Pan. 3.1; canon not found ID.

38 ID 6.20; Pan. 3.41.

39 Pan. 3.32; canon not found in ID.

40 ID 6.74, 5.69a, 6.21; Pan. 3.25, 12, 21.

41 ID 6.26; Pan. 3.27.

TABLE 2.1 Hugh of St. Victor's use of legal thought in chapter on door-keepers in the *De Sacramentis Christianae Fidei*.

Hugh of St. Victor, De Sacramentis, Bk. 2 pt. 3 cap. 6	*Ivo of Chartres, De excellentia ordinum* (Sermon 2)	*Ivo of Chartres, Decretum*	*Panormia, Bk. 3*
De ostiariis.			
Inter hos septem gradus spiritualis officii primus est eorum quo ostiarii dicuntur, qui in Veteri Testamento olim janitores vocabantur.	In his septem officiis primus gradus est ostiariorum qui		
Ad officium ostiarii pertinent claves ecclesiae, ut claudater et aperiat horis cempetentibus templum Dei et omnia quae sunt intus extraque custodiat fideles recipiat, excommunicatos et infideles ejuciat.		c.20: Ad ostiarium namque pertinent claves ecclesie, ut claudat et aperiat templum Dei, et omnia que sunt intus extraque custodiat, fideles recipiat, excommunicatos et infideles excipiat.	c.41: Ad ostiarium namque pertinent claves ecclesie, ut claudat et aperiat templum Dei, et omnia que sunt intus extraque custodiat, fideles recipiat, excommunicatos et infideles excipiat.
Ostiarius cum ordinatur postquam ab archidiacono instructus fuerit, qualiter in domo Dei dehabeat conversari, ad suggeationem archidiaconi tradit ei episcopus claves Ecclesiae de altario dicens ei: Sic age quasi redditurus Deo rationem pro his rebus quae his clavibus recluduntur.		c.18: Ostiarius, cum ordinatur, postquam ab archidiacono instructus fuerit qualiter in domo Dei debeat conversari, ad suggestionem archidiaconi tradit ei episcopus claves ecclesie de altario, dicens ei, Sic age, quasi redditurus Deo rationem pro his rebus, que istis clavibus recluduntur.	c.39: Ostiarius cum ordinatur, postquam ab archidiacono instructus fuerit qualiter in domo Dei debeat conversari, ad suggestionem archidiaconi tradit ei episcopus claves ecclesie de altario dicens ei, Sic age quasi redditurus Deo rationem, pro his rebus que istis clavibus recluduntur.
Hoc officium Dominus in sua persona suscepit, quando flagello de funiculis facto vendentes et ementes de templo ejecit.	Hoc officium Dominus noster nobis initiavit, quando flagello de funiculis facto, 'vendentes et ementes de templo ejecit.'		
Ipse quippe ostiarius dicit: 'Ego sum ostium. Per me si quis, introierit salvabitur, et ingredietur, et ingredietur et pascua inveniet.'	Unde et ipse ostiarius praetaxatus dicit: 'Ego sum ostium. Per me si quis, intreicrit, ingredietur, et egredietur.'		

elected to the sacred orders[42]; and reasons for changing one's ordination status.[43] Hugh may have found that the *Panormia* was more accessible than Ivo's *Decretum*. The texts upon which he relied are all found in a limited section of Book 3 of the *Panormia* whereas they are scattered throughout Book 6 of Ivo's *Decretum* with some being found in Book 5. Furthermore, the *Decretum* does not contain all of the texts on which Hugh relied, whereas the *Panormia* does.

The largest concentration of legal sources explicitly cited by Hugh of St. Victor in his *De Sacramentis Christianae Fidei* can be found in the sections devoted to consanguinity, affinity, and spiritual relationships. Hugh concluded his description of consanguinity by including nine texts found in legal sources: seven papal decretals, one text from the *Lex Romana canonice compta*, and one text from Bede's *Ecclesiastical History*. All but one of the texts on marriage that Hugh included in this chapter experienced wide circulation in canonical collections.[44] The lone exception, attributed to the *Institutes*, can be found only in the *Lex Romana canonice compta* (ca. 825–882), a collection of Roman law dealing with ecclesiastical matters; it survives in one manuscript from northeastern France.[45] Hugh's section on affinity simply comprises a list of three legal sources as one might see in a legal collection: two conciliar decrees and one papal decretal.[46] His chapter on spiritual relationships, also presented as one might find in a legal collection, comprises of five legal texts: three conciliar canons and two papal decretals.[47] While the texts, minus one, circulated in as many as 18–20 collections, not all of them were included in Gratian's *Decretum*.[48]

Peter Lombard likewise drew upon canonical thought sparingly, though when he had cause to do so he took advantage of his access to Gratian's *Decretum*. Compiled as a work of systematic theology for teaching at the University of Paris, canonical thought did not factor significantly into Books 1–3 of the *Sentences* and it played a limited role in Book 4. Book 1 addresses the nature of the Trinity, that is, three persons in the one Godhead. Book 2

42 Sections of Pan. 3.43–63; ID 6.58, 6.118, 6.95b, 6.126, 6.37, 6.41, 6.410, 6.107, 6.374, 6.60b, 6.134, 6.136, 6.138, 6.139. ID contains no parallels for Pan. 3.50, 3.52, 3.53, 3.54, 3.57, 3.63.

43 Pan. 3.69 (ID 5.138 contains similar ideas but is not a direct parallel), 3.89 (no parallel in ID), 3.74 (ID 6.176), 3.73 (ID 6.173), 3.75 (ID 6.270), and 3.24 (ID 6.22). For each, text Weisweiler meticulously detailed from which canons Hugh drew his text; see Weisweiler, "Die Arbeitsmethode Hugos von St. Viktor," 81–82 for parallels to the *Panormia*.

44 De Sac. 2.11.14 (PL 176: 540–546).

45 L. Fowler-Magerl, *Clavis Canonum Clavis Canonum: Selected Canon Law Collections Before 1140* (Hannover, 2005), 70.

46 De Sac. 2.11.15 (PL 176: 546–547).

47 De Sac. 2.11.16 (PL 176: 547–548).

48 De Sac. 2.11.14 (PL 176: 545): two canons from a decretal of Pope Zachary, one from a decretal of younger Gregory, and one from Bede's *History of the English* (1.37.4); cap. 15 (PL 176: 546): a canon from Gregory's decretal to Venerius, Bishop of Cagliari, is longer in Hugh's text than in Gratian's (GD C.35 q.10 c.1 ends with "numquid erit humanum").

treats creation, the state of man in Eden prior to lapsing, the Fall, as well as original and actual sin. Book 3 deals with Christology, different views on hypostatic union, soteriology, charity, and virtues. Book 4, finally, treats the sacraments as signs of grace and the last judgment.[49]

With the limited use of law noted, we must again remember the common intellectual culture and the links between theology and law as sciences that both relied heavily on the Bible and the Church Fathers. After all, Book 20 of Burchard of Worms' *Decretum* (ca. 1012–ca. 1022) was known as the *Speculator* and it deals with speculative theology.[50] Book 1 of the decretal collection *Liber extra* (1245) specifically addresses the Trinity. The *De consecratione*, which circulated with Gratian's *Decretum* as Part III, deals with the sacraments. Peter Lombard owned a copy of the *Decretum* and he used it. He drew a canon from John Chrysostom, via C.22 q.1 c.11, regarding whether an oath was more binding if sworn by God, the Gospels, or by creatures. Since God imbued holiness on the Scripture and made creatures, naturally, it is best to swear by God.[51] As Atria Larson has shown in her study of Gratian's *De penitentia*, Peter Lombard did not always treat the canons or the *dicta* in the same way. He could copy the text word for word, truncate or abbreviate the text, or paraphrase it. Sometimes his use of the material was to support a particular point, but he also used the texts to support a point unrelated to that found in the *De penitentia*. Other times, he did not accept Gratian's stance.[52] This was not an uncommon trend, as we will see. Peter the Chanter and his circle treated the legal sources upon which they drew for their *Libri penitentiales* in a similar manner. They adapted the law to suit their needs.

Hugh of St. Victor, Ivo, the compiler of the *Panormia*, Peter Lombard, and Gratian traveled in the same intellectual circles, drawing on similar sources and arguments. For example, in asking whether something that is not a lie can be perjury, Lombard cites Jerome's *On Jeremias*: "It is to be noted that the swearing of an oath has three components: truth, judgment, and justice. If these are lacking there is no oath, but perjury. Where a falsehood is sworn, truth is lacking."[53] The text is found in Ivo of Chartres' *Decretum*, the *Panormia*, and

49 For a detailed discussion of each book, sometimes with contradictory interpretations, see M. Colish, *Peter Lombard*, and P. Rosemann, *Peter Lombard.*

50 de Ghellinck, *Le Mouvement Thèlogique du XIIe Siècle*, 277–278, 283–287.

51 Lombard 3.39.6; GD C.22 q.1 c.11.

52 See Larson, *Master of Penance*, 319–332. Larson maintained that "Peter Lombard would not have thought of Gratian and Hugh or Peter Abelard as belonging in different disciplines…" (319). I am not sure that I would go this far, though I think they would have appreciated one's expertise in particular areas of thought. I do agree that these *litterati* relied on a common set of sources and utilized similar dialectic methods. They were part of the same intellectual climate.

53 Lombard 3.39.2.1: "Advertendum est, quod iusiurandum tres habet comites: veritatem, iudicium et iustitiam. Si ista defuerint, non erit iuramentum, sed periurium. Ubi autem falsum iuratur, veritas deest; …"

Gratian's *Decretum*.[54] Augustine's sermon on the triple manner of perjury is also found in all four collections.[55] Lombard included Augustine's famous comments on the eight types of lies, followed by Augustine's words that a person sins much less when the lie is not a capital lie that is used in teaching religion. But whoever thinks that there is any sort of lie which is not sin deceives himself terribly since he is judged honest though he is a deceiver of others.[56] The text is also found in Ivo, the *Panormia*, and Gratian.[57] Lombard's text does not replicate that found in the canonical collections but rather addresses the point under discussion, that is, the eight types of lies and the overall danger of lying while omitting the text found in the collections on the different types of lying. A final example of the overlapping intellectual climate is Lombard's use of a text from Isidore of Seville's *Sentences* on one who swore with verbal artfulness. While the text is found in Ivo's *Decretum*, the *Panormia*, and Gratian's *Decretum*, it is only the *Panormia* and Gratian that includes the version of the text found in Lombard's *Sentences*; the version found in Ivo is longer.[58]

Hugh of St. Victor and Peter Lombard were more than comfortable drawing upon sources from legal collections when they saw fit to do so. Occasionally they would include a full text. Most of the time, however, they were content with drawing from a particular sentence or two. As Peter Lombard illustrates, it was not uncommon for theologians to paraphrase a concept similar to that found in the law without directly citing a particular legal source. Lombard and Hugh of St. Victor reflect de Ghellinck's view that canonists and theologians studied topics, engaged with sources from similar angles, and shared their thoughts with each other.[59] For example, in setting out the shapes lies can take—for the safety or advantage of others, as amusement, and those that stem from malignity and duplicity—Lombard implicitly alluded to Augustine's *Enarrationes in Psalmos*.[60] Ivo, the compiler of the *Panormia*, and Gratian both expressed similar concepts, though Lombard did not directly quote them.[61] In questioning oaths sworn by creatures, Lombard draws on Jerome and Augustine to argue that Christ forbade swearing by creatures lest there should be believed to be something divine in them. Similar arguments and examples are found in C.22 q.1 c.16 and d.p.c.16.[62] Lombard's discussion of what it means to swear by God, also rooted in Augustine, echoes points made by Ivo and the compiler

54 ID 12.22; Pan. 8.123; GD C.22 q.2 c.2.
55 Lombard 3.39.3.1; ID 12.39; Pan. 8.111; GD C.22 q.2 c.3.
56 Lombard 3.38.2.
57 ID 12.1; Pan. 8.82a; GD C.22 q.2 c.8.
58 Lombard 3.39.11; Pan. 8.112; GD C.22 q.5 c.9; ID 12.36. The text in ID is the same as that in Pan. 8.112 and 8.113.
59 de Ghellinck, *Le Mouvement Thèlogique du XIIe Siècle*, 280.
60 Lombard 3.38.1.1.
61 ID 10.46; Pan. 8.130; GD C.22 q.2 c.14. The texts in the canonical collections were the same.
62 Lombard 3.39.5.2.

of the *Panormia*.[63] Sometimes theologians felt moved to use canonical texts directly. Even when they were not, they were still acquainted with the source material.

At the turn of the thirteenth century when papal decretals were all the rage, both Robert of Flamborough and Bartholomew of Exeter, upon whose work Robert leaned, drew from Burchard of Worms, Ivo of Chartres, in addition to Gratian, for their *Libri penitentiales*. This would make sense as Bartholomew's penitential was a source for Robert's *Liber penitentialis*. With that said, they may not have utilized the authorities to the same degree.[64] Chapters 41–135 of Bartholomew's penitential have more parallels with the *Decretum* of Ivo of Chartres and the more contemporary *Decretum* of Gratian.[65] Forty-eight canons in Bartholomew's penitential parallel Ivo's collection on penance for the sick, 33 canons on marriage, 14 canons on incest and fornications, 24 canons on drunkenness and other sins, 22 canons on lying and perjury, 14 canons on magic, 13 canons on goods of the church and ecclesiastical property, 12 canons on baptism, 12 canons on the ordination of clerics, and 11 canons on the Eucharist.

Robert of Flamborough's penitential, despite being compiled after that of Bartholomew, continued to regard the *Decretum* of Burchard of Worms and the *Decretum* of Ivo of Chartres as particularly useful. As bishops, both Burchard and Ivo would have had to oversee the satisfaction of transgressions. As his primary interest was in pastoral theology, Robert's interest in the law lay with homicide, marriage, lying/perjury, magic, the Eucharist, and drunkenness. He drew 29 canons from Burchard's Book 19 on penance, 27 canons on homicide, 26 canons on magic, 16 canons on fornication and incest, 14 canons on excommunication, 11 canons on perjury, and ten canons on the Eucharist. From Ivo of Chartres's *Decretum*, he drew 35 canons on homicide, 34 canons from the section on penance for the sick, 28 canons on drunkenness and other sins, 22 canons on marriage, 17 canons on fornication and incest, 22 canons on perjury, 22 canons on magic, and 11 canons on the Eucharist.

The direct parallels between the two penitentials as they relate to the use of Ivo of Chartres's *Decretum* provide a good example of Robert having drawn some, but not all, of his texts from Bartholomew. For example, 17 of the 35

63 Lombard 3.39.7; ID 12.34; Pan. 8.115.

64 What follows is a statistical comparison of the indices found in editions of Morey and Firth. Taliadoros noted that Morey's edition is not a critical edition in that he attempted to identify the formal sources, but rather he only suggested parallels to texts found in Burchard, Ivo, Gratian, and Peter Lombard. According to Taliadoros, Burchard is arguably the most important source. See "Bartholomew of Exeter's Penitential," 460–461.

65 Gerard of Cambrai, *Opera* VII, 57 by way of S. Kuttner and E. Rathbone, "Anglo-Norman Canonists of the Twelfth-Century: An Introductory Study," *Traditio* 7 (1951): 279–358, here 295; J. Longère "Quelques 'Summa de poenitentia' à la fin du XIIe siècle et au début du XIIIe siècle," in *La piété populaire au Moyen Âge*, ed. E. Delaruelle (Paris, 1975), 45–58, here 46.

canons on homicide are in common with Bartholomew, 16 of the 34 canons from the section on penance for the sick are in common, 16 of the 28 canons on drunkenness and other sins are in common, 12 of the 22 canons on marriage and seven of the 17 canons on fornication and incest are in common, 13 of the 22 canons on perjury are in common, six of the 21 canons on magic are in common, and four of the 11 canons on the Eucharist are in common. These numbers suggest that Robert did not draw blindly from the penitential of Bartholomew of Exeter, but rather he also returned to the original source, in this case, the *Decretum* of Ivo of Chartres, and selected texts that best suited his purpose.

While Biblical quotations from the Old and New Testament are found in virtually every paragraph of Peter the Chanter's *Summa de sacramentis et animae consiliis*—a work that addresses the efficacy of the sacraments, baptism, confirmation, extreme unction (last rights), dedication and consecration of churches, and the Eucharist—that reliance does not negate the role legal thought played as examples from Part I on the sacraments suggest. In these cases, Peter made explicit reference to the law. In his discussion of what makes baptism effective, Peter specifically referenced the Council of Seville (Hispalense)—"Diffinit enim Hispalense concilium"—which decreed that the [holy] orders should not be conferred on those whom the bishop ignorantly laid his hands, and another priest should give and advance the benediction.[66] The canon as found in Gratian's *Decretum*, attributed to c.5 of the Second Council of Seville (ca. 619), recounts a bishop's ordination of unworthy candidates.[67] Peter did not quote the canon verbatim but rather drew out the essential implications: the bishop's responsibility is to ordain worthy candidates, and in the event that an ordination is unworthy another should perform the sacrament. In his discussion of the preparatory states to baptism, such as exorcism and catechism, Peter questioned briefly how spiritual affinity is restricted on account of

66 Chanter I §35, p. 102: "Diffinit enim Hispalense concilium, ordines non esse collatos illis quibus episcopus cecutiens manum imposuit, et sacerdos alius benedictionem dedit et protulit."

67 GD D.23 c.13:

> Ad cognitionem nostri examinis Gabrenensis diaconi relatu peruenit de quibusdam ipsius ecclesiae clericis, quorum cum unus ad presbiterium, duo ad Levitarum ministerium consecrarentur, episcopus eorum, oculorum dolore detentus, fertur manum suam super eos tantum posuisse, et presbiter quidam illis contra ecclesiasticum ordinem benedictionem dedisse; qui propter tantam presumptionis audaciam poterat accusatus iudicio presenti dampnari, si adhuc in corpore positus, non fuisset mortis vocatione preventus. Sed quia iam ille examini divino relictus humano iudicio accusari non potest, hi, qui supersunt, et ab eo non consecrationis titulum, sed ignominiae potius elogium acceperunt, ne sibi licentiam talis ultra usurpatio faciat, decrevimus, ut a gradu sacerdotalis vel levitici ordinis, quem perverse adepti sunt, depositi equo iudicio abiciantur. Tales enim merito iudicati sunt removendi, quia prave inventi sunt constituti.

Letter of Pope Simplicius to Bishops Severus and Florentinus (Jaffé no. 339).

the holy sacraments, as is held in the canon(s) ("in canone habetur").[68] Causa 30 q.1 of Gratian's *Decretum* explicitly addresses spiritual affinity.[69] Peter asked in what way spiritual paternity is restricted since he who is called a spiritual son has not been brought forth again / regenerated (*regeneratus*).[70] His question parallels Gratian's conclusion that a husband and a wife should not be separated should one receive their own or their spouse's child from the baptismal font.[71] In both cases, spiritual affinity does not negate a holy sacrament, be it baptism or marriage. Peter Lombard likewise addressed spiritual affinity as an impediment to marriage.[72] Some of his material sources echo those used by Gratian, though in most cases he pulls a select quotation rather than relying on the entire canon.[73] In other instances, Peter Lombard drew from legal texts not utilized by Gratian.[74] Theology and law asked similar questions about the sacraments and they drew upon similar, if not the same, material sources.

Peter the Chanter included a wide swath of material found in the legal tradition, particularly in Parts II and III. This material can be found in each of the sections of Gratian's *Decretum*, that is, the *distinctiones*, *causae*, and tractates *De penitentia* and *De consecratione*. He also incorporated concepts found in conciliar canons, primarily from the eleventh and twelfth century, such as from the councils of Rome (1078), Reims (1119, 1131, and 1148), Rouen (1128 and 1190), Tours (1163), and from the Second Lateran (1139) and Third Lateran (1179) Councils. What strikes one's eye is that the councils drawn upon were held in or around the Paris region. Peter also drew, though somewhat sparingly, from papal letters, such as those from Gregory VII, Urban II, Alexander III, and Innocent III. These letters could be found in decretal collections such as the *Collectio Brugensis*, the *Collectio Peterhusensis*, the *Collectio Sangermanensis*, and *Compilationes I* and *II*. Finally, he was familiar with

68 Chanter I §21, p. 61: "Per ea spiritualis proximitas contrahitur scilicet compaternitas, sicut in canone habetur."

69 GD C.30 q.1 c.1–c.10.

70 Chanter I §21, p. 61: "Sed quomodo paternitas spiritualis contrahitur, cum non sit regeneratus ille qui filius spiritualis dicitur?"

71 GD C.30 q.1 d.p.c.10: "His itaque auctoritatibus apparet, quod sive proprium, sive tantummodo viri filium mulier de sacro fonte susceperit, non ideo a viro suo est separanda. Quod et de viro similiter oportet intellegi."

72 See Lombard 4.42.1–6.

73 Pope Symachus (Lombard 4.42.2; GD C.30 q.1 c.8), Council of Mainz (Lombard 4.42.2; GD C.30 q.1 c.5), Pope Nicholas I to the Bishop of Salona (Lombard 4.42.2; GD C.30 q.1 c.3), Second Council of Chalon-sur-Saône (813) (Lombard 4.42.2; GD C.30 q.1 c.4), Pope John to Bishop Anselm of Limoges (Lombard 4.42.2; GD C.30 q.1 c.7), Pope Deusdedit to Bishop Gordianus of Seville (Lombard 4.42.2; GD C.30 q.1 c.1), Capitulare Compendiense (757) misattributed to the Council of Verberie (Lombard 4.42.2; GD C.30 q.1 c.2) [Lombards leaves out that the canon applies equally to women].

74 Pope Nicholas I to the Bulgarians (Lombard 4.42.3), Pope Urban II (Lombard 4.42.4, 6), Council of Tribur (895) (Lombard 4.42.4, 5), Pope Nicholas I to the Bishop of Constantinople (Lombard 4.42.5).

Roman law as he incorporated ideas found principally in Justinian's *Digest*, as well as a smattering of texts in the *Institutes*, *Codex*, one from the *Authentica*, as well as three texts from the *Theodosian Code*.[75]

The Chanter also explicitly referenced councils and papal pronouncements. In his section on simony, he indirectly referenced councils on three occasions—c.4 and c.7 of the Third Lateran Council (1179) and c.2 of the Council of Tours (1163)—presided over by Pope Alexander III in which he banned simony. In the case of the canons from the Third Lateran Council, Peter simply named the council, "Lateranensis concilli," or Alexander as the pope.[76] He provided no further information, expecting the reader to know the legal source. In the case of the Council of Tours, Peter provided the incipit of the canon and the council: "Plures clericorum ex concilio Turonensi."[77]

Peter the Chanter's discussion on the redemption of benefices and their commutation offers an example of how he drew upon but did not cite the law. Here, Peter asked "[a]fter, having been led to penance, he asked for money from the bishop as he discussed, offering to him the resigned prebend. It is asked whether the bishop is able to ransom a prebend."[78] To present the contra stance, that the bishop was not able to bestow a prebend in exchange for money, Peter noted that by giving money he made himself unworthy, and, therefore, he was not able to receive the benefice. Furthermore, he who accepts the money is not able to retain his benefice.[79] Justinian's *Digest* treats a similar issue in Book 12 title 5 "The *condictio* for immoral or illegal payments." To offer a few examples: According to Ulpian, if a thief pays to avoid being given away, there is no recovery, for both parties are tainted.[80] According to Paul, if both parties, giver

75 Chanter, Table of citations for ecclesiastical and secular authors found in II, pp. 497–505; III.2a and III.2b, pp. 799–817.

76 The Third Lateran Council (c.7) in 1179 was referenced as "...decretum Lateranensis concilli quo constitutum est, ne quid exigatur pro benedictione nuptiali et huiusmodi, ita determinandum, ne quid exigatur ante, sed post licet." See Chanter III.2a §74, p. 67 ln. 19. The Third Lateran Council (c.4) was referenced as "... Videtur hoc symonia, et dominus Alexander papa hoc prohibuit." See Chanter III.2a §179, p. 79 ln. 50.

77 The Council of Tours c.2 in 1163 was referenced as "...canonis Plures clericorum ex concilio Turonensi ubi dicitur quod licet clericis recipere supra sortem ad redimendum beneficium ecclesiasticum de manu laici." See Chanter III.2a §180, p. 82 ln. 25.

78 Chanter III.2a §176, p. 69: "Post, penitentia ductus, petit ab episcopo pecuniam quam contulit, illi offerens resignationem prebende. Querit an episcopus possit ita redimere prebendam"

79 Chanter III.2a §176, p. 70 ln. 5–11:

> Contra. Ille dando pecuniam facit se indignum pecunia. Ergo eam recipere non potest. Preterea, *in pari causa turpitudinis potior est conditio possidentis*, sed in quo potior nisi a retinendum? At qui accepit, retinere, non potest, quia *non dimittetur ei peccatum nisi* reicerit *turpiter acceptum*, maximie in tanta turpitudine. Ergo nec ille qui dedit potest recipere multior fortius quod concessibile uidetur.

80 Dig. 12.5.4.1: "Item si dederit fur, ne proderetur, quoniam utriusque turpitudo versatur, cessat repetitio." See also Dig. 1.378.

and recipient, are tainted, the possessor is stronger, and no recovery is therefore possible even though the payment is made under a stipulation.[81] Paul also noted that when the evil taints both the giver and recipient, recovery is excluded as where money is given to pervert a judgment.[82] Peter the Chanter could be seen as drawing upon legal principles found in Roman law, though he never explicitly cited it.

Sometimes, the Chanter heavily abbreviated references to Gratian's *Decretum*, simply referencing the causa and nothing else.[83] On one occasion, he references Gratian's text by the rubric. In his section concerning the redemption of ecclesiastical law and agreements about the tithes, Peter included the rubric "Usura enim est quicquid sorti accredit"as evidence that those involved in casting lots are guilty of usury.[84] In one case, Peter simply included one sentence—"Quisquis alterum eorum venit sine quo alterum non provenit, neutrum invenditum dereliquit"—from C.1 q.3 c.7 without further attribution to reinforce the point that those who buy an ecclesiastical benefice, also are proven to buy churches.[85]

Other times he combined attributions in order to provide the reader with a greater sense of location within the *Decretum*. For example, Peter might cite the material sources (*fontes materiales*) and the incipit of the canon, as in the cases of C.1 q.3 c.8 by citing "Salvator, Urbanus" and C.8 q.1 c.6 by citing "in illa auctoritate Iheronimi, scilicet *Moyses*"[86] He might also cite the causa and the incipit, as in the case of C.12 q.2 c.67 where Peter improperly cited causa but correctly cited the incipit as "ca. XI *Ecclesiasticis*" and D.63 c.21 where Peter improperly cited the distinction but correctly cited the incipit as "Agatho, D. LX."[87] Finally, Peter cited the causa and question as in the case of C.1 q.5.[88]

In some instances, the Chanter felt it necessary to include complete citations to the *Decretum*. In his section concerning those who bought a benefice or religious habit, Peter cites C.1 q.2 c.2 by "C.1 q.2 *Quam pio*" to argue that nothing is to be exacted from those who have been accepted to religious orders.[89] Peter again cited C.8 q.1 *Moyses* (c.2) to argue that a bishop cannot appoint his successor.[90] This would be the only canon where Peter included the

81 Dig. 12.5.8: "...porro autem si et dantis et accipientis turpis causa sit, possessorem potiorem esse et ideo repetitionem cessare, tametsi ex stipulatione solutum est." See also Dig. 1.378.

82 Dig. 12.5.3: "Ubi autem et dantis et accipientis turpitudo versatur, non posse repeti dicimus: veluti si pecunia detur, ut male iudicetur." See also Dig. 1.378.

83 Chanter III.2a §169, p. 49 ln. 56 references GD C.1; p. 79 ln. 42 incorrectly cites Causa 7 when referencing C.10; p. 81 ln. 19 references C.16.

84 Chanter III.2a §178, p. 75 ln. 12.

85 Chanter III.2a §166, p. 43 ln. 13.

86 Chanter III.2a §162, p. 37 ln. 109; III.2a, §160, p. 27 ln. 56.

87 Chanter III.2a §178, p. 77 ln. 47; III.2a, §187, p. 105 ln. 3.

88 Chanter III.2a §184, p. 100 ln. 122.

89 Chanter III.2a §168, p. 46 ln. 10.

90 Chanter III.2a §182, p. 92 ln. 37.

entire text—material source as Jerome in a letter to Titus, causa, question, and complete canon—in his discussion of the definition of simony and the various forms it took.[91] Also in that discussion was the one time that Peter included the material source, the causa, question, and incipit *Sunt nonnulli* to C.1 q.1 c.114, incorrectly cited as q.6, on the multiple types of simony.[92]

Robert of Courçon's *Summa* likewise drew upon Gratian's *Decretum* while also drawing on papal decretals if needed. Although he relied less on Roman law, Robert was not unfamiliar with it. As a papal judge-delegate, Roman law may have proven convenient or necessary as a supplement. Robert's reliance on the law varied between explicit citation, a general reference, and no reference at all, but his thoughts were grounded in it. Chapters 11 and 12 on usury illustrate these usages. In his articulation of what it means to exact interest, Robert quotes from Gratian, C.14 q.3 *Plerique* (c.3): "Usura est quicquid sorti accedit."[93] Whether borrowed from Peter the Chanter or taken directly from the *Decretum*, Robert saw the law as important for corroborating his position.[94]

Posing the argument that one could charge interest, Courçon simply provided a loose reference to the "lex Justinana" as evidence. In this case, he noted that the "lex Justinana" permitted interest to be charged at 1%.[95] Robert did not explicitly cite the law to which he referred and, while Roman law called for what could be considered reasonable rates, the cited rate of 1% was not this generous. The *Digest* noted 6% as an example in cases where debtors' loan was transferred to the treasury, a rate that would continue to be owed.[96] The *Codex* provided more nuance. Persons of higher rank could stipulate no more than 4% interest for any contract, no matter the size. Managers of shops and persons who carry on any lawful business could exact no more than 8% interest. Maritime contracts or loans of property in species could carry an interest rate of no more than 12%. All other contracts were limited to 6% interest, the percentage reflected in the *Digest*. Furthermore, a judge was prohibited from increasing rates for any reason in any region.[97] The *Novella* would add to the nuances found in the *Codex* by stipulating that bankers could not loan money at more than 8% interest per year.[98] Robert had presented a generous interpretation of Roman law to make the point that even at an interest rate of 1%, the charging of interest was in no way permitted. In his *solutio*, he notes Peter the Chanter's

91 Chanter III.2a §156, p. 5 ln. 30.
92 Chanter III.2a §156, p. 6 ln. 49.
93 Courçon 11.1 (fol. 51va); G. Lefèvre, ed. and trans., *Le Traité "De Usura" de Robert de Courçon* (Lille, 1902), 3; edF., col. 734.
94 Chanter III.2a §213, p. 179 ln. 2. It should be noted that Peter the Chanter did not explicitly cite the causa-question-incipit but simply included the quotation from c.3.
95 Courçon 11.2 (fol. 51va); Lefèvre, ed. and trans., *Le Traité "De Usura" de Robert de Courçon*, 5.
96 Dig. 22.1.17.6.
97 Cod. 4.32.26.2.
98 Nov. 136 c.4.

stance that while the charging of interest is not permitted against one's brother, it could be in cases in which a foreigner asked you to lend to him.[99]

Robert of Courçon did not always reference the legal tradition, but it did factor into this thinking. Take, for example, his questioning of whether a prince, a prelate, or any entity could accept something from someone who had charged interest. The second part of the *questio* is clearly grounded in legal thought. It questions whether prelates, abbots, and religious houses were permitted to accept items from interest to defend themselves.[100] In his *solutio*, Robert concludes that abbots and religious houses cannot legitimately accept anything from usurers unless they have tried to return what they have taken. If the usurer cannot restore the goods to those from whom he took them, they can be donated by the hand of the Church for the benefit of the souls of their victims and the aid of the poor.[101] Such falls in line with that set forth in the latter half of C.14 q.5 where Gratian notes that every effort should be made to return the ill-gotten possessions to those wrongly affected. If that is not possible, they may be used for the benefit of those in need, especially for the relief of the poor.[102]

The first part of this *questio* represents the changing realities of the legal landscape. Robert began under the premise: "Videtur quod princeps possit iure principum regni quod decretum est, si constiterit christianum fieri feneratorem omnia bona eius cedere in ius et arbitrium principis."[103] According to this, the prince was able to invoke the a sovereign right of the princes, which held that if a Christian has become a lender at interest, all his property falls under the law and judgment of the prince. Robert's *solutio* would go on to conclude that neither princes, prelates, abbots, nor religious houses can receive something from a known usurer or someone with a reputation for being one. The prince of the territory must take away from the usurer all the property gained from his actions and return it to those who had been despoiled, as it is the prince's responsibility to render justice. Should the prince keep the property for himself, he has sinned.[104] While the core of the resolution—that attempts should be

99 Courçon 11.3 (fol. 51vb):

> Per has et consimiles rationes, videtur quod in nullo casu admittenda est usura. ... Cantor sic exposuit illam auctoritatem: 'non feneraberis fratri tuo in terra sancta; sed ibi adeo abundans eris quod feneraberis alieno, id est, alieni petent a te fenerari.'

Lefèvre, ed. and trans., *Le Traité "De Usura" de Robert de Courçon*, 7: See for example, Chanter III.2a §213, p. 182 ln. 80: "Si autem prorsus alieni, non est usura."

100 Courçon 11.6 (fol. 53ra): "...se defendere prelati, abbates, et domus religiose quibus contendunt se talibus posse accipere aliquid..." Lefèvre, ed. and trans., *Le Traité "De Usura" de Robert de Courçon*, 21. Exod. 12:36; Luc 16:9, Tob. 2:18–21 are used as support.

101 Courçon 11.7 (fol. 53rb); Lefèvre, ed. and trans., *Le Traité "De Usura" de Robert de Courçon*, 23.

102 GD C.14 q.5 d.p.c.13–c.15.

103 Courçon 11.6 (fol. 53ra); Lefèvre, ed. and trans., *Le Traité "De Usura" de Robert de Courçon*, 21.

104 Courçon 11.7 (fol. 53rb); Lefèvre, ed. and trans., *Le Traité "De Usura" de Robert de Courçon*, 23.

made to return the ill-gotten possessions to those wrongly affected—reflects C.14 q.5, nowhere is there mention in the canon of the secular authority as the party responsible for ensuring this happened. The closest proximity seems to be a decretal from Pope Innocent III to the Archbishop of Narbonne (1198), which stated that Jews are compelled to make restitution for usury by their removal from the Christian community by secular princes.[105] While not a viewpoint held in canon law, Robert of Courçon was acknowledging that secular, as well as ecclesiastical, courts adjudicated usury cases.[106]

Courçon's response to the question of what timid priests should do concerning lenders whom public infamy accuses reflects a legal tradition on the cusp of change. He notes that these lenders—who are incorrigible and do not want to restore anything—are supported by the bishop, archdeacon, and rural dean. Such supporters remark that because they have not confessed, they must be tolerated. The simple faithful, however, cry out that these supporters are usurers themselves who have allowed themselves to be corrupted by others. Robert's solution, which did not explicitly cite any legal principle, is that the priest should bring together the simple parishioners of his church and enjoin them to accuse all these usurers. This way the malefactors can be convinced to accept correction or be cut off from the church if they do not want to come to correction.[107] Robert's solution bears some semblance to accusatory procedure, the process whereby an accuser, in this case, the simple faithful, came forward and publicly accused another of a crime. The "full proof" (*plena probatio*) provided of the crime necessary to convict would either be a confession from the accused or statements of two credible witnesses under oath that they personally witnessed the crime.[108] Yet, Robert was aided by inquisitorial procedure, which Pope Innocent III's *Qualiter et quando* integrated into the formal legal structure of the Western Church as a replacement for accusatory procedure. With inquisitorial procedure, the "frequent outcries" and "public reports" were sufficient to begin the judicial process. Again, the denunciation of the

105 III Comp. 5.10.2 (X 5.19.12). Note 2 indicates that the letter was also addressed to the archbishop's suffragans, the counts, the barons, and all the people of the province of Narbonne (edF. 2, col. 814).

106 As it will be discussed in Chapter 7 on Thomas of Chobham's treatment of greed, courts, both secular and ecclesiastical, dealt with overt cases of usury. Cases of "cloaked usury"—such as those found in *venditio* and *emptio ad tempus / ad terminum* resulting in surreptitious profits, were left to the internal forum of confession. See, T. P. McLaughlin, "The Teaching of the Canonists of Usury," *Mediaeval Studies* 1 (1939): 81–147, here 119–120.

107 Courçon 12.12 (fol. 58ra–58rb); Lefèvre, ed. and trans., *Le Traité "De Usura" de Robert de Courçon*, 81.

108 M. H. Eichbauer, *Medieval Canon Law*, 2nd edn. Expanded and revised version of the First Edition by James A. Brundage (London, 2023), 106–118 for the *ordo iuris*; J. Brundage, "Full and Partial Proof in Classical Canonical Procedure," *The Jurist* 67, no. 1 (2007): 58–71, here 60, 67; H. A. Kelly, "Inquisitorial Due Process and the Status of Secret Crimes," in *Proceedings San Diego 1988*, ed. S. Chodorow (Vatican City, 1992), 407–427, here 407.

simple faithful was sufficient. Innocent III had grounded inquisitorial procedure in Genesis 18:21 whereby God responded to the ill repute of Sodom and Gomorrah: "I will go down and see whether they have done according to the cry that is come to me." Based on the inquiry (*inquisitio*), a judge could proceed with the judicial process and determine if there was enough evidence to deem the accused guilty of the reported crimes.[109] Inquisitorial procedure had made initiating the process easier, though the basic procedural elements of due process were to remain unaltered. Despite the possible road to redemption, Robert's *solutio* holds little hope that the usurer would take advantage of it. He cites an example of a man who confessed that all he possessed was gained on account of his father's usury and plunder. He admitted that neither he nor others could be saved unless they returned everything in so far as possible. Yet, when knowing that salvation hung in the balance, he stated that he would rather have "you take me from here naked and throw me into manure, then make all those palaces and other riches be returned."[110]

Robert of Courçon's reliance on the law, and his citation of it, depended very much on the topic at hand. That is, he did not include legal sources simply for the sake of using them but only did so when they were germane to the discussion. In some cases, where the law added to, but was not the center of, his point, he attributed a less specific reference. Such can be seen in the *solutio* and, though less frequently, the *objectio* of chapter 1 on penance. As one would expect, Biblical citations and references to the Church Fathers (Jerome, Augustine, and Ambrose) feature predominately. When Robert does draw on legal principles, especially those from the *Decretum*, he rarely cites them explicitly. Rather he uses phrases such as "cum auctoritas clamet," "dicit canon," "tradit decretales," or "dicit auctoritas." Chapter 1.25 addresses the remedies of penance which should be rendered in alms with the last quarter rendered by the wearing down of the flesh. As part of his justification for the weakening of the flesh as a component of repayment, Robert briefly noted that, "cum auctoritas clamet," a sin cannot be dismissed unless what was taken has been restored. That last quarter was important for restoration echoes C.14 q.6 c.1. which deals with whether usurers were able to perform penance if they had not restored what they had taken.[111] In chapter 1.33 on the immunity of animals in the law, Robert shifts to the question of what would you say to a cleric or anyone from among the clergy who approached you in the penitential forum

109 III Comp. 5.1.3 (X 5.1.17); Potthast 1824. See also Brundage, "Full and Partial Proof in Classical Canonical Procedure," 68; Kelly, "Inquisitorial Due Process and the Status of Secret Crimes," 408, 409.

110 Courçon 12.12 (fol. 58rb): "…ut me nudum asportetis et in sterquilinis prociciatis et omnia illa palatia et cetera restitui faciatis." Lefèvre, ed. and trans., *Le Traité "De Usura" de Robert de Courçon*, 83.

111 Courçon 1.25 (fol. 10va); V. L. Kennedy, "Robert of Courson on Penance," *Mediaeval Studies* 7, no. 1 (1945): 291–336, edition 294–336, here 307.

having served in the army for a long time under some prince and having not resisted but either consented or cooperated in his exactions? Robert simply uses "dicit canon" to reiterate the principle that should someone start a fire, cause it to be started, or knowingly provide counsel or help to those starting one, he first has to make reparations for the loss according to his means as part of his. He then references the principle "iuxta illud" that those who consented should restore everything seized, for he approves of an error when he does not resist it.[112] The texts alluded to in "dicit canon" and in "iuxta illud" are found, respectively, in the *palea* C.23 q.8 c.32 and in D.83 c.3 of the *Decretum*. Robert's *solutio* to the issue would reference a decretal of Pope Clement III—that those who lay hands on a cleric or were incendiaries could only be absolved by the pope—simply as "tradit decretalis." Incendiaries and others promoting sedition in the city were to be sent to the pope because it was irregular to flog them and difficult to determine the appropriate penance.[113] As a final example from chapter 1.39, Robert asks what should be responded to in the cloistered penitential forum when particular demons rear their head, such as usury, theft, simony, or any illicit acquisition of something. In his *objectio*, Robert questions what should happen if the confessor hands him over to the council of the abbot. He should be struck with a sentence of excommunication and he ought not to rise up against his pastor. "[D]icit canon" reflects the legal principle that both a just and an unjust sentence of excommunication stands.[114] In his discussion of theft and robbery, Robert uses "auctoritas dicit" to include the principle that it was not permitted for the Egyptians to seize the possessions of another as it was theft from the Israelites.[115] In each of these examples, the legal principle was not the most important component of the dialogue and thus did not warrant a specific reference. Law, rather, served an auxiliary role, a role which only necessitated a generic mention.

As we saw above, the *Libri penitentiales* of Bartholomew of Exeter and Robert of Flamborough were drawn from the earlier canonical collections of Burchard of Worms and Ivo of Chartres. Bartholomew also drew heavily upon Gratian's *Decretum*, having 92 more canons as parallels with Gratian's *Decretum*—77 of which are found in the *causae*—than does the penitential of Robert of Flamborough. Bartholomew's chapter on perjury parallels 17

112 Courçon 1.33 (fol. 12rb): "Si enim clericus aliquis uel alius quicumque diu militavit sub tali principe non resistendo eius exactionibus aut consentiendo aut cooperando, tibi accesserit in foro penitentiali, quid dices ei?"; Kennedy, "Robert of Courson on Penance," 311.

113 Courçon 1.33 (fol. 12va); Kennedy, "Robert of Courson on Penance," 312; II Comp. 5.18.8 (X 5.39.19); Jaffé 10238.

114 Courçon 1.39 (fol. 14rb–14va): "...preterea sententia excommunicationis sive iuste sive iniuste lata fuerit a pastore tenet. Hoc dicit canon; sicut nosti"; Kennedy, "Robert of Courson on Penance," 317; GD C.11 q.3 c.27.

115 Courçon 1.39 (fol. 14va): "...et auctoritas dicit: Spoliandi sunt Egyptii et ditandi sunt Hebrei." Kennedy, "Robert of Courson on Penance," 317; GD C.14 q.5 c.12.

canons with Causa 22 of Gratian's *Decretum*, with 11 canons paralleling C.22 q.5 on whether a bishop who compelled his archdeacon to go against his oath is guilty of perjury. Parallels exist between 13 canons from C.24 q.3 on whether an entire family ought to be excommunicated for the sin of one, and 12 canons from C.11 q.3 on whether a cleric who held his bishop's sentence in contempt be deposed without hope of restitution. Adrian Morey noted that Bartholomew's two chapters on schism and simony were exclusively drawn from Gratian.[116]

Robert of Flamborough used Gratian's *Decretum* rather sparingly despite explicitly cross-referencing the collection. He drew most heavily from Causa 22 where he borrowed nine canons from q.5 on whether one who compels another to go against his oath is guilty of perjury, seven of which Bartholomew also used; and six canons from C.22 q.4 on whether an illicit oath ought to be upheld, three of which are also in common with Bartholomew. From Causa 33, he drew five canons from q.3, four of which he shares with Bartholomew, on whether a crime can be remitted through confession in the heart alone; and four canons, three of which are in common with Bartholomew, from q.4 on whether the conjugal debt can be rendered during times of prayer. He borrowed eight canons from D.50 dealing with clerical crimes, three of which are in common with Bartholomew. He borrowed seven canons from C.1 q.1 on simony, none of which were in common with Bartholomew. He borrowed seven canons from C.17 q.4 on whether an abbot could retain the possessions of a monk who left without permission, seven of which are in common with Bartholomew. He borrowed five canons both from C.11 q.3 on whether one who held his bishop's sentence in contempt could be deposed without hope of restitution and from C.12 q.2 on whether belongings given to a church should remain in perpetuity with that church. In both cases, Robert shares only one canon with Bartholomew. Finally, Robert drew six canons from Distinction 4 of the *De consecratione*. Four of these texts are in common with Bartholomew, who only drew eight texts from this section for his penitential. Aside from these instances, Robert might only include one, two, or three canons from any particular distinction or question of the *Decretum* if he included any at all.

Robert of Flamborough supplemented his use of Gratian's *Decretum* with Huguccio's *Summa decretorum*. In fact, Robert referenced Huguccio by name in his discussion of spiritual affinity and homicide.[117] Huguccio was one of the most famous of the Bolognese canonists. A student at Bologna, he remained after his studies as a *magister* teaching canon law. While at Bologna he compiled his commentary on the *Decretum* in the 1180s. Huguccio was elevated to the bishopric of Ferrara in 1190, a position which he held until his death in

116 A. Morey, ed., *Bartholomew of Exeter, Bishop and Canonist: A Study in the Twelfth Century* (Cambridge, 1937), 174.
117 Flamborough 2.3 §45, p. 82; 3.3 §107, p. 122.

1210.[118] The apparatus of Firth's edition reveals that Robert leaned upon Huguccio for the rendering of the law and legal theory, particularly as it pertained to matrimonial law (Bk. 2) and ecclesiastical ordination (Bk. 3).[119] Robert's interest lay in the jurisprudence a *penitentiarius* or confessor would need to know in order for him to execute his duties.

Huguccio's commentary is reflected in the third section of Book 2, which addresses the impediments and diriments to marriage.[120] The nature of vows, whether simple vows that could be broken or solemn vows that could not be broken,[121] was important as they factored into marriage. For example, a man could revoke a simple vow to marriage prior to the marriage taking place, just as an abbot could revoke a monk's simple vow of abstinence prior to his conversion to the religious life.[122] Confessors, no doubt, had to grapple with vows made between spouses. Could, for example, a husband revoke a solemn vow to live a chaste life when his wife gave consent? Is a husband responsible for fulfilling his wife's vow to undertake a pilgrimage after her death?[123] Sometimes a vow to enter either a clerical (*de ordine*) or monastic order (*de habitu*) intersected with marriage. Sacred and religious orders are an impediment and diriment to marriage. Nevertheless, if one wanted to leave religious life and return to the world so as to be able to marry, s/he could do so during the probation period and s/he announce publicly that they did not want to be in a religious or clerical order. If one was placed in an order while a minor, the decision can be made at the age of 15 to leave and return to the world.[124] Aside from vows, the question of consent could impede a marriage. A legitimate marriage was not valid until the age of puberty had been reached, yet betrothals could be arranged by the parents at the age of seven.[125] Also serving as impediments were blood or spiritual relations. The calculation of consanguinity up to the

118 On Huguccio and his *summa*, see W. P. Müller, *Huguccio: The Life, Works, and Thought of a Twelfth-Century Jurist* (Washington D.C., 1994); K. Pennington and W. P. Müller, "The Decretists: The Italian School," in HMCL 2, 121–173, here 142–160.

119 J. Longère "Quelques 'Summa de poenitentia' à la fin du XIIe siècle et au début du XIIIe siècle," 45–58, here 48. See Bk. 2 sections 11–72, and Bk. 3 sections 197–233.

120 See Flamborough Book 2 on what constitutes a marriage and impediments to marriage, pp. 63–98.

121 Flamborough 2.3 §17, p. 67; Huguccio, *Summa decretorum*, ad C.27 q.1 d.a.c.1 (Paris, BnF, lat. 3892, fol. 282ra). Firth has conducted excellent work on Robert of Flamborough's drawings from Huguccio.

122 Flamborough 2.3 §18; p. 68; Huguccio, *Summa decretorum*, ad C.20 q.4 c.2 s.v. *frangendum* (Paris, BnF 3892, fol. 255ra).

123 Flamborough 2.3 §19, pp. 68–69; Huguccio, *Summa decretorum*, ad C.33 q.5 c.10 s.v. *sed similiter convertatur* (Paris, BnF 3892, fol. 343va–343vb).

124 Flamborough 2.3 §31, p. 75; Huguccio, *Summa decretorum*, ad C.27 q.1 c.21 s.v. *proposito* (Paris, BnF 3892, fol. 284ra bottom margin). Flamborough 2.3 §32–§33, pp. 75–76; Huguccio, *Summa decretorum*, ad C.20 q.1 d.a.c.1 (Paris, BnF 3892, fol. 253ra–253rb).

125 Flamborough 2.3 §53–§54, pp. 86–87; Huguccio, *Summa decretorum*, ad C.30 q.2 c.1 s.v. *consensus utriusque* (Paris, BnF 3892, fol. 300vb–301rb).

seventh degree was of keen importance. Dispensations could be made but only by the pope and only until the third degree.[126] Spiritual affinity through baptism proved to be an impediment both to marriage as well as to the issuing of penance.[127] In addition to spiritual affinity and consanguinity between the first and third degrees, the killing of a wife (*uxorcide*), matricide, adultery, and *raptus* impeded a marriage. Clandestine marriages were in the same category as fornication and necessitated penance, but they were still marriages.[128]

As a second example, Book 3 echoes Huguccio's commentary in the section addressing excommunication as an impediment to entering an order and executing one's office.[129] Robert is most concerned with the types of excommunication, as the sentence impedes promotion, the ability to execute one's office, and the entity responsible for issuing the sentence. Excommunication separates the individual from those among the faithful. It is found in two types: anathema, which is a solemn excommunication, and simple excommunication.[130] Both types can occur either *a decreto* or *a persona*. The former has been established by the canons of the Church. The latter comes at the judgment of a bishop or the pope and often occurs in cases of solemn, also referred to as major, excommunication.[131] Both major and minor excommunication constitute a *datae sententiae* whereby a canon or an authority has issued the sentence.[132] Robert's concern becomes the authority responsible for absolving sentences of excommunication. In cases of excommunication *a decreto*, a simple priest or a bishop can absolve.[133] In cases of excommunication *a persona*

126 Flamborough 2.3 §38–§41, pp. 78–80; Huguccio, *Summa decretorum*, ad C.35 q.2–3 d.a.c.1 (Paris, BnF 3892, fol. 346rb–346vb), ad C.35 q.8 d.a.c.1 (Paris, BnF 3892, fol. 354rb).

127 Flamborough 2.3 §45–§48, pp. 82–84; Huguccio, *Summa decretorum*, ad C.30 q.4 d.a.c.1 (Paris, BnF 3892, fol. 302ra–302ra), ad C.30 q.4 c.3 s.v. *suscepit de sacro fonte* (Paris, BnF 3892, fol. 302rb–302va), ad C.30 q.4 c.3 s.v. *effecti una caro* (Paris, BnF 3892, fol. 302va), ad C.30 q.4 c.6 s.v. *set ut puritas…infamia* (Paris, BnF 3892, fol. 303ra–303rb), ad C.30 q.3 d.a.c.1 (Paris, BnF 3892, fol. 301rb–301va), ad C.30 q.1 c.1 s.v. *septem dona baptismi* (Paris, BnF 3892, fol. 299va–300ra), ad C.30 q.1 c.7 s.v. *nec deb<ere> separari quod esset contra prae<fatas> auctoritates* (Paris, BnF 3892, fol. 300rb), ad C.30 q.1 c.8 s.v. *quia scriptum est* (Paris, BnF 3892, fol. 300rb).

128 Flamborough 2.3 §69–§70, pp. 96–97; Huguccio, *Summa decretorum*, ad C.30 q.5 c.1 s.v. *non dubitantur* (Paris, BnF 3892, fol. 303va).

129 See Flamborough 3.3 on impediments to the order and execution of one's order pp. 117–168, esp. pp. 144–158.

130 Flamborough 3.3 §142, pp. 145–146; Huguccio, *Summa decretorum*, ad C.3 q.4 d.p.c.11 (Paris, BnF 3892, fol. 148vb).

131 Flamborough 3.3 §143, pp. 146–147; Huguccio, *Summa decretorum*, ad C.11 q.3 *d.p.c.15 Quia* (Paris, BnF 3892, fol. 189vb). Canon 15 in Friedberg's edition (col. 647) does not include a d.p.c.15 but rather reference is made to the *tractactus ordinandorum*, in this case D.93 c.1.

132 Flamborough 3.3 §144, p. 147; Huguccio, *Summa decretorum*, ad C.11 q.3 d.p.c.24 s.v. *anathemati* (Paris, BnF 3892, fol. 191ra), ad C.17 q.4 c.29 s.v. *mandatum* (Paris, BnF 3892, fol. 247va), ad D.93 c.1 s.v. *commotione* (Paris, BnF 3892, fol. 98vb).

133 Flamborough 3.3 §146, pp. 148–149; Huguccio, *Summa decretorum*, ad C.11 q. 3 d.p.c.15 s.v. *Quia* (Paris, BnF 3892, fol. 189vb; see above, n.131), ad C.11 q.3 c.29 s.v. *regulare iudicium sui*

there are some, including Huguccio, who believe that the sentence cannot be reversed by the executor or his success unless the sentence was given in anger.[134] In cases where a priest has a prebend in two episcopates and one bishop excommunicates him, he is not able to be absolved by the other bishop.[135] Robert, again drawing upon Huguccio, notes eight instances where laying hands on a man of the cloth would not result in excommunication: the attacker was under 14; the religious' status was not known; the religious was hit lightly in jest; he was hit as a disciplinary measure; in cases of self-defense; the religious was the attacker; the attack occurred while preventing a disturbance; or the religious was harming the attacker's mother, daughter, sister, or wife.[136]

As a final example, Book 3 provides an example of Robert's supplementing his use of Huguccio's *Summa* with papal decretals that were also contained in the collection *Compilatio prima*, also known as the *Breviarium extravagantium*. Compiled by Bernard of Pavia between 1189 and 1190 while serving as the provost of Pavia, the *Breviarium* was a collection of papal decretals and other texts Gratian excluded. It would become known as *Compilatio prima* after the circulation of *Compiliationes secunda* and *tertia* after ca. 1210.[137] Both Huguccio and *Compilatio prima* feature prominently in the section devoted to simony as an impediment to entering an order and executing one's office.[138] Huguccio's commentary provided the definition of simony as the buying (also referred to as *giezia*) or selling of an office or spirituality or something linked to a spirituality. There were also three types of simony: *a manu* which occurred with an exchange of money, *a lingua* which occurred with promises and adulations, and *ab obsequium* which had attached obligations or duties. Simony came as an effect: a transaction needed to have occurred because "si voluisti et non fecisti, non es simonia."[139] Huguccio also proved useful in parsing the difference between knowingly committing simony, for which penance to retain the benefice or position was not an option, ignorantly committing simony, for which penance was available, and knowing that some sort of irregularity was taking place, for which papal dispensation was required.[140] Robert's use of

---

episcopi (Paris, BnF 3892, fol. 191va), ad C.17 q.4 c.29 s.v. *absolvere* (Paris, BnF 3892, fol. 247rb), ad C.11 q.3 c.16 s.v. *communione* (Paris, BnF 3892, fol. 190ra).

134 Flamborough 3.3 §147, p. 149; Huguccio, *Summa decretorum*, ad C.11 q.3 c.40 s.v. *successori* (Paris, BnF 3892, fol. 192rb).

135 Flamborough 3.3 §152, p. 153; Huguccio, *Summa decretorum*, ad C.11 q.3 c.2 s.v. *ab aliis* (Paris, BnF 3892, fol. 188rb).

136 Flamborough 3.3 §157, pp. 156–157; Huguccio, *Summa decretorum*, ad C.17 q.4 c.29 s.v. *mandatum* (Paris, BnF 3892, fol. 247va).

137 K. Pennington, "The Decretalists, 1190–1210," in HMCL 2, 211–245, here 212.

138 See Flamborough 3.3 on impediments to the order and execution of one's order pp. 117–168, esp. pp. 123–144.

139 Flamborough 3.3 §110, pp. 123–124; Huguccio, *Summa decretorum*, ad C.1 hypothetical (Paris, BnF 3892, fol. 106vb–107ra).

140 Flamborough 3.3 §111–3.3 §112, pp. 124–125; Huguccio, *Summa decretorum*, ad C.1

decretals that could be found in *Compilatio prima* comes through in the back-and-forth between the *penitens* and the *sacerdos*. These are brief situational conversations with the *penitens* bringing an issue before the *sacerdos*, with an assessment being offered and a path forward being found. Echoes from the decretal collections appear in the *sacerdos* portion. For example, the priest notes that one cannot be promised a vacancy. If simony did not occur, but it was at worst an intrusion, the penitent would still not be able to retain the prebend.[141] The holding of multiple benefices—plurality—was also forbidden.[142] To name a successor to a church by granting him the pension constituted simony.[143] It was also simonical to give or to receive the right of patronage (*ius patronatus*) in exchange for something as was it to pay a yearly fee for a deconate.[144]

Thomas of Chobham, who served as an *officialis* and subdean of Salisbury, distilled the law for his reader either by quoting a text or by providing a summary of the concept. As the last of Peter the Chanter's circle, he drew upon sources familiar to his peers. As will be discussed in Chapter 7, Thomas echoed Roman law for this discussion of theft. His positions on usury, the *ius patronus*, and tithing reflected positions found in Gratian's *Decretum*, the commentary of the Decretists, and papal decretals.

Irrespective of whether he quoted a text or provided a summary of the concept, it was not uncommon for Thomas to introduce the law with a generic, non-descript reference. That is, at no point did Thomas provide a specific reference to the formal legal text where the information could be found or to the material source being used. For example, in bringing readers into contact with the law pertaining to the murder of a family member, Thomas merely cited "penitentia talis est" or "penitentia hec est" to reference the penitential of Bartholomew of Exeter, the source from where he quoted these texts.[145] He neither attributed the text to Bartholomew's penitential nor did not cite the material source, be it a conciliar decree or papal decree. References then were often very generic. Thomas introduced a long quote from D.25 d.p.c.3 of Gratian's *Decretum* with "it is said" (*dicit*). The text Thomas selected centered on the Gratian's synthesis of Bede, Augustine, and the Apostle Paul on the difference

hypothetical (Paris, BnF 3892, fol. 106vb–107ra), ad C.1 q.5 c.3 s.v. *ex concessione episcopi sui* (Paris, BnF 3892, fol. 124vb), ad C.1 q.5 c.1 (Paris, BnF 3892, fol. 124rb), ad C.1 q.5 c.3 (Paris, BnF 3892, fol. 124va).

141 Flamborough 3.3 §119, p. 130; I Comp. 3.8.2 (X 3.8.2).

142 Flamborough 3.3 §128, p. 134; I Comp. 3.4.3, 3.5.6, 5.27.1 (X 3.4.3, 3.5.5, 5.31.1, respectively).

143 Flamborough 3.3 §120, p. 130; I Comp. 1.26.6 (X 3.39.11).

144 Flamborough 3.3 §131, pp. 136–137; I Comp. 3.33.19, I Comp. 3.33.20 (X 3.38.16), I Comp. 3.39.9 (X 3.38.7). Flamborough 3.3 §132, p. 137; I Comp. 5.3.1, 5.3.2 (X 5.4.1, 5.4.2, respectively).

145 Chobham 7.4.9.3–12, pp. 452–461, quotes heavily from Bartholomew of Exeter, which in turn relies on texts found in the collections of Gratian, Ivo of Chartres, and Burchard of Worms. For example, Chobham 7.4.9.5–6 quotes from Bartholomew c.49, which Bartholomew took from ID 10.177–178.

between moral and venal sins in the course of examining a candidate for ordination.[146] In setting forth what a priest ought to know, particularly as it concerns the books that should be learned, Thomas introduced another quotation from Gratian's *Decretum*, here D.38 c.5, with "[e]st autem canon talis."[147] In his discussion on prostitution, Thomas again drew directly from Gratian, noting "in canonibus" to define a prostitute as a woman who is open to the lust of many.[148] Thomas tended to reference Roman law as "lex secularis," such as in his quote from Gratian's *Decretum* that bishops, treasurers, and provincial governors or their officials should see to it that anyone who rapes, solicits, or corrupts an assistant, deaconess, nun, or other women of religious life or habit, have their goods, and those of anyone else implicated in this sin, be sold to found a religious house where the woman can live. The man himself is subject to capital punishment. The woman should be thoroughly investigated and placed in a secure monastery with her goods. If she was a deaconess with legitimate children, they were to receive their share of the legal inheritance.[149] In quoting from Ulpian, as found in the *Digest* regarding the praetor's comment that he would not hold valid what has been done by force or under duress, Thomas simply used "in lege."[150] In setting forth the punishment to be mettled out for rape, Thomas quoted a series of texts from Causa 36 of Gratian's *Decretum*, simply stating, "these are the words of the canons."[151] Introducing a quoted decretal of Alexander III regarding the ability to excommunicate clerics refusing to abjure their concubine, Thomas simply noted "cum decretalis statuat."[152]

Thomas did not alter his citation technique when he chose to capture the essence of the legal concept. A paraphrased decretal misattributed to Pope Eugenius regarding a priest who knew that someone was guilty of a crime but had not been judged was simply referenced as "sicut dicit decretalis" to capture the concept that the priest cannot excommunicate him.[153] In setting up one view that those in the minor orders who contract a marriage are to be deprived of their benefices, Thomas simply leaned on the reference "hanc

146 Chobham 3.1.2, pp. 17–19; GD D.25 d.p.c.3: "Unde Bede super epistolam Iacobi…criminale, dum placet. … etsi non omnia, vel aliqua…regnum Dei possidebunt."
147 Chobham 4.2.1, p. 86: "que ipsis sacerdotibus…in foveam cadent"; GD D.38 c.5.
148 Chobham 7.2.6, p. 346: "Vidua est, cuius maritus defunctus (GD: mortuus) est. Eiecta, que a marito viventi proicitur. Meretrix, que multorum libidini patet"; GD D.34 c.16:
149 Chobham 7.2.16.3, p. 391; Nov. 123.43; GD C.27 q.1 c.30. In this case, Thomas most likely took the canon from Gratian as he notes "Lex etiam secularis sed tamen canonical ita de his statuit."
150 Chobham 7.11.9.8, p. 557: "'quod vi vel metu fit, ratum, non habeo ait pretor'"; Dig. 4.2.1.
151 Chobham 7.2.7, p. 354: "Verba autem canonum hec sunt". Thomas draws on GD C.36 q.1 c.2, C.36 q.1 c.3, C.36 q.2 c.10, and C.36 q.2 c.1.
152 Chobham 7.2.16.4, p. 382: "'clericos in sacris…a similibus arceantur'"; I Comp. 3.2.4 (X 3.2.3).
153 Chobham 5.1.10, p. 211: "Et nullus nominatim…debet eum excommunicare"; I Comp. 1.23.6 (X 1.31.23). The letter attributed to Alexander III can be found in Jaffé 9092.

constitutionem canonicam hodie" before countering it.[154] In summarizing what Roman law stated ("secundum leges seculars") regarding the contumacious, Thomas noted the ability of the victim to put their own value on the wrong committed. The judge could condemn on account of the victim's estimation or for a lesser sum as seemed right to him.[155] In these examples, Thomas brought his readers into contact with the legal tradition of Burchard of Worms and Ivo of Chartres, Gratian, Decretists, the decretales, and Roman law, giving them the nuggets of information important to the discussion underway. Sometimes he felt a quotation was best, other times a synthesis of the concept was all that was needed. It was important that the reader knew what the legal tradition held, not the specifics of the legal source itself. For this reason, Thomas focused on the concept rather than the citation.

Rev. Bloomfield struggled with Thomas's treatment of the canons from the Fourth Lateran Council (1215). Even though a number of topics discussed by Thomas were the subject of the council's legislation, Bloomfield felt that his *Summa confessorum* did not engage with the canons, showing a superficial knowledge of the material at best, evidence which he used to date the text. He analyzed the conciliar decrees c.21 (requirement to confess and receive communion once a year at or around Easter), c.28 (clerics cannot serve in cases where sentence of death or mutilation is passed, e.g., ordeals), c.25 (a patron kills or mutilates a cleric belonging to his church), c.16 (on clerical dress), c.66 (avarice of clerics), and c.3 (heresy) to argue that Thomas completed his *Summa* prior to receiving a copy of the canons or consulting anyone who attended the council.[156]

Recent scholarship has done much to shed light on the transmission of normative versions of conciliar canons. Danica Summerlin painstakingly studied three manuscripts that transmitted the canons of the Third Lateran Council. The British Library, Cotton Claudius, A.iv, and the Berlin, Staatsbibliothek Preussischer Kulturbesitz, Savigny 3 manuscripts reveal that copyists extracted the information that was legally pertinent from the canons for their particular needs. The Vatican Library Reg. lat. 984 manuscript meanwhile suggests that drafts of the canons accidentally circulated, masquerading as the canons themselves. Summerlin concluded that there most likely was not a single version of the conciliar text used across Latin Christendom and that the canons were not

154 Chobham 7.2.16.1, p. 377: "Contra hanc constitutionem canonicam hodie obtinet consuetudo quod statim ex quo acolythus contahit matrimonium, privatur omni beneficio ecclesliastico, cum canon precipiat ipsum de beneficio debere sustenari."; I Comp. 3.3.1–3 (X 3.3.1–3).

155 Chobham 7.4.1, p. 419; Inst. 4.4.7: "…praetors permittebant ipsis qui iniuriam passi sunt eam aestimare, ut iudex vel tanti condemnet, quanti iniuriam passus aestimaverit, vel minoris, prout ei visum fuerit…."

156 Revd. F. Bloomfield, ed., *Thomae de Chobham Summa confessorum* (Louvain, 1968), xl–lx.

considered to be untouchable authorities.[157] Akin to Summerlin, Jeffrey Wayno's study of the canons from the Fourth Lateran Council and their transmission in the Angers compilation (1216–1219) of diocesan and synod statutes, in the statutes of Richard Poore—who served as bishop of Chichester from 1215 to 1217, of Salisbury from 1217 to 1228, and Durham from 1228 to 1237—, and in Rouen has suggested that the conciliar canons most likely did not circulate in a normative version. Diocesan legislation from the years immediately following the council reveals that bishops frequently altered the texts or could ignore some of them altogether. For example, Richard Poore's statute on the care of the sick borrowed heavily from the original language of c.22 of the Lateran council, as did statutes 4 and 55 in preserving the essence and critical language of c.1 on the Trinity and the doctrine of transubstantiation. Other statutes, however, changed the thrust of the canon by omitting important language. For example, statute 8, which prohibited clerical fornication, reiterates passages from c.14 on clerical incontinence but then in other places softens the language from the council as well as the punishments it prescribed. In the end, Wayno concluded that the process of communicating the canons from the Fourth Lateran Council was plagued by problems largely caused by members of the episcopate who were supposed to implement the decrees issued at the council.[158]

Recent scholarship both supports and complicates Bloomfield's dating of the *Summa*. As noted above, the lack of engagement with the canons of the Fourth Lateran Council led him to date the text to possibly completed by ca. 1215 and in circulation by ca. 1216. Since normative versions of the canons were not in circulation, this date remains plausible. So too does a possibly later date as he could have altered the canons or omitted them to fit the needs of Salisbury. What is certain is that Thomas was not disengaged from the law; he, rather, was very much engaged when it suited his purpose.

Conclusion

Bec and Laon were at the fore of using new techniques, such as *questiones* and *disputationes*, to delve into Scripture. Following the path laid, Peter Lombard used dialectic to bring attention to discordant texts to explore questions pertaining to faith. This climate was also one in which legal thought held a prominent place. Ivo of Chartres was the most prominent canonist of his time, and around his influence, legal collections flourished. Prelates and diocesan administrators took a renewed interest in procedure and sought out texts from the

157 D. Summerlin, "Three Manuscripts Containing the Canons of the 279 Lateran Council," BMCL 30 (2013): 21–43.

158 J. M. Wayno, "Rethinking the Fourth Lateran Council of 1215," *Speculum* 93 (2018): 611–637.

Roman legal tradition. The *Via Francigena* facilitated this interest further as people and texts traveled between stations in northern France and Rome. The *Via* influenced the production of law as it helped to quicken the pace at which legal collections were produced. Places such as Chartres, Reims, Thérouanne, and Châlon-sur-Marne were centers of production. Collections were used to produce new collections that better suited the needs of its users.

Northern France was an incubator of inquiry in the twelfth century. A common intellectual tradition acted as an adhesive. *Litterati*—whether renowned for law or for theology—worked with a similar source base, explored similar questions, and engaged in a dialogue. Writings of the Church Fathers played a particularly important role. Questions about marriage, simony, heresy, homicide, and sins associated with greed were ubiquitous. In such a climate, it should come as no surprise that those known for their theology, such as Peter Lombard, Hugh of St. Victor, Peter the Chanter, Robert Courçon, Robert of Flamborough, and Thomas of Chobham, would be familiar with the legal tradition. Whether canons, papal decretals, conciliar texts, or commentaries, theologians chose the material relevant to their argument and adapted it to suit their purpose. Subsequent chapters aim to flesh out, using specific case studies, how each adapted and used that legal thought in service of their duties. As a canon regular at St. Victor, Hugh approached marriage from the standpoint of monastic theology as the *De Sacramentis* both served as an exegetical treatise and provided spiritual instruction. While both Hugh of St. Victor and Peter Lombard were teachers and committed to pastoral care, Peter approached the topics from the vantage point of a secular cleric and his role as archdeacon of Reims. Often using legal sources to do so, he tended to discuss specific situations that a cleric might come across ministering to the laity or in adjudicating a case. Peter the Chanter, Robert of Courçon, Robert of Flamborough, and Thomas of Chobham pragmatically used law in service of teaching, for answering jurisdictional and procedural questions, for urban pastoral care, and for diocesan management.

3

HUGH OF ST. VICTOR, PETER LOMBARD, AND NORTHERN FRENCH CANONICAL COLLECTIONS

Intellectual Interplay on Marriage

Introduction

Northern French theologians and canonists at the turn of the twelfth century did not necessarily see the disciplines as airtight but rather drew upon each as needed. Their texts circulated within the region (and beyond), and they gathered at councils to discuss the issues facing the Church and the faith. The careers of Hugh of St. Victor (d. 1141) and Peter Lombard (d. 1160) were situated between the proliferation of legal texts in early twelfth-century Paris, marked by Ivo of Chartres and his orbit, and the circulation of Gratian's *Decretum* and the "French" school of canon law.[1]

Hugh of St. Victor compiled his *De Sacramentis Christianae Fidei* (*On the Sacraments of the Christian Faith*) in 1134. He spent his career as a canon at the Augustinian house of St. Victor, which was founded by William of Champeaux. As an institution, St. Victor took full advantage of the intellectual renaissance taking place in northern France and the spirit of

1 Stephan of Tournai has been seen as laying the foundation for the "French" school of canon law. He studied canon and Roman law at Bologna and then returned to France where he compiled his influential *Summa* on Gratian's *Decretum* ca. 1166 while a canon at the Victorine abbey of St. Euverte in Orléans. Stephan would serve as abbot of the house from 1168 to 1176 and then became the abbot of Ste. Geneviève in Paris from 1176 to 1192, also a Victorine abbey of regular canons. He would end his career as bishop of Tournai from 1192 until his death in 1203. See K. Pennington, "Stephen of Tournai (Étienne de Tournai), 1128–1203," in *Great Christian Jurists in French History*, eds. O. Descamps and R. Domingo (Cambridge, 2019), 35–51; R. Weigand, "Studien zum kanonistischen Werk Stephans von Tournai," ZRG Kan. Abt. 72 (1986): 350–361; H. Kalb, *Studien zur Summa Stephans von Tournai: Ein Beitrag zur kanonistischen Wissenschaftsgeschichte des späten 12. Jahrhunderts* (Innsbruck, 1983).

DOI: 10.4324/9781003465096-4

religious reform from which canons regular benefited. Hailing (possibly) from Hamersleben in Saxony, he joined St. Victor between 1115 and 1118 during the abbacy of Gilduin, who had continued to expand the monastery's reputation through his close connections with Pope Innocent II and King Louis VI. Hugh had earned the title of "master" by at least 1127 and he was the head of the school by 1133. Philosophy and reason as ways of approaching God framed Hugh's thoughts. Scripture was the most important of his sources; followed by Augustine, Gregory the Great, Jerome, and John Cassian, and in third place sat the writings of Origen, Ambrose, Cassiodorus, Isidore of Seville, and Bede. He also drew upon the philosophies of Plato, Plotinus, Aristotle, the Stoics, and the Pythagoreans, along with the grammar of Cicero and Virgil. Texts from the patristic fathers and councils were drawn from legal sources, such as the *Panormia*.[2]

Having most likely studied at the Cathedral of St. Mary's in Novara and then probably at Lucca,[3] Peter Lombard arrived in France in 1133/1134 to study at the cathedral school at Reims, which happened to coincide with Alberic's tenure as master. Alberic, who had left Laon in 1177 with the death of Anselm of Laon, taught (possibly Roman) law between 1118 and 1136.[4] Lombard studied there until 1136 when he would become a master at the cathedral school at Notre Dame. He compiled his *Sententiae in IV libris distinctae* (*Sentences*) between 1155 and 1157 while also serving as archdeacon at Reims. The Fourth Lateran Council's affirmation of Lombard's singularity of each member of the Trinity was also an affirmation of the *Sentences*, which had undergone sustained criticism.[5] Peter Lombard knew and worked deeply

2 P. Rorem, *Hugh of Saint Victor* (Oxford, 2009), 7–11; Z. Petersen, "Hugh of St. Victor (1096–1141)," in *The Rise of the Medieval World 500–1300: A Biographical Dictionary*, ed. J. K. Schulman (Westport, 2002), 226–228; D. Poirel, *Hugues de Saint-Victor* (Paris, 1998), esp. chap. 1, and pp. 67–69.

3 Constant Mews noted the importance of the schools in northern Italy, especially in places such as Pistoia and Milan, for studying law. This is not to suggest that Peter Lombard formally studied law while studying in northern Italy but simply that he was immersed in the culture both there and in northern France. See, C. Mews, "The Schools and Intellectual Renewal in the Twelfth Century: A Social Approach," in *A Companion to Twelfth-Century Schools*, ed. C. Giraud (Leiden, 2020), 10–29, here 16–19.

4 J. R. Williams, "Cathedral School of Reims in the Time of Master Alberic, 1118–1136," *Traditio* 20 (1964): 93–114, here 96; W. Uruszczak, "Albéric et l'enseignement du droit roman à Reims au XIIe siècle," in *Confluence des droits savants et des pratiques juridiques: Actes du colloque de Montpellier: Colloque tenu du 12 au 14 décembre 1977, sous le patronage et avec le financement du C.N.R.S./Max-Planck-Institut für europäische Rechtsgeschichte, Istituto di storia del diritto italiano (Università degli Studi di Milano), Institut d'Histoire des anciens pays de droit écrit (Université de Montpellier I)* (Milan, 1979), 39–68.

5 C. Monagle, "Theology, Practice, and Policy at the Turn of the Thirteenth Century: The Papacy and Peter Lombard," *Journal of Religious History* 37, no. 4 (2013): 441–456, here 445.

with Gratian's *Decretum*.[6] He would end his career serving a short tenure as bishop of Paris, beginning in 1159 and ending in 1160 with his death.[7] He bequeathed a copy of the *Sentences* and Gratian's *Decretum* to the Cathedral of Notre Dame,[8] a gift that alludes to the connectedness of the disciplines.

As noted in the previous chapter, Hugh of St. Victor and Peter Lombard drew upon the legal tradition sparingly. Peter Lombard's most consistent use of legal sources comes in Book 4 of his *Sentences* where he addresses the sacraments. Joseph de Ghellinck long ago noted Lombard's use of the canons from Book 1 of the *Panormia* (c.113–c.122) that treated the sacraments. He also noted Lombard's use of Ivo of Chartres's sermon, *De excellentia ecclesiasticorum ordinum*, as a model for Dist. 24 on the seven ecclesiastical orders.[9] More recently, Atria Larson has analyzed Lombard's treatment of Gratian's *De penitentia* (C.33 q.3 of the *Decretum*), finding that Lombard did not simply copy the text as found in the order as it was set forth in the *Decretum*. Lombard, rather, adopted what he needed and adapted it to suit his needs.[10] It is in his distinctions on marriage (Dist. 26–41) though that the slippage between theology and law is most prevalent, as here Lombard drew most heavily upon the legal tradition. Using Gratian for comparison, both he and Lombard discussed marriage from similar vantage points and espoused the same source base as authoritative: Scripture, writings of the Church Fathers, conciliar canons, papal decretals, and, on a few occasions, Roman law, as authorities.[11] Framed in a manner

6 Larson has underscored scholarly acknowledgment of the extent to which Peter Lombard was indebted to Gratian for his thoughts on and treatment of penance. See A. Larson, *Master of Penance: Gratian and the Development of Penitential Thought and Law in the Twelfth Century* (Washington D.C., 2014), 317, 338–342. See also, P. Fournier, "Deux controverses sur les origins du Décret de Gratien. Primière Partie: Gratien et Pierre Lombard," *Revue d'histoire et de littérature religieuses* 3 (1898): 97–116. Furthermore, Larson has demonstrated that Peter Lombard "fully absorbed" Gratian's *De penitentia* even if Lombard did not always treat Gratian's *auctoritates* or *dicta* in the same way and even if he did not work through the *De penitentia* in order, see pg. 319–338.

7 J. Longère, *Oeuvres oratoires de maitres Parisiens au XIIe siècle: Études historique et doctrinale*, 2 vols. (Paris, 1975), 1.13–14; P. W. Rosemann, *Peter Lombard* (Oxford, 2004), 34–39. On Lombard's teaching, see L. Hödl, *Die Geschichte der Scholastischen Literatur und der Theologie der Schlüsselewalt, Teil I* (Münster, 1960), 187–217.

8 J. R. Ginther, "Peter Lombard (ca. 1100–1160)," in *The Rise of the Medieval World 500–1300: A Biographical Dictionary*, ed. J. K. Schulman (Westport, 2002), 342–343; N. Haring, "Chartres and Paris Revisited," in *Essays in Honor of Anton Charles Pegis*, ed. J. R. O'Donnell (Toronto, 1974), 268–329, here 286–287, 291–292; For Lombard's donation, see M. Guérard, ed., *Cartulaire de l'église Notre-Dame de Paris* (Paris, 1850), 1.60.

9 J. de Ghellinck, *Le Mouvement Thèlogique du XIIe Siècle*, 2nd edn. (Paris, 1948), 198, 205–206; Ivo of Chartres, Sermon II (*De excellentia ecclesiasticorum ordinum excellentia*), in PL 162.513–519.

10 Larson, *Master of Penance*, chap. 8 (pp. 315–342). See also A. Larson, "The Reception of Gratian's *Tractatus de penitentia* and the Relationship between Canon Law and Theology in the Second Half of the Twelfth Century," *Journal of Religious History* 37, no. 4 (2013): 457–473.

11 For Gratian's use of patristic texts in his marriage causae, see J. Gaudemet, "L'apport de la patristique latine au Décret de Gratien en matière de mariage," *Studia Gratiana* 2 (1954): 290–319. For a general introduction, see, P. L. Reynolds, *Marriage in the Western Church: The Christianization of Marriage during the Patristic and Early Medieval Periods* (Leiden, 1994).

similar to Walter of Mortagne's *De coniugio*, he wove in conciliar canons and papal decretals alongside patristic and Biblical sources. Hugh of St. Victor, by contrast, drew most heavily on the Bible, the *Sententiae Magistri A.*, and on *Cum omnia sacramenta II*—a second recension of the work that was more succinct and better organized than the first recension—for his *De Sacramentis*.[12] Yet, he leans upon the legal tradition—particularly conciliar canons—for his discussion of consanguinity and affinity in his discussion of marriage.

To that end, marriage serves as an excellent lens through which to understand the intellectual interplay and porous boundaries between theology and law on the cusp of the growth of the University of Paris. Hugh of St. Victor and Peter Lombard were very much a part of the dialogue surrounding marriage as a sacrament. Yet, both were very much engaged in an intellectual climate in which the legalities of marriage were at the forefront of conversations among and between theologians and canonists. Ivo of Chartres's *Decretum*, the *Collectio canonum* of St. Victor (hereafter *Collectio St. Victor*), and the *Collectio decem partium* provide a sampling of the legal thought circulating in northern France in the first half of the twelfth century.[13] A comprehensive collection of law, Ivo completed his *Decretum* ca. 1095. The *Collectio canonum* was compiled at the Augustinian abbey of St. Victor ca. 1125, possibly under the inspiration of the abbey's founder, William of Champeaux. Around the same time, between 1125 and 1130, the *Collectio decem partium* was compiled for use in diocesan administration in Thérouanne, possibly by Walter who served as its archdeacon. By the time Peter Lombard was teaching at Paris in the 1150s, Gratian's *Decretum* had circulated far from its origins at Bologna.[14] Putting the thought of Hugh of St. Victor and Peter Lombard into dialogue with these legal collections reveals a common

12 P. L. Reynolds, *How Marriage Became One of the Sacraments: The Sacramental Theology of Marriage from its Medieval Origins to the Council of Trent* (Cambridge, 2016), 312–313, 362. The *Cum omnia sacramenta II* has been edited by F. P. Bliemetzrieder, see "Théologie et théologiens de l'école épiscopale de Paris avant Pierre Lombard," *Recherches de théologie ancienne et medieval* 3 (1931): 273–291.

13 For an overview of marriage in canon law, particularly as it concerns equality and gender inequality, see S. McDougall, "Women and Gender in Canon Law," in *The Oxford Handbook of Women and Gender in Medieval Europe*, eds. J. Bennett and R. Karras (Oxford, 2013), 163–178. McDougall pointed to a balance between gender equalities and inequalities in marriage in legal theory (canon law) and legal practice (church courts). She noted the equalities in the formation of marriage, remarriage, rendering of the conjugal debt, adultery, legal separation, and the dissolution of marriages. Inequalities could be found in the age at which a marriage could be contracted (14 for boys and 12 for girls), a wife's duty to obey her husband, the required ritual of purification for a woman to return to church after birth, and that a husband could seek a legal separation from his wife for the simply the suspicion of adultery whereas a wife needed grounds on which to base her accusation.

14 It was common for the same canon to circulate in multiple collections. The *Collectio St. Victor* drew from Burchard of Worms' *Decretum*; the *Collectio decem partium* drew from the *Panormia*, which in turn drew from Ivo of Chartres' *Decretum*; Gratian's *Decretum* likewise drew from Ivo of Chartres. My interest is not in how many collections a particular canon circulated but rather in the treatment of the topics stressed in that collection.

intellectual space in which questions of how the Church should regulate marriage were fleshed out.

Topics discussed included: marriage as a sacrament, the definition of a legitimate marriage, when a marriage begins, the conjugal debt, clandestine marriages, the goods of marriage, separation, marriage of unbelievers, and consanguinity and affinity. Within each of these central themes, a variety of connected subthemes were addressed. On the whole, Hugh and Peter echoed one another, which, to some extent, makes sense as the latter drew on the former. How the topics were treated, however, differed, which, again, makes sense considering each's primary duties. A similar observation could be made of Ivo of Chartres, the author of the *Collectio St. Victor*, and Walter of Thérouanne. As a canon regular at St. Victor, Hugh approached marriage from the standpoint of monastic theology as the *De Sacramentis* both served as an exegetical treatise and provided spiritual instruction.[15] A monastic framework offers a backdrop to the *Collectio St. Victor* which covers the high points of marital law quickly and efficiently. While both Hugh of St. Victor and Peter Lombard were teachers and committed to pastoral care, Peter approached the topics from the vantage point of a secular cleric and his role as archdeacon of Reims. Often using legal sources to do so, he tended to discuss specific situations that a cleric might come across ministering to the laity or in adjudicating a case. He delved into error of fortune and error of quality, death of a spouse, the number of marriages, captivity, the killing of a spouse, and abortion; topics Hugh of St. Victor did not address. Similarly, the compiler of the *Collectio decem partium*, presumably Walter, archdeacon of Thérouanne, drilled into specific situations that could be missed in a detailed corpus of canon law such as Ivo's *Decretum*. Between theology and law there were a number of topics, such as consent, upon which there was agreement. In other cases, such as *de futuro* and *de presenti* marriage, theology seemed to set the tone with the legal tradition taking those ideas in a different direction. This could lead, as with Lombard and Gratian, to theology and law not always espousing the same point of view. Finally, both the legal and theological traditions treated sexual sins, but to varying degrees. Marriage reveals a complex interplay between theology, law, and the respective vantage point of the author.

Marriage as a Sacrament and Definition of Marriage

As a sacrament, marriage serves two purposes: as a function and as a remedy. Instituted by God, the sacrament of marriage existed before sin as a function for the propagation of man. Because man did not avoid fornication, marriage's purpose as a sacrament after sin was as a remedy, an indulgence, to prevent

15 Reynolds, *How Marriage Became One of the Sacraments*, 363.

fornication. Both Hugh of St. Victor and Peter Lombard drew upon imagery to explain marriage's function and remedy. Marriage, which takes place between a man and a woman, is a sacrament existing in spirit, a compact of love between God and the soul. Marriage is also a sacrament existing in the flesh between Christ and the Church. While the sacrament in the flesh is great, the sacrament exiting in the spirit is greater. Thus, the true sacrament of marriage can exist even if carnal intercourse does not follow.[16] While the canonists recognized marriage as a function for having children and as a prevention of fornication, they did not seem to engage in the imagery which would, by the time of Gratian, have profound implications on the debate of whether consent or consummation makes a true marriage.

All thinkers discussed in this chapter defined marriage as one in which a man and a woman consent to live an undivided way of life. The definition had roots in Roman law.[17] While they both should live, neither may join with another, and each should treat the other according to the "Golden Rule"—do unto others as you would have done unto yourself.[18] There were four types of marriages according to the canonical tradition. The first is when a woman is given to a man as a virgin. The second is when a man seizes her and she is joined with him by force. They can have a legitimate marriage if the father so wishes and the abductor endows her and compensates her father for the price of her modesty. The third type of legitimate marriage occurs if a man seizes her by force, but her father objects and gives her in marriage to another. Finally, a fourth type of legitimate marriage is when a spouse dies; the widow(er) can remarry if the other is free to do so.[19]

Certain exceptions prevented some from entering into a legitimate marriage. The *Collectio St. Victor* paid particular attention to the importance of virginity before marriage and the inability of the religious and penitent widows to

16 De Sacr. 2.11.1–3; Lombard 4.26.1–4. See also G. Silano, "Peter Lombard," in *Christianity and Family Law: An Introduction*, eds. J. Witte, Jr. and G. S. Hauk (Cambridge, 2017), 146–160, here 150–151.

17 De Sacr. 2.11.4; Lombard 4.27.2; ID 8.1; Cdp 7.1.1 "Nuptie sive" (fol. 108rb); GD C.27 q.2 d.a.c.1; Dig. 23.2.1; see also Gaudemet, "Le marriage en droit romain: Justum matrimonium," in *Sociétés et marriage*, 46– 103, here 47–49; and Gaudemet, "Les legs du droit romaine n matière matrimoniale," in *Sociétés et marriage*, 338–378.

18 Lombard 4.27.2.

19 ID 8.40–41; Cdp 7.6.5 "Hieronimus ait"–7.6.6 "Hieronimus ait" (fol. 110ra); GD C.36 q. 2 d.p.c.6–d.p.c.11: Having presented the viewpoint that an abductor cannot marry the girl he abducted, Gratian put forth the viewpoint that once the girl is returned to the control of her father and penance has been served for the sin of abduction, they are permitted to marry each other if the parents' consent. While Jerome's authority supported this view, councils at Meaux and Aachen did not. The councils allowed them to marry after penance, just not marry each other. Gratian's final viewpoint again leaned on the consent of the girl's father. Once penance was complete and if the father consented to the marriage, the abductor may lawfully marry the girl he abducted. The father, however, could refuse the marriage and give her to another.

marry.[20] Hugh and Peter drilled in on bishops, priests who professed celibacy, and those who had taken vows as persons not free to marry. Hugh condemns the violation of a celibacy pledge as a falling away from a higher good. It is damnable, especially for monks and holy virgins, to take a spouse or even want to marry. He explicitly states that monks and holy virgins are forbidden to take a spouse. Peter draws on a decretal of Pope Leo I and canons from the Council of Carthage and the Sixth Synod to drill into the specific offices as it pertains to marriage: deacons and subdeacons were forbidden to marry; lectors, doorkeepers, exorcists, and acolytes are able to take a virgin wife if they were not bound by a vow, wore a monastic habit, and did not wish to profess continence. If a bishop, priest, deacon, or subdeacon had a wife from when they were laymen or in these minor orders and could lawfully marry, they must abstain from their wife. If any of those who entered the clergy wished to be joined to a wife in lawful marriage, he should do so before he was ordained subdeacon.[21] Hugh was especially in tune with the idea that "no reasonable cause"—a hidden cause, unacknowledged by the judgment of the Church—could either prohibit a marriage from taking place or undermine it after it had taken place.[22] The right to enter into a legitimate marriage was sacred, and once done so, it was binding. What was unclear to the Church beforehand should not be used later to dissolve a legitimate union.

Peter Lombard and the canonical collections would include mental illness as preventing someone from entering into a legitimate marriage. Those who suffered from insanity could not contract a marriage while in the throes of their illness. However, if a marriage was contracted they were not to be separated. For those who contracted marriage while healthy and then suffered some dementia, insanity, or a different illness befell one or both of them, the marriage could not be dissolved because of the infirmity. The same was true of those who were blinded or maimed by their enemies, or who had been castrated by barbarians.[23]

Of particular interest were the solemnities associated with contracting a legitimate marriage. Pope Evaristus's decretal, cited by canonists and theologians alike, stated that a lawful marriage is one in which the wife is sought by those who have dominion over her and espoused by her parents. She is dowered in accordance with the law. A priest blesses the marriage with prayers and

20 CSV 8.54 "Virgines que" (fol. 250va), 8.55 "Virgines que" (fol. 205va–vb), 8.67 "Qui penitenti" (fol. 251rb), 9.5 "Qualis esse" (fol. 252vb^1), 9.3.7 "Uxor est" (fol. 254vb). The pagination of fol. 252v/253r is duplicated in Paris, Bibliothèque de l'Arsenal, lat. 721. To lessen confusion 252v^1 and 235r^1 denote the first showing, while 252v^2 and 235r^2 denote the second showing.

21 De Sacr. 2.11.12; Lombard 4.37.1.

22 De Sacr. 2.11.4.

23 Lombard 4.34.4; ID 8.168; CSV 9.13 "Si qui" (fol. 253rb^1–252va^2), 9.14 "Neque furiosus" (fol. 252vb^2), 9.38 "Si mulier" (fol. 254vb–255ra). For impediments to marriage in Peter Lombard, see Silano, "Peter Lombard," 156–159.

offerings. She is escorted by bridesmaids at which point she is received. The couple then give themselves to prayer for two or three days, keeping chastity.[24] The *Collectio St. Victor* further emphasized such solemnities, the dowry, and benediction by the priest.[25] Ivo's *Decretum* emphasized the importance of a dowry and the exchange of oaths sworn by both parties. Legitimate marriages must be contracted publicly and formally with proper trappings: public exchange of vows, gifts, wedding rings, and a priest's blessing.[26] As a collection that might have been used in diocesan courts, the *Collectio decem partium* noted that a wife was one taken according to the law as a chaste virgin, betrothed in her virginity, lawfully endowed, bestowed on the bridegroom by her parents, received by the bridesmaids, and taken openly into marriage with public nuptials, according to the law and the Gospel. She should never separate from her husband so long as she lived (except with his consent to undertake a religious life).[27] Provided that a marriage was conducted according to the proper form with the associated ceremonies, oath, and benediction—a man shall swear by the divine, holding the woman's hand, and given in the oratory of the sacrament—she was his lawful wife. Such was the case even if she did not have a dowry.[28]

The attention paid to the ceremony seemed to come from two directions. Peter Lombard and Hugh of St. Victor reveal a concern with limiting clandestine marriages.[29] With an eye to realities on the ground, Peter noted that without such solemnities a marriage did not have the due decorum and decency but was still a marriage. All that was needed for the sacrament of marriage was present consent. Everything else was for dignity of the sacrament. In fact, Peter's comments on clandestine marriages were short and sweet: present consent, even in secret, was just that—a secret. If one dismissed the other, the Church could not step in because there were no witnesses. That is why it was important to publicly reaffirm what was made in secret.[30] It was Hugh of St. Victor who seemed to be more concerned with clandestine marriages. He delved into an often-repeated trope. A man marries a woman in secret, but then he regrets his decision and marries another openly with pomp and

24 De Sacr. 2.11.5; Lombard 4.28.1.4; ID 8.4; CSV 9.36 "Aliter legitimum" (fol. 254vb); Cdp 7.6.3 "Aliter legitimum" (fol. 109vb–110ra).

25 CSV 9.5 "Qualis esse" (fol. 252vb[1]), 9.8 "Nullum sine" (fol. 253ra[1]), 9.7 "Sponsus et" (fol. 253ra[1]), 9.9 "In primo" (fol. 253ra[1]), 9.36 "Aliter legitimum" (fol. 254vb).

26 ID 8.4–6, 41–41, 44, 144.

27 Cdp 7.7.2 "Qualis esse" (fol. 110rb).

28 Cdp 7.2.1–4 "Si quis," "Quod femine," "Quod imprimis," "Nostrates tam" (108va–vb). Epitome Juliani 67.4 (see S. Corcoran, "UCL Volterra Project," available at https://www.ucl.ac.uk/volterra/texts/epitome-iuliani).

29 On consent and clandestine marriages, see J. Gaudemet, *Le marriage in occident: Les moeurs et le droit* (Paris, 1987). Strict consensualism favors clandestinity, an issue that theologians and lawyers had to address.

30 Lombard 4.28.2.

circumstance. This couple then had children. The man's first wife, whom he had married in secret, protested, claiming that he had married her. He denies this marriage. The Church validates the second marriage because it was done in public with solemnities. Hugh then frames this trope against confession. The man regrets his second marriage and confesses to the priest that he had consented to the first marriage and he wishes to return to his first wife. Hugh wrestled with the fact that while he confessed for fear of his soul, granting his request would lead to great scandal which should be avoided. Thus, the Church should deny the request because (a) he changed his story, and (b) the second marriage was legitimate with witnesses.[31] Coming from the second direction, canonical collections sought to eliminate concubinage.[32] As the *Collectio decem partium* noted, no one may have a concubine. A wife was different from a concubine, just as the slave girl was different from the free woman. Being lawfully endowed and made an honest woman by public nuptials played a central role.[33] The solemnities were critical for distinguishing lawful marriages from concubinage. The curtailment of clandestine marriages and eradication of concubinage were not mutually exclusive concepts. The twelfth-century Church was working to bring marriage more concretely under its purview, whereby legitimate marriages were those with witnesses and celebrated before a priest. Theologians and canonists addressed the same issue by emphasizing different facets of the problem.

The Point at Which Marriage Begins and the Importance of Consent

Of particular concern for theologians and canonists was the point at which a marriage began. The consent of both parties was critical. Children had to be seven years old in order to be betrothed. This was considered the age of reason at which point one could understand and agree with what was happening.[34] Ivo's *Decretum* noted that consent was to be given by the partners; betrothal, and thus the marriage pact, began at that point. A betrothal, not deflowering, made a marriage. It was a union of minds, not a union of bodies. A valid betrothal binds the partners together indissolubly. Having the status of a valid contract, those who had made such agreements were prohibited from marrying anyone else but to whom they were pledged.[35] In short, Ivo took the position held by the theologians: consent made a valid and true marriage.

31 De Sacr. 2.11.6.
32 ID 8.30–32, 60–65, 154–155; CSV 9.4 "Non omnis" (fol. 252va–vb[1]), 9.10 "Audite karissmi" (fol. 253ra–rb[1]).
33 Cdp 7.7.1 "Non omnis" (fol. 110ra–rb), 7.7.7 "Audite karissmi" (fol. 110va–vb).
34 Cdp 7.3.2.3 "Quapropter a primordio etatis sponsalia effici possunt, si modo id fieri ab utraque persona intelligatur, id est si non sint minores quam septem annis" (fol. 109ra). Dig. 23.1.14.
35 ID 8.2–3, 17, 20, 169.

The conviction that a betrothal was binding did not leave much wiggle room. The *Collectio decem partium* noted the binding nature of betrothals and anathematized a marriage in which a second man received a girl betrothed to another. A betrothed girl whom another had abducted should be returned to the man to whom she was first betrothed, even if the abductor used force on her.[36] The *Collectio St. Victor* called for parents to abstain from communion for three years if they broke the faith of a betrothal.[37] Hugh of St. Victor and Peter Lombard grappled with the pickle posed by indissolubility, and it was the theologians who devised a solution: *de futuro* and *de presenti* consent. Future consent, "are going" or "will," makes the partners spouses; they are espoused to enter into a true marriage at an arranged point in the future. Both contend that her guardians, who have power over her, should also be asked for their consent. However, while this should be done, if the bride and groom exchange consent in the present tense, it is a true marriage. A true marriage begins when the bride and groom exchange consent in the present tense, regardless of whether consummation of the marriage follows.[38] Peter did counter the notion—espoused by Gratian—that carnal joining completed the marriage and that before carnal joining the "spouses" could choose a monastic life without the other's permission, but after carnal joining the "marriage partners" could not. He reiterated the view that the distinction between espousal and true marriage lay in the tense of the consent, not in whether there was a conjugal act.[39] Leaning on a text found in the *Novella*, Peter explicitly noted that because a promise to marry in the future was the same as present consent, if another marriage was contracted it, not the first which was in the future tense, was binding.[40]

If [present] consent is the foundation of a true marriage, what nullifies that consent? Showing his concern for practicalities on the ground, Peter addressed this question more fully than Hugh. Hugh noted that when consent was lacking sexual intercourse and everything else was in vain.[41] Peter tackled head-on the importance of free consent, that the unwilling and resistant should not be compelled to marry. Leaning on a decretal of Pope Urban I and on the *Digest*, Peter stated that she must manifestly dissent, visibly resisting her father's will. Anything short of visible resistance was deemed consent. If the opportunity for objection had been given and the couple had cohabitated for some length of

36 Cdp 7.4.1–2 "De coniugiali," "De sponsatas" (fol. 109ra–rb).
37 CSV 9.51 "Si qui" (fol. 255va–vb).
38 De Sacr. 2.11.5; Lombard 4.28.1. See also Silano, "Peter Lombard," 151–152.
39 Lombard 4.27.5. Guilio Silano noted that Peter Lombard was a stronger proponent of consent as the sole constituent of marriage. According to him, it was not that Gratian and Peter disagreed regarding the importance of both consent and consummation but that Peter seemed readier than Gratian to suggest that marriage was fully and finally constituted when consent in words of present effect is uttered. See Silano, "Peter Lombard," 159.
40 Lombard 4.28.1.3; Nov. 75.5.
41 De Sacr. 2.11.5.

time without complaint, then consent was considered given. Letters of Pope Urban II sent to Prince Jordan and to Sancho, king of Aragon, reinforced that a girl could not be forced to marry another against her will or that of her parents. A girl—or boy—coerced into marriage may want to separate later or may fall into fornication. In either case, their sin fell on the shoulders of the one who coerced them.[42] The *Collectio decem partium* had echoed a similar sentiment to that of Peter Lombard: a daughter must consent to the betrothal, and, if she did not oppose her father, she was held to consent. She could only withhold consent, however, if her father chose someone unfit for betrothal on account of his bad behavior or character. Similarly, a betrothal of a son could not be carried out in his name if he refused his consent.[43] One could imagine situations in which the Church would have to adjudicate claims of coerced consent.

One could also imagine situations in which the Church would have to adjudicate claims of misplaced consent. Here, the theologians and canonists appear to be on the same page, which, in turn, Gratian synthesizes. Error came in four forms—of person, condition, quality, and fortune. [44] Error of person nullified consent. Error of person occurred when a person was thought to be one person, but he was, in fact, someone else. Thus, if someone agreed to marry person A but married person B unknowingly, the marriage was deemed invalid should s/he not agree to it when the truth was discovered. The person had not agreed to marry *that* person. Consent was nullified because the person had consented to one person/type of person but got another instead. Error of condition—when one who was a slave was thought to be free—also nullified consent. If one married a person in a servile state but was told they were free, when the deceit was later discovered the marriage could be dissolved because the person did not consent to marry someone in a servile state. While passed over by Hugh as not necessary to address, Peter explicitly stated types of error that did *not* nullify consent. For example, error of fortune—when one who was rich was thought poor and vice versa—did not preclude or overturn marriage consent. Neither did error of quality—when one who was wicked was thought to be good or thought to be a virgin but was not—nullify consent.[45] The *Collectio*

42 Lombard 4.29.1; GD C.31 q.2 c.1, c.3; Jaffé 4311, Jaffé 4113; Dig. 23.1.1.7.

43 Cdp 7.3.2 "In sponsalibus" (fol. 108vb–109ra). Dig.23.1.11–13.

44 Dig. 2.14.1. See especially, J. Gaudemet, "Droit canonique et droit romain: A propos de l'erreur sur la personne en matière de marriage (C. XXIX, qu. 1)," in *Sociétés et marriage*, 320–337; K. Pennington, "The 'Big Bang': Roman Law in the Early Twelfth-Century," RIDC 18 (2007): 43–70, here 58–62.

45 De Sacr. 2.11.18–19; Lombard 4.30.1. Lombard synthesized the thrust of C.29 q.1 d.a.c.1 minus the examples Gratian provided to illustrate the concepts. Lombard again raised error of condition in Lombard 4.36.1 where he cited the council of Verberie, also found in the *Decretum* (C.29 q.2 c.4), which decreed that if a man married another believing her to be freeborn but she was in fact of servile status he could marry another if he could not procure her freedom. C.29 q.2 c.5, from the same council, applies the principle equally to women. Lombard followed with a decretal attributed to Pope Zachary that if their condition was known, there was no error, and thus the marriage stood, see Lombard 4.36.2. See also Silano, "Peter Lombard," 152–153.

decem partium included the comparison of error of quality to a horse that loved its mate. If either was changed, the other did not know how to carry the yoke and thought it was not whole.[46]

Peter took the opportunity to delve more deeply than Hugh into situations that might arise in error of condition cases, cases which bled into questions involving the marriage of those in a servile state. Canonical thought—such as that found in Ivo's *Decretum*, the *Collectio decem partium*, and later Gratian's *Decretum*—proved helpful on this matter. A free-born person could marry one of servile condition, but, as noted above, if the condition was not known then s/he could be dismissed freely when it was discovered. But in cases when a free man took another's serving girl as his wife and mistakenly believed her to be free-born, once discovered he should try to redeem her from her servile status if he was able. If he could not, he could marry another should he so wish. In cases in which a master gave a slave girl her freedom and then married her, the marriage was lawful so long as the two parties consented. Should, however, a free-born person marry someone in a servile condition, knowing of their condition, s/he could not be dismissed. The stipulations held true for both men and women as there was one law for both.[47] The *Collectio decem partium* would also note other situations involving valid marriages of those in a servile state. Such included a lord arranging the marriage between a slave woman and a free-born man to whom he presented a dowry so that the lord could profit either wholly or in part from the marriage; and a lord not promoting, but also not preventing, a marriage of a free-born man and a slave woman. In both cases, the children were legitimate because of the special circumstances and the presumption was that the slave woman would become free.[48] Following canonical thought, Peter Lombard noted that should one man's serf take another man's serving girl in marriage, the marriage should not be dissolved even if they were of different lords and they should continue to serve their lords. The lords, however, must have consented to the marriage. If the lords did not give their consent, there could not be a lawfully contracted marriage.[49] Similarly, the *Collectio decem partium* had noted that if a servant and slave both of the same master were joined in marriage and after one of them was freed, the marriage was not dissolved.[50] The collection also noted that, in a legal union having the owners' consent, the marriages of slaves could not be annulled even if they had different owners. Rather, in order to preserve the unity of marriage, they were

46 Cdp 7.22.2: "Comparem suum et equus diligit, et si mutetur alius, trahere iugum nescit. Compar alterius et se non totum putat" (118rb).

47 Cdp 7.24.2 "Si quis" (119r); GD C.29 q.4 d.p.c.3–c.7.

48 Cdp 7.24.1 "Si quis" (fol. 118vb–119ra); Epitome Iuliani 36.3.

49 Lombard 4.36.1. Hugh leaned on the texts from the Capit. Vermeriense and Pope Zacharias. ID 8.52–56, 164–165, 167; CSV 9.46 "Quicumque ex" (fol. 255rb-va); Cdp 7.24.1 "Si quis" (fol. 118vb–119ra); GD C.29 q.2 c.8; Epitome Iuliani 36.3.

50 Cdp 7.7.4 "Si servum" (fol. 110va).

to serve their different owners.[51] Peter, however, went on to acknowledge that there was disagreement on this view as there were some who said that there could be a marriage between them without their lords' knowledge.[52] Also following the canonical tradition, Peter offered the scenario of a woman marrying a free man and, in order to procure a divorce, he made himself the serf of another. In such cases, the marriage should continue to stand, and she should retain her status as free.[53] Personally, I give credit to the husband for his creative plot to procure a divorce.

Hugh focused less on the factors surrounding consent than on what a couple was consenting to. It is here that consent to carnal union weighed heavily. As noted above, both Hugh and Peter distinguished between two forms of consent: consent to marital union which mirrored the relationship between God and the soul, and consent to the conjugal debt which mirrored the relationship between Christ and the Church. Mary consented to the former but not to the latter which illustrated that as long as consent to live an undivided way of life was given, a love of souls, the marriage was a legitimate and true marriage. However, those who consented only to carnal intercourse could not be said to consent to a true marriage. Hugh then drilled into the two forms of consent. He emphasized that if they consented to carnal relations when they consented to marriage, they were bound to render the debt. If they pledged equally to forego carnal relations, neither could ask the debt of the other though the sacrament of the marriage remained. To explore this idea, he uses the marriage of Mary and Joseph as an example. Mary gave one form of consent: she consented to marry but she did not consent to carnal relations. She thus had made two vows: a vow to marry but also a vow to remain a virgin. Consent to carnal relations was an accompaniment to marriage; it was not the cause of marriage. Marriage is defined as a legitimate association between a man and a woman. Hugh thus explained the marital debt in two ways: (1) to keep one's self for the other and not move into another society; (2) to have carnal intercourse. According to Hugh, marriage was all the more holy when the conjugal debt was not desired. But even if there was no intercourse, they are still debtors to each other; two become one in mind and one in heart. The principal cause of marriage is the indivisible bond of love with the reciprocity of a unique love. The duty of generating children was added later.[54] Hugh essentially set forth the essence of what is found in modern marriage vows: Spouses were to have

51 Cdp 7.7.5 "Dictum est" (fol. 110va).
52 Lombard 4.36.2. Hugh leaned on the texts from the Second Council of Cabillon.
53 Cdp 7.21.1 "Per latum" (fol. 116rb); Lombard 4.36.3. Hugh leaned on the texts attributed to the Council of Tribur.
54 De Sacr. 2.11.4; BVM 1.1, 1.3, 1.7–8; Lombard 4.26.6.3, 4.28.3.1, 4.30.2.

> all sincerity of love, in the responsibility of solicitude, in every tender feeling, in every zealous compassion, in every strength of consolation and faithful devotion. Thus, each regards the other as one with his or her self, in all good things and in all bad ones, as a companion and sharer in consolation. Thus, they also show themselves inseparable in tribulation and suffering. Finally, regarding what pertains outwardly to the needs of the body, they both undertake to foster the other's flesh as though it were their own. Regarding what pertains internally to love of the heart, they both take care to keep the other, as if their own soul (*animum*), in peace and tranquility and without upset, insofar as they can.[55]

While the canonists did not delve into the two forms of consent—consent to marital union which mirrored the relationship between God and the soul, and consent to the conjugal debt which mirrored the relationship between Christ and the Church—they did wrangle with the place of coitus in the formation of marriage. As we have seen above, Ivo's *Decretum* stressed consent in the formation of a marriage. The *Collectio decem partium*, however, struggled with the role coitus played. The compiler, presumably Walter of Thérouanne, noted the view that when a marriage is initiated, the name of marriage is given to it. They are truly called married after the first pledge of betrothal, although conjugal intercourse is as yet unknown to them. Not the deflowering of virginity, but the conjugal contract makes a marriage. When a woman is united to a man there is a marriage, not when she has intercourse with him.[56] A marriage is when anyone has been betrothed, handed over, and enjoyed (*utatur*).[57] The ambiguous meaning of "enjoyed" (*utatur*) seems to open the door to pose the contra stance: A woman has not entered into a marriage unless there has been sexual intercourse. Marriages are not held as a sacrament of Christ and the Church if they are not followed by the comixing of the sexes. From the beginning, the marriage bond was instituted in such a manner that without sexual intercourse it would not possess the sacrament of Christ and the Church. Thus, a woman who has not experienced the nuptial mystery has not entered marriage.[58]

The difference between Gratian and Peter Lombard on the role of coitus in the formation of a marriage would epitomize the (Bolognese) legal tradition versus the (northern French) theological tradition. Gratian presented sources maintaining that the betrothed were married,[59] followed by presenting sources

55 BVM 1.9 in Feiss, *On the Sacraments*, 259.

56 Cdp 7.3.3–5 "De sponsata," "Coniuges verius," "Coniux vocatur" (fol. 109ra).

57 Cdp 7.3.6 "Si quis" (fol. 109ra).

58 Cdp 7.5.2–4 "Non est," "Non habent," "Cum societas" (fol. 109rb).

59 GD C.27 q.2 c.2 (Nicholas I), c.4 (Pseudo-Chrysostom), and c.5 (Ambrose) are the same sources as those used by Lombard (Lombard 4.27.3.2).

maintaining that the betrothed were not married.[60] He presented evidence that those who are betrothed both may keep continence and may enter a monastery without seeking the consent of the other to suggest that no valid marriage exists between the betrothed. Those who have a valid marriage must seek the consent of the other before either undertaking a vow of continence or entering a monastery.[61] Gratian concluded that a betrothal began the marriage and made them spouses not simply because words were spoken but because of the fidelity which each gave by their words to be faithful. The marriage was completed and ratified, however, with coitus.[62] Reflecting theology's *de futuro/de presenti* distinction, the betrothed were considered married because of future hope, not because of a present reality. Yet, neither does intercourse without intention to contract a marriage, nor does deflowering without a conjugal agreement make marriage. Rather, the intention to contract marriage and the rendering of the conjugal contract bring about the marriage.[63]

For Gratian, both consent and coitus were necessary to make a marriage. Gratian implicitly acknowledged some differences between present and future consent. He, however, did not drill into the tense of the verb used—present or future—when the consent was given; "I shall take" or "I take" seemed to be one and the same.[64] A marriage had begun and neither could contract another marriage, though, as stated above, one was still permitted to enter a monastery.[65] Furthermore, Gratian emphasized the need for the father's consent to the marriage,[66] which follows the Roman law definition of marriage,[67] and is a point not raised at all by Lombard. The betrothed were considered married because of future hope, though they were not presently married on account of not having consummated the union.

Lombard and Gratian's differing views on consent and the relevance of consummation are on display in each of their interpretations of the marriage of Mary and Joseph. For Lombard, present consent was necessary for the validity of their marriage. If one held that coitus was necessary, they could not be

60 See GD C.27 q.2 c.1–c.9 for consent validating the marriage and c.16–c.18 for consummation validating the marriage.

61 GD C.27 q.2 d.p.c.26.

62 GD C.27 q.2 d.p.c.34 followed by c.35–c.38; GD C.27 q.2 d.p.c.45: "Sed a prima fide desponsationis coniunx dicitur appellari, non quod in ipsa desponsatione fiat coniunx, sed quia ex fide, quam ex desponsatione sibi inuicem debent, postea efficiuntur coniuges, ..."

63 GD C.27 q.2 d.p.c.45.

64 J. Brundage, *Law, Sex, and Christian Society in Medieval Europe* (Chicago, 1987), 237 Fig. 6.1.

65 See GD C.27 q.2 c.50–c.51.

66 GD C.31 q.3 c.1, d.p.c.1; GD C.32 q.2 d.p.c.12–c.14. GD C.32 q.3 c.1, d.p.c.1 argue that a free uncle, as opposed to a slave father, may decide whom a girl can marry, thus demonstrating the importance of the "head of household" in granting consent.

67 Inst. 1.10 notes that unless the persons are independent authorities, consent of the head of their family is needed. See also Gaudemet, "Le marriage en droit romain," in *Sociétés et marriage*, 56–58.

regarded as married; their union was incomplete and less than perfect. This would be the wrong interpretation: Even though there was no sharing of the marriage bed, they were truly marriage partners.[68] Gratian presented the contra stance: Mary and Joseph were not married...as such. As the argument goes: If the consent was to a carnal union, then a marriage did not exist between them. Mary had vowed to remain a virgin. Had she vowed to a carnal union later, she would have been guilty of breaking her vow of virginity. Mary, rather, had intended in her heart to keep her vow of virginity even if she had not expressed it in words. Furthermore, if Mary and Joseph had been married, then the Lord would not have separated Mary from Joseph and entrusted her to John as this would have been considered a divorce and the Lord would not have orchestrated a divorce. Joseph had not known Mary and so they could not be considered to have been married.[69] Presenting the pro stance, as put forth by Augustine: Mary and Joseph had a "complete marriage,"[70] even though Augustine had also stipulated that a woman had not entered into a "complete marriage" unless she and her husband had had coitus.[71] Gratian had to reconcile these viewpoints. As would Hugh of St. Victor and Lombard,[72] Gratian stated that in the case of Mary and Joseph a "complete marriage" should be understood not as to the use of marriage but as to those things that accompany it, that is, fidelity, sacrament, and offspring.[73] Mary and Joseph's marriage represented fidelity in that there was no adultery; it represented the sacrament in that they did not divorce, and they had offspring, the Lord Himself. Furthermore, even if they were not spouses in the flesh, they were by their intention.[74] Joseph provided for Mary's well-being and gave her his undivided affection. As such, she should be considered his spouse because she was a future wife. Even though they were not married, it was customary to refer to a betrothed as a spouse.[75] Gratian conceded that Mary and Joseph were considered spouses because they were betrothed. And, despite their marriage not being consummated, it was complete on account of fidelity, sacrament, and

68 Lombard 4.26.6.3, 4.30.2 (Cf. C.27 q.2 c.3).

69 GD C.27 q.2 d.p.c.2, C.27 q.2 c.3, C.27 q.2 d.p.c.29 [John 19:26–27], C.27 q.2 c.43. See also, I. M. Resnick, "Marriage in Medieval Culture: Consent Theory and the Case of Joseph and Mary," *Church History* 69, no. 2 (2000): 350–371, esp. 355–367.

70 GD C.27 q.2 c.3.

71 GD C.27 q.2 c.16.

72 Essence of BVM 1; Lombard 4.30.2.

73 GD C.27 q.2 d.p.c.39. See also J. Werckmeister, "La fidélité conjugale dans le droit canonique medieval," *Revue de droit canonique* 44 (1994): 17–34, here 29–34; idem, "Le Mariage sacrament dans le Decret de Gratien," *Revue de droit canonique* 42 (1992): 237–267.

74 GD C.27 q.2 c.10, C.27 q.2 c.9.

75 GD C.27 q.2 c.40 (Matthew 1:16, 1:18, 1:20), C.27 q.2 c.42 (Chrysostom); C.27 q.2 c.44 (Origen); C.27 q.2 c.45 (Gregory I).

offspring.[76] With his focus on present consent alone to make a valid marriage, Lombard puts forth that of Mary and Joseph as an example for us all. We enter into marriage by consenting to take another as our spouse and live an undivided way of life. For Gratian, the marriage of Mary and Joseph was an anomaly and not the norm. While they were spouses because of their betrothal and had a "complete marriage" on account of fidelity, the sacrament, and offspring, it was unlikely that any of us would experience the immaculate conception that was required to make it complete. For us, consummation was required.

Conjugal Debt and the Goods of Marriage

The two forms of consent—consent to a true marriage and consent to render the conjugal debt—had profound impacts on the conjugal debt and the ability to take a vow of chastity. Taking a 30,000-foot view, Hugh emphasized the marital couple as debtors to each other in mind and heart. He noted that conjugal love was a sacrament, representing love that existed in spirit between God and the soul. So too was sexual intercourse of the married a sacrament, representing participation that existed in the flesh between Christ and the Church. As debtors to one another, a distinction must be made between a hidden and a public vow of continence. If a hidden vow was made and the person married, the Church could not prohibit or void the union because it did not know about the vow. If the vow was public and the person married, the violator was to be returned to their original state (widowhood or monastic life), and if the person refused then s/he was to be excommunicated and not to be admitted to penance until s/he withdrew from the marriage.[77]

Peter brought this 30,000-foot view to the ground level. Drawing from the legal tradition, he devoted more attention than Hugh to the rendering of the conjugal debt itself: each was equally bound to do so and to do so was not a crime, but to request it beyond procreating was a venial (not mortal) sin. He keenly noted that couples should abstain from coitus on days of procession or feasts. Marriages should not be celebrated from Septuagesima until the Octave of Easter, for the three weeks before the feast of St. John, and from the Advent of the Lord until after the Epiphany. Marriage partners *could not* profess continence or enter a monastery without the other's consent. If a marriage partner denies the request, this was not grounds for divorce, and if they did consent, the bishop must be notified. If either professed continence or enters monastery without permission of the other, s/he is to be recalled. Those espoused, however, *could* profess continence or enter a monastery without other's consent.

76 GD C.27 q.2 d.p.c.45. According to Silano, Gratian was not especially worried if their marriage were found to have been annulled. For Peter Lombard, this would have been unthinkable as their marriage exemplified Christian spouses. See "Peter Lombard," 159.

77 BVM 1.9–10; De Sacr. 2.11.12.

Peter also distinguishes between a private (hidden) singular vow and a solemn (public) singular vow. Like Hugh, he noted that those who made a solemn (public) vow were to be returned to their original state (widowhood or monastic life) or be denied penance, but Peter noted that if they wanted to enter penance worthily, they should not be denied the ability to do so. In the case of unveiled virgins who made a solemn (public) vow but changed their mind and married, they were to do penance and not receive communion until satisfaction was made.[78] While Hugh emphasized conjugal love between spouses and deemphasized coitus, Peter felt obliged to more concretely address the realities of the latter.

As suggested above by Gratian's reconciliation of the marriage of Mary and Joseph, three goods earmark a true marriage: fidelity, offspring, and the sacrament. As a remedy against evil, the marriage bond provides an outlet for sexual desire. This outlet should be for the hope of offspring, but if it goes beyond the necessity for procreation, Hugh warns, they are guilty of lust. Marriage as a sacrament is witnessed by the devotion to one another and no divorce. As noted above, Mary and Joseph's marriage met these criteria as they had offspring in the Lord; they were faithful in that there was no adultery, and they upheld the sacrament by never divorcing. These three goods, according to Hugh and Peter, excuse coitus.[79] The *Collectio decem partium* expressed a similar sentiment: true marriage does not consist merely of intercourse between a male and a female, although, without that, marriages could not procreate children. Other elements are essential to marriage, which also distinguish marriage from adultery. Examples are fidelity to the conjugal yoke; actions directed to the procreation of children; and the good use of something evil, that is, the good use of carnal desire which the adulterer misuses.[80] With the realities on the ground in mind, Peter also noted some other honorable causes, secondary benefits, of marriage: the reconciliation of enemies and bringing about peace. Less honorable causes include marrying because of the other's beauty. Peter also recognized the advantage and possession of riches as realities for contracting marriages. Regardless of the reason behind contracting the marriage, if it was legitimately contracted, it was a legitimate marriage.[81]

78 Lombard 4.27.6–8, 4.32.2, 4.38.2. Similar views are expressed in ID 8.316–321; CSV 9.18 "Si quis" (fol. 252vb^2–253^{2}ra), 9.18 "Agothosa latrix" (fol. 253ra–rb^2). See Silano, "Peter Lombard," 154–155.

79 De Sacr. 2.11.7–9; Lombard 4.30.2.4, 4.31.5–8. Cdp 7.6.2 "Omne itaque" (fol. 109vb) marked a similar sentiment: the goods of marriage were complete in the parents of Christ—fidelity, sacrament, and offspring. Only nuptial intercourse was lacking. On account of sinful flesh this could not have occurred without the fleshly concupiscence that resulted from sin, and He without sin wished to be conceived without that.

80 Cdp 7.5.9 "Non in" (109vb).

81 Lombard 4.30.3.

Betraying its practical use, the *Collectio decem partium* took a stance on the mother's rights to her children by collating into one place texts scattered in Ivo's *Decretum*. Should a man live with a free woman and have children with her out of wedlock, he may have them deemed legitimate and placed under his power by arranging a dowry for their mother. Stated another way: entering into a legitimate marriage with the children's mother made them legitimate. Even though born out of wedlock, they fall under the power of the father with the giving of a dowry—thus making a legitimate marriage between the parents.[82] If, however, a mother wished to retain governance over her minor children after the death of her husband, she may reject a second marriage in a judgment without swearing an oath. The judgment binds goods to her until her son reaches puberty, and thus, she was regarded as his tutor (*tutela*).[83] If a woman served as the guardian over her minor children and, after the start of the governance, she wanted to forego it and contract a second marriage, she first ought to arrange for a tutor for the minor children and set aside funds for their care. If it was apparent that she was in debt, it ought to be paid. At that point, she could arrange a second marriage. If this method of contracting a second marriage brings scorn, both the goods of the mother and stepfather may be set aside for the children.[84]

Separation and Divorce

Theologians and canonists were compelled to reconcile separations (divorce) with the permanent bonds of a true marriage. Hugh of St. Victor simply notes that in cases of blame or lack of offspring, they do not cease to be marriages. Should a divorce occur the marital covenant is not abolished; they are spouses even if they are separated.[85] For the canonical tradition and Peter Lombard, sterility and its impacts on a true marriage were a keen area of concern. As noted above, Hugh of St. Victor treats the matter quite quickly: in the event there is no offspring, it remains a true marriage. Ivo's *Decretum*, the *Collectio St. Victor*, and the *Collectio decem partium* echo this emphasis. Ivo explicitly excluded sterility as a basis for separation.[86] Illustrative of the canonical tradition, the *Collectio decem partium* emphasized that if a man took a wife who was sterile, deformed in body, weak in the members, blind, deaf, dumb, affected by some disease or by pains and labors, he should remain with her for the sake of union and fidelity; a point that would be echoed by Peter Lombard.[87] While it is not lawful for a man to send away a sterile wife for the sake of procreation,[88]

82 Cdp 7.8.12 "Si quis" (fol. 111rb); Epitome Juliani 67.1.
83 Cdp 7.12.6 "Si mater" (fol. 113ra); Epitome Juliani 87.1.
84 Cdp 7.11.5 "Si mulier" (fol. 112vb–113ra); Epitome Juliani 36.27; ID 16.129.
85 De Sacr. 2.11.11.
86 ID 8.254.
87 Cdp 7.22.3 "Si uxorem" (fol. 118rb); Lombard 4.34.6.
88 Cdp 7.22.4 "Tantum valet" (fol. 118rb).

spouses who know that they will never have children may not lawfully separate and unite with others for the sake of children. If they do, they are committing adultery with those to whom they have joined themselves because the previous marriage still exists.[89] While the door permitting separation on account of sterility seemed closed for the most part, the canonical tradition left open a window. The *Collectio decem partium*, for example, included a canon, a letter from Gregory III to Bishop Boniface, allowing for a husband whose wife could not render the debt and he could not remain abstinent to remarry. He, however, should continue to support the woman disabled by illness and not cast her aside entirely.[90] Ivo's *Decretum*, the *Collectio St. Victor*, and the *Collectio decem partium* included a letter of Pope Gregory to Bishop John of Ravenna that if a husband could not have relations with his wife on account of his frigid nature, he should keep her as his sister. However, if she wanted to have children, they should swear on sacred relics in the presence of seven relatives serving as witnesses that they never engaged in intercourse. She could then remarry, though he could not. Should he do so, all involved were guilty of perjury, and, after penance, the first marriage was reinstated.[91]

Both Lombard and Gratian reaffirmed this position. They saw the highest good of marriage as the procreation of offspring. A secondary reason was the avoidance of fornication. Lombard drew almost directly from Gratian's text, which comprises letters from Pope Gregory and a conciliar canon from the Council of Compendium (757), for the policy regarding natural impotence. Should he not be able to render the debt on account of impotence, they should remain together unless she expressed a desire to have children. In that case, she was able to contract a second marriage, though he could not take another. If there was disagreement as to whether he ever rendered the debt, he was to be believed.[92] Lombard again drew from Gratian's text, a letter from the archbishop of Reims, regarding the possibility that some sort of sorcery was used to bring about impotence. If his ability to perform was not restored through the partners' penance, they could separate and marry others. However, should the ability to perform be restored later, those second marriages stood as valid.[93] It was clear that Lombard had Gratian's text in front of him. Gratian simply

89 Cdp 7.22.4.1 "Manet vinculum" (fol. 118rb–va).

90 CSV 9.38 "Si mulier" (fol. 254vb–255ra); Cdp 7.24.3 "Quod posuistis" (fol. 119ra–rb).

91 ID 8.182; CSV 9.17 "De his" (fol. 252va–vb[2]); Cdp 7.24.6 "Quod autem" (fol. 119rb).

92 Lombard 4.34.2, 4.34.2.1 + 4.34.2.3 = GD C.33 q.1 c.2; Lombard 4.34.2.2 = GD C.33 q.1 c.1; Lombard 4.34.2.4 = GD C.33 q.1 d.p.c.2, c.3. On the legitimacy of remarriages and the place of the marriage blessing in such cases, see D. L. d'Avray, *Medieval Marriages: Symbolism and Society* (Oxford, 2005), 142–152.

93 Lombard 4.34.3.1; GD C.33 q.1 c.3. See C. Rider, *Magic and Impotence in the Middle Ages* (Oxford, 2006), 53–75 for views of Gratian and Peter Lombard. She points to Hincmar of Reims as a founding father of the impotence caused by magic. While outside the scope of this chapter, see pp. 90–112 for the treatment of the topic in thirteenth- and fourteenth-century pastoral literature, such as the *Summa confessorum* of Thomas of Chobham.

commented in his *dictum* after this canon that this appeared to contradict the previous chapter of Gregory (C.33 q.1 c.2) which rendered the second marriage invalid should he regain his ability to perform. In such cases, she was to return to her first husband.[94] Gratian did not reconcile the contradiction but simply noted it existed. Lombard, however, posited that either this precept is understood more from rigor than from canonical authority, or that they could not be reconciled to their former spouse unless by a judgment from the Church which separated them in the first place.[95]

Fornication/adultery was a permissible reason for divorce. Courtesy of Isidore of Seville (though misattributed to a Pope Alexander), Peter Lombard offered the definition of fornication as all illicit coitus done apart from one's wife—understood especially as intercourse with widows, prostitutes, or concubines—and adultery as the violation of another's marriage-bed. In the case of fornication, it was permissible for the husband and wife to dismiss the other for the offense. Peter Lombard, Ivo of Chartres, and the compilers of the *Collectio St. Victor* and the *Collectio decem partium* were in agreement that what was unlawful for one was unlawful for the other, but if either was dismissed for fornication s/he must remain unmarried. A husband could not dismiss a fornicating wife unless he were innocent of the same offense and vice versa. Those separated because of fornication could be reconciled. If an innocent husband dismissed his wife for fornication, he could not join with another; he must practice continence or return to the wife he dismissed. The same was true of a wife.[96] For the canonical tradition, only heresy surpassed adultery in the seriousness of offenses.[97] One could not commit adultery for children, and one could not marry the individual with whom they committed adultery.[98] While adultery was condemned for both sexes, Peter does note that wives do not easily accuse their husbands of adultery. Husbands have been more freely accustomed to bringing their adulterous wives before the priests. If his crime was detected, he should be removed from communion. Adulterous husbands were subject to the same penalties as adulterous wives, though they should be published more harshly because they were to surpass women in virtue and rule them by example.[99]

94 GD C.33 q.1 d.p.c.3.

95 Lombard 4.34.3.2.

96 Lombard 4.34.5.4; ID 8.109–110, 127, 199, 208, 233, 237, 239, 240, 242, 243; CSV 9.26 "Placuit ut" (fol. 253va), 9.27 "Quod si" (fol. 253va–vb), 9.28 "Apostolus Paulus" (fol. 253vb), 9.35 "Amodo in" (fol. 254va), 9.55 "Preceptum domini" (fol. 256rb); Cdp 8.1.1 "Preceptum Domini" (fol. 121rb–vb); Cdp 8.3.1–9 "Apostolus Paulus," "Precepit Dominus," "Inter virum," "Et illud," "Dominus ad," "Licite dimittitur," "Interveniente divortio," "Ait dominus," "Sicut autem" (fol. 122ra–vb); Cdp 8.8.1 "Quod tibi" (fol. 125ra–rb).

97 ID 8.99; Cdp 8.5.3 "Quid in" (fol. 124ra).

98 ID 8.201–202, 211; Cdp 8.4.2 "Illud vero" (fol. 122vb), 8.5.2 "Sic non" (fol. 124ra).

99 Lombard 4.35.1–3. See also Silano, "Peter Lombard," 154–155.

Marriage of Unbelievers

The marriage of unbelievers followed a similar course as the three goods of marriages: it was valid if they married for progeny, maintained fidelity, and loved and cared for each other. If they were lawful persons, unbelievers could have lawful marriages. Hugh of St. Victor emphasized the spiritual effects of marriage. The sacrament of marriage was not denied to unbelievers, though they did not receive the spiritual effect. In the case of a wife who could not follow her husband because he became Christian, he was permitted to marry another without sin. The unbeliever was not to remarry and committed adultery if s/he did so. If the believer was remarried before the unbeliever converted, s/he was not bound by the first union. If, however, the believer was unmarried at the time and the unbeliever converted, then the first marriage remained in force.[100] Hugh's position was not dissimilar from the canonical tradition. If an unbeliever sent away his wife before baptism, he may decide, after baptism, either to have her or not have her. But if a man married a virgin before baptism, he could not take another wife after baptism so long as she lived. Baptism wiped out sins, not marriages. In the event that one of the spouses was baptized but not the other and the unbeliever chose to leave, s/he should be allowed to do so if that was their desire.[101]

Interfaith marriages were of keen interest to both theologians and canonists. The *Collectio St. Victor* and Lombard, for example, worked under the premise that a Christian man may not enter into a marriage with a pagan or Jewish woman. A marriage could not be contracted by those of different religions and faiths. Lombard maintained that two infidels, like two Christians, could enter into a valid marriage. Should one convert and the other remain an unbeliever, the marriage should remain because it was contracted when both of them were of the same infidel faith. Unbelief alone did not dismiss a marriage, which existed even among the infidels so long as they were lawful persons but not approved because it was without faith. It was thus lawful if it was contracted in accordance with the legal institutes or the customs of the province and not against the Lord's command. The unbeliever could be saved through the believer. If one of them should leave the region, the other was not required to follow and could remarry. In cases in which one of the partners converted and the other did not, the marriage remained valid as the unbeliever may convert at some point. However, as noted in Ivo's *Decretum*, the believer could dismiss the unbeliever because idolatry and noxious superstition equated to fornication of the mind (as opposed to physical fornication). The believer could dismiss the unbeliever if s/he were trying to turn them back to the infidel faith or blasphemies

100 De Sacr. 2.11.13; Lombard 4.39.6–7. Such is held in the canonical tradition, such as Cdp 7.18.1 "Nunquid non" (fol. 115ra).

101 ID 8.195–197; Cdp 7.18.2–4 "Si quis," "Simili modo," "Sic non" (fol. 115rb–va).

God, though the believer should not dismiss an unbeliever who wished to live together and did not call the believer away from God.[102] In the event the believer did dismiss the unbeliever, Peter questioned whether the believer could remarry. He presented two viewpoints espoused: the contra that the believer could not remarry so long as the unbeliever was alive; and the pro that the believer could remarry. His determination rested with whether the unbeliever abhorred Christ or was willing to live with the believer and not fuss over the newfound faith. So long as the marriage was contracted when they were both unbelievers and the unbeliever abhorred Christ, the believer could remarry. If the unbeliever did not abhor Christ and was willing to allow the believer to practice their faith unobstructed, s/he should not be dismissed. If both were believers when they married or both had converted, and one left the faith and abandoned the other, the one dismissed should not follow the abandoner but also could not remarry because the marriage had been contracted when they were both believers.[103]

Lombard presented the information in such a way that interfaith marriages could remain in the hopes the unbeliever would convert or the unbeliever could be dismissed. While Lombard echoed the position found in Gratian, Gratian, however, directly engaged with the particulars involving Jews in a way that Lombard did not. He included texts advocating for the separation from a Jewish spouse. Not only should a Jew and a believer not remain married, but a believer should not associate in any with the Jews and there should not be marriages between them.[104] The reason, Gratian maintained, was "lest the believer who sought the unbeliever's salvation perish in unbelief along with the believer."[105]

Consanguinity and Affinity

Both Hugh and Peter ground their sections on consanguinity and affinity (both familial and spiritual) in legal sources, whether they are conciliar canons in the case of the former or papal decretals in the case of the latter. Both Hugh and Peter reiterated that consanguinity and affinity, the latter of which constituted familial relationships formed with in-laws, extend to the seventh degree. Both present, even if in different ways, the method of counting found in Isidore of Seville's *Etymologies*. Hugh counted the degrees of consanguinity with higher, lower, and transverse lines beginning with the first degree as father and mother in the higher line and the son and daughter in the lower line. He also considered the maternal and paternal lines. By the time the sixth degree is reached, relations have extended to grandfather and grandmother four times removed

102 Lombard 4.39.1.2. This is one of the few places where Lombard mentions Jews specifically. CSV 8.64 "Si quis" (fol. 251ra), 9.53 "Iudei qui" (fol. 255vb–256ra).

103 Lombard 4.39.2–5, 7; ID 8.248–250. Cf. C.28 q.2 d.p.c.2.

104 GD C.28 q.1. c.10–c.17.

105 GD C.28 q.1 d.p.c.10: "…dum fidelis salutem querit infidelis, pocius ipse cum eo infidelitatis perditionem inveniat."

and grandson and granddaughter four times removed. Peter's rendition of Isidore's method of counting is that of a tree with the son or daughter or brother and sister as the trunk. By the time the sixth degree is reached, relations have extended to the grandson and granddaughter five times removed. Both noted that there were different ways to count degrees. Peter pointed to (a) father in the first degree and children in the second degree; (b) children in the first degree; (c) father and brothers in the first degree. Hugh pointed to the canonical method and the Justinian method. He reconciled them by showing that Justinian's was for the purpose of inheriting property, not of marriage.[106]

Gratian echoed the same methods of counting as Peter Lombard and Hugh of St. Victor, which depended upon whether the children were counted as the trunk or in the first degree. He likewise included the letter from Pope Zacharias and Isidore's explanation in his *Etymologies*.[107] Gratian also included the lengthy decretal of Pope Alexander II to the Italian bishops and clerics that outlined yet another method of counting, that according to secular Roman law for the purpose of succession. According to the pope, this method counted natural siblings as the second degree, their children as the fourth, and their grandchildren as the sixth. The Roman method of counting continued by adding one degree for each person born but succession was limited to the tenth degree.[108] Alexander went on to note that while the canons differed from this method on account of use, that it is used for the purpose of marriage and not succession, they did not differ as a result: two degrees in Roman law were equivalent to one degree in the canons. Thus, the sixth and seventh degrees by the canons are the twelfth and fourteenth degrees in Roman law.[109]

106 De Sacr. 2.11.14; Lombard 4.40.1–2. The texts Hugh drew upon—largely conciliar decrees—circulated widely and he would include 5 texts not included in Gratian's *Decretum*. The texts are from Pope Zachary, Gregory II, Bede, and Gregory's reply to Augustine. They circulated in several northern French collections, such as Ivo's *Decretum* and *Panormia*. See K. Ubl, *Inzestverbot und Gesetzgebung: Die Konstruktion eines Verbrechens (300–1100)* (Berlin, 2008) on the historical development of consanguinity and its dialogue with power and the functions of law.

107 GD C.35 q.5 c.1, c.4.

108 The Roman way of counting degrees up to the common ancestor and then down to the relative had been abandoned by the ninth century, if not earlier, and replaced by the canonical method of counting up to the common ancestor and stopping. A brother and sister were related in the second degree in the Roman way of counting but in the first degree according to canon law. A couple with common grandparents—first cousins—were related in the fourth degree in the Roman method of counting but only in the second decree in the canonical method of counting in the canonical tradition. The sixth degree in the canonical method equated to fifth cousins while the seventh degree was sixth cousins. On this, see D. d'Avray, *Papacy, Monarchy and Marriage, 860–1600* (Cambridge, 2015), 65. On the historical development of consanguinity and its dialogue with power and the functions of law, see K. Ubl, *Inzestverbot und Gesetzgebung: Die Konstruktion eines Verbrechens (300–1100)* (Berlin, 2008).

109 GD C.35 q.5 c.2; Jaffé 3476; Inst. 3.6.1–7. Gratian echoed the same argument in GD C.35 qq.2&3 d.p.c.19 and d.p.c.21. See Gaudemet, "Le marriage en droit romain," in *Sociétés et marriage*, 59–64.

The canonical tradition was greatly concerned with consanguinity and affinity. Ivo devoted Book 9 of the *Decretum* and the *Collectio decem partium* devoted Book 8 to the subject. The *Collectio St. Victor* focused on the bonds of affinity formed through marriage and prohibitions on fornication with anyone who falls under these bonds.[110] The *Collectio decem partium* paid particular attention to the investigation of accusations of consanguinity. Members of the family, or, if not available, two or three reputable persons of mature years who know of the relationship, should testify under oath of the consanguineous relationship before a synod. If the couple is found to be related, they are to be separated. The couple could also confess to the relationship. If they were separated by the bishops' judgment, the young were not forbidden to contract another marriage.[111]

Consanguineous relationships were a second reason, aside from fornication, to dissolve a union. Hugh conceded that a consanguineous relationship having been made public warranted the separation of a couple legitimately married and blessed by the Church.[112] His concern lay with the children born from such unions. In his view, it would be harsh to call them illegitimate as long as the disqualifying facts remained hidden at the time of the marriage. Thus, if the children were deemed legitimate in some respect, the marriage from which they took their existence likewise had legitimacy in some respect.[113] Peter likewise acknowledged such separations but, leaning on a text from Pope Urban II and a spurious text of Pope Fabian, he more directly acknowledged the disagreement as to whether the union was legitimate. Some say no because it was unlawful for them to marry. Others say yes because the Church lawfully married them without knowing of the relationship. In the end, such marriages were dissolved by the testimony of two or three men under oath, preferably that of close relatives but otherwise elders with knowledge of the relationship. The bishop could also call the spouses to determine what they know, at which point they could confess to the consanguineous relationship. If the bishop separated the union for ignorance of consanguinity, both could remarry.[114]

Gratian, akin to the *Collectio decem partium*, was far more concerned with process and procedure. Separation, he argued, was a punishment that only a judge could inflict because only a judge inflicts punishment. No one, therefore, could lawfully send away a wife for any reason—be it adultery or consanguinity—without judgment having been rendered.[115] Gratian had laid the foundation for

110 See in particular CSV 8.1–19 (fol. 244rb–245va).

111 Cdp 8.15.2–7 "Consanguineos extraneorum," "Convenit Troie," "Notificamus tibi," "De parentela," "Illud sacramentum," "Ab isto" (fol. 129va–130ra). The Cdp also includes example oaths to be used at the trial.

112 De Sacr. 2.11.11.

113 De Sacr. 2.11.4.

114 Lombard 4.41.3–4; GD C.35 q.6 c.1, c.3, c.4, d.p.c.11.

115 GD C.33 q.3 c.1–d.p.c.4; C.35 q.6 d.p.c.9, c.10.

Lombard, holding that two or three men should attest to the consanguinity of a relationship under oath or the couple could confess. If neither should happen, the bishop could call the spouses as witnesses to determine what they know.[116] Yet, Gratian went further by including a number of sample oaths, such as that to be taken before the synod where the case was being heard,[117] to be taken by those denouncing the marriage,[118] and by those serving as witnesses.[119] Should the court order a separation, Gratian provided an example of the oath of separation,[120] and should the wife have been found to be unjustly sent away, he provided an example of the oath of reconciliation.[121] Lombard had no use for such examples in his work, but he knew where to find them should he need them. It is also understandable that Gratian would be more concerned with remedying legal mistakes. Should the Church order the separation of a couple based on the deceitful or false testimony of witnesses, the Church should overturn the initial ruling and reinstate the validity of the marriage. In such instances, the Church would be correcting something that had occurred because of another's fraud. In the event that the couple had contracted a second marriage, that marriage would be dissolved and they should return to their first spouse.[122] Again, Lombard may not have addressed the matter specifically, but assuredly he knew the policy. Finally, Gratian, like Hugh of St. Victor, addressed the status of children born from consanguineous marriages. Contrary to Hugh of St. Victor, however, Gratian, in one canon, set forth an argument that such children should not be regarded as legitimate children.[123] Lombard seemed not to have an appetite for this issue as he did not address it.

While in agreement with the canonical tradition that the same considerations for consanguinity apply to affinity, that is, one's in-laws, Hugh and Peter diverge on what is of interest to them. Hugh's interest lay in emphasizing that the death of a spouse did not dissolve the affinity of the relationship. That meant a survivor could not marry the family member of a deceased spouse, and the children of the first marriage could not marry the children of a first marriage.[124] Peter likewise acknowledged this simply by noting that if a couple was espoused and death prevented them from marrying, none of his family could marry her.[125] Both Gratian and Peter would note that a woman who entered into a second marriage kept her affinity with her first husband, as such the

116 GD C.35 q.6 c.1, c.3, c.4, d.p.c.11; Lombard 4.41.4.
117 GD C.35 q.6 c.7.
118 GD C.35 q.6 c.5.
119 GD C.35 q.6 c.6, c. 8.
120 GD C.35 q.6 d.p.c.9, c.10.
121 GD C.35 q.6 d.p.c.10, c.11.
122 GD C.35 q.9 c.1–d.p.c.9.
123 GD C.35 q.7 d.a.c.1, c.1.
124 De Sacr. 2.11.15.
125 Lombard 4.27.9.

children of the first marriage could not marry blood relatives of the first marriage.[126] Peter also noted that affinity does not extend to the in-law's spouse.[127] Peter honed in on the possibility of obtaining a dispensation. For example, there are those who appear to concede that marriage may be contracted between people related by affinity in the fifth degree. As another example, if a marriage had been contracted between those related in the fourth degree they were not to be separated. Also, if the relationship was in the third degree, it was not unlawful to take the other's wife after death. Thus, the Church could grant dispensation in the union of persons linked by affinity, beginning at the third degree of affinity and in the fourth degree for consanguinity, as Gregory did.[128]

Representing the canonical tradition, Gratian did not see a distinction between relations by blood or by affinity. Those joined by consanguinity or affinity could not marry within seven degrees, and the Church should order the separation of those joined in the fourth or fifth degree. He did not seem to espouse the ability for dispensation.[129] Gratian argued further that affinity extended to a woman's second marriage and that her children from the second marriage cannot marry relatives from her first marriage.[130] Lombard's inclusion of Innocent's text demonstrates that views within the canonical tradition were conflicted. This text is one of two paleae added later. The first is a spurious letter from a Pope Hyginus and the second is a spurious letter cited by Lombard from Pope Innocent. Both qualify and soften Gratian's original argument to maintain that the offspring of a woman's second marriage could not marry the relatives from her first marriage up to the third/fourth generation.[131] Lombard had no way of knowing that these were texts added later and not Gratian's original argument, but it shows that Lombard was engaged in the calculation of affinity, both of in-laws of a first marriage and the extent to which a second marriage was to be considered consanguineous.

On the matter of spiritual affinity, Hugh again took a 30,000-foot view whereas Peter delved more into specifics. Hugh noted that one could not be joined to one's godparent or godparent of his spouse. Should a woman hold up her own children before the bishop in the hopes of dissolving her marriage, her plot would not work; the marriage would continue to stand.[132] Peter, following the canonical tradition, delved a bit more into the subject, clearly defining spiritual proximity

126 Lombard 4.41.2.5; GD C.35 q.10 c.1.
127 Lombard 4.41.5–4.41.9.3 for a definition of affinity.
128 Lombard 4.41.2.
129 GD C.35 qq.2&3 c.12–d.p.c.19, C.35 q.5 c.3–c.6, C.35 q.8 d.a.c.1–d.p.c.3.
130 GD C.35 q.10 d.p.c.1–c.3.
131 Lombard 4.41.2.6; GD C.35 q.10 c.4–c.5.
132 De Sacr. 2.11.16. Gregory II at the Council of Rome in 720 banned marriages between godparent and godchild or the widowed mother of the godchild. Pope Zachary extended the ban on marriage between the godchild and the real child of the godparent. As David d'Avray noted, godparenting was quite popular as it provided a vehicle for forging social links. See, d'Avray, *Papacy, Monarchy and Marriage*, 113.

as the relationship between godfather and godmother, those who raised him or her from the baptismal font, those who sponsored him or her in catechism or confirmation, and between a priest and those who confessed to him. Such marriages were not permitted. Peter also noted that spiritual or adopted children could not be joined. Peter would concur with Hugh that those who treacherously seek to use spiritual affinity as a loophole to dissolve a marriage should be prevented from doing so. However, he did present the view that there were those who thought the marriage should be dissolved. He also noted that there was no prohibition against a husband and wife from raising their child from the baptismal font, but they should not aspire to do this. If necessity led to the baptizing of the child, sons and daughters of spiritual co-parents could marry. A man may marry a goddaughter and godmother in succession with consideration given to the timing of becoming a godparent, and if her husband had abandoned her and she had not had intercourse with him afterwards.[133] The fleshing out of the details would have proven helpful to those navigating cases of consanguinity and affinity coming before Church courts.

Such consanguinity and affinity policies left shrewd couples a certain amount of flexibility to manipulate the system. David d'Avray has pointed to c.50 of the Fourth Lateran, which narrowed the degrees of consanguinity from seven to four (i.e., from sixth cousin to third cousin) as a mechanism by which to curb frequent annulments. Similarly, relations from affinity were reduced to only former spouses or the sexual partners of persons related in the forbidden degrees. As d'Avray observed, whatever latitude may have been allowed in the past, c.50 set a realistic "incest taboo" for enforcement, thus cutting out the traditional grey area—, the fifth, sixth, or seventh degrees— which had fallen at the periphery of what could be easily proven as within the forbidden degrees.[134]

Realities of Pastoral Care

As we have seen, Peter Lombard, who had served as an archdeacon of Reims, delved into plausible real-life situations a cleric might face. To that end, there were a few topics pertaining to marriage that Peter addressed but Hugh did not as they lay outside the scope of his conceptual framework. Peter explicitly noted that since the Apostles did not limit the number of times someone could marry neither could the Church.[135] Following the canonical tradition, he also discussed the issue of captivity and instances when a wife feared her husband dead or would never be released so she remarries only to have him return. In such cases, the first marriage was to be restored. So long as it was held certain that a woman's husband was still alive, though he could be held in captivity, she

133 Lombard 4.42.1–6; Cdp 7.26.1–5 "Ita diligere," "Nosse desideras," "Ad limina," "Si quis," "De his" (fol. 119vb–120va).

134 d'Avray, *Papacy, Monarchy and Marriage*, 69, 72, 76, 105.

135 Lombard 4.42.7. Augustine, Jerome, Council of (Neo) Caesarea.

may not contract a second marriage. Peter also set forth the plausible scenario of a man who left his wife, moved to another area, and remarried. This man repented his sin and wanted to return to his first wife. Peter noted that he was unable to do so and he was to stay with his second wife but never request the conjugal debt from her. She, however, could request it from him.[136] In a case in which a fiancé(e) died, the surviving partner was not considered a widow(er) because they were espoused in the future tense. One could be considered a widow only if they were married in the present tense. As such, should the fiancé marry, he could still enter the major orders later if he wished as he was not a bigamist.[137] However, should someone kill their wife without process of law and cause—such as being adulterous—he is to do public penance and be anathematized if he is contumacious. He loses any right to remarry.[138]

Lombard, like canonical collections, treated the issue of abortion. The *Collectio St. Victor* focused keenly on the sin of women who ended a pregnancy resulting from ill-conceived or adulterous liaisons.[139] The collection also addressed the killing of children and infanticide by leaving children exposed to the elements.[140] Lombard drew upon the same material sources as Gratian: Augustine's *Questions on Exodus*, Augustine's *Questions on the Old and New Testament*, and Jerome's letter to Algasia. Lombard did not copy the texts exactly as they were found in the *Decretum*. Rather, he chose the portion of the text that illustrated his point: abortion was considered homicide if the unborn child was formed—received in their features and members—and has a soul. Before then it was not.[141] Gratian, however, included a portion of text from Augustine's *Questions on Exodus*, passed over by Lombard:

> For even if an unformed embryo had, in some as yet unformed way, a soul (and one should not plunge into this great question and give a rash unreflective opinion), the law would not call it murder, because one cannot tell when a body that lacks sensation has a living soul.[142]

136 Lombard 4.38.3; ID 8.189–193, 244–246; Cdp 7.16.5 "Generaliter diffiniendum" (fol. 115ra). Dig. 23.2.6.
137 Lombard 4.27.10.
138 Lombard 4.37.2. See also Cdp 8.4.4–7 "Si cuius," "Inter hec," "Interfectores suarum," "Ammonere te" (fol. 123rb–vb).
139 CSV 8.41 "Si qua" (fol. 248vb), 8.42 "Hi vero" (fol. 248vb), 8.43 "Mulieres quedam" (fol. 248vb–249ra), 8.70 "Si qua" (fol. 251va).
140 CSV 8.45 "Si qui" (fol. 249ra), 8.48 "Si quis" (fol. 250ra), 8.49 "De infantibus" (fol. 250ra–rb), 8.50 "De expositis" (fol. 250rb).
141 Lombard 4.31.4; Silano, "Peter Lombard," 154. Cf. C.32 q.2 d.p.c.7–c.10.
142 GD C.32 q.2 c.8 §1:

> Si illud informe puerperium iam quidem fuerat sed adhuc informiter quodammodo animatum (quoniam magna de anima questio non est) precipitanda indiscussa temeritate sentenciae, ideo lex noluit ad homicidium pertinere, quia nondum dici potest anima uiua in eo corpore, quod sensu caret.

See also W. P. Müller, *The Criminalization of Abortion in the West: Its Origins in Medieval Law* (New York, 2012), 23–25.

This portion of the text seems to suggest that it remained unknown when the fetus was fully formed and thus the point at which the soul was imbued. Both Lombard and Gratian emphasize the need for the embryo to have formed all of its parts in order for abortion to be considered murder. Gratian, however, seems to qualify the role of the soul's formation and the point at which that took place.

Sexual Sins

Sexual sins were a concern but to varying degrees. Ivo, Gratian, and Peter Lombard repeated the basic definition of rape as illicit intercourse whereby the abductor engaged in debauchery. The treatment of rape engaged both unmarried virgins and married women. They noted that abduction with force occurred when a virgin without a preceding marriage contract was subjected to unlawful intercourse.[143] As such, she was corrupted by the will of both men: the rapist and the father who, having discovered that she had been seduced did not immediately take injury to heart.[144] Ivo's *Decretum* followed by the *Collectio decem partium* identified rape as it applied to married woman: if the victim was married and her husband tried to kill her, the bishop should step in and help to relocate her to a place of her choosing to ensure her safety.[145] Grounded in Roman law, Gratian would explain that rape was akin to robbery, which was a greater sin than theft as force was used to steal the item. The abductor did not seize the thing, but forcibly seized the use of the thing, and therefore admitted the robbery because he forcibly snatched the chastity.[146] Gratian was abundantly clear that so long as the woman—virgin or married—has a virtuous mind, she could not be sullied by defilement. Such women who have suffered violence have not lost their modesty and thus could not be accused of fornication or adultery.[147] The *Collectio canonum Saint Victor* treated rape as if with an ear to what might be heard in a confessional. Addressed in one canon, a man raped a woman, who later married the rapist's brother. The rapist had

143 Ex., ID 8.26; GD C.27 q.2 c.48, C.36 q.1 d.p.c.2; Lombard 41.5–9, p. 226.

144 ID 8.26; GD C.27 q.2 c.48; GD C.36 q.1 c.1; GD C.36 q.1 d.p.c.2: "Stuprum autem est proprie virginum illicita defloratio, quando videlicet non precedente coniugali pactione utriusque voluntate virgo corrumpitur, patre iniuriam ad animum statim post cognitionem non revocante."

145 ID 8.210; Cdp 8.4.4 "Si cuius uxor" (fol. 123ra–123rb).

146 GD C.36 q.1 d.p.c.3:

> Sed rapina dupliciter fieri dicitur; aliquando enim res ipsa rapitur, aliquando ipsius rei usus tantummodo violenter eripitur. Res ipsa tunc rapitur, cum violenter domino eripitur, ut in perpetuum teneatur; aliquando vero non res ipsa affectatur, sed usus eius domino prohibente violenter usurpatur. Hic ergo raptum admisit, quia florem virginitatis puellae renitenti violenter eripuit.

147 GD C.32 q.5 d.a.c.2–c.9, d.p.c.14: "Cum ergo hec, que violentiam passa est, pudicitiam amisisse probari non potest, nullo modo convincitur fornicationis vel adulterii crimen incurrisse."

doubly sinned and was subject to a doubly severe penance: he had raped the girl and hide the act from his brother. Should the marriage be dissolved, the woman could not remarry but the brothers could marry after penance.[148]

Seemingly more so than theologians, collections drilled into unnatural sexual acts. Peter Lombard had simply noted that the evil of adultery surpassed fornication and was surpassed by incest. But the worst of these was what was done against nature, as when a husband used the part of his wife's body not allowed for this end (e.g., sodomy).[149] Ivo of Chartres had included a number of canons condemning sodomy, bestiality, pederasty, transvestitism, fellatio, and masturbation.[150] The *Collectio St. Victor*, for example, drilled into any number of sexual sins such as a woman who fornicates with herself or with another woman[151]; relations between those who are professed religious[152]; relations with lepers[153]; bestiality[154]; and pedophilia[155]; particularly by the religious[156]; and nocturnal emissions.[157]

Conclusion

At the dawn of the University of Paris, conceptions about marriage put on display the intellectual interplay between canonists and theologians. Ivo of Chartres, the compiler of the *Collectio St. Victor*, Walter of Thérouanne who presumably compiled the *Collectio decem partium*, Hugh of St. Victor, Peter Lombard, and Gratian thought and taught at a time questions about the formation of and ability to dissolve a marriage were bubbling to the forefront of conversations among and between theologians and canonists. The implicit and explicit back and forth reveals the porous boundaries between the disciplines.

The theologians and canonists discussed in this chapter each defined marriage as a union of man and woman consenting to keep an undivided way of life.

148 CSV 8.15 (fol. 245va):

> Item indicatum est quemdam stuprasse quamdam feminam, quam postea frater eius accepit uxorem. Statuerunt eum qui stupravit et a se stupratam fratri celavit, quia geminavit peccatum, penitentia districtiori castigandum. Coniugium tale dissolvi oportere, et mulieri quidem nunquam dari potestatem nubendi; illis autem pro misericordia coniugium indulgere, sed cum penitentia.

149 Lombard 4.38.2.10.

150 ID 8.111–113; ID 9.85–95, 105–107.

151 CSV 8.22 "Mulier quocumque" (fol. 246rb), 8.24 "Mulier si" (fol. 246rb).

152 CSV 8.23 "Si sanctimonialis" (fol. 246rb).

153 CSV 8.26 "Hos qui" (fol. 246va).

154 CSV 8.27 "Qui cum" (fol. 246va), part of 8.27 "Si inventi" (fol. 246va), 8.32 "Si quis" (fol. 246va–247ra), 8.71 "Si quis" (fol. 251va–vb).

155 CSV 8.30 "Si quis" (fol. 246vb), 8.62 "Stupratoribus puerorum" (fol. 251ra).

156 CSV 8.29 "Clericus vel" (fol. 246va–vb), 8.31 "Si deprehensus" (fol. 246vb).

157 CSV 8.35 "Item in sompno" (fol. 247vb), 8.37 "Clericus si" (fol. 248ra).

The intersections between the disciplines come through in the evolution of respective ideas. Hugh, Peter Lombard, and Ivo of Chartres saw consent as making them spouses. It was the theologians though who contributed significantly to the concept of when a true marriage began and what it entailed. The emphasis on verb tense helped to solve the indissolubility of betrothals. Future tense— "I shall take"—made them betrothed, which in turn left open the possibility of breaking the contract. Present tense—"I take"—made the marriage valid and binding. Hugh of St. Victor used the "complete marriage" of Mary and Joseph as an example of the two forms of consent needed for a marriage: consent to marry and consent to carnal relations. It mattered not whether coitus factored into it. While Ivo of Chartres followed the thought of Hugh of St. Victor, consent of the two parties alone made a marriage; canonists, such as Walter of Thérouanne, would struggle with the role of coitus. Gratian would maintain that once consent was given they were spouses and coitus validated the marriage. In an effort to curb clandestine marriages, the canonists turned to emphasizing the importance of the family's involvement in the marriage, witnesses, and benediction of the priest as evidence of a valid marriage.

One's respective duties played a role in how one approached topics related to marriage, even if the respective positions did not differ. Hugh intertwines monastic theology with pastoral care though he is most concerned with the conceptual aspects as opposed to delving into specific examples. Along the lines of the *Collectio St. Victor*, users of the text learned the foundational principles that governed marriage, but not necessarily specific examples. Peter Lombard, on the other hand, drew upon legal sources to provide examples of how policy applied to specific situations. He, like Walter of Thérouanne and Gratian, may have had more work-a-day situations in mind, commonplace enough to feel the need to focus on how to handle them. Peter, more so than Hugh, directly addressed coitus in the marriage. The rendering of the debt was central to the ability to have children and take a vow of continence. Peter, like the canonists, felt compelled to deal with abortion. The marriage of unbelievers also garnered attention, particularly as it pertained to interfaith marriages. So too did consanguineous relationships formed between in-laws and godparents/godchildren. More so the concern of canonists was sexual sins stemming from abduction and unnatural acts.

Theologians and canonists engaged in implicit and explicit dialogue regarding the definition of a legitimate marriage, when a marriage begins, the conjugal debt, clandestine marriages, the good of marriage, separation, marriage of unbelievers, and consanguinity and affinity. As Hugh of St. Victor and Peter Lombard illustrate, theologians thought about these topics—and their subthemes—not simply through a singular disciplinary framework, but within an intellectual climate that brought the disciplines together, which they then adapted, as needed, to their working environment.

4

PETER THE CHANTER

Using Excommunication to Teach the Pragmatics of Pastoral Care

Introduction

The previous chapters have set forth an intellectual climate in northern France built upon a foundation of porous boundaries between law and theology. Texts, and people, moved freely along the *Via Francigena*. Theologians and canonists gathered at councils to discuss the most pressing issues facing the Church and the faith. A vibrant legal culture, for which Ivo of Chartres receives a lion's share of the credit, saw the proliferation and circulation of canonical texts. In the center of it all lay the schools of Paris—Notre Dame, St. Victor, and Ste. Geneviève. Masters such as Hugh of St. Victor and Peter Lombard may have focused their writings on theological texts, but these texts reveal an implicit and explicit dialogue with legal thought. Pastoral care, on the one hand, and the realities of administrative service outside of the schools, on the other hand, made familiarity with the law advantageous. Nowhere is this more apparent than with Peter the Chanter and his circle (Robert of Courçon, Robert of Flamborough, and Thomas of Chobham, as it pertains to this book). Careers were not isolated to the classroom. Masters not only trained the next generation of priests and administrators but also were actively involved in ecclesiastical affairs, which warranted a comfortability in both theology and law.

Peter the Chanter's education exposed him to canonistic thought, and it was something with which he was quite familiar. He was schooled at Reims, known for its teaching of dialectic, rhetoric, and grammar, which were essential to the study of both theology and law. While there he most likely received the educational background that would allow him to carry out his two-fold duties: confessor and judge. Master Alberic, who was known to have taught at Reims, was

DOI: 10.4324/9781003465096-5

renowned for his knowledge of Roman law.[1] Peter applied the division of cause, person, place, time, quality, quantity, and effect found in Gratian's *Decretum* to who, what, where, by what means, why, how, and when a sin was committed and the appropriate penance that should be levied. He also relied upon the *casus* as a teaching device as well as the *sic et non* methods being uitlized by both canon law and theology as a means of contextualizing and developing a moral law adequate to the new situations of the time.[2]

Peter the Chanter and those around him adhered to a pattern in northern French intellectual circles that blurred the boundaries between law and theology, a porosity that was on full display in discussions of rights, entitlements, obligations, and moral imperatives. The practical questions they addressed put Scripture into practice. Peter became a master in Paris in the 1170s and chanter of the Cathedral of Notre Dame—a position dedicated to the liturgy and instruction of the choir boys—in 1183. As Jason Taliadoros commented, Peter's main aim was to advise penitents on the most appropriate means of expediting sin. He was thus one of the first to distinguish between penalties imposed by the priest in the name of God and those imposed by an ecclesiastical judge for damages against the Church. This distinction eventually manifested in the "internal" forum, in which the priest secretly heard confession and administered penance, and the "external" forum of the ecclesiastical court that openly heard, tried, and punished crimes.[3] Yet, Peter's influence extended beyond the classroom where he taught moral theology and practical ethics. His views served as influences for shifting ecclesiastical policy regarding ordeals and as an influence on Pope Innocent III and papal policy regarding interdict.[4]

Peter's *Summa de sacramentis et animae conciliis* is a work of pastoral theology that relied heavily upon Scripture for the texts. Peter and his colleagues, such as Peter Comestor and Stephen Langton, used the Bible for the lessons it imparted, lessons that would prepare their students for active ministry.[5] Peter's *Summa*, which records his lectures in theology at the end of the twelfth

1 J. Baldwin, *Masters, Princes and Merchants: The Social Views of Peter the Chanter and His Circle*, 2 vols. (Princeton, 1970), 1.49.

2 J. Baldwin, *Masters, Princes and Merchants*, 1.56; J. Goering, "The *Summa* of Master Serlo and Thirteenth-Century Penitential Literature," *Mediaeval Studies* 40 (1978): 290–311, here 299–300.

3 J. Taliadoros, "Law, Theology, and Morality: Conceptions of the Rights to Relief of the Poor in the Twelfth and Thirteenth Centuries," *Journal of Religious History* 37, no. 4 (2013): 474–493, here 476–480.

4 C. Monagle, "Theology, Practice, and Policy at the Turn of the Thirteenth Century: The Papacy and Peter Lombard," *Journal of Religious History* 37, no. 4 (2013): 441–456; P. D. Clarke, "Peter the Chanter, Innocent III and Theological Views on Collective Guilt and Punishment," *Journal of Ecclesiastical History* 52 (2001): 1–20.

5 See B. Smalley, *The Study of the Bible in the Middle Ages*, 3rd edn. (Notre Dame, 2006; originally published Oxford, 1940).

century,[6] comprises three parts: the *De sacramentis legalibus et de effectu sacramentorum*; the *Tractatus de penitentia et excommuncatione*; and the *Liber casuum conscientie, sive subtilium questionum circa simoniam, furtum, usuram, matrimonia*, etc. Composed in stages between 1191 and his death in 1197, it is a composite of Peter's own thoughts and a series of *reportationes*, reports of Peter's teachings made by his students. Jean-Albert Dugauquier reached the conclusion that the work was very much a collaborative effort resulting from Peter himself, as seen by the use of the first person, and that of his students, as seen by the use of the third person. For example, Part 2 cap. 4 on the power of the keys includes a number of uses of the first person plural ("dicimus" and "excommunicamus"). The portion of cap. 4 focused on excommunication, however, is largely in the third person. Similarly, Part 3 cap. 11 on excommunication is also in the third person with only a few uses of the first person plural.[7] Peter's intention with his *Summa* was not so much to present the abstract legal formulations espoused by the canonists but rather to provide solutions to real-world problems generated by confession. In many respects, Peter looked at the intersection of life and law and the conflict created when they do not necessarily mesh. As a teacher and practitioner, Peter knew that the priest needed to find a solution to the challenges posed in the confessional and he sought to show his students how to go about finding pragmatic resolutions.[8]

Peter the Chanter cited his legal sources in different ways, as an examination of the section on simony in Part 3, the *Liber casuum conscientie*, reveals. Sometimes, he incorporated the essence of contemporary legal thinking. For example, in his analysis of what constituted simony, Chanter noted that, based on what had been stated before, both administering the sacraments as well as carrying the cross and ringing the bells for the burial of the dead for a price mounted to simony: "Ex supradictis, patet quod ponere sub pretio sacramenta, symoniacum est. Similiter sacramentalia, ut sepelire, crucem ad mortuum deferre, campanas pulsare, et huiusmodi."[9] Peter did not specify to what "ex supradictis" referred but rather used the phrasing to bring attention to the accepted thought. For example, the Council of Limoges (c.12) in 1031 decreed that a cleric could not accept money for baptism, burial, or to offer penance unless it was spontaneously and voluntarily given.[10] The Council of Reims

6 On the teaching of Peter the Chanter, see L. Hödl, *Die Geschichte der Scholastischen Literatur und der Theologie der Schlüsselewalt, Teil I* (Münster, 1960), 306–339.

7 Examples of the use of the first-person plural Part II cap. IV portion addressing the power of the keys: II, pp. 329, 331, 333, 334, 335, 336, 337, 343. In the portion of cap. IV addressing excommunication, the first person is found on p. 383. There are a few examples of the use of the first-person plural Part III cap. XI addressing excommunication: III.2a, pp. 238 and 241.

8 E. Corran, *Lying and Perjury in Medieval Practical Thought: A Study in the History of Casuistry* (Oxford, 2018), 20, 40, 66–75. Following Corran, I too will be referring to Peter the Chanter, irrespective of the part, in order to avoid confusion.

9 Chanter III.2a, §156, p. 9.

10 Mansi 19:504–505.

(c.4) in 1119 echoed a similar sentiment, decreeing that a price could not be exacted for baptism, the chrism, holy oil, burial, or visitation of the sick.[11] As a final example, the Third Lateran Council (c.6) in 1179 prohibited the selling of burials, the chrism, and holy oil.[12] Peter then gave a highly paraphrased citation: "Non intelligis hoc de labore illo qui exercetur in pulsatione campanarum et faciendis fossis, et huiusmodi, cuius venditio licita est; set de venditione dandi licentiam, pulsandi campagans et huiusmodi faciendi, que omnino illicita est."[13] Peter essentially put into his own words a version what can be found in c.6 of Alexander III's Council of Tours (1163): "Pro sepultura quoque, chrismatis, et olei sacri perceptione, nulla cuiusquam pretii exactio intercedat: neque sub obtentu alicuius consuetudinis reatum suum quis quam tueatur: quia divturnitas non minuit peccatum, sed auget."[14] Peter neither felt it necessary to cite his specific legal source nor to go into further detail regarding the law; rather, he simply presented the gist of an established and accepted legal principle.

Peter's treatment of simony in Part 3 demonstrates his comfort with the legal thought. He drew upon legal sources when they supplemented his argument. Yet, his citations to the law suggest two observations, both of which are equally plausible. On the one hand, Peter could have assumed that the reader already knew the law and thus it was not necessary to give fuller details. On the other hand, Peter could have felt that fuller details were not necessary. His purpose was to impart practical pastoral knowledge not the intricacies of the law, thus his students did not need more depth. Peter knew the source, even if his attribution was not entirely correct, but there was no need for his students to get lost in the weeds. In both scenarios, there was no need to belabor the citations: either his students would have known the legal citations or they would not.[15]

Peter relied on legal texts most heavily in the sections dealing with the power of the keys, excommunication, simony, theft and restoration, and marriage. He did draw upon legal thinking, though more sparingly, in the sections dealing with churches and cemeteries, the dismissal of fornicating priests, and usury. As a teacher at the cathedral school of Notre Dame and as a practitioner serving as a papal judge-delegate, Peter the Chanter knew that the priest needed to find a solution to delicate issues, and he sought to show his students how to go about finding pragmatic resolutions. While legal principles sketched the contours of Peter's thought, he did not slavishly follow the law. As his discussion of excommunication demonstrates, he selected the legal principle most fitting

11 Mansi 21:236.
12 COGD 2.1, pp. 131–132.
13 Chanter III.2a, §156, p. 9.
14 Mansi 21:1178.
15 The same point could be made regarding Peter the Chanter's use of Peter Lombard's *Sentences*.

to the point he wanted to make and, if needed, adapted it to the practicality of activity ministry. Peter's discussion falls into topics concerned with establishing the parameters for who can excommunicate, jurisdictional questions, offenses, sentences and their implications, communication with the excommunicated, and the ability to excommunicate those who have died.

Parameters for Who Can Excommunicate and Jurisdiction

For Peter the Chanter, the ability to excommunicate hinged directly on the one being tasked with the care of souls. He laid this foundation at the opening of chapter four on the power of the keys and excommunication with the comment that "the strength of confession resides in the power of the keys,"[16] which is found in Part 2, referred to as the *Tractatus de penitentia et excommunicatione*. Those who hold the keys must exercise knowledge and discretion in order to bind by the imposition of penance and to loosen through absolution.[17] The ability to bind was the ability to punish wrongs and to provide a mechanism by which one could make amends for those wrongs. The ability to loosen was the ability to recognize when those wrongs have been satisfied. The keys thus come with a two-pronged obligation: one must first have the right to possess them, and second one must use those keys with wise discretion.

Peter applied the connection between the ability to excommunicate and possessing the care of souls to situations in which that connection was broken, specifically in the cases of a vacant metropolitan see and when an excommunicated superior excommunicated a subordinate. In the case of a vacant metropolitan see, how should subordinates from the parish and suffragan bishops approach the issue of excommunication since they are subjected to the precepts of that see? Peter noted Pope Alexander III's rebuke of a suffragan of the see of Sens who did not want to obey.[18] Similarly, he noted the rebuke of the abbot of St. Remigius for disobedience during the vacancy of the see of Reims. Who, Peter questioned, has the ability to excommunicate: the archdeacon tasked with the care of parishes or the head of the cathedral chapter who possesses a higher ranking within the ecclesiastical hierarchy? In providing an answer, Peter appeared to draw from principles found in Roman law, specifically that of the *materfamilias* and that of *sui heredes*. In the case of *materfamilias*, the wife with her children succeeded in the *ius patrisfamilias*.[19] In the case of *sui heredes*, the wife *in manu*, in addition to sons and daughters *in*

16 Chanter II, §140, p. 327: "Confessionis vis residet penes claves."

17 Chanter II, §140, p. 330.

18 Until 1622, the archbishopric of Sens numbered seven suffragan (subordinate) dioceses: the dioceses of Chartres, Auxerre, Meaux, Paris, Orléans, Nevers, and Troyes.

19 Chanter II, §154, p. 377: "Ipsa est quasi materfamilias que succedit in ius patrisfamilias, ipsa scilicet cum filiis suis." See PL 200:218 for Pope Alexander III's rebuke of the abbot.

potestate, are able to succeed to property upon the death of the *paterfamilias*.[20] He used these examples to present the viewpoint that with the metropolitan see vacant, subordinates from the parish and suffragan bishops could exercise more independence. Yet, that authority resided in the hands of the collective, the head of the cathedral chapter and the archdeacon, and not in the hands of the singular alone. The collective is able to judge and excommunicate, but not ordain.[21] The cathedral canons resembled the *mater* in that they worked in conjunction with the bishop to impose a sentence, but they did not do so independent from the bishop. Pope Celestine III noted in his letter to the bishop of Clermont regarding the placing of a church under interdict that a canon could not do so, but the bishop should do so with two or more of the canons giving their approval.[22] The archdeacon resembled the child in that he was connected to the *mater*, the cathedral canons, and both were subordinate to the *pater*, the bishop. The bishop had to grant the archdeacon the authority to care for souls, thus the ability to bind and to loosen. As Pope Alexander III set out, the bishop

20 B. Nicholas, *An Introduction to Roman Law* (Oxford, 1962), 238. See also R. P. Saller, "Pater Familias, Mater Familias, and the Gendered Semantics of the Roman Household," *Classical Philology* 94, no. 2 (1992): 182–197 for an interesting discussion cautioning against reading too much into the gendered language and losing sight of the fact that women could make wills and in fact did serve as heads of household.

Gaius's *Institutes*, 3.2 and 3.3 articulated this point most succinctly: "Children who were under the control of the deceased at the time of his death are held to be proper heirs… (3.2)" and "A wife who is in the hand of her husband is a proper heir because she occupies the position of his daughter (3.3)." Gaius's text, however, was not known to have been studied at the schools in northern France. It is more likely that he knew of Ulpian's reiteration of the same concept found in the *Digest* (Dig. 50.16.195.2):

> Familiae appellatio refertur et ad corporis cuiusdam significationem, quod aut iure proprio ipsorum aut communi universae cognationis continetur. Iure proprio familiam dicimus plures personas, quae sunt sub unius potestate aut natura aut iure subiectae, ut puta patrem familias, matrem familias, filium familias, filiam familias quique deinceps uicem eorum sequuntur, ut puta nepotes et neptes et deinceps. Pater autem familias appellatur, qui in domo dominium habet, recteque hoc nomine appellatur, … Et cum pater familias moritur, quotquot capita ei subiecta fuerint, singulas familias incipiunt habere: singuli enim patrum familiarum nomen subeunt.

(We talk of several persons as a household under a peculiar legal status if they are naturally or legally subjected to the power of a single person as in the case of a head of a household, the wife of a head of a household, a son-in-power, a daughter-in-power, and those who thereafter follow them in turn, as, for instance, grandsons and granddaughters, and so on. … Someone is called the head of a household if he holds sway in a house, … And when the head of a household dies, all the individuals who were subjected to him begin to hold their own households for as individuals they enter into the category of heads of households.) Taking a different view was the Roman jurist Paul (Dig. 37.4.4.2) espoused the view that women did not have *sui heredes*: "Ad testamenta feminarum edictum contra tabulas bonorum possessionis non pertinet, quia suos heredes non habent.".

21 Chanter II, §154, pp. 376–379: "Item. Auctoritas sedes residere videtur penes universitatem non penes singulos. Item. Iudicare potest, excommunicare potest, ordinare non, qui insacratus ordinare non potest."

22 II Comp. 3.9.2 (X. 3.11.2).

conferred upon the archdeacon the authority to care for souls. The office alone does not give an archdeacon the right to excommunicate.[23] In the end, the collective was necessary to exercise authority.

Someone could be in the priesthood though not have the power to bind and loose, a point that Peter used to argue that an excommunicated superior could not excommunicate his subordinates. The power of the keys was tied to his charge and not to the mere fact of being a member of the priesthood (*sacerdos*).[24] Peter explicitly cited C.24 q.1 c.4 of Gratian's *Decretum*. Stemming from a letter of Pope Alexander II to Bishop William of Marche, Alexander wrote of hearing that Henry, the said Archbishop of Ravenna, had endeavored to excommunicate William. But in truth, because Henry had been excommunicated he was not able to excommunicate William. Alexander absolved him and those around him by apostolic authority and ordered them never to care thereafter.[25] Essentially, the Pope absolved William and his circle and ordered them to pay no attention to Henry's sentence.

Peter drew upon this text as an example of both the *pro* and *contra* stance of the position that an excommunicated superior cannot excommunicate his subordinates. C.24 q.1 c.4 reads:

> Audivimus, quod Henricus, Ravennas dictus archiepiscopus, nisus sit te excommunicare. Verum, quia excommunicatus ***te*** [bold emphasis mine] non potuit excommunicare, apostolica auctoritate *te tuosque absolvendo* mandamus exinde ***numquam curare***.[26]

Peter maintained that *te tuosque absoluendo* proved the *pro* stance—he who is absolved is freed from the bond—and ***Te nunquam [oportet] curare*** proved the *contra* stance—if there is no ability to care [for souls], there is no ability to absolve.[27] Peter construed the text to tie the keys to the care of souls. In its entirety, the canon simply argues that the excommunicated bishop is not able to excommunicate his subordinates. The pope had absolved the bishop of the illicit sentence.

23 I Comp. 1.15.4 (X 1.23.4), I Comp. 1.15.5 (X 1.23.5).

24 Chanter II, §152, pp. 369–370: "Unde etiam potestas sepe videtur committi in causarum delegatione non sacerdotibus. Sed secundum hoc videtur quod quis possit esse sacerdos absque potestate solvendi vel ligandi."

25 GD C.24 q.1 c.4.

26 edF., col. 967.

27 Chanter II, §152, pp. 369 ln. 3–7:

> Finis illius capitula *Audiumus*, Ca. XXIIIIa, Q. Ia, facit pro et contra. Pro, cum dicitur *te tuosque absolvendo*; qui enim absolvitur a vinculo liberatur. Contra vero, cum dicitur: *Te nunquam oportet curare*; si enim non est curandum, non habet absolutionem.

To support further the viewpoint that the excommunicated cannot excommunicate others, Peter pointed to C.24 q.1 c.38 and c.39 of Gratian's *Decretum*. Both of these texts stem from letters of Augustine in which he states that those excommunicated for heretical behavior are not to be received by Catholics.[28] If he cannot be received by Catholics he cannot excommunicate Catholics. Finally, Peter highlighted C.15 q.6 c.5 in the *Decretum*, a letter from Pope Urban II maintaining that no one is compelled to serve those who are excommunicated from the faith until they are reconciled. In this case, the soldiers of a Count Hugh were released from their oath to him until he was again in the good graces of the Church.[29] Peter grounded his conclusion in law: the power of the keys were associated with the appointment to his position, not simply with his ordination. Thus, one was able to be a priest without having the power to bind and loose.[30]

Peter emphasized the care of souls as the key criterion for being able to use the keys. A priest (*sacerdos*) ordained without a title, such as a monk or anyone who was not charged with the care of souls, could not receive the keys. Simply being in the sacred orders did not automatically grant the means (*materia*) to use the keys. The ability to use the keys derived more from pastoral care than from order.[31] Peter seemed to echo contemporary thought. The school of Laon, and Anselm of Laon in particular, had divided the keys into two parts: the key of knowledge (i.e., discretion) and the key of power. One who was consecrated as a priest without receiving the *cura pastoralis* did not receive the power of the keys. Stated another way: in his ordination, the priest received the power to perform the sacraments, but he received the power of the keys only when the bishop committed a parish to him.[32] Thus, if he did not possess the care of souls, he did not possess the keys. Just as he who conferred the order conferred the appurtenances of the order, he who conferred the care of souls conferred the appurtenances of care.[33] The school of St. Victor, as represented by the anonymous work the *Vae vobis pharisaesis*, held that the key of knowledge (i.e., discretion) included all the sacramental power held by the *sacerdos*. These powers included preaching, instructing, correcting, baptizing, curing the infirm, chasing demons, and the Eucharist. The key of power was the power of

28 GD C.24 q.1 c.38 and c.39.

29 JL 4291.

30 Chanter II, §152, pp. 369–370: "Unde etiam potestas sepe videtur committi in causarum delegatione non sacerdotibus. Sed secundum hoc videtur quod quis possit esse sacerdos absque potestate solundi vel ligandi."

31 Chanter II, §142, p. 335: "Ex cura namque pastorali videtur potius oriri talis obnoxietas quam ex ordine. Unde dicimus talem clavem habere, sed non materiam in qua clavibus utatur."

32 S. Chodorow, *Christian Political Theory and Church Politics in the Mid-Twelfth Century: The Ecclesiology of Gratian's Decretum* (Berkeley, 1972), 159, 162–163.

33 Chanter II, §142, p. 336: "Nonne potestates iste ligandi et solvendi sunt ex ordine, et qui ordinem contulit, nonne appenditia ordinis contulit; qui curam animarum dedit, nonne appenditia cure contuilt."

binding and loosing, which permitted the priest to excommunicate and absolve. While all of the powers of the priesthood were contained in the keys, the priest only received the power to use the keys with the *licentia episcopi*.[34] Gratian's understanding of the ability to use the keys encapsulates that of Laon and St. Victor, distinguishing between the *potestas* that came from God through the sacramental orders and the *executio potestatis* that derived from the *licentia episcopi*. Gratian maintained that the priest received his powers in the sacrament of the orders and that the bishop only gave him the right to use his powers when he committed a parish to his care. The bishop did not transmit any substantive power to the priest when he granted him the *cura animarum*, but now the *sacerdos* could use that power.[35]

A *sacerdos* thus possessed the full powers of the keys and, with his responsibility to care for souls, the ability to use the keys. A parish priest, Peter the Chanter thus argued, could suspend parishioners from entering the church without the order of a superior as long as there was evidence of contumacy.[36] By extension, a more minor priest could, in general, absolve the excommunicated provided he had made satisfaction for that which he committed.[37] If someone was bound by a general excommunication, a simple priest was able to absolve him after he had rendered satisfaction. If bound by a special excommunication, he should return to where he committed the crime. By allowing him to travel elsewhere, to the place where he committed the crime, his prelate is seen to have granted interim jurisdiction to the bishop of that location.[38] If someone under special excommunication died without confession but with sufficient grief, the special excommunication was downgraded to a general excommunication.[39]

Peter's stance regarding the ability of the priest to use the keys as it pertains to excommunication and absolution reflects a change taking place in ecclesiastical thought. The law traditionally had held that the power to bind and loose lay in the hands of the bishop. Canon 56 of the Council of Laodicea (343–381), included in the *Distinctiones* of Gratian's *Decretum*, made clear that priests were to accompany or follow bishops, they were not to be ahead of them. Priests were subordinate to bishops. For example, priests were not to enter or be seated before bishops at tribunals.[40] Gratian reiterated that priests' were to obey bishops, as children were to obey parents.[41] Gratian reiterated

34 Chodorow, *Christian Political Theory and Church Politics in the Mid-Twelfth Century*, 161–164.

35 See GD D.20 d.a.c.1, De pen. D.1 d.p.c.60 and d.p.c.87, and C.16 q.1 d.a.c.1. See also Chodorow, *Christian Political Theory and Church Politics in the Mid-Twelfth Century*, 168–171.

36 Chanter II, §142, p. 335: "Unde videtur quod possit suspendere parrochianum suum ab introitu ecclesie absque precepto sui superioris, quotiens apparet inobediens per contumatiam."

37 Chanter II, §144, p. 343: "… generaliter potest absolvi a minoir sacerdote dummodo satisfaciat ei in quem commisit."

38 Chanter II, §143, pp. 339–340.

39 Chanter II, §143, p. 341.

40 GD D.95 c.8.

41 GD D.95 d.a.c.1.

that priests' were conferred with the ability to offer communion at the altar, say prayers, and to bless the gifts of God.[42] Pope Leo I prohibited co-bishops and priests from performing certain tasks, such as the public reconciliation of a penitent.[43] If a priest did not possess the power to reconcile the penitent, it stands according to the old law that he did not possess the power of correction either. Correction was associated with the bishop's responsibility.[44] However, canon law did permit a priest to baptize with the permission of the bishop. For example, a priest could baptize in the absence of a bishop, by permission, when compelled by extreme necessity, such as the point of death.[45] Causa 26 q.6 reiterated this stance, maintaining that a priest was not able to restore someone excommunicated by a bishop without his permission. The only exception was when the bishop was not available and death was imminent.[46] Gratian distinguished between the episcopate and the presbyterate. Bishops performed sacraments that presbyters were not permitted to perform. The bishop confirmed those into the orders, consecrated churches and shrines, and blessed the holy chrism. The bishop also excommunicated the delinquent from the Church and then reconciled the penitent with it. The bishop and presbyter, however, share the power to perform baptisms, bestow the Eucharist, issue penitence, preach, and enjoy ecclesiastical benefices.[47]

Peter was not engaging with the law as it had been, but rather with the law as it was becoming. The canonical tradition was evolving to distinguish between major, which Peter referred to as "special," and minor, which Peter referred to as "general," excommunication. Major excommunication entailed full social exclusion from the church. This punishment fell under the purview of ecclesiastical courts. Minor excommunication excluded the condemned from the sacraments but not from the community. This punishment fell under the purview of the parish priest and derived from his duties associated with the penitential forum.[48] In a letter to Walter of Coutances, archbishop of Rouen, Pope Clement III instructed a minor excommunicate (*minor excommunicatio*) to be barred from the Eucharist, though he also added that the faithful were to avoid all contact with such an individual.[49] Clement III's letter is the first time papal legislation used the term minor excommunicate.[50] Pope Innocent III alluded to minor

42 GD D.25 c.1: "Ad presbiterum pertinent sacramentum corporis et sanguinis Domini in altario conficere, orations dicere, et benedicere dona Dei."

43 GD D.68 c.4.

44 GD D.45 c.1–c.3, c.8.

45 GD D.95 d.p.c.2. GD De cons. D.4 c.19, however, grants a priest (*sacerdos*) the right to baptize. Deacons, however, could not do so unless in the presence of a bishop or priest (*presbiterus*).

46 GD C.26 q.6.

47 Chodorow, *Christian Political Theory and Church Politics in the Mid-Twelfth Century*, 175–176, esp. n30. For excommunication see GD C.26 q.6 d.p.c.11 and d.p.c.13.

48 E. Vodola, *Excommunication in the Middle Ages* (Berkeley, 1986), 41–42, 56. For references to major excommunication, see X 2.2.5, 5.39.30, and 5.39.55.

49 Mansi 22:617. The letter is undated but must have been sent between 1187 and 1191, which are the dates for Clement's pontificate.

50 Vodola, *Excommunication in the Middle Ages*, 42 fn. 54.

excommunication in his letter to the bishop of Breslau when he wrote that communication with the excommunicated was a sin to be confessed to the parish priest.[51] Peter's *Summa*, dating between 1191 and 1197, sat in the center of these papal decretals, which dated between 1187 and 1191 for that of Clement III and 1199 for that of Innocent III. Peter was on the cusp of change and he applied this new law to the practical needs of pastoral care.

Jurisdiction is connected to the care of souls. If one is charged with the care of souls, he possesses jurisdiction to exercise the keys. This connection led Peter the Chanter to ask whether someone excommunicated for a crime in one diocese, such as Paris, could perform their penance in another diocese, such as Cologne, and, as a result, be absolved in Cologne for the crime committed in Paris? Peter maintained that he could not. He had not satisfied the conditions for absolution, and therefore it was a just sentence both from order and from character (*animus*).[52] As established in question 3 of Causa 11 of the *Decretum*, a bishop could not receive in communion a person excommunicated by his own bishop.[53] Distinctions 70–72 firmly established that a bishop in one diocese could not ordain someone who belonged to the diocese of another.[54] Peter's view thus reflects a legal understanding of ecclesiastical jurisdiction. In his comments on prescription found in Causa 16 of Gratian's *Decretum*, Stephan of Tournai distinguished between temporalities and spiritualities associated with a bishop's diocese. He argued that the 30/40-year rule associated with the rules of prescription meant that a bishop could lose the property and tithing rights to a church in his diocese to another bishop. The bishop, however, could not lose his spiritual rights to that church. In an example given, the bishop of Bologna owned a *villa* in the diocese of the bishop of Ferrara, where he wanted to build a church. While the bishop of Bologna would retain the temporal revenues, the bishop of Ferrara would retain the spiritual rights of the consecration of clerics, excommunication, and absolution.[55] Thus, another bishop could not usurp the spiritualities of another bishop. The bishop of Paris had placed the individual under excommunication, and he was responsible for absolving the excommunicate once the bishop felt that penance was served.

The jurisdiction for punishment, however, possessed a caveat not seen with reconciliation. To elucidate the caveat, Peter used a hypothetical case: someone plundering lands in the episcopate of Paris and then returning to his territory. Peter set forth the position that a sentence bound no one not under his judgment, save in the case of plundering. He cited C.6 q.3 c.4 of the *Decretum* in which a bishop was unable to excommunicate the parishioner of another,

51 III Comp. 5.21.3 (X 5.39.29). The letter is dated 1199.
52 Chanter II, §144, pp. 343–344.
53 GD C.11 q.3 c.2, c.73.
54 edF., col. 256–260.
55 Stephan of Tournai, *Summa*, ad. C.16 q.2 c.9 s.v. *conventum* (Munich, Bayerische Staatsbibliothek, Clm 17162, fol. 117ra).

except in the case of plundering.[56] The Church of Paris thus could excommunicate the one plundering.[57] He then posed the question of before whom ought he stand for justice. It was said that he should stand before his judge unless he was found in the parish of Paris. Since the sentence of Paris bound him according to the canon, the plunderer was thus subject to the bishop of Paris. As such, the bishop of Paris had the right to judge him by the authority of the pope, who produced that canon.[58] Peter would eventually allude to the actual circumstances that underpinned this hypothetical: the Archbishop of Reims's excommunication of the Count of Champagne, who technically fell under the jurisdiction of the Bishop of Châlons. Archbishop Henry of Reims (d. 1175) had excommunicated Count Henry of Champagne (1127–1181) when the latter had plundered territory in the parish of the former.[59] The two Henries had a contentious relationship despite being brothers-in-law. The Archbishop lashed out at the Count when the latter sided with Philip of Flanders to broker a peace when the commune of Reims revolted against the Archbishop in 1167. The Count would exacerbate matters when he extended his influence into the northern portion of the Marne Valley, which encroached upon the county of Reims held by the Archbishop. By 1171, the two would be at war, with each invading the other's territory and killing each other's men. The Archbishop accused the Count's men of plundering episcopal villages and killing villagers along the road between Reims and Châlons. The Archbishop responded by killing men in the territory of the Count. The Count, in turn, retaliated by ravaging episcopal lands. The hostilities continued with the Count building towers on the Archbishop's lands and capturing the Archbishop's men. The Archbishop excommunicated the Count, but he did not announce the sentence publicly. The hostilities would require both King Louis VII and Pope Alexander III to quell.[60]

Ecclesiastical courts meted out sentences of major excommunication, and, to that end, Peter briefly addressed the question of a court's jurisdiction. He asked if one layman has a case against another layman though each resides in different parishes, and if the first layman has an ecclesiastical action, before whom ought the action be tried? Could he bring it before whomever he wanted, or did the jurisdiction lay where first man made the citation, and, if so, why? The first man making the citation does not preclude another from hearing the case because the issue

56 edF., col. 563.

57 Chanter II, §143, p. 339: "Esto quod ecclesia parisiensis excommunicet eum."

58 Chanter II, §143, p. 339: "Parisiensis enim habet ius in eum auctoritate summi pontifices, qui canonem illum tulit."

59 Chanter II, §143, p. 342: "...ecclesia Remensis consueuit excommunicare comitem Henricum, cum depredatus est in alia parrochia, scilicet si deseratur querimonia ad ipsam, et hoc ratione territorii quod habet in archiepiscopatu remensi."

60 T. Evergates, *Henry the Liberal: Count of Champagne, 1127–1181* (Philadelphia, 2016), 130–133.

remains undecided before the *litis contestatio*, unless one considers Urban's decretal where a *litis contesatio* began with a citation.[61] Peter may be referring to Pope Urban III's letter to the bishop and deacon of Rouen in which he noted that an edict of citation (*citationis edicto*) began litigation. With the *citatio* issued, the case was underway, and thus a judge-delegate could continue his work despite the death of the one who assigned the case.[62]

Peter the Chanter deftly navigated the legal tradition, even as it was in the midst of change, to offer solutions for some of the more problematic examples posed by the ability to use the keys of binding and loosing. He drew upon a long legal tradition that argued an excommunicate could not excommunicate others. He drew upon ideas found in Roman law to argue for a collective judgment involving the cathedral canons and archdeacon in the case of a vacant metropolitan. He deftly navigated the law that preserved the right of a bishop to absolve despite someone moving into the diocese of another, though he used the legal loophole to punish someone for plundering in another diocese. For Peter, being tasked with the care of souls was the necessary ingredient for exercising the power associated with the keys. It is here that he engaged in a changing legal tradition, changing from a tradition that had reserved the right to bind and loose for the bishop to one that distinguished between minor excommunication afforded by the penitential forum to the priest and major excommunication reserved for bishops and ecclesiastical court.

Offenses

Peter the Chanter certainly did not list every offense that could lead to excommunication. In fact, he did not spend time a lot of time discussing offenses at all. However, the offenses he did mention shed light on those issues he felt were pressing enough to discuss. For example, he outlined a few offenses that endangered public morals, offenders who included rope-dancers, notorious drinkers, hired champions, and thieves.[63] Peter would offer a qualification for theft. If the thief was poor and did not have enough to sustain himself, excommunication should not be imposed.[64] He also outlined a few of the more common reasons for excommunication: usury and notorious public financiers, sorcery, laying violent hands on a cleric, arson, and poisoning (*venefici*).[65] He did not

61 Chanter II, §143, p. 342.

62 I Comp. 1.21.23 (X 1.29.20). See also R. H. Helmholz, "Citations and Construction of Procedural Law in the Ius Commune," in *The Creation of the Ius Commune: From Casus to Regula*, ed. J. W. Cairns (Edinburgh, 2012), 247–276, here 251.

63 Chanter III.2a, §264, pp. 278–279.

64 Chanter III.2a, §265, pp. 279–280. See also J. Taliadoros, "Law, Theology, and Morality: Conceptions of the Rights to Relief of the Poor in the Twelfth and Thirteenth Centuries," *Journal of Religious History* 37, no. 4 (2013): 474–493.

65 Chanter II, §147, pp. 349–350.

elaborate on these offenses but simply listed them as excommunicable. Since the law had already established them as such, there was no need to delve into them further. The question of usury was well established, being covered in both D.47 and D.48 of Gratian's *Decretum* as well as in C.14 q.3, which questioned what was meant by exacting interest, and in q.4, which asked whether it was permitted for clerics or laymen to exact interest.[66] Likewise, Pope Alexander III amply addressed the issue as his responses comprise approximately 50% of title 19 on usury in the *Liber extra*.[67] Magic likewise received a fair amount of attention in the *Decretum*, with C.24 q.1–q.5 focused on the topic and q.5 specifically addressing the excommunication of practitioners.[68] The *Liber extra* briefly returned to the subject in title 21 of book 5.[69] The murder of Thomas Becket, archbishop of Canterbury, by the hands of, presumably, men of King Henry II would bring the subject of laying violent hands on clerics to the fore. Letters from Pope Alexander III to the archbishop of Sens and the bishops throughout Gaul made it clear that those who did so were not only excommunicated but also could only be absolved by the pope.[70] Causa 23 q.8 had made it clear that the mutilation of limbs, murder, and the burning of houses were all forbidden without judicial authority. Offenders were excommunicated.[71]

While Peter the Chanter's list of excommunicable offenses, such as usury and violence against clerics, seems to fall in line with legal thought, he did include one curious addition: that of a courtesan (*meretrix publica*) who prostituted herself in public. He pointed to the Apostle Peter who damned Ananias and Sapphira, having them convicted and excommunicated because neither confessed before the law of engaging in such a notorious crime. According to Peter public courtesans were not to receive the Eucharist as they were separated from the body and blood of the Lord. Furthermore, he excommunicated ordinary men who had undoubted knowledge of their crime.[72] There was no danger in excommunicating prostitutes because the multitude would not fall into prostitution, thus resulting in a schism.[73] While prostitutes, like public actors, should not be offered the Eucharist, they did warrant prayers as they were not to be shunned from the church. Neither Gratian's *Decretum* nor the decretals that would be collated into the *Liber extra* directly addressed the excommunication of prostitutes. The discussion of prostitutes in the *Decretum* centered on

66 GD D.46 c.9–c.10, D.47 c.4–c.8, C.14 q.3 and q.4.
67 I Comp. 5.15.1–.4, 5.15.8–11 (respectively, X 5.19.1–.9).
68 edF., col. 1020–1036.
69 edF. 2, col. 822–823.
70 I Comp. 5.34.6 (X 5.39.5); I Comp. 5.34.9 (X 5.39.7), I Comp. 5.34.10 (X 5.39.8), I Comp. 5.34.14 (X 5.39.9).
71 GD C.23 q.8 d.p.c.30–c.34.
72 Chanter II, §147, pp. 351–352.
73 Chanter III.2a, §242, p. 242 ln. 24–27.

whether they were permitted a legal marriage, which they were.[74] A legal marriage would not be valid if one of the spouses were under a sentence of excommunication. In the title on simony, the *Liber extra* included a text attributed to Deusdedit which stated that every sinner, even a prostitute, could sing the mass and accuse someone of simony.[75] While every excommunicate was a sinner, not every sinner was an excommunicate. A prostitute was a sinner, but there does not seem to be mention of her being excommunicated.

Peter felt pressed to address groups that fell outside of the Catholic Church but nonetheless were not considered excommunicated. *Ethnici* (gentiles) and *publicani* (public tax collectors) were specifically mentioned as those who should not be shunned.[76] Peter did not elaborate on who this group could be, but the task of public tax collection often fell to the Jews. The Jews, Peter maintained, were to be tolerated.[77] A second group worthy of mention was the Greeks, who were schismatics because they took themselves away from the obedience of the Roman church. Peter questioned why the Latin Church communicated with them welcomely.[78] Peter referenced Pope Telesphorus's letter to all bishops, which included those in the East, that clerics were supposed to fast from meat and delicacies for seven full weeks before Easter.[79] The two churches shared a common past and common rights, such as that seen in Telephorus's command that clerics undertake a 50-day fast. The Greeks held a precarious position for Catholics, but they were not excommunicated.

A central—and practical—consideration for Peter the Chanter regarding excommunication was whether the crime was hidden and the percentage of people engaged in the crime. In line with legal thought, a grounding principle was the crime could be proven, and the percentage of people engaged in the crime. For example, if the crime was hidden from all, such as those who imitated the form of the devil, they could not be excommunicated despite such actions being a mortal sin. If the crime was open, such as a dice thrower, boxer, or *balistarius*, then the perpetrators could be excommunicated. We saw above how this principle was applied to prostitutes as well. Key considerations for excommunication, however, were whether there was a fear of retaliation from

74 GD C.32 q.1 d.p.c.13–c.14.
75 I Comp. 5.2.16 (X 5.3.7).
76 Chanter III.2a, §262, p. 275: "Ethnici gentiles sunt. Publicani dicuntur conductores publicorum vestigalium. … Valde nos movet quid sit vitare aliquem ut ethnicum et publicanum."
77 See J. Watt, "Parsian Theologians and the Jews: Peter Lombard and Peter Cantor," in *The Medieval Church: Universities, Heresy, and Christian Life: Essays in Honour of Gordon Leff*, eds. P. Biller and B Dobson (Woodbridge, 1999), 55–76, esp. 68–76; G. Dahan, "Les interprétations juives dans les commentaires du Pentateuque de Pierre le Chantre," in *The Bible in the Medieval World: Essays in Honour of Beryl Smalley*, eds. K. Walsh and D. Wood (Oxford, 1985), 131–155.
78 Chanter III.2a, §240, pp. 237–238.
79 GD D.4 c.4.

the prince or if the multitude were involved in the sin.[80] The latter exception was of particular concern. Peter drew upon C.23 q.4 d.p.c.31, in which Gratian held that if the majority were involved in sin, they should not be sentenced for fear of creating a schism.[81] For Peter, this particular position was important for the laity holding the tithe. He maintained that they were not to be denied the Eucharist because the Church ignored this transgression. He did acknowledge the position taken at the Third Lateran Council (c.14), which excommunicated the laity who held the tithe and thus endangered the ability of the Church to fulfill its charge of caring for souls. But then he discounted this view by stating that the sentence is perhaps abolished today on account of the dissimulation of the church.[82] Peter honed in on Gratian's view that if the majority were engaged in the crime, no punishment should be rendered. To him, while a sin, the pervasiveness of the laity holding the tithe was not worth punishing. Interestingly, Peter set aside plenty of legal texts that both focused on the bishops' responsibility to distribute the tithe to priests and not to the laity and prohibited the laity from holding the tithe. Pope Gregory VII maintained that bishops were simoniacs who distributed tithes and oblations to the laity as opposed to the clergy.[83] Pope Paschal II condemned those clerics of simony who sold the tithes and altars for money.[84] The laity should not hold oblations or tithes, and they should not give them to those outside of baptism without the consent of the bishop.[85] Yet, as Gratian pointed out, even if they had the bishop's permission, they were still deemed irreprehensible.[86] Tithes were to be given by the laity and distributed by the bishop to priests for the benefit of their flock.[87] Gratian maintained that the laity could not possess tithes or churches either themselves or by the authority of the bishop.[88] Pope Alexander III followed suit. Tithes could not be conceded to laity by hereditary right.[89] Furthermore, tithes and oblations of a church were not able to be conceded to the laity, and a prelate

80 Chanter III.2a, §242, pp. 241–242: "...quia viles persone sunt, de facili possunt cogi ab ecclesia, nec habent sociam multitudinem, nisi timeatur offensa alicuius principis, debet repelli ab eucharistia. Eodem modo deberent balistarii et pugillatores repelli, quia non est crimen occultatum."

81 GD C.23 q.4 d.p.c.31: "Similiter non est ferenda sentencia, quando multitudo est in causa, vel quando ille peccat, qui sociam habet multitudinem."

82 I Comp. 3.26.23 (X 3.30.19), COGD 2.1, pp. 137–138; Chanter III.2a, §242, p. 241: "...quia *multitudo est in culpa*, tamen excommunicati sunt in concilio lateranensi omnes decimarum detentores, sed forte abolita est sententia hodie propter dissimulationem ecclesie."

83 GD C.1 q.3 c.13.

84 GD C.1 q.3 c.14; Jaffé 4867.

85 GD C.16 q.1 c.55–c.57.

86 GD C.16 q.1 d.p.c.56: "...si episcopo disponente hoc fecerint, inreprehensibiles inveniantur."

87 GD C.16 q.1 c.66, C.16 q.2 c.3.

88 GD C.16 q.7 d.a.c.1: "Laici autem nec sua, nec episcoporum auctoritate decimas vel ecclesias possidere possunt." GD C.16 q.7 c.1–c.9 proved the point that tithes should not be given to the laity.

89 I Comp. 3.26.27 (X 3.30.15).

doing so was to be punished.[90] Pope Innocent III likewise maintained that the laity was not able to give churches or tithes even if they were the king.[91] The laity could neither possess nor give tithes or church property. Despite the clear articulations in the law, Peter the Chanter was willing to overlook the issue as a lost cause.

Peter approached excommunication from a practical stance.[92] The examples he provided were not exhaustive but shed light on issues that he felt were most pressing in society. Two issues felt more pressing: laying violent hands on a cleric and prostitution. His treatment of the former fell within the lines of the law; his treatment of the latter, however, seems to have imposed the law onto it. Since excommunication was a means by which to organize society, a grounding principle for Peter was whether the crime could be proven and the percentage of people engaged in the crime. Excommunication could lead to turmoil when imposed both on that which was not obvious, such as accusations of dressing up like the devil, and on that in which the majority of people engaged, such as the laity possessing the tithes. The former could not be proven, and the latter would amount to winning a battle but losing the war.

Sentences and Their Implication

As noted above, the canonical tradition was evolving to distinguish between major and minor excommunication. Pope Clement III was the first to explicitly refer to minor excommunication, while Pope Innocent III would speak of major excommunication.[93] Peter was in the thick of this evolution as seen by his use of terms. Rather than using the terms "major" and "minor," Peter wrote of "special" and "general" excommunication. Neither general nor special excommunication could be removed without confession or without contrition.[94] Such suggests that the exact phrasing was not yet crystallized. Irrespective of the discrepancy with the precise terminology, Peter, in step with the legal climate, distinguished between two types of excommunication. Essentially, Peter distinguished between a liturgical exclusion and a social exclusion. The former prevented one from partaking in the Eucharist but not from partaking in the community. The latter prevented both and anyone who associated with

90 II Comp. 3.17.2 (X 3.30.17).

91 IV Comp. 3.9.3 (X 3.30.31).

92 Corran noted Chanter's focus on wide-ranging dilemmas that threatened one's conscience; see Corran, *Lying and Perjury in Medieval Practical Thought*, 73–75.

93 See pp. 121–122 above.

94 Chanter II, §143, p. 340: "Querit item de excommunicato in genera quando decessit absque confessione, non sine contribitione tamen, an ei subtrahantur ecclesie suffragia, generalia et specialia? Dicit non. Specialia non subtrahuntur ei quia orabitur pro eo nominatim si amicos habuerit, generalia multo fortius."

the excommunicated likewise could be excommunicated.[95] Some crimes were heinous enough to exclude one from society; otherwise, as someone engaged actively in the *cura animarum*, he understood that excluding someone from society may not be the most effective method of getting someone to repent.

Central to Peter's discussion of excommunication was the concept of being "named" (*nominatio*); that is, the individual has been named as a sinner and their name has been called out by the bishop as excommunicated. If the crime was known but he had not been named as excommunicated, there was doubt as to whether he should be shunned.[96] In other words, the crime might be known, but he had not yet been found guilty and thus not yet excommunicated. In cases where the crime was hidden but easily able to be proven, the precept outlined in Mathew 18:15 should be applied: since the fault is between the two individuals, the one trespassed against should confront the trespasser and seek to resolve the matter.[97] For one to be a named excommunicate with a noted sentence, he had to have been found guilty in a secular or ecclesiastical court, a conviction brought about by due process.[98] If he has been noted by a precise sentence, he was not to take the food of the holy Eucharist, nor communal food, nor communicate in prayer until corrected.[99] If the crime for which the individual was excommunicated was evident but not notorious, he ought to be avoided in private but not in public; rather, he should be beseeched in the church to amend his ways. If the crime for which the individual was excommunicated was evident and notorious, such as for participating in tournaments or committing violence against clerics, he was to be shunned in every way.[100] The notoriety associated with tournaments and violence against clerics had a long tradition in the law. The Third Lateran Council (c.20) banned tournaments, repeating prohibitions established at the Council of Reims in 1131 (c.12), the Second Lateran Council in 1139 (c.14), and the Council of Reims in 1148 (c.2).[101] Gratian's *Decretum* recorded the long legal tradition prohibiting violence against clerics and ecclesiastical property.[102] Yet, not every evident and notorious crime warranted complete shunning. Prostitutes and actors are offered as examples. They warrant prayers as they are not to be shunned from

95 See Vodola, *Excommunication in the Middle Ages*, 8.

96 Chanter III.2a, §240, p. 238 ln. 27–28.

97 Chanter III.2a, §240, p. 238 ln. 21–23; Matt. 18:15: "Si autem peccaverit in te frater tuus vade et corripe eum inter te et ipsum solum si te audierit lucratus es fratrem tuum."

98 Vodola, *Excommunication in the Middle Ages*, 10–11; R. H. Helmholz, "Excommunication as a Legal Sanction: The Attitudes of the Medieval Canonists," ZRK Kan. Abt. 68 (1982) 202–218.

99 Chanter III.2a, §240, pp. 23 ln. 12–15.

100 Chanter III.2a, §240, pp. 237–239; see also II, §147, p. 354.

101 For the Third Lateran Council c.20, see I Comp. 5.13.1 (X 5.13.1), COGD 2.1, p. 142. For the Council of Reims (1131) c.12, see Mansi 12:460. For the Second Lateran Council (1139) c.14, see COGD 2.1, p. 109. For the Council of Reims (1148) c.2, see Mansi 21:716.

102 GD C.17 q.4 c. 21, c.23–c.29.

the church, but they are shunned from the Eucharist. Those who receive them at the table, unless there is some great necessity, commit a moral sin.[103]

Peter most clearly grappled with the distinction between liturgical and social exclusion in his discussion of interdict. An interdict occurred when a land or family of someone suffered for the guilt of the lord and it only impacted the churches found in the lands of the lord who was placed under interdict. Churches outside of those lands remained in communion.[104] If a castle was under interdict on account of the guilt of the lord, baptism and last right could be given.[105] Interdict was different from suspension, which applied when he was kept from entering a church on account of his guilt though it was possible to communicate with him at the table, in greeting, and in other ways besides the church. If he should approach a church while suspended, he ought to be shunned, even if he was standing outside of the church in the arc to hear the mass because his guilt had accompanied him. He could, however, enter the church when mass was not being celebrated.[106]

Interestingly, Peter drew upon feudal principles for his phrasing of churches placed under interdict. Churches were placed under interdict because every church ought to supply mutual council and aid (*auxilium et consilium*) to ecclesiastical offices with complete charity.[107] The reference echoed the oath of fidelity outlined by Fulbert of Chartres in his letter to William V, which Gratian included, "...ut in eisdem sex supradictis consilium et auxilium domino suo fideliter prestet, si beneficio dignus videri vult, et salvus esse de fidelitate, quam iuravit...."[108] A church owned fidelity to the papacy under pain of being placed under interdict.

Peter recognized that unjust sentences could occur, and they occurred either *ex causa et ex animo*, or *ex ordine*. Peter concluded that though the sentence was unjust *ex animo et ex causa*, or *ex ordine*, it justly bound him although with unjust consideration.[109] Peter deftly engaged with the categories of unjust sentences set forth in the *Decretum*. C.11 q.3 d.p.c.65 distinguished between different reasons for a sentence being unjust: *ex causa* as when either no sin had been

103 Chanter III.2a, §240, pp. 237–239; see also II, §147, p. 354 and III.2a, §264, p. 278 ln. 3–5.

104 Chanter III.2a, §267, p. 282 ln. 1–5.

105 Chanter III.2a, §267, p. 283 ln. 20–22: "Quandoque interdicitur castrum aliquod ab omni sacramento ecclesie excepto baptismo nascentium et viatico morientium, et hoc pro culpa domni sui."

106 Chanter III.2a, §267, pp. 282–283 ln. 6–13.

107 Chanter II, §150, p. 364: "...quia omnes ecclesie mutuum sibi auxilium et consilium debent prebere ad officia ecclesiastica caritate peragenda."

108 GD C.22 q.5 c.18; F. Behrends, ed. and trans., *The Letters and Poems of Fulbert of Chartres* (Oxford, 1976), no. 51, pp. 90–93: "It remains that he faithfully give his lord counsel and help in the aforementioned matters, if he wishes to be worthy of his benefice (fief) and safe in the fidelity that he has sworn."

109 Chanter II, §141, p. 334: "Cum sententia sit iniusta ex animo et causa, ex ordine tamen iusta, dicimus quod iuste ligat eum, alia consideratione iniuste."

committed or a sin other than that for which the sentence was imposed; *ex animo* as when the judge made his decision not from love of justice, but due to hatred, bribes, or partiality; or *ex ordine* as when there was a procedural error.[110] A sentence *ex animo* engaged with bans against judgments based on wrath and bribes.[111] Even though a sentence was imposed on someone not out of love for justice but for some other reasons, it should humbly be obeyed.[112] In cases when a sentence was unjust *ex causa*, there might not be a crime that was worthy of damning him at all. Sometimes, the crime for which the sentence was passed did not pertain to him but should have been attributed to another.[113] Similar to *ex animo*, Gratian stated, within the context of *ex ordine* but with *ex causa* in mind, that sometimes there was no crime, yet he still received a sentence of damnation either due to the hatred of the judge or due to the plotting of enemies.[114] A sentence was unjust *ex ordine* when someone was damned for his sin without a judicial order.[115] Gratian supported this stance by pointing to procedural norms: dubious cases that could not be determined through a certain judgment, cases that could not be proven by certain evidence should not be believed, and that judgment may not be passed before proper examination.[116] Despite violations of procedural norms, Gratian held that the sentence should be observed because the condemned may still bear a hidden guilt. Though the sentence for the crime was unjust because it pertained to a sin for which the accused was innocent, the sentence remained just because he could already be excommunicated in God's eyes for another sin. Drawing upon a homily of Pope Gregory I, the pastor's sentence should be feared whether it is just or not: either the unjustly sentenced person deserved the sentence on account of some other crime, or, if he protested, he deserved

110 GD C.11 q.3 d.p.c.65: "…quod sententia aliquando est iniusta ex animo proferentis, iusta vero ex ordine et causa; aliquando est iusta ex animo et causa, sed non ex ordine; aliquando est iusta ex animo et ex ordine sed non ex causa." See also Anders Winroth, *The Making of Gratian's Decretum* (Cambridge, 2000), 105–107.

111 GD C.11 q.3 c.66–c.72.

112 GD C.11 q.3 d.p.c.72: "Huic itaque sententiae, que non amore iustitiae, sed ex alia qualibet causa fertur in quemquam, humiliter obediendum est."

113 GD C.11 q.3 d.p.c.65:

> Cum autem ex causa iniusta fuerit, aliquando nullum in eo omnino delictum est, quod sit dampnatione dignum: aliquando non est in eo illud, super quod fertur sententia, sed ex alio nominandus est. Ex animo est iniusta, cum aliquis seruata integritate iudiciarii ordinis in adulterum vel in quemlibet criminosum non amore iustitiae, sed livore odii, vel precio, aut favore adversariorum inductus sententiam profert.

114 GD C.11 q.3 d.p.c.77: "Aliquando nullum subest crimen, et tamen vel odio iudicis, vel factione inimicorum obpositam sibi sententiam dampnationis in se excipit."

115 GD C.11 q.3 d.p.c.73: "Item sententia est iniusta ex ordine, quando non servato iudiciali ordine quilibet pro culpa sua dampnatur."

116 GD C.11 q.3 c.74–c.76.

the sentence even if he was not guilty of any crime, because, in protesting, he was now guilty of the sin of pride.[117] Peter the Chanter likewise asked whether or not an unjust sentence, in this case an unjust sentence *ex causa*, should be obeyed. Akin to Gratian, he concluded that it should be obeyed, though noting "until which time it is retracted." Every order of a prelate should be obeyed in every lawful manner.[118] As Pope Alexander III wrote to the archbishop of York, when a case is appealed and the sentence is considered unjust, it is proper that it be vacated. A clearly unjust sentence ought not to remain.[119] While Gratian did not appear to discuss the retraction of an unjust sentence, contemporary legal thought had addressed just such a possibility.

Peter the Chanter knew that one size did not fit all with respect to excommunication. There were shades of grey depending upon the nature and severity of the crime. Both would determine whether one was banned from the Eucharist or whether he was banned from both the Eucharist and from society. Peter used a similar framework to discuss the difference between suspension and interdict; the former allowed some latitude to engage in society, whereas the latter cut the impacted individuals off from the world around them. It was the prevailing social framework of feudalism, however, from which Peter drew to explain an interdict placed on churches. He likewise engaged in contemporary legal thought when providing a pathway to have unjust sentences retracted. Excommunications, Peter recognized, were not always justly pronounced.

Communication with the Excommunicated

Peter the Chanter fell in line with the evolving legal discourse which distinguished between general and special excommunication, that is, between minor and major excommunication. This distinction carried with it implications for whether the excommunicate was shunned from the Eucharist but not from the community, or from both the Eucharist and from the community. Yet, Peter

117 GD C.11 q.3 d.p.c.77:

> Cum ergo sententia ex ordine iniusta est, nec tunc ab ea recedendum est, quia etiam ante, quam sententia daretur in eum pro qualitate sui reatus ligatus apud Deum tenebatur. … Iustam sententiam vocat, quando crimen subest, super quod fertur: iniustam, quando illud non subest, que tamen timenda vel seruanda est, quia ex alio iam dudum dampnandus erat. Unde, cum premisisset Gregorius: 'Utrum iuste an iniuste obliget pastor, pastoris tamen sententia timenda est gregi,' subsecutus adiecit: 'Ne is, qui subest, et cum iniuste forsitan ligatur, ipsam obligationis suae sententiam ex alia culpa mereatur. Pastor ergo vel absolvere indiscrete timeat, vel ligare. Is autem, qui sub manu pastoris est ligari timeat vel iniuste nec pastoris sui iudicium temere reprehendat: ne, etsi iniuste ligatus est, ex ipsa tumidae reprehensionis superbia culpa, que non erat, fiat.'

118 Chanter II, §141, p. 334: "…quousque retractetur…"
119 I Comp. 2.20.17 (X 2.27.9).

seemed to revert back to the thinking of the old law in his discussion of communication with the excommunicated. Whether minor excommunication or major excommunication, the ability of the excommunicate to engage in the world around him was curtailed in the eyes of Peter. If the excommunicated entered a church while a prelate was saying the divine services, the priest should stop those services.[120] If the excommunicated approached a priest to say the mass for him and his wife was with him, knowing that he was excommunicated and allowed the mass to be said, she too should be excommunicated. In fact, it was the wife's duty to see to it that her husband performed the necessary satisfaction to return him to church.[121] If the excommunicated had a son in the sacred orders, that son, having been ordained, was emancipated from the power of his father. Should the son communicate with this excommunicated father, he too would be excommunicated.[122]

Peter stressed that there were four key ways in which it was not permitted to communicate with the excommunicated: table, prayer, greeting, and kiss of peace.[123] He drew upon C.11 q.3 c.17 and c.18 of the *Decretum*, which state that those who communicate with the excommunicates over prayer, food or drink, or the kiss incurred the same punishment of excommunication.[124] Canon 19 deposed clerics.[125] Peter noted that neither the poor nor lepers should take alms from the excommunicated nor communicate with them.[126] Furthermore, it was a sin to accept, buy, sell, or deal with the excommunicated in any other way.[127] Peter essentially wrote of knowingly communicating with the excommunicated and ignoring the sentence imposed. He leaned upon Pope Gregory VII's Roman council of 1078 where it was decreed that anyone not part of the circle of the excommunicated was not excused for conducting business with the excommunicated.[128]

Pope Gregory VII, however, also maintained that there were those who deserved the mercy of the Church for communicating with the excommunicated: those within the Church who gave humanitarian aid, wives, children, slaves, and freedmen of the excommunicated with whom communication was unavoidable.[129] Peter the Chanter concurred as one interested in active ministry.

120 Chanter III.2a, §268, p. 284 ln. 19–21.
121 Chanter III.2a, §268, p. 284 ln. 23–29.
122 Chanter III.2a, §268, p. 284 ln. 30–33.
123 Chanter II, §153, p. 371: "Cum excommunicatis non licet communicare in quatuor: mensa, oratione, salutatione, osculo pacis." See also Vodola, *Excommunication in the Middle Ages* 52–53, where she discusses the importance of the kiss as a symbol of incorporation and the concern regarding pollution spread at the communal table over food and drink.
124 GD C.11 q.3 c.17, c.18.
125 GD C.11 q.3 c.19.
126 Chanter III.2a, §268, p. 284 ln. 4–10.
127 Chanter II, §153, p. 374.
128 GD C.11 q.3 c.103.
129 GD C.11 q.3 c.103.

Peter drew attention to Augustine's commentary on the Apostle Paul's first letter to the Corinthians, which Gratian included in his *Decretum*. Augustine recollected that if the Apostle did not pass judgment on a woman who remarried after the death of her husband, neither should he, even if she ended up remarrying a number of times.[130] Peter used this example to justify that judgment should not be passed on to a woman who communicated with her excommunicated husband.[131] Gregory VII also noted that travelers or pilgrims who entered the land of the excommunicated and were in need of buying goods could do so without incurring punishment.[132] Peter the Chanter commented that travelers on a journey could ask someone who was excommunicated for directions. They also could ask the excommunicated for defense if accosted by a robber. In cases of imminent need, they could ask the excommunicated for legal counsel.[133] Yet, instances occurred when exceptions did not apply, such as if a doctor was treating a sick individual and that doctor was subsequently excommunicated. In this case, the sick should discontinue seeking care from him. Similarly, if someone sent his sons to another for education and the teacher would subsequently be excommunicated, the sons should not remain under his tutelage.[134]

Peter the Chanter's discussion of communicating with the excommunicated seemed to send a mixed message. He seemed to ground the discussion more in the old law that banned communication with the excommunicated rather than in the new law that seemed to qualify between those sentenced to minor or major excommunication. In the preceding discussion on named sentences, he noted that for a person to be completely shunned, that is, incur a sentence of major excommunication, the crime must be evident and notorious. If the crime was simply evident but not notorious, he incurred a sentence of minor excommunication and was banned from the Eucharist but not from society. Yet, not only did he not refer to general (minor) or special (major) excommunication, he did not make a distinction between crimes that were evident but not notorious and crimes that were evident and notorious. Here, a sentence of excommunication brought excommunication both from the Eucharist and from society, except for certain unavoidable circumstances or in cases where it was not possible to know the individual was excommunicated.

Excommunication after Death

Peter briefly posed the question of whether he who had died in a state of excommunication would remain excommunicated in death.[135] Peter posited the

130 GD C.31 q.1 c.13.
131 Chanter III.2a, §268, p. 285 ln. 50–58.
132 GD C.11 q.3 c.103.
133 Chanter III.2a, §268, p. 285 ln. 38–43.
134 Chanter III.2a, §268, p. 285 ln. 44–49.
135 Chanter II, §146, p. 345.

contra stance, that excommunication did not follow one into death and thus did not retain its efficacy. He cited a portion of C.24 q.2 c.2, a letter from Pope Gelasius to Master Faustus on administering the office of ambassador to Constantinople. In his letter, Gelasius quoted Peter, "'You will be able to bind whatever on earth,'" and commented, "Upon the earth, he said."[136] Death, Peter noted, occurred on earth. For Peter no one, if he had been saved, was withdrawn from God by excommunication. If he had been damned, he did not feel the effect of the punishment.[137] At first blush, Peter's comments seemed to run counter to the remainder of C.24 q.2 c.2 which stated that on no occasion must someone who has died while bound be absolved.[138] Peter, however, did not declare the condemned absolved but simply that the effects of the punishment were no longer felt. Gratian would go on to argue that while the living were able to be bound and loosened, the dead were not...in most cases. For certain crimes, such as that of heresy, people were able to be accused or damned even after death, such as for heresy.[139] Peter seemed to follow the view expressed by Gratian maintaining that: "It is certain that just as the Church communicates with the living, they ought to also communicate with the dead, unless an undisputed reason made against him regarding the faith. It is doubted."[140]

Conclusion

Peter the Chanter was clearly comfortable working with legal sources, and he anchored some of his teachings, such as simony and excommunication, in them. He drew upon principles contained in Roman law, the law compiled in Gratian's *Decretum*, and the papal and conciliar legislation compiled in decretal collections. Yet, Peter was not teaching law; he was teaching to prepare his students for active ministry. A complete repetition of a particular text was not always necessary or desirable. It is for this reason that one might find some combination of reference to a specific location, to a material source, to the incipit, or to a particular portion of the text. Other times, there might not be a specific reference at all, simply an illusion to a pope's decretal or a conciliar

136 GD C.24 q.2 c.2: "B. Petro apostolo principaliter mandauit: 'Quodcumque ligaveris super terram etc.' Super terram, inquit. Nam alligatione defunctum nusquam dixit esse absoluendum."

137 Chanter II, §146, p. 346.

138 GD C.24 q.2 c.2: "Nam alligatione defunctum nusquam dixit esse absolvendum."

139 GD C.24 q.2 d.p.c.5: "His auctoritatibus probatur, quod viventes, non mortuos solvere possumus vel ligare. Verum hoc non de omni crimine intelligendum est. Sunt enim quedam crimina, de quibus etiam post mortem accusari possunt quilibet uel dampnari, veluti heresis."

140 Chanter II, §146, p. 348: "Certo certius est quod *sicut communicauit ecclesia vivo, mortuo quoque communicare deberet*, nisi inuibitata ratio fidem faceret contra eum. Dubitat." The italicized portion is a mis-rendering of GD C.24 q.2 c.1 which reads: "Nos autem quibus viventibus non conmunicamus mortuis conmunicare non possumus." The canon argues that those who did not want to be absolved by it in this life are not able to be loosened by the Church after death.

canon. He was quite keen to present only—or students were quite keen only to record—the elements of the law that needed to be conveyed.

Peter's use of the law demonstrates that he was not so much interested in incorporating legal texts for the purpose of presenting the *pro et contra* but rather in providing support for the position taken. He possessed enough familiarity with the legal tradition to select the text(s) that justified the handling of a particular issue. That position could be anchored in a long-standing legal tradition, such as the ability of a superior to excommunicate a subordinate. It could be engaging in a changing climate, such as minor versus major excommunication. It could be a focus on a particular point, which, while valid, disregarded the long-standing legal precedent, such as the laity possessing the tithe. Finally, that position could impose a stance on which the law was silent, such as prostitution. Peter possessed enough familiarity with the law to apply, bend, disregard, or manipulate it as needed.

Peter the Chanter's use of law demonstrates that the penitential and judicial fora remained intrinsically linked. Established legal principles laid a foundation for both, even as the Church was beginning to reconsider the nature of excommunication. While the distinction between major and minor excommunication bestowed on priests a function previously reserved for bishops, they still had to possess the legal right to execute that function. That power rested in the *cura animarum*. Major and minor excommunication would each have parallel and complimentary spheres of correction. The law underpinned the penitential forum. Yet, we also see areas where the penitential forum was reconsidering the efficacy of the law, and, as a result, areas in which penitential thought, as seen with Peter the Chanter, was beginning to deviate from the canonical legal tradition. Such was the case with the excommunication of prostitutes and choosing not to excommunicate the laity who held the tithe. From the pastoral theologian's viewpoint, the former was a societal threat that needed to be addressed, while the latter was simply too pervasive to be addressed. For Peter, the law was necessary and useful...to a point.

5

ROBERT OF COURÇON

Administering Crusading Activity and the Fight Against Heresy

Introduction

Like Robert of Flamborough (Chapter 6), Robert of Courçon was an Englishman affiliated with Paris. Originally from Keddleston in Derbyshire, he studied under Peter the Chanter in the 1190s.[1] He would teach theology at Notre Dame in the first decade of the thirteenth century,[2] during which time he compiled his *Summa penitentiae*.[3] Robert also held prebends as a canon at Noyon (from ca.1204) and at Notre Dame in Paris (ca. 1209–ca. 1211).[4]

1 M. Dickson, and C. Dickson, "Le Cardinal Robert de Courson: Sa Vie," *Archives d'histoire doctrinale et littéraire du Moyen Âge* 9 (1934): 53–142, here 61–65.

2 Ferruolo states that Robert taught theology from 1208 to 1212; see S. Ferruolo, *The Origins of the University: The Schools of Paris and Their Critics, 1100–1215* (Stanford, 1985), 301. Bermon states that he taught from 1204 to 1210, though we know he was teaching between 1207 and 1209, see P. Bermon, trans. *La fondation de l'Université de Paris (1200–1260)* (Paris, 2017), 68 n6, 118. Gorochov, however, points to Robert as among the masters of theology from Paris involved in a trial in 1201 (Courçon section 30 chapter 2 [hereafter referenced as section.chapter, fol. 104vb–105rb]) in which the heretic Évrard de Châteauneuf was condemned to be burned, see *Naissance de l'université*, 169. On the teaching of Robert of Courçon, see L. Hödl, *Die Geschichte der Scholastischen Literatur und der Theologie der Schlüsselewalt, Teil I* (Münster, 1960), 306–339.

3 Ferruolo simply states that Robert wrote his *Summa* toward the end of his teaching career, see *The Origins of the University*, 301. Gorochov dates his *Summa* to 1204–1208, see *Naissance de l'université*, 272. Bermon dates it to 1204–1207, see *La Fondation de l'Université de Paris*, 119. Dickson and Dickson date the penitential to 1204–1208; see "Le Cardinal Robert de Courson," 67.

4 Dickson and Dickson, "Le Cardinal Robert de Courson," 67, 71. Robert was not in residence at Noyon because of his duties as judge-delegate and/or because of teaching (68–70). See also J. Taliadoros, "Law, Theology, and Morality: Conceptions of the Rights to Relief of the Poor in the Twelfth and Thirteenth Centuries," *Journal of Religious History* 37, no. 4 (2013): 474–493, here 485–486.

DOI: 10.4324/9781003465096-6

Of the secular masters studied here, Robert of Courçon (d. 1219) was arguably the most active in the institutional affairs of the Church. He was frequently called upon to serve as a papal judge-delegate and, from March 1212 to November 1215, he served as a papal legate to France, having been appointed by Pope Innocent III. From 1213, he also held the title of cardinal-priest of St. Stephen in Monte Celio.[5] Among Robert's numerous duties were preaching against the Albigensians and preparing for what would be the Fourth Lateran Council (1215). He also presided over councils held at Paris (1213), Reims (1213), Clermont (1214), Bordeaux (1214), Rouen (1214), and Montpellier (1215). In 1218, Robert left on the Fifth Crusade as the papal legate for Pope Honorius III; however, he fell ill and died in Damietta on 6 February 1219.[6]

Among Robert's administrative tasks was his instrumental role in the drafting of the statutes that organized the University of Paris while serving as chancellor. These statutes, dating from 1215, established the requirements for a master in arts and a master in theology to lecture. They also set forth which books of Aristotle could be read and which books, primarily pertaining to natural philosophy, were not to be read. They banned the doctrines of Almaric and of David de Dinant. Finally, the statutes granted each master jurisdiction over his students.[7] This provision was an extension of a synod held in Paris in 1210 in which Robert took part. Presided over by Peter of Corbeil, archbishop of Sens (1200–1222), the synod ordered the surrender of theological works written in French and prohibited the teachings of Aristotle's works on natural philosophy. It also condemned to burning the writings of David de Dinant. Finally, it condemned Amalric of Bène and his followers, the Amalricians. Amalric, a priest at Chartres and regent of the school of liberal arts, and the Amalricians were charged with pantheism, that is, a focus on the divine presence of God in the physical world and their tendency to ignore the distinction between God and creation. They believed that they had attained spiritual perfection on earth and were granted a special gift of understanding, both of which secured them salvation. Their beliefs drew further criticism for their antinomian and anti-sacramental implications.[8]

5 Epistolae Papae Innocentii III, Lib. 15, no. 106; Potthast 4529; Potthast 4711; Dickson and Dickson, "Le Cardinal Robert de Courson," 77.

6 Dickson and Dickson, "Le Cardinal Robert de Courson," 130–134.

7 H. Denifle, ed. *Chartularium Universitatis Parisiensis*, 4 vols. (rpt. Bruxelles, 1964), 1.20, pp. 78–80; see also Dickson and Dickson, "Le Cardinal Robert de Courson," 114–124.

8 J. M. M. H. Thijssen, "Master Amalric and the Amalricians: Inquisitorial Procedure and the Suppression of Heresy at the University of Paris," *Speculum* 71, no.1 (1996): 43–65, here 43, 46–47. For more on David de Dinant, see Bermon, *La Fondation de l'Université de Paris*, 75–78; Gorochov, *Naissance de l'université*, 277–288. For more on Amalric of Bène, see Bermon, *La Fondation de l'Université de Paris*, 84–87; Gorochov, *Naissance de l'université*, 184–192, 263–266. Thijssen (pp. 48, 53, 60) notes that the trial reflected Innocent III's articulation of inquisitorial procedure for suppressing heresy (*Nichil est pene* [1199], *Licet Heli* [1199], and *Qualiter et quando* [1206]), the placing of heresy on the same legal footing as treason (*Vergentis in senium*), and the delivery of criminous clergy to secular justice (*Novimus*).

The statutes that Robert of Courçon spearheaded solidified regulatory measures and jurisdictional questions negotiated in 1213 by Hervé, bishop of Troyes (1207–1223), between the masters and students and the local ecclesiastical authorities John of Candeilles, chancellor of the university (1210–1214), and Peter of Nemours, bishop of Paris (1208–1219). As outlined by Pope Innocent III in his letter to Bishop Hervé, the masters and students had complained to the pope about the manner in which John of Candeilles was exercising his right to grant licenses to teach. John would no longer be permitted to extract an oath of fidelity nor to charge a fee. He was to promise to grant a license to whomever the masters deemed fit, although he could still grant a license to those who did not have the masters' support. Furthermore, John was no longer permitted to imprison and then fine scholars. It was argued that he was imprisoning them for even minor offenses and then he would charge them a fine, which he kept, before allowing them to be released. John was only permitted to incarcerate them in just and evident cases. If the case was not just and evident, the accused would have recourse to the *officialis* who should make a determination. If it was determined that the cleric should be incarcerated, he was to be freed from prison in exchange for sufficient bail as a guarantee. The fine charged was to be paid directly to the aggrieved party. Clerics arrested or summoned to court were not to be done so by public officials if his own (i.e., ecclesiastical) officials were able to do so.[9] John had claimed for himself as chancellor broad powers to punish. The chancellor of the university was, in effect, the chancellor of the cathedral of Notre Dame. He granted licenses to teach. The chancellor of Notre Dame was also the head of the cathedral chapter and, as such, he could, with the bishop's permission, exercise ordinary jurisdiction on behalf of the bishop. John of Candeilles had appended this right to exercise jurisdictional authority as head of the cathedral to his role as chancellor of the university. He thus claimed for himself the right to not only issue licenses to teach but also to discipline the masters and students of Paris.[10] Collectively, such measures based on the work of Bishop Hervé and reinforced by Robert mitigated the jurisdictional powers of the chancellor of the university.

Robert of Courçon compiled his *Summa penitentiae* probably between 1208 and 1213, on the cusp of his full-time papal appointment. It contains 46 sections and each section comprises chapters structured as a question (*questio*), which begins the discussion, followed by an objection (*obiectio*) or objections. Finally, he would provide a solution (*solutio*) whereby he gave his own position and answers to the objections. He begins his *Summa penitentiae* with a lengthy

9 Denifle, ed., *Chartularium Universitatis Parisiensis*, 1.14, pp. 73–74, 1.16–18, pp. 75–77; Bermon, *La Fondation de l'Université de Paris*, 102–103, 106; Gorochov, *Naissance de l'université*, 299–316; I. Wei, *Intellectual Culture in Medieval Paris: Theologians and the University c.1100–1330* (Cambridge, 2014), 94–95; Ferruolo, *The Origins of the University*, 295–300, 308.

10 Bermon, *La Fondation de l'Université de Paris*, 110.

section on penance, which comprises 46 chapters. Robert then follows with sections on absolution/remission (2), the keys (3), excommunication (4–6), the return of sins (7), simony (8–10), usury (11–12), tithes (13–14), seizure and the use of property (15–16), benefices (17), prescription (18), patronage (19), fraternal correction (20), vows (21–24), scandal (25), that which is confusing (*de perplexitate*) (26), oaths and perjury (27), lies (28–29), clerics and capital punishment (30), promotion and demotion of clerics (31), procedure (32–36), sacraments (37), baptism (38–41), marriage (42), Eucharist (43), confirmation (44), extreme unction (45), and the dedication of churches (46).[11]

As noted in the previous chapter, the use of the first person—singular and plural—in Peter the Chanter's *Summa de sacramentis et animae consiliis* gives the sense of a lecture scenario. It is the recording of a magister teaching his students, providing his interpretation of the material and the topic under discussion. Robert of Courçon's use of the first person in the *solutio*, however, provides the feel of a judge rendering a verdict. It is in the *solutio*, though sometimes in the *objectio* as well, where he tended to incorporate legal sources most often. Section 35, which deals with judicial procedure, serves as a case in point. Section 35 chapter 4 addresses the numerous differences between accusations.[12] In the course of his response, he draws on Gratian's *Decretum* C.2 q.1 c.19 from Augustine and C.2 q.1 c.14 from the *Digest* 48.2.3—both of which were referenced by causa-question-incipit—to set forth who could and could not bring forth accusations and when a judge could not preside over a case. Robert concluded the topic by commenting on when someone has been condemned without an accusation: "[t]hat we concede when they are notorious criminals, as we discussed before, as someone labors in public infamy, as it is clearly shown above."[13] Here, as he frequently does throughout his *Summa*, Robert provided an explanation in the manner of a judge explaining why he and his fellow judges ruled as they did.

An author's work thus reflects their frame of mind at that time, the environment that occupied their thoughts. In an analysis of the rights of the poor, Jason Taliadoros showed that both theologians and lawyers thought

11 V. L. Kennedy, "The Content of Courson's *Summa*," *Mediaeval Studies* 9, no. 1 (1947): 82, for a list of the chapters, see 83–107. Kennedy notes of the manuscripts examined, three ended with section XLVI. She noted that four manuscripts contain an additional chapter on the sacrament of the orders (Paris, BnF, lat. 3258, 3259, 14,524; Bruges, Museum Kings, 9 E xiv. Two of those manuscripts (Paris, BnF, 14,524; Bruges, Museum Kings, 9 E xiv) add yet another additional chapter on prayer. One of the manuscripts (Bruges, Museum Kings, 9 E xiv) adds yet another chapter on the afterlife. See "The Content of Courson's *Summa*," 83.

12 Courçon 35.4 (fol. 116ra): "Item accusationum multiplex est diversitas…" Paris, BnF, lat. 14524 originated from the abbey of St. Victor in Paris.

13 Courçon 35.4 (fol. 116rb): "Quod concedimus, ubi crimina sunt notoria ut prediximus, velut quis publica laborat infamia, sicut plene ostensum est supra."

deeply about the language of rights and *ius* as practitioners who linked "social thought and social action" in order to find solutions to specific cases.[14] Each author thought about the space in which he worked and how best to navigate those waters. The penitential of Peter the Chanter reflected his teachings. How he addressed his subjects rose out of confession and was intended to help penitents and priests make decisions about their actions. While following Peter the Chanter's structure of a teaching text—making use of the dialectical method involving question, objection, and solution—Robert of Courçon's *Summa*, as Emily Corran has noted, is arranged in a more orderly fashion and thus more accessible than Peter's *Summa*.[15] The penitential of Robert of Flamborough, as will be discussed in the next chapter, was tailored for practical use in service of a bustling city with university students. While addressing similar topics to Robert of Flamborough, such as simony and usury, Robert of Courçon did so in much more detail.[16] Such topics were more of a concern for someone on the cusp of a full-time papal appointment. He also addressed benefices, prescription, and patronage in more depth than either Peter the Chanter or Robert of Flamborough. Yet, unlike them, Robert of Courçon did not appear overly concerned with magic or homicide. Finally, he focused on procedure more so than Peter the Chanter or Robert of Flamborough. He discussed the cleric's ability to participate in any aspect of a trial where capital punishment was at stake. He defined a legal case and discussed the methods by which one could be opened. He discussed both the *ordo iudicarius* and its elements from peremptory edicts, to witnesses, to judges, to sentences. Robert devoted entire sections to appeals and the circumstances under which they could and could not be made; the legal designation of infamy; evidence, the types, and its veracity; and the issuance of rescripts. He found it necessary to do so "since an ecclesiastic of our day is assailed from all sides by litigation and lawsuits."[17] Robert of Courçon's *Summa* reflects the environment of a papal judge-delegate, a future cardinal whose principal task would be to resolve disputes and correct abuses.

14 Taliadoros, "Law, Theology, and Morality," 493.

15 Emily Corran, *Lying and Perjury in Medieval Practical Thought: A Study in the History of Casuistry* (Oxford, 2018), 41–43, 86.

16 Robert of Courçon also wrote a treatise on usury. See Georges Lefèvre, ed. and trans, *Le Traité "De Usura" de Robert de Courçon: Texte et traduction publiés avec une introduction* (Lille, 1902).

17 Kennedy, "The Content of Courson's *Summa*," 81, n. 7:

> Quoniam vir ecclesiasticus hodie undique pulsatur litigiis et causis, ut facilius se a nexibus eorum expediat, dubia de iudicio et ordine iudiciario, de sententiis, de iudiciis, de testibus, de recriptis, de appellationibus, quorum cognitio sacerdotibus et pastoribus ecclesiae admodum est necessaria, breviter discutimus.

Crusading Activity

Peter the Chanter and Robert of Flamborough, in all fairness, also served as a judge-delegate at some point or another. Yet, administrative and judicial tasks on behalf of the papacy were secondary duties for them. For Robert of Courçon, they would become his principal charge. His knowledge of and manner in which he wove Gratian's *Decretum*, decretal law, conciliar decisions, and the Justinianic corpus into his penitential led V. L. Kennedy to note the *Summa's* concern with the external forum,[18] a forum in which his principle charge would, in one way or another, frequently engage him. Robert's engagement in papal administration and justice is an excellent opportunity to examine how a mental framework or working environment could influence the shape of a text. It also underscores that the difference between the penitential of Robert of Courçon and those of Peter the Chanter and Robert of Flamborough seems to lie not in their knowledge of law, as each possessed a firm grasp of legal principles. Robert of Courçon used his penitential, on occasion, as a space to directly and indirectly address current events, as a space to delve into points where the rubber met the road.

The early thirteenth century brought a flurry of crusading activity. The Fourth Crusade was launched in 1202 by the papacy. Pope Innocent III, however, quickly lost control over the enterprise. The true leaders, Count Theobald of Champagne, followed by Boniface of Montferrat after Theobald's death in May 1201, would divert crusading efforts first to Zara (modern-day Zadar) in order to pay debts owed to the doge of Venice, Enrico Dandolo, and then to Constantinople in order to help Prince Alexius assume the throne as Alexius IV. When Alexius IV was not forthcoming with the payment promised, the crusaders sacked the city in 1204. Meanwhile, Innocent III remained deeply concerned with the state of the Church in southern France and the spread of heresy.[19] Over the course of his 18-year pontificate, Innocent III dispatched 21 legates to the region. Eighteen of the legates preached against or investigated heresy, and were to ensure that French clergy worked in conjunction with papal

18 Kennedy, "The Content of Courson's *Summa*," 81.

19 As Elaine Graham-Leigh has brought to bear, all aspects of noble and episcopal behavior as it related to the Church were a central concern. A charge of heresy did not necessarily reflect heretical beliefs but rather could reflect opposition to the Church and the objectives of the Cistercians tasked with dealing with Cathars in the regions. Local bishops regarded as opposing Cistercian efforts against heresy were often removed and replaced with prelates from the ranks of legates and their associates. Pope Innocent III, however, remained concerned that the Church not be enriched from the illicit seizure of lands. Compounding matters were the struggles for control of southern France involving Trencavels and the crown of Aragon. See *The Southern French Nobility and the Albigensian Crusade* (Woodbridge, 2005), 58–112.

initiatives on the matter, and, eventually, to manage crusading efforts.[20] Increasingly dissatisfied with the lack of progress against the Cathars and suspicious that Raymond VI, count of Toulouse, had a hand in the murder of the papal legate Peter of Castelnau (1208), Innocent III launched the Albigensian Crusade in 1209, which lasted until 1218. With this endeavor, he sought to reassert papal oversight over the crusading movement, that is, to assert a chain of command that tied the leaders and local bishops to the papacy. In July 1209, Arnaud Amaury—abbot of Cîteaux, archbishop (and duke) of Narbonne, and papal legate—commanded the attack on Béziers, an attack that history would regard as a massacre.[21] Illusions to events that had transpired, and foreshadowing those that were on the verge of transpiring, may have provided Robert with the topic for section 26 chapter 9 and section 26 chapter 10.

The extent of a legate's obligation to follow the letter of a pope's mandate, in this case as it pertains to war, connects section 26 chapters 9 and 10. Collectively, Robert uses these two chapters to argue that a legate may delay imposing a pope's mandate or he may follow the spirit—though not necessarily the letter—of the mandate. In both cases, the legate was in a position to have information that was not available to the pope when he issued his order and when the pope became aware of this information he would change his mind as to how to handle the matter. Section 26 chapter 9 wove in the additional concern of the feudal-bishop and his actions in a military setting. Roberts posed the case of the pope, via his legate to the kingdom of the Franks, excommunicating all of the soldiers and barons following the flag of the king in war, which at that point was between two kings. The pope, via his legate, further ordered all bishops of the kingdom under the punishment of excommunication to excommunicate all opponents and place their lands under interdict. Complicating the situation, however, were new facts—about which had the pope known would have led him to alter his judgment—that proved sufficient to delay imposing the sentence. Should the bishops impose the mandate of the pope? The king was charged with defending his kingdom and the Church, though, as noted above, the war in question was between two kings and thus, presumably, not on behalf of the Church. If they do not impose the pope's order, they could be proven disobedient and, as such, the pope could suspend them from their office or benefice according to the law. Yet, bishops have soldiers and barons bound to them and under whom there are cases of Arianism.

20 Claire Maria Dutton, "Aspects of Institutional History of the Albigensian Crusade, 1198–1229," (PhD diss., Royal Halloway and Bedford New College, 1993), 126–132. Between 1217 and 1230, Pope Honorius III sent six legates to southern France, three of whom were charged with reconciling the south with the Church (pp. 133–135).

21 Colin Morris, *The Papal Monarchy: The Western Church from 1050 to 1250* (Oxford, 1989), 439–447; Rebecca Rist, *Papacy and Crusading in Europe, 1198–1245* (London, 2009), 7, 46.

They are doubly bound: bound by their lord but also bound by their pastor, the pope.[22] Therefore, either they are unfaithful to the king or they are disobedient to the lord pope. If the bishops follow the order of the shepherd (the pope), then they would not follow their king into war, even though they owe obedience and should serve him with fidelity by the law of regality. If they follow the order of the shepherd (the pope) and excommunicate everyone who clearly follows under the royal flag, then they diminish the regality of the king. They owe all of what pertains to the regalia of the king because of his prestige. But if they are disobedient against the lord pope they are now excommunicated because the pope warned them to obey under penalty of excommunication. If they are excommunicated, they are not able to excommunicate others, and thus they are not able to bring a sentence of excommunication against those soldiers if they are disobedient.[23]

Robert's solution in this case lay in whether a war between kings was deemed just or unjust. If it was deemed unjust, then they ought to attend personally but not with soldiers. If the war was deemed just, they were not to consult with the soldiers bound to them or go with their king—whose flag they were held to follow—to restrain the barons of the kingdom, even as it pertains to the

22 Courçon 26.9 (fol. 92ra–92rb):

> Item de facto accidit quod dominus papa distri[n]cte iniunxit cuidam legato ad regnum francorum destinato, ut excommunicaret omnes milites et barones sequentes vexilla regis in guerra, que tunc erat inter reges, et precepit omnibus episcopis regni sub pena excommunicationes ut premissa ammonitione omnes contradictores excommunicarent, et terras illorum interdictio supponerent; preterea nova causa que suffecit ad sententiam illam differendam, domino papa nesciente intervenit, quam si sciret nullatenus lxx mandasset; hic prelati et episcopi sibi perplexi videntur, quia aut ipsi exequentur mandatum domini pape aut non; si non exequentur, inobediente argu[un]entur, et de iure dominus papa poterit eos ab omni officio vel beneficio suspendere tamquam inobedientes. Si autem exequentur mandatum eius secundum formam eius. Contra sic. Prelati habent milites illos et barones sub se qui sunt homines ligii ipsorum, et quorum causas Arianarum habent. Ergo tenentur eis consulere dupliciter scilicet eo modo quo veri dominum habent consulere homnibus suis, et eo modo quo iure pastores habent consulere ovibus suis.

23 Courçon 26.9 (fol. 92ra–92rb):

> Si dicant eis ratione dominii nolite sequi regem vestrem in guerra, quam habet pro defendendo regno suo et ecclesia, cui debetis servare omnem fidelitatem. Idem est ac si dicat, nolite obedire dominis vestris in licitis et debitis obsequiis, et si hoc dicunt eis derogant regi, in hoc quod iure regalitatis debent ei fidelitatem; preterea si intuitu pastoris excommunicet omnes qui secuntur manifeste vexilla regalia; regalitatem quam a rege tenant diminuunt. Set ipsi debent omnia que spectant ad regalia regi ex prestito regi sacramenta; aut ergo erunt per iuri et infideles contra regem; aut inobedientes contra dominum papam; set si sunt inobedientes contra dominum papam; ex ipsa inobedientia iam excommunicati sunt, quia precepit eis obedire sub pena excommucationis; preterea si excommunicati sunt; alios excommunicare non possunt, ergo super subditos non possunt ferre senteniam excommunicationis, si inobedientes fuerunt.

defense of the kingdom and Church.[24] Robert seems to suggest that if the war was unjust, the prelate could take part but without soldiers, possibly to serve in a spiritual capacity. If the war was just, he could send soldiers, but he himself should not personally fight.

Though not explicitly cited, Causa 23 and Causa 24 of Gratian's *Decretum* echoed the position taken by Robert: a bishop could accompany his lord in an unjust war, but only in a spiritual capacity; in the case of a just war he could send soldiers, but he could not participate himself. The involvement of the major orders—subdeacon, deacon, priest, and bishop—in military endeavors ranged from recruiting troops to engaging in physical combat. Craig Nakashian has set forth a variety of reasons for clerical involvement in military action: royal service, obligations based on land- and office-holding, growing awareness of Roman law's construct defense of the *patria*, political partisanship, a sense of elite culture shared by prelates and secular nobles, and clerical engagement in a construct of masculinity that valued military action.[25] Along with Causa 25 and Causa 26, Causa 23 and Causa 24 used heresy as a springboard to discuss obedience and the execution of one's office.[26] Heterdoxy introduced the broader topic of the navigation of one's ecclesiastical office and the extent of one's powers. Causa 23 set forth that a bishop had to fulfill his duties to the pope and the emperor. The pope had to accept the bishop's holding of secular properties, and to the emperor—as the feudal lord—had to offer protection. With Causa 24 the bishop's ability to bind and to lose was intertwined with adherence to the bishop of Rome as the latter was the keeper of orthodoxy.[27]

The case statement of Causa 23 is that of heretical bishops who took the offensive to compel those from the surrounding regions to espouse their heresy. From here, we get into the heart of the case: the bishops who were ordered by the pope—and already had civil jurisdiction from the emperor—to defend the faithful from the heretics however they could and, when they

24 Courçon 26.9 (fol. 92rb): Solutio. Aut iniustum est bellum inter reges aut non; si constat eis quod iniustum est, tunc uero per se nec per subditos debent ille vires ministrare si iustum fuerit bellum tunc non possunt consulere ligiis homnibus; vel baronibus regni inhibere ne eant cum domino suo, cuius vexilla sequi tenentur, maxime pro defensione regni et ecclesie; et dominus papa precipere non potest contra, cum ipse non sit supra apostolam dicentem.

25 C. M. Nakashian, *Warrior Churchmen of Medieval England, 1000–1250: Theory and Reality* (Woodbridge, 2016), 7–10. Nakashian divides the historiography of clerical warfare into four main trends: from the perspective of canon law, within the context of the crusades, biographies, and contextualized within larger studies of military history (14–18).

26 Rather than the *Causae hereticorum*, I have argued that we should think more broadly about the purpose these cases served and that it might prove more fruitful to consider Causae 23–26, along with the preceding case (Causa 22) on the oath and perjury, as a thematic unit addressing obedience and the execution of one's office. See "Rethinking Causae 23–26 as the *Causae hereticorum*," ZRG Kan. Abt. 101 (2015): 86–149.

27 Rebecca Rist has maintained that Causae 23 and 24 were important to the pope's authorization of a crusade against "internal enemies," that is, an internal crusade against heretics. See *Papacy and Crusading in Europe*, 29–35.

were able, compel them to return to the righteousness of the faith. Having received the prerequisite authority from both the sacred and secular realms, the bishops called together soldiers and began to fight openly and through ambushes. Finally, with some heretics handed over to be killed and with others placed in jails and dungeons, those who remained were forced to return to the faith.[28]

Causa 23 juxtaposed the duties owed by a bishop to his secular lord as a feudal-bishop (e.g., to serve as judge and to engage in war) with those owed to the pope as his spiritual lord. Having defined and justified military service and war in Questions 1 and 2 as for the recovery of lost goods and the repulsion of injury,[29] Question 3 argues that a just war could be waged by the edict of a legitimate authority to aid an ally (*socius*).[30] The use of the word *socius* is telling. While it can be translated as friend or neighbor, Gratian's use suggests some relationship solidified by an oath. The language of C.22 q.5 lends support to this interpretation. C.22 q.5 c.1, from the Penitential of Theodore, refers to *dominus* and *miles*;[31] C.22 q.5 d.p.c.17 reads "de forma fidelitatis et quid quisque debeat domino vel e conversion;"[32] C.22 q.5 c.18 is Fulbert of Chartres's letter to William V.[33] The bishop and the emperor could become *socii* in a couple of different ways. First, as seen in the Concordat of Worms, the emperor could swear to protect the Church.[34] The Church thus could seek help from the emperor in matters of defense.[35] Second, an emperor or king would invest a bishop with a secular fief, thereby making the bishop his vassal and a lay lord in his own right. Such was the case here as the bishops "had received civil jurisdiction from the emperor" ("…qui ab inperatore civilem iurisdictionem acceperant …"). Reflecting upon the principles laid out in Causa 22, the bishop and the emperor have entered into a relationship solidified by an oath, which entails the rendering of certain services.

As a *socius* the enfeoffed bishop would have both secular and ecclesiastical jurisdictions. Remembering that it was the pope who ordered the army to be raised, possibly from the resources of the bishops' secular benefice, Question 8 focuses on the bishop's military responsibilities. Those bishops who were content with the tithe were free from the laws of the emperor. Those who held

28 GD C.23 hypothetical.
29 edF., col. 889–895.
30 edF., col. 895–898.
31 edF., col. 883.
32 edF., col. 887.
33 edF., col. 887.
34 Heinrici V Imp. *Constitutiones, Concordatum Wormatiense*, MGH, Leges II, p. 76.
35 GD C.23 q.3 d.p.c.1.

benefices (*predia, villas, castella, et civitates*) were bound by his law.[36] Should a bishop purchase property or receive it as a gift, then he owed the customary obedience attached to the land to the prince (i.e., taxes and the associated military obligations). Gratian offered two examples of acceptable conduct. As Pope Leo IV (847–855) did, serving as the secular ruler of Rome, a bishop may encourage anyone to his defense (i.e., he can raise an army). As Pope Gregory I (ca. 540–604) did when he called upon a faithful leader for assistance, a bishop may request defense from his *socius*. While a bishop may raise an army and accompany the soldiers, under no circumstances could he engage in battle.[37] The ability of the feudal-bishop, however, was limited to serving his spiritual functions; he could not serve in a secular capacity.[38] Causa 23 q.3, q.4, and q.5 would repeatedly emphasize that the secular realm was charged with the duty of assisting the Church when called upon, particularly in matters of correction.[39]

Causa 24 would emphasize the bishop's spiritual functions, particularly as they relate to his administrative ability to excommunicate and reconcile. The ability to execute his powers was inherently linked to his good standing with Rome as the keeper of orthodoxy. The case statement of Causa 24 again weaves in the question of heresy, this time for the purpose of using his power to excommunicate. A heretical bishop deprived some priests of their office and excommunicated them. After his death, the bishop along with his followers and their families were accused of heresy and condemned.[40] A bishop's ability to execute his powers to bind and to loosen was contingent upon his obedience to Rome. Papal primacy answers the question of why a bishop of another locale, such as

36 GD C.23 q.8 d.p.c.20 and d.p.c.22. Stanley Chodorow has suggested that C.23 q.8 d.p.c.20 was taken in part from the Agreement of Sutri in February 1111 (= Heinrici V Imp., *Tractatus cum Paschali II et Coronatio Romana* [nos. 83–101], MGH Const. I, pp. 134–152) in which Pope Paschal II granted to Emperor Henry V the right of investiture and thus reveals Gratian's sympathies for the pope. The ensuing Crisis of 1111 questioned the legality of Paschal II's concession. Placidus of Nonantula, Girard of Angoulême, and others argued that the pope should repudiate the privilege as it countered the canons and previous decrees. In response to their calls, Paschal II reiterated his desire to uphold the pronouncements of his predecessors, especially those of Pope Gregory VII and Pope Urban II. He bowed to the pressure and issued a statement nullifying the concession at the Lenten Council in March 1112, see Mansi 21:50–51. See Chodorow, *Christian Political Theory and Church Politics in the Mid-Twelfth Century: The Ecclesiology of Gratian's Decretum* (Berkeley, 1972), 151–152; idem, "Ecclesiastical Politics and the Ending of the Investiture Contest: The Papal Election of 1119 and the Negotiations of Mouzon," *Speculum* 46 (1971): 613–640.

37 GD C.23 q.8 d.p.c.25, d.p.c.27, d.p.c.28.

38 GD C.23 q.8 c.4–c.6, c.26. GD C.23 q.8 c.1–d.p.c.3 likewise reiterate that a cleric cannot be involved in warfare.

39 GD C.23 q.3 c.9 "si ecclesiasticam–profecto nocebitur," c.10; C.23 q.4 c.41, c.45–c.49; C.23 q.5 c.20–c.26, c.32, c.39–c.41, c.43.

40 GD C.24 hypothetical.

Paris, must obey the bishop of Rome and not *vice versa*. The Holy Spirit is found in the Church; therefore, one must be a member of the latter to possess the former. Because the Holy Spirit is found in the Church, those outside of the Church do not possess the Holy Spirit and are heretical. Since Christ gave Peter the keys to the kingdom of heaven, the one true Church—where the Holy Spirit is found—is the church which Peter founded in Rome. The Holy Spirit, therefore, has its headquarters in Rome with Peter. Just as the Holy Spirit did not descend upon those not gathered at Pentecost, the work of the Holy Spirit and the power of Christ did not grant the ability to bind and loose to those outside of the Church. A bishop who counters the Roman See cannot take an oath, cannot consecrate, cannot excommunicate, and cannot reconcile. He cannot judge those inside, those who possess the Spirit, as if he were equal to them.[41] Heresy was a failure to adhere to Rome; heresy was disobedience to Rome.[42] For deviating from that dictated by Rome, the bishop relinquished his episcopal powers. A bishop must himself be in good standing with the Church and has no power to excommunicate or to refuse communion to someone neither accused of a crime, nor convicted publicly by a judge, nor having confessed according to the law.[43] Faith and fulfillment of one's duty (that is, adherence) to Rome go hand-in-hand with excommunication playing a necessary corrective role.

Robert would continue with the theme of war in section 26 chapter 10. Having stated that the justness or unjustness of a war declared by the prince should be discussed, not by the soldiers but rather by the prince's counselors, Robert then posed two seemingly opposing scenarios. In the first scenario, the Edomites had refused Moses and the Israelites passage under the pain of the sword. The Israelites did not press the matter further and they went away. In the second scenario, Sihon, king of the Amorites, also refused the Israelites' passage. Yet, in this case, the Israelites took the cities of the Amorites.[44] Robert then put forth the position, stemming from Augustine, that just wars were waged when a harmless passage, which is owed by the law of human society, was denied. The difference between the two events lies in God's promise. Edom had not been promised to the Israelites, and thus it was not to be conquered. God had promised the land of the Amorites to Israelites, and thus the war

41 Gratian previews the argument constructed by c.5 through c.36 in d.p.c.4. GD C.24 q.1 d.p.c.4.
42 GD C.24 q.3 c.26–c.29 equated schism with heresy.
43 GD C.24 q.3 d.a.c.1, c.1, d.p.c.1.
44 Num. 20:14–35.

waged to conquer King Sihon's lands was just.[45] Robert then returned to the before-mentioned legate: he ought to attend to the intention of the pope in his legation rather than implementing the pope's wishes exactly. Should the pope issue a mandate without key information, the legate ought to delay implementation until which time the pope could issue a new mandate based on the new information.[46] A legate could respect the intent of the papal order but not necessarily follow the letter of that order. while he awaits updated instructions.

Section 26 chapters 9 and 10 are connected by whether a war is just and the legate's obligation to home in on the spirit of the pope's order if the pope might not have all of the information when he issued the order. The Fourth Crusade brought these issues to bear. Count Theobald of Champagne and the French nobility had made arrangements with Doge Enrico Dandolo in 1201 to provide supplies and naval transportation. However, the significantly lower-than-expected number of crusaders who met at the rendezvous point of Venice in 1202 meant that the debt incurred could not be paid. As a way of allowing the crusaders to reconcile their debt and get the crusade underway, the Doge proposed an assault on the city of Zara. Zara, however, was a Christian city that recognized King Bela III of Hungary, who himself had taken the cross, as their overlord, having broken free from Venetian control. The crusaders, now under the leadership of Boniface of Montferrat, fulfilled the Doge's wishes despite Pope Innocent III's command not to attack the city, a command which his legate Peter of Capuano ignored. As a result, the crusaders—soldiers under the king's banner on a mission for the Church—were excommunicated for the

45 Courçon 26.10 (fol. 92rb-92va):

> Obedite dominis vestris et quod hec distinctio pocius sit indiscusse tenenda quam traditio legis humane que dicit quod non spectat ad subditos discutere utrum iustum vel iniustum sit bellum; probamus auctoritate legis divine contra quam nichil potest lex humana. Legimus enim libro numero quod misit Israel nuntios ad Seon regem Amorreorum ut concederet ei licitum transitum per terram suam quem contradicentem expugnauit et civitatem eius et terram legitime possedit, sed hoc noluit facere contra regem edom qui quamvis negaret ei transitum; noluit contra eum aggredi bellum. Unde super illum locum ait Augustinus. Notandum quomodo bella iusta gerantur. Innoxius enim transitus negabatur, qui iure humane societatis debebatur. Sed ut deus sua promissa compleret adiuunt israelitas quibus Amorreorum terras dari oportebat. Sed Edom ubi israel transitus negabatur non expugnauit, quia terram illam israel non promiserat. Ecce contra Seon regem bellum erat iustum quia dominis ita constituit et promisit ut terra ipsius redderetur populo israleitico, cui competebat aut iure hereditario; aut ordinatione divina. Sed contra edom iniustum erat bellum et ideo ab ydu meis negantibus eis transitum declinauunt.

46 Courçon 26.10 (fol. 92va):

> De predicto legato dicimus quod debere pocius mentem domini pape attendere in sua legatione quam superficiem scripti, debere etiam attendere causam. Quare emanauerit tale mandatum, et si viderit quod postmodum contraria causa emerserit, cuius cognitio totam mentem domini pape immutaret, ad horam differre debet sententiam, quousque secundum novum eventum novum emanaverit mandatum.

actions taken against another king. Innocent III would lift the sentence placed on the crusaders when he learned that the Venetians had put the crusaders into the position on account of the debt owed to the Doge. While such a conquering was unjust, further information led the pope to reverse his decision.[47] Robert's mention of Arians may have simply been a way to indirectly confront what had happened. The events at Zara had been viewed with skepticism—Simon de Montfort disagreed with the attack entirely. The insinuation to the events at Zara may offer context to the juxtaposition of an unjustified war against the Edomites and the justified war against the Amorites in section 26 chapter 10. While the conquering of Zara, like the conquering of the Edomites, was illicit, the conquering of Constantinople, like the conquering of the Amorites, was licit. God had promised the Israelites the land; Emperor Alexius IV had reneged on the promise of payment to place him on the throne and had become increasingly belligerent toward the crusaders, and, furthermore, the Greeks were schismatics from the one true faith. Despite initially viewing the capture of the city positively, Innocent III would become angered once he learned of the atrocities from visitors to Rome. However, in the end, Innocent accepted the conquering of Constantinople as God's will.[48] Like the taking of the Amorites' land, the taking of Constantinople was deemed just.

Robert himself would be in the position to implement his view that the pope's ability to judge the justness of a war could be impaired by his distance from the events. He actively preached for the campaign against the Albigensians at a time when Pope Innocent III had suspended the crusading effort in southern France. Robert also took part in the siege of Morlhn where Waldensians were burned, in the battle at Casseneuil, and in the battle at Sainte-Livrade. It was at this last battle in 1214 that he would grant swaths of land belonging to Count Raymond VI of Toulouse to Simon of Montfort.[49] By doing so, Robert had ignored Innocent III's command to postpone the fate of these lands until the convening of what would be the Fourth Lateran Council.[50] Some prelates at the Council of Montpellier (1215) concurred with Robert's decision. Some Bolognese trained canonist Peter Beneventano, who also served as legate for southern France and

47 J. Phillips, *The Crusades, 1095–1204*, 2nd edn. (London, 2014), 183–190; J. Phillips, *The Fourth Crusade and the Sack of Constantinople* (New York, 2004), 56–70; R. H. Schmandt, "The Fourth Crusade and the Just-War Theory," *Catholic Historical Review* 61, no. 2 (1975): 191–221.

48 Phillips, *The Crusades, 1095–1204*, 195–201; Phillips, *The Fourth Crusade and the Sack of Constantinople*, 102–126; Schmandt, "The Fourth Crusade and the Just-War Theory," 216–218.

49 Dutton, "Aspects of Institutional History of the Albigensian Crusade," 100–102.

50 Dutton, "Aspects of Institutional History of the Albigensian Crusade," 45–46.

the kingdom of Aragon-Catalonia between 1214 and 1215, presided over the council, and, despite the council's view, overturned the decision.[51]

The juxtaposition between sanctioned killing and the clerical office was a quagmire posed by crusading efforts.[52] Robert reflects upon this subject in section 31 chapter 7 where he poses the issue of *irregulares* who followed the pope's order to take up the cross and kill many Saracens. *Irregulares* contravene the provisions of canon law.[53] Robert points to the Apostle Paul's letter to Titus which instructs a bishop or priest to be without crime, and his letter to Timothy which makes such men irreprehensible. His solution concludes that every moral sin, in addition to other irregularities which Robert would address, impedes promotion as they upend the rigor of the law.[54] Yet, after a lengthy digression examining other irregularities, such as infamy and concubines, Robert returns to the original subject to elaborate upon this position. Although there are those who kill meritoriously, having taken the cross against the Saracens at the request of the pope, the Church has decided that those who do so are not permitted to be promoted in the event that such men took delight in the act. Despite noting that position, Robert concludes that if they truly repentant, that is, sinners of whatever type were moved, not compelled, to seek dispensation then they are tolerably permitted to execute their office.[55]

51 Dutton, "Aspects of Institutional History of the Albigensian Crusade," 104–105; J. L. Bird, "Paris Masters and the Justification of the Albigensian Crusade," *Crusades* 6 (2007): 117–156, esp. 131–132.

52 Courçon Chapters 30–36 (fol. 104ra–118ra) deal with procedural matters. Chapter 30 deals with clerics involved in capital crimes.

53 See entry for *irregularis* in *Lexicon mediae latintatis*.

54 Courçon 31.7 (fol. 107vb–108ra):

> Et unde est quod dominus papa reputat eos irregulares, qui ad mandatum eius assumentes crucem multos sarracenos interfecerunt, cum ipsi executi sint bonum obedientie, et meritorie maleficos interfecernitur. Solutio. Sicut dicit apostulus ad Titum [1 Tit. 7–11]. Oportet episcopum uel quemcumque sacerdotum sine crimine esse et ad Thimotheum [1 Tim.:3] hominem irreprehensibilem esse. Omne crimen quod est peccatum mortale et impedit per movendum et deicit iam permotum de rigore iuris sicut dicit augustinus lxxxi d. capitulo aposotlis et insequentibus illis capitulis et non solum crimina set irregularitates impediunt promovendum, …

Robert references D.81 of Gratian's *Decretum*, which addresses that clerics cannot be ordained by a bishop outside of his diocese and he cannot preach in the diocese unless he has permission from that bishop. The subject matter of GD D.50 is more closely aligned with what Robert is addressing.

55 Courçon 31.7 (fol. 108rb–108va):

> Unde nulla in occidente remanet irregularitas post baptismum, et quamvis meritoire occidant multi ut cruce signati Sarracenos ad mandatum domini, tamen propter horrorem sanguinis, scilicet ne homines delectet effundere sanguinem alienum instituit ecclesia ne tales ex rigore iuris promoveantur. Sed si vere peniteant tales vel quicumque peccatores non de rigore sed de dispensatione possunt promoveri et in executione sui officii tolerari, sicut habetur in q. vii capitulo. Si quis omnem.

Robert cites C.1 q.7 c.2 ("q. vii capitulo Si quis omnem") of the *Decretum* in support of this position, which, at first blush makes sense as the rubric reads "De his, qui pro muneribus ordinationem faciunt, et qui redeuntes ab heresi in suis ordinibus recipiuntur" ("Concerning those who perform an ordination for gifts, and who are accepted into their order returning from heresy"). Yet, this example is provided either out of carelessness or purposeful distortion. Robert essentially leaned on the canon's rubric and a comment Gratian made in C.1 q.7 d.p.c.4 where he states that "…when they will have detested their heresy in true penance, they are not prohibited by the aforementioned authorities to be received in their grade."[56] Yet, Gratian immediately goes on to state "[b]ut nevertheless as," which he follows with a list of examples one of which was C.1 q.7 c.2, "they are ordered to be damned unrestorably."[57] C.1 q.7 c.2 states that those who violate the written and non-written tradition of the Church were to be anathematized. Those who lapse into fornication after baptism should not be received into the priesthood. Every bishop, priest, and deacon having been convicted of giving or accepting ordination for gifts is degraded from the priesthood. He who has been ordained by simony, whether bishop, priest, or deacon is alienated from the priesthood. If someone knew that another entered into the priesthood in such a manner, he too would be degraded. Essentially, he who ordains, is ordained, or has been ordained, by money—whether he is a bishop, priest, or deacon—is repelled from the priesthood. A bishop, priest, deacon, or anyone who is a murderer is deposed. He who has been ordained by a secular power and obtains a church is deposed; he is expelled if he obtains a religious house.[58] Robert's citation did not support his position that those who kill unbelievers in accordance with the pope's crusading order can remain in their rank, provided they have voluntarily sought remediation.

Robert seems to have felt pressure to address the ethical quandary of clerical involvement in the crusading effort. Pope Honorius III would address the matter a few years later in his response to a priest named Pelagius. Enemies of the Lord's cross and those blasphemous of the Christian name had attacked a certain castle and inhabitants, both clerical and lay, died fighting against the enemy. The priest had inquired what a cleric should do if he engaged in warfare. Honorius III responded that if his conscience nagged him from the murder of someone in that conflict, he should respectfully abstain from the ministry of the alter, as it is more prudent to abstain when in doubt than to celebrate rashly.[59] Though preceding Honorius III's letter, Robert similarly seems to give

56 GD C.1 q.7 d.p.c.4: "Unde cum heresim suam veraci penitentia detestati fuerint, premissis auctoritatibus non prohibentur recipi in suis gradibus."

57 GD C.1 q.7 d.p.c.4: "Verumtamen capitulo illo Nicenae sinodi: 'Si quis per pecuniam etc.' et illo alio septimae sinodi, 'Si quis omnem traditionem etc.' et Innocentii, et aliorum multorum auctoritatibus inreparabiliter dampnari iubentur."

58 GD C.1 q.7 c.2.

59 Potthast 7837 (24 July 1216–18 March 1227); V Comp. 5.6.4 (X 5.12.24).

leniency to those who kill the infidel, Muslim or Cathar, so long as they willingly seek penance for their actions. In such cases, they can resume their clerical duties. While Robert stretches his citation to Gratian to the breaking point, it does not mean that his interpretation of the law was incorrect. Rather, he did not cite the particular section of the *Decretum* that would have supported his position. Distinction 50 addressed the reality that clerics could, and did, commit crimes. The distinction asks whether after having performed penance, they are able to remain at their rank or advance into the major orders.[60] It begins with the premise that those in the major orders who committed capital crimes, gave false testimony, or made a false claim were to be deposed and put into a monastery essentially at the rank of laity.[61] Yet, a qualification would be made to take intent into consideration. Pope Nicholas I permitted clerics who had killed a pagan in self-defense to return to their rank and progress to another after penance was served. Though he did point out that under normal circumstances, it was in no way lawful to kill a man.[62] In another example, a cleric who committed murder when besieged with no hope of escape could be purged by a two-year penance of vigils, prayer, and alms, after which point he could return to his office and communion.[63] A series of examples were offered—Maria being cured of her leprosy, Peter denying Christ and yet remaining an apostle, and those reunited with faith who fell back into heresy and eventually becoming bishops—to show that it was possible to return to one's rank after penance.[64] Those who fell were admonished and, after having accepted that admonishment, could stand up again.

The key issue was whether the cleric came to penance, was forced to penance, or performed penance for self-serving reasons. If he came to penance, he could be restored. If he was forced to penance or performed it for self-serving

60 GD D.50 d.a.c.1: "...quod variis criminibus irretiti in sacerdotes ordinari non possunt. Nunc autem des hisdem queritur, utrum post actam penitenciam vel in propriis ordinibus remanere, aut ad maiores gradus conscendere valeant?"

61 GD D.50 c.7.

62 GD D.50 c.6.

63 GD D.50 c.36.

64 GD D.50 d.p.c.12:

> Econtra exemplis et auctoritate probatur, post actam penitenciam proprios gradus licite posse administrare, et ad maiores conscendere. Maria enim, soror Aaron, postquam lepra percussa est, quia in Moysen murmuraverat, acta penitencia mundata est, et pristinam gratiam prophetandi recepit. Aaron post conflatum vitulum etiam in summum sacerdotem est consecratus. David post adulterium et homicidium spiritum prophetiae recepit, et in proprio gradu permansit. Achab post mortem Nabuthae viri sanctissimi per penitenciam humiliatus in regia sede remansit. Et, ut pretereamus multa exempla veteris testamenti, Petrus negavit Christum, et tamen postea princeps apostolorum factus est; Paulus Stephanum lapidavit, et tamen a Deo in apostolum electus est. Multi quoque ab heresi ad unitatem catholicae fidei revertentes in suis ordinibus recepti sunt, alii vero ad episcopalem etiam gradum sunt promoti.

reasons, then he could not be restored.[65] In other words, those called to, that is, ordered to do, penance for any crime could not be accepted into or remain among the clergy. Likewise, if one was moved to penance in the spirit of pride after the crime was found out, he was not to be admitted to the clergy after penance. Those who offered false penance out of fear of poverty (i.e., losing benefice) or ambition were not to be restored to former their rank because they did not do their penance out of disgust of the crime. However, those who *offered* penance to God for crimes were able to return to their rank. It was a question of the motive driving the penance. While one could return to his rank if he performed solemn penance, which should only be performed once, then he could not advance to or within the major orders.[66] Distinction 50 supports the position Robert advocated, but for whatever reason he did not cite it.

Robert also took up the issue of clerics involved in a murder in section 30 chapter 5 where he addressed the calling upon others to take up arms. There, he posed a scenario in which you, presumably a cleric, are in a church. Incendiaries force their way into the church with the intention of burning it to the ground. This would no doubt this would happen unless you call upon the village for help. Yet, if you do, you know that everyone would be seized immediately by force, and thus you will be the cause of their death. If you remain silent, however, you will incur death and the church will be destroyed. While you know that all laws and rights permit you to repel them by force, you choose rather to be killed and leave us, presumably the judges, to sentence the malefactors to death.[67] Robert cited C.23 q.5 c.3 of the *Decretum* in support of the position taken. Gratian had begun question five, which dealt with the death penalty, citing Exodus and Matthew, both of which forbade one person from killing another.[68] Canon 3 stemmed from Augustine's letter to Donatus in which he calls for the correction, but not the killing of, the impious wicked.

65 GD D.50 d.p.c.24: "Sunt quidam, quos non odium criminis, sed timor vilitatis, amissio proprii gradus et ambitio celsioris ad penitenciam cogit. Hos sacri canones irrecuperabiliter deiciunt, quia qui simulatione penitenciae vel affectione honoris adeo non consequitur veniam, nec ab ecclesia meretur reparationem."

66 GD D.50 d.p.c.54, d.p.c.61–c.63, d.p.c.64–c.66.

67 Courçon 30.5 (fol. 106ra):

> Item tu es in ecclesia aliqua, et vides irruere incendiarios in eam ut illam incendant, vel te interficiant nisi clames et convoces uiciniam. Quod si facias tu scis quod omnes statim rapientur ad furcas, et ita eris causa mortis illorum, si taces incurris mortem et ecclesia subvertetur, et tu scis quod omnes leges et omnia iura permittunt uim repellere, set dicit Augustinus. Pocius occidi eligamus, quam maleficos occidendos aliquorum iudiciis inferamus, et hoc habetur. xxiii. q. v capitulo unum solum.

68 GD C.23 q.5 d.a.c.1: "Quod autem nulli liceat aliquem occidere, illo precepto probatur, quo Dominus in lege homicidium prohibuit, dicens (Exod. 20:13): 'Non occides.' Item in euangelio (Matth. 26:52): 'Omnis, qui gladium acceperit, gladio peribit.'" While Gratian began question five under the premise that the death penalty was forbidden, he would, in the course of the question, justify its use in certain circumstances.

While he does not want discipline to be neglected, he does not want them to be coerced to repent by, presumably physical, punishment.[69]

In his solution, Robert distinguished between the perfect and the imperfect. Those who are perfect would rather die than bring about the death of others. Those who are imperfect would repel by force, and call together the village for the defense of the church and public goods, working in every and all ways in so far it was possible out of a zeal for justice.[70] Precedents of clerics calling upon secular authorities to protect the church could easily be found to offer the justification required for such actions. The king of France had received a mandate from the pope to take up arms against the Albigensians and other heretics having sprung up in the kingdom.[71] Arms were also permitted in the taking of the cross and fighting against Saracens, which the pope likewise ordered.[72] Thus, it was permitted to kill such people by the authority of the Church. He referenced Pope Lucius III's decretal *Ad abolendam* in support of the view the Church was able to kill such people meritoriously. Other unbelievers could be handed over to the curia for punishment as was done at the Council of Paris under legate Octavian,[73] a council which also involved the masters of Paris who issued a death sentence.

Possibly at the forefront of Robert's mind was the situation addressed in c.27 of the Third Lateran Council (1179). This canon excommunicated heretics and those who protected them. In addition, it excommunicated mercenaries who despoiled an unnamed church and harmed the unarmed in southern France. Those who employed the mercenaries were also excommunicated and their vassals were no longer required to follow them. Prelates were to call upon secular princes to confiscate the lands of these recalcitrant excommunicates in return

69 GD C.23 q.5 c.3: "…corrigi eos cupimus, non necari; nec disciplinam circa eos negligi volumus, nec suppliciis, quibus sunt digni, coherceri."

70 Courçon 30.5 (fol. 106ra):

> Distinguendum est ut supra, aut tu es perfe[c]tus aut imperfectus. Si tu es perfectus, eligas potius mori quam aliquos prodere ad mortem, sicut dicit predictum capitulum. Si vero imperfectus es licet tibi vim repellere, et in viciniam convocare pro defensione ecclesie et rei pubice, et tunc modis omnibus laborare quantum in te est…set tamen zelo iusticie.

71 Ex. Potthast 2682 Innocent III (1 Feb. 1206).

72 Ex. Potthast 924 Innocent III (10–31 Dec. 1199) called upon Philip to assist against the Saracens.

73 Courçon 30.5 (fol. 106ra):

> Item de novo emanavit mandatum a domino papa ad regem Francorum, ut armata manu impugnaret albigentes et alios hereticos in regno suo pululantes … Nonne auctoritate domini pape hoc facit. Sic ergo licet interficere tales auctoritate ecclesiae. Et ita ecclesia potest interficere tales meritorie vel tradere curie puniendos, sicut habetur in illa constitutione Lucii iii Ad abolendam. Eadem permissa est questio de assumentibus crucem et impugnatibus sarrace nos ad mandatum domini pape et ibi soluta est questio, est similis questio soluta est a concilio parisiensi sub Octouiano legato….

for crusading privileges and an indulgence, a remission of sins, to be at the local bishop's discretion. It also provided an indulgence, for those who fought against heretics. An eternal reward was granted to those who died fighting.[74] Robert would draw upon this canon at the Council of Bordeaux (1214) over which he presided as legate. He offered a 60-day indulgence to all who resisted heretics, *routiers*, and their supporters to incentivize secular authorities to suppress heresy in Bordeaux and confiscate their lands. If harborers of the heretics had not moved to seek absolution within 40 days, their vassals were to support them no longer.[75]

The Fight Against Heresy

Robert was deeply committed to enforcing the most recent procedural norms in his fight against heresy.[76] Not only was there the perception that heresy, particularly the Cathar heresy, was spreading uncontrollably in southern France but it was also perceived as a problem in the diocese of Auxerre and in northern France in general. Masters of the schools of Paris showed a particular interest in the matter. William of Auxerre's *Summa aurea* and William of Auvergne's *De legibus* both demonstrated an interest in the heresy. Prévostin of Cremona, who served as chancellor of the schools of Paris from 1206 to 1209, had spent a significant amount of time around the Cathars.[77] Robert questioned whether a priest should require the penitent to swear that he would not repeat the sin to which he confessed prior to imposing penance. Robert concluded that the priest should not demand an oath from the one confessing, save one exception: heresy. As "dicit canon" sets up, this was in the event that he fell back into heresy, it could then be proven he perjured his oath.[78] The oath alluded to can be found in the formula provided in C.1 q.7 c.9 of the *Decretum*, which was provided as an example of an oath for those returning to the Church from engaging in a schism.[79] If he should fall back into his heresy later and is

74 COGD 2.1, 145–147.

75 Bird, "Paris Masters and the Justification of the Albigensian Crusade," 121–122; Rist, *Papacy and Crusading in Europe*, 27.

76 The Paris manuscript omits the last question in chapter 2 (on absolution and remission) entirely. This question asks what penance should be imposed if a heretic confessed or is convicted. Courçon (fol. 21va); Kennedy, "The Content of Courson's *Summa*," 85 n4.

77 P. Biller, "Northern Cathars and Higher Learning," in *The Medieval Church: Universities, Heresy, and The Religious Life: Essays in Honour of Gordon Leff*, eds. P. Biller and B. Dobson (Rochester, 1999), 25–53, here 40–51, esp. 46–47. Biller has posited that concern with the Cathar heresy may have had some role, even if a minor role, in the concern with heresy and Aristotle's works on natural philosophy (p. 49).

78 Courçon 1.44 (fol. 17va): "Exigere non debet sacerdos votum a confitente nisi in casu ut dicit canon scilicet ubi confitetur heresim suam, quia tunc sacerdos compellere debet penitentem ut abiuret eam." Kennedy, "Robert of Courson on Penance," 325.

79 GD C.1 q.7 c.9; Gregory I, Epp., Bk. 12, letter 33.

convicted for it, he is handed over to be punished by the curia according to the decree *Ad abolendam* issued at the Council of Verona in 1184.[80]

Pope Lucius III's decretal *Ad abolendam* is often seen as one of two decretals, Pope Innocent III's *Vergentis in senium* being the other, that changed the legal process as it pertains to heresy. Because of its importance, a summary of *Ad abolendam*'s contents may prove useful. Regarding those notoriously convicted of heresy, if he should be an ecclesiastic—cleric or religious—he will be deposed from his order and despoiled of his benefice. Essentially, losing his ecclesiastical status he will be delivered to the secular arm for punishment. He may, however, avoid such outcomes if he should renounce his errors as soon as he is found to be in error and submit himself to the bishop of the diocese for correction. If the notoriously convicted was a layman, whether convicted publicly or privately, he is handed over to the secular arm for punishment unless he abjures his heresy, makes satisfaction, and immediately returns to the Catholic faith. Those suspected of heresy are to provide full evidence of their innocence according to the level of suspicion against them and their status. Otherwise, they are subject to the same sentence as those convicted. Those who have been found to relapse after having either abjured themselves or have been cleared upon examination are to be delivered to the secular arm without any further hearing, and their goods confiscated for the use of the Church. Excommunication should be renewed and repeated at all major festivals, at every public solemnity, or on any other occasion. If any bishop neglects or is slow to prosecute heresy, he is suspended for three years from his episcopal dignity and administration. All secular leaders should swear with an oath to assist the Church in rooting out and prosecuting heretics. If any should refuse, they are deprived of their status and sentenced with excommunication, and their goods confiscated for the use of the Church. Those who are accomplices to heretics are under the stigma of perpetual infamy, unable to serve as attorneys or witnesses, or of bearing any public office whatsoever. Those who are exempt from diocesan jurisdiction in normal circumstances and thus are under the protection of the pope are subject to the judgment of the archbishop and bishops in matters involving heresy.[81] Robert would have occasion to draw upon Lucius III's *Ad abolendam* more than once.

Robert explicitly engaged with the decision of the Council of Paris (1201), a council in which he was directly involved, against Évrard of Châteauneuf. Évrard was a knight who first served Peter of Courtenay—cousin of the king of France and of the count of Auxerre—and then served Hervé, count of Nevers. Hugh of Noyers, bishop of Auxerre from 1183 to 1206 and to whom

80 Courçon 1.44 (fol. 17va): "Unde si postmodum relabatur in eam et comunicatur super hoc tradi debet curie puniendus, sicut dicit illud consilium veronense, ad abolendam"; Kennedy, "Robert of Courson on Penance," 325. I Comp. 5.6.5 (X 5.7.9).

81 I Comp. 5.6.5 (X 5.7.9).

the *Gesta* of the bishops of Auxerre referred as a *hereticorum malleus* ("hammer of heretics"), accused Évrard of heresy and aggressively pursued the charges.[82] The papal legate Octavian called the council to hear the case. Évrard would be deemed guilty and handed over to the count of Nevers for punishment (burning). Évrard's conviction at the council involved Robert, masters of theology from Paris, and the canonist Rodoicus Modicipassus (d. ca. 1201–1204),[83] in addition to the legate archbishops and bishops throughout France. These clerics had all had a part in his trial, a trial that resulted in a man's death. Robert noted that Évrard had been judged a heretic and that he lapsed and then relapsed. He also noted that the process set forth by Pope Lucius III's decretal, *Ad abolendam* (1189), had been followed. That is, an ecclesiastical tribunal examined the case and the charge of heresy had been proven.[84] The guilty was handed over to the lay officials (i.e., the count of Nevers) who executed the punishment.

Robert himself commented, "I am prepared for this malefactor to be hung, or burned, [or] dismissed, or die."[85] It is almost as if he was coming to grips with the realities of the case, despite a similar procedure having been used in 1200 when the heretics of Troyes were burned. It was *he*, along with his fellow judges, who were responsible for not only finding Évrard guilty of heresy, but also, drawing on Roman law, of having condemned him to death.[86] While Robert referenced C.23 q.5 c.1 and c.2, canons stemming from Augustine's letters to Emperor Marcellinus asking that the Donatists be punished but not killed,[87] Robert followed those canons with the decree of Emperors Arcadius and Honorius and Theodosius which called for the search for Manicheans and

82 Biller, "Northern Cathars and Higher Learning," 34–35.

83 Mansi 22:739; Courçon 30.2 (fol. 105ra) where he was cited explicitly. See Stephan Kuttner, "Rodoicus ou Rotbertus Modicipassus (Parvipassus)," in DDC (1965): 7.701–702.

84 Courçon 30.2 (fol. 104vb). Interestingly, on this occasion, Robert did not draw from Pope Innocent III's bull *Vergentis in senium* (1199). The decretal excommunicated heretics and brought the crime of heresy under the umbrella of Roman law's *crimen laesae majestatis* (treason). Their property was confiscated, and they were banned from holding public office, giving testimony in court, making wills, or inheriting. A condemnation for heresy condemned their children to a life of poverty. Innocent also applied these provisions to those who supported, defended, and harbored heretics, which was an extension of previous policies applied to heretics. For the decretal, see III Comp. 3.4.1 (X 5.7.10). For Innocent III's innovative legal thinking, as heresy did not constitute treason in Roman law, see W. Ullmann, "The Significance of Innocent III's Decretal *Vergentis*," in *The Papacy and Political Ideas in the Middle Ages*, ed. Ullmann (London, 1976), 729–741; and G. M. Cantarella, "L'evoluzione della normativa antiereticale di Innocenzo III dalla *Vergentis in senium* (1199) al IV concilio lateranense (1215)," *Bullettino dell'Istituto storico italiano per il Medio Evo* 106, no. 2 (2004): 207–240. For the impacts of Innocent III's decretal, see K. Pennington, "'Pro Peccatis Patrum': A Moral and Legal Problem of the Inquisition," *Church History* 47, no. 2 (1978): 137–154.

85 Courçon 30.2 (fol. 104vb): "Ego paratus sum hunc maleficum suspendere uel comburere uel dimittere [uel] abire."

86 Gorochov, *Naissance de l'université*, 168–174.

87 Courçon 30.2 (fol. 105rb).

Donatists, even after death. Because the memory of the deceased found guilty of treason could be denounced, it was not unreasonable that a heretic should undergo the same sentence. He also referenced a decree of Emperors Leo and Anthenius that allowed accusations of high treason, of public crimes, and of simony, which was deemed a heresy, to be put forward equally.[88] Cases involving exceptional crimes (*crimen exceptum*)—treason, heresy, sorcery, and other crimes that varied depending upon the time—permitted judges to suspend the accused's procedural rights.[89] Robert drew further upon C.23 q.5 d.p.c.7, the key *dictum* in which Gratian, having set for the contra stance, as seen with c.1 and c.2, shifts to the pro stance. Here, Gratian notes that while the wicked must be coerced by scourges, they must not be beaten to the point of maiming their limbs or temporal death. He then cites various Old Testament examples involving Moses, Samuel, and Phinehas, all of whom had justly put someone to death for various crimes. Gratian concludes that while it is prohibited for anyone armed with his own authority to kill another, it is not prohibited to hand over the defendants to be killed by the order of the law. For he who under public authority kills the wicked by the order of his own law does not transgress the precept "do not kill."[90] Again drawing on Augustine, Robert references C.23 q.5 c.8 and c.10 of the *Decretum*, canons which support the position taken by Gratian in d.p.c.7: those who have the authority and responsibility are waging just wars on behalf of God are not guilty of murder and have not violated the Ten Commandments.[91] Robert not only explained the legal justification for applying the death penalty in cases of heresy, but he also justified clerical involvement in such trials. More importantly, Robert seems to have cleared his conscience.

88 Courçon 30.2 (fol. 105rb–105va); Cod. 1.4.4; Cod. 1.3.29 (also included in the *Decretum* as C.15 q.3 c.4). Such supports Bermon's observation that Robert had knowledge of Roman law in Justinian's corpus, see *La Fondation de l'Univerité de Paris*, 119.

89 E. Peters, "Crimen exceptum: The History of an Idea," in *Proceedings Syracuse 1996*, eds. K. Pennington, S. Chodorow, and K. Kendall (Vatican City, 2001), 137–194.

90 GD C.23 q.5 d.p.c.7:

> Hinc apparet, quod mali flagellis sunt cohercendi, non membrorum truncatione vel temporali morteplectendi. §. 1. Sed obicitur illud, quod ait Dominus ad Moysen: 'Maleficos non patieris vivere'; item: 'Qui coierit cum iumento morte moriatur.' Adulterii etiam vel blasphemiae crimine notatus inmisericorditer lapidari iubetur. Item Moyses, qui legem acceperat, cultores idoli morte puniuit. Samuel etiam Agag regem pinguissimum in frusta conscidit. Finees quoque Iudeum cum Madianita coeuntem gladio transfixit, quod ei reputatum est ad iusticiam. Similiter nonnulli in veteri testamento inueniuntur malos trucidasse, nec transgressores legis, sed defensores appellantur. §. 2. Prohibetur ergo illo precepto quisque sua auctoritate in necem alicuius armari, non legis inperio reos morti tradere. Qui enim, publica potestate functus, ipsius legis inperio malos perimit, nec illius precepti transgressor, nec a celesti patria alienus habetur.

91 GD C.23 q.5 c.8, c.10.

Robert also explicitly addresses the fate of the heretic Amalric of Bène and his followers, the Amalricians. As a whole, chapter 4 addresses a variety of issues dealing with the concept and practical consequences of excommunication. For example, Robert explores: whether the excommunicated should be shunned by the family; whether an excommunicated noble should be shunned by his inferiors; whether an excommunicated abbot should be shunned by his monks; what should someone do if he knows that a knight entering a noble's hall has been excommunicated for fighting in a tournament; who is entitled to excommunicate; what is excommunication's binding force; and what are the court procedures.[92] Amalric and the Amalricians were an excellent case study. Amalric was a master of arts at Paris whose controversial teachings led to his condemnation at Rome; he fell ill and died in 1206 under a sentence of excommunication. A synod held in Paris in 1210 sentenced four of his followers to incarceration and condemned ten others to burn. Amalric's body was to be removed from its burial place on sacred ground and reburied on unconsecrated ground.[93]

Robert questions whether an excommunication pronounced in several churches has more binding force than an excommunication pronounced in a single church. After all, the Amalricians had moved about and were active in more than one area. He concludes that an excommunicate in more than one church has a greater binding force. If excommunicated were to be absolved in one church, the excommunication would still be in effect in another.[94] With respect to Amalric's postmortem excommunication, Robert took up the issue of whether someone could be lawfully excommunicated after his death. He drew upon C.24 q.2 of the *Decretum* where it was stated that heretics in whose books heresies were to be found ought to be excommunicated even if dead.[95] Pope Alexander III

92 Courçon 4 (fol. 26rb–30ra).

93 See W. J. Courtenay, *Rituals for the Dead: Religion and Community in the Medieval University of Paris* (Notre Dame, 2019), 11. Courtenay notes that Amalric was most likely buried originally in the garden of the priory of Saint-Nicolas-des-Champs just north of the city wall.

94 Courçon 4.5 (fol. 27rb); Thijssen, "Master Amalric and the Amalricians," 43–65. Thijssen includes a very partial edition of Robert of Courçon's question 4 on pp. 63–64 with commentary on pp. 50–51.

95 GD C.24 q.2 c.6:

> Sane profertur a quibusdam, qui dicunt oportere post mortem hereticos anathematizari, et sequi doctrinam in hoc sanctorum Patrum, qui non solum viventes hereticos condempnauerunt, sed etiam mortuos, sicut eos, qui iniuste condempnati sunt, revocaverunt post mortem, et in sacris dipticis scripserunt. … Sancta sinodus dixit: Sufficiunt que dicta et prolata sunt ecclesiasticam traditionem demonstrare, quod oportet hereticos etiam post mortem anathematizari. Item in actione IV.: §10. Sancta sinodus dixit: Augustini sanctae memoriae, qui inter Affricanos episcopos splenduit, diversae epistolae sunt recitatae, significantes, quod hereticos oportet etiam post mortem anathematizari. Talem autem ecclesiasticam traditionem et alii Affricani reverentissimi episcopi servaverunt; sed et Romana sancta ecclesia quosdam episcopos etiam post mortem anathematizavit, licet pro fide in vita sua non essent accusati, et utrumque apud nos gesta habita significant.

had written to the archbishop of Sens that a church or cemetery was polluted if someone having been excommunicated is buried there.[96] Pope Honorius III decreed that if the bones of the excommunicated have been buried in an ecclesiastical cemetery, they were to be disinterred, removed, and cast away.[97] Yet, Robert raised the point that since death brought an end to someone's life, there was nobody liable for the crime and thus there could not be a trial. Furthermore, a legitimate excommunication requires a conviction, a confession, contumacy, or notoriety on the part of the accused. None of these categories apply in the case of an accused who is already dead. Hence, such persons should not be excommunicated. To resolve the conflict posed, Robert turned to a decretal from Pope Alexander III to the archbishop of Sens that maintained a special privilege could, in some cases, supersede a general privilege.[98] Robert argued that due to the enormity of the crime of heresy, a restriction of the general rule should apply. Heretics, therefore, could be excommunicated after death.[99]

Conclusion

Robert of Courçon actively engaged in the world around him. He, for example, navigated conflict at the schools of Paris and implemented statutes that established the parameters for the University of Paris. Unlike Peter the Chanter and Robert of Flamborough, administrative efforts on behalf of papal business would come to occupy his time. In addition to frequently serving as a papal judge-delegate, he, as a papal legate, convened councils and addressed issues of immediate importance. Such business would have necessitated a working knowledge of the law. He demonstrated this knowledge both in direct citations but also in his solutions that feel in line with contemporary legal thought.

Robert's penitential, more so than the others studied here, seemed particularly concerned with the external forum and judicial procedure. Both of these concerns were brought to bear in his implicit and explicit reference to contemporary events. Of particular interest were clerical involvement in crusading activities and the sentencing of heretics. A bit less penitential in tone and a bit more juridical, Robert seems to have felt the need to justify actions taken by clerics. He navigated the bishop's secular and spiritual obligations. He justified the ability of a legate on how best to "interpret" the pope's instructions based on what was happening on the ground. He legitimized clerical involvement in heresy cases that resulted in death. Robert did not skirt the realities of his time: clerics were involved in the world around them, and sometimes the world around them was unpleasant.

96 IV Comp. 3.15.1 (X 3.40.7).
97 III Comp. 3.21.3 (X 3.28.12).
98 I Comp. 1.2.1 (X 1.3.1).
99 Courçon 4.13 (fol. 29va–30ra).

6

ROBERT OF FLAMBOROUGH

Penitentiarius to the Students of Paris and Homicide

Introduction

Robert of Flamborough was English by birth, possibly from Yorkshire. He was among Peter the Chanter's circle and was close friends with Richard Poore (dean of Salisbury, 1198–1214) who lived and taught in Paris between ca.1208 and 1213.[1] Between 1205 and 1207, Flamborough became associated with Robert of Courçon as a papal judge-delegate. Robert's penitential was truly a work tailored for the *cura animarum*. As a canon at the abbey of St. Victor from 1205, his principal charge would be to serve as *penitentiarius* (confessor-general).[2] The *penitentiarius* was responsible for hearing the confessions and administering penance to the students of Paris, all of whom held the status of clergy. As St. Victor had assumed this important pastoral responsibility, Robert addressed all matters concerning penitential discipline for the University of Paris.[3]

It is prudent to treat Robert's penitential in tandem with that of the canonist Bartholomew of Exeter. Robert leaned heavily upon Bartholomew's penitential to compile his and both were more interested than Peter the Chanter in drawing upon the older law found in the collections of Ivo of Chartres and Burchard of Worms (d. 1025). Peter the Chanter took an interest in teaching students how to think

1 Thomas of Chobham, discussed in the next chapter, served as subdean during Richard Poore's tenure both as dean and then as bishop of Salisbury.

2 Robert of Flamborough, *Liber Poenitentialis: A Critical Edition with Introduction and Notes*, ed. J. J. Francis Firth (Toronto, 1971), 3, 8; J. Baldwin, *Masters, Princes, and Merchants: The Social Views of Peter the Chanter and His Circle*, 2 vols. (Princeton, 1970), 1:32–34.

3 Flamborough, *Liber poenitentialis*, 12; J. Goering, "The Internal Forum and the Literature of Penance and Confession," in HMCL 2, 380, 385–387; idem, "The Internal Forum and the Literature of Penance and Confession," *Traditio* 59 (2004): 175–227.

DOI: 10.4324/9781003465096-7

through legal exceptions so they could better perform their penitential duties; Bartholomew and Robert took a ground-level interest in the practical orientation of how the law was used. This practical orientation may have been the reason why they were drawn to the collections of Ivo of Chartres and Burchard of Worms. Those collections were systematically structured by topic. A hallmark of the "old law," as Kathleen Cushing has noted, was that users and compilers looked beyond the texts and into the real-world contexts in which law fit. The structure of Burchard's *Decretum* (ca. 1012–ca. 1022) and its practical orientation toward administration contributed to its value.[4] A similar observation can be made of Ivo's *Decretum*. Gratian's *Decretum*, on the other hand, was harder to wade through to obtain the desired information. Each causa addressed multiple questions that may—or may not—be closely linked to the topic at hand.

Bartholomew compiled his penitential at Exeter between 1155 and 1170, quite possibly in the early 1160s, during his service as archdeacon or possibly in his early years serving as bishop.[5] It was a tremendously popular work. While not divided into books, Bartholomew divided his penitential into numbered chapters devoted to a particular subject. The first part of the work, chapters 1–40, is more theologically based, dealing with topics such as confession, penance, satisfaction, remission, and the nature of sin. The second part, beginning with chapter 41, is a list of sins and their associated penances. Each chapter includes the inscription to the original source followed by the text. Sometimes, the chapter contains multiple sources and texts. The original material sources selected derive from the Church Fathers, conciliar canons, papal decretals, and, on occasion, the Roman penitential and penitentials of Bede and Theodore. As with canonical collections like the *Decreta* of Burchard, Ivo of Chartres, and Gratian, Bartholomew referenced the material sources upon which he relied. The inclusion of the material source and the nature of the sources he used combine to give his penitential the feel of a canonical collection.

Bartholomew was renowned for his legal learning though his written and professional work, as Jason Taliadoros has noted, combined law and theology. He studied the arts and theology, quite possibly in Paris in the 1140s, but he was known for his knowledge of Roman law. He was considered a member of Archbishop Theobald of Canterbury's (1138–1161) *familia*, and he was a member of Thomas Becket's circle. He served as archdeacon of Exeter before becoming bishop of Exeter in 1161, a position which he held until his death in 1184. His most frequent area of activity was as a papal judge-delegate and he was employed as one more so than any other English bishop. One-fifth of the

4 K. Cushing, "Law and Reform: The Transmission of Burchard of Worms' *Liber decretorum*," in *New Discourses in Medieval Canon Law Research: Challenging the Master Narrative*, ed. C. Rolker (Leiden, 2019) 33–43, here 40, 43.

5 J. Taliadoros, "Bartholomew of Exeter's Penitential: Some Observations on his Personal Dicta," in *Proceedings Esztergom 2008*, eds. P. Erdő and S. A. Szuromi (Vatican City, 2010), 457–473, here 457–459.

decretals written by Pope Alexander III to English prelates and incorporated into the *Liber extra* (41 of 219) include Bartholomew among the addressees.[6] Bartholomew's activities as a papal judge-delegate centered on cases involving clerical conduct, ecclesiastical property, and marriage.[7] As bishop, he would have served as the judge-ordinary in the court of first instance for the diocese. Routine activities would have included administration and diocesan life: disputes between village persons and parishioners and between religious house and local landowners; the rights of patronage attached to a parish church; government and good behavior of his clergy; organization of the Cathedral Chapter, church, and its income.[8] Thus, as Taliadoros commented:

> Bartholomew applied his learning in the law to matters that were, strictly speaking, outside law. But despite this supra-legal application to theology, sacramental, or ecclesiological matters, the link to law was clear in that the overriding aim was to resolve conflict through pragmatic, practical, pastoral means by means of a discourse that crossed between these higher disciplines of law and theology.[9]

Robert of Flamborough compiled his *Liber penitentialis* between 1208 and 1213. He divided his penitential into books followed by numbered chapters applying moral rules to particular transgressions. It begins with general instructions (Bk. 1); and then addresses marriage (Bk. 2); simony (Bk. 3); sin according to the seven vices (Bk. 4); and ends with penitential texts found in the penitential of Bartholomew of Exeter, Burchard of Worm's *Decretum*, and the

6 Adrian Morey, ed., (*Bartholomew of Exeter, Bishop and Canonist: A Study in the Twelfth Century*((Cambridge: Cambridge University Press, 1937), 44–46.

7 Morey, ed., *Bartholomew of Exeter, Bishop and Canonist*, (54–72, 91–97. Bartholomew served as judge in cases involving: a clerk murdering the father of another clerk; a canon accusing a prior of being uncanonically elected; a priest accusing monks of trying to dispossess a church he held for 30 years; disputes between an abbey and the chapel of an abbey; the chaplain of king versus a clerk arguing about who possessed a church; disposing of worthless abbots; exemption of monastery from the bishop's advowsons, esp. the appropriation of churches by religious houses abbot versus bishop over rights of churches in lay hands; simony; rights of *matrix ecclesia* over chapels founded within parochial boundaries; subdeacons contracted marriage and lived like laymen not clerks; hereditary succession to benefices and married clergy; impediments and diriments to marriage. Bartholomew brought at least 16 cases (the number of cases preserved) before the pope because marriage law was still in flux. He brought cases involving the remarriage of a widow within one year of the husband's death; the legitimacy of children bore before parents married; procedure for marriage cases with prohibited degrees; and consummation versus consent.

8 Morey, ed., *Bartholomew of Exeter, Bishop and Canonist*, 79–81, 87.

9 Taliadoros, "Bartholomew of Exeter's Penitential," 471.

Decretum of Ivo of Chartres (Bk. 5).[10] Unlike the penitential of Bartholomew of Exeter, Robert's penitential tends not to include the material source. Akin to the penitential of Peter the Chanter, however, Robert would cross-reference a legal authority, such as Gratian's *Decretum* by distinction/causa-question and canon incipit or a decretal of Pope Alexander III, in support of the particular point being made.[11]

In a similar vein to Peter the Chanter, Bartholomew of Exeter and Robert of Flamborough sought to render relevant legal theory usable in their penitentials. As observed by Jason Taliadoros, Bartholomew's aim was pedagogic and pastoral. Rather than delving into the fine points of canonistic theory, he drew upon the law and rendered it in such a way as to provide a simple, accessible, and practical guide for ministering to parishioners.[12] A similar observation can be made of Robert of Flamborough. As Firth noted in his critical edition of the penitential, there was a need for a short, orderly, readable book if confessors were to learn how to proceed according to canon law. For Robert, in particular, this was of utmost importance. As an expert in penitential law and theology, he had received episcopal dispensatory powers from two successive bishops of Paris, Odo of Sully and Peter of Nemours.[13] He thus heard confessions of the diocesan clergy, adjudicated cases reserved for bishops from the local confessors, and supervised the imposition of public penances in the bishop's stead. Robert's duty as *penitentiarius* is particularly interesting as the task of caring for the souls of university students is not for the faint of heart.

As discussed in Chapter 2 of this work, Robert of Flamborough leaned on the penitential of Bartholomew of Exeter to compile his. With that noted, Robert did not slavishly follow Bartholomew. Bartholomew found both the *Decretum* of Ivo of Chartres and the *Decretum* of Gratian particularly useful.[14] Robert continued to regard the *Decreta* of Burchard of Worms and Ivo of

10 Flamborough, *Liber Poenitentialis*, 11, 16–17; Baldwin, *Masters, Princes, and Merchants*, 1:32–34. Rev. Bloomfield maintained that Robert's penitential concentrated on casuistry, which is a fair point. However, he also maintained that this was "typical of manuals written by the canonists and shows their authors' legal bias and predominance of the aspects of trial and punishment" (*Thomae de Chobham Summa Confessorum*, xviii). Despite his knowledge of the law, Robert is best known as a theologian, not a canonist.

11 Robert, for example, referenced Gratian's *Decretum* as "Causa xxii quaest. v. c. Parvuli" = GD C.22 q.5 c.14 (Flamborough 2.2 §52, p. 86), "i. quaest. i. Si qui confugerint" = GD C.1 q.1 c.52 (Flamborough 3.2 §81, p. 105), and "…ut Dist. xxv c.1" (Flamborough 3.3 §107, p. 122, though he notes a possible error for GD D.24 c.7). He referenced Pope Alexander III, as "Unde, si vult, cum homicida dispensare potest papa, sicut fecit Alexander tertius; …" (Flamborough 3.3 §100, p. 117).

12 Taliadoros, "Bartholomew of Exeter's Penitential," 460, 468–469, 471.

13 Flamborough 3.3 §108, p. 122: "Ego autem ad istud vitandum inconveniens a duobus parisiensibus episcopis Odone et Petro habui ut ubique eorum auctoritate dispensarem, ubi et ipsi dispensarent." See A. Larson, "Killing a Career: Homicide and the Development of Medieval Clerical Discipline," *The Jurist* 74 (2014): 265–288, here 285.

14 Ivo of Chartres's *Decretum* and Gratian's *Decretum* proved useful for canons on penance for the sick, marriage, incest and fornications, drunkenness, lying and perjury, excommunication, magic, the goods of the church and ecclesiastical property, clerical obedience, baptism, ordination of clerics, and the Eucharist. The chapters on schism and simony were most likely drawn exclusively from Gratian's *Decretum*.

Chartres as useful complements to more recent material. While he drew some, but not all, of his texts from Bartholomew, Robert also turned to the collections themselves and selected texts that best suited his purpose.[15]

While Robert relied on Bartholomew's penitential for material, each ordered the topics to tailor their penitential to their particular working environment. With their audience in mind—students at the University of Paris for Robert and diocesan life for Bartholomew—each emphasized topics in a manner conducive to their administrative work. Table 6.1 compares homicide related topics addressed by Robert of Flamborough in Book 5 of his penitential against those treated by Bartholomew of Exeter in his penitential (murder in chapters 41–57 and manslaughter in chapters 58–60).

Two observations stand out. First, both cover similar, but not identical, topics. Second, the order of the topics is not the same in each penitential. The two are entwined. Robert emphasized topics in such a way as would be conducive to the pastoral care of university students and the environment that the university occupied. Suicide; murder of or by clerics; and infanticide, abortion, and contraception are covered at length early in the discussion. Robert also included unique topics: committing murder with poison (5.2.14), the killing of someone by the accusation/denunciation of another (5.2.15), and leading away a freed Christian only to resell them into slavery (5.2.17). Bartholomew's treatment of homicide has more of a lay focus at heart. He begins voluntary homicide and, after briefly touching on the murder of clerics and murder committed by clerics, he spends time focusing on the murder of family members and spouses. Bartholomew would end his section on homicide by noting that not all who kill men are guilty of homicide (c.60), a subject Robert passed over.

An analysis of suicide, the violence against and by clergy, and the murder of spouses and the intention behind a homicide—issues with a particular lay focus—suggest that Robert of Flamborough and Bartholomew of Exter had *whose* souls they were tasked with caring for at the forefront of their minds when organizing and delving into the topics. Robert may have dealt with suicide at the outset because, as *penitentiarius*, he knew students were a vulnerable population both subject to the stresses of university life and prone to conflicts with city residents that could end poorly. With that also in mind, it is no

15 The penitential canons in Book 5—borrowed from the penitential of Bartholomew of Exeter, Burchard of Worm's *Decretum*, and the *Decretum* of Ivo of Chartres—deal with homicide, fornication, perjury and lying, those who cause damage, magic, and drunkenness and gluttony. Gratian's *Decretum* proved useful for oaths and perjury, whether confession in the heart alone can remit sins, whether the conjugal debt can be rendered during times of prayer, simony, clerical crimes, ecclesiastical property, and whether an abbot could retain the possessions of a monk who left without permission. Canonistic commentary, such as Huguccio's *Summa decretorum*, was useful for matrimonial law and the impediments to valid marriage, ecclesiastical ordination and addressing excommunication as an impediment to entering an order and executing one's office, and simony. *Compilatio Prima* provided decretals on ecclesiastical ordination and simony.

TABLE 6.1 Homicide related topics as treated in the penitentials of Robert of Flamborough and Bartholomew of Exeter

Robert of Flamborough	*5.2*	*Bartholomew of Exeter*	*cap. 41–60*
he who kills himself (suicide)	1	voluntary homicide	41–45
killers of priests [244–249; clerics committing homicides 250–251]	2	killers of priests	46
parricide (killing near relatives) [252; 253–257: matricide, patricide, and fratricide also included]	3	clerics committing homicides	47
crushing an infant	4	parricide (killing near relatives)[a]	48
dishonoring father and mother	5	kills his mother	49
women who fornicate / prostitute and kill their offspring (abortion)	6	husband kills wife or wife kills husband	50
impeding of conception (using contraception)	7	he who kills himself (suicide)	51
voluntary homicide	8	killing someone a penitent in public	52
husband kills wife or wife kills husband	9	those of your council who commit murder	53
killing someone who is a penitent in public	10	homicide committed in war	54
homicide committed out of vengeance	11	a female lord (*domina*) killed her slave girl in anger	55
involuntary homicide	12	undertaking an abortion	56
commits homicide by instruction of the lord	13	homicide committed out of vengeance	57
commits a murder by poisoning (*veneficio*)	14	involuntary homicide[b]	58
someone killed by the accusation/ denunciation (*delatio*) of another	15	crushing an infant	59
homicide committed in war	16	not all who kill men are guilty of homicide	60
lead away a freed (*mancipium*) Christian and then resell them	17		
a female lord (*domina*) killed her slave girl in anger	18		

a This chapter, which is but a few lines describing patricide as the killing of family members, is, in fact, one of Bartholomew's *dictum*. See Taliadoros, "Bartholomew of Exeter's Penitential," Appendix, p. 473.

b Bartholomew includes a *dictum* (ll. 14–19) noting that those who exercised all due diligence are not guilty of murder. See Taliadoros, "Bartholomew of Exeter's Penitential," Appendix, p. 473.

surprise that he would delve deeply into the murder of and by clerics. Yet, he tilted in a direction slightly different from Bartholomew, who also dealt with the subject early in his section. Robert was more amenable to allowing clerics to return to their rank after serving penance for violence, whereas Bartholomew tilted in the direction of the cleric remaining degraded. Whereas Robert seemed most concerned with clerics and their environment, Bartholomew addressed with force issues of particular concern for the laity, such as the murder of spouses and the intention behind a homicide. Here he had delved into more detail than Robert, particularly as it pertained to adultery and secular justice. He also considered the intention behind homicide, realizing the nuances of human emotion and their role in interpersonal conflict.

Self-Murder (Suicide)

Robert began his section on homicide with the topic of self-murder. An interesting choice, to be sure, but one that fits under the umbrella of homicide. First, the deliberate and willful act of killing oneself carried with it the stigma of "murder."[16] Second, as Alan Murray noted, "the result from suicide and from murder look very much the same."[17] Yet, texts addressing suicide, the voluntary killing of oneself, were not abundant. The subject does not seem to leave a trail in decretal law; neither the *Compilationes antiquae* nor *Liber extra* includes any references to it. Ecclesiastical legal collections—especially those compiled in northern France prior to 1140 in addition to Gratian's *Decretum*[18]—and twelfth-century penitentials drew from the same small handful of early medieval texts, namely from the works of Augustine, and from canons issued at the First Council of Braga (561) and at the Council of Auxerre (ca. 561–ca. 605). Chapters 17, 20, 21, and 26 from Book 1 of Augustine's *On the City of God* were condensed into a lengthy canon expounding on the heinous and illicit nature of the act.[19] Chapter 49 from Book 2 of Augustine's letter against Petilianus reinforces the concept that those who hang themselves—commit suicide—are not to be revered as martyrs.[20] Canon 16 from the First Council of Braga decreed

16 A. Bähr, "Between 'Self-Murder' and 'Suicide': The Modern Etymology of Self-Killing," *Journal of Social History* 46, no. 3 (2013): 620–632, here 622.

17 Alexander Murray, *Suicide in the Middle Ages, Vol. 1: The Violent Against Themselves* (Oxford, 1998), 120.

18 GD C.23 q.5 d.p.c.8–c.12. All texts pertaining to suicide were added in the second recension. At first blush, suicide may not seem to fit with the question which asks whether it is a sin for a judge or his official to put guilty defendants to death. The other additions to the second recension focus on the secular realm's role in correction. Suicide falls into place when one considers that those condemned to death might commit suicide to avoid punishment.

19 GD C.23 q.5 c.9; ID 10.4; Ivo of Chartres, *Tripartita*, 3.20.2; Pan. 8.2; *Collectio canonum* in Paris Arsenal MS 713, 1353a; Cdp 9.2.1. The *Clavis canonum* database is indispensable for visualizing the transmission of a particular text in pre-Gratian collections.

20 GD C.23 q.5 c.10; ID 2.99g, 10.7; Ivo of Chartres, *Tripartita*, 3.2.14h and 3.20.3; *Collectio canonum* in Paris Arsenal MS 713, 1356; *Collectio Catalaunensis I*, 2.10e.

that those who inflict death upon themselves voluntarily either by way of a sword, or by way of poison, or by way of a fall or by way of hanging, or by any other means should have no commemoration in the form of prayers, and the corpses should not be led to their burial with psalms. Such provisions could also apply to those executed for their crimes. The canon seems to be countering the practice in which people were wrongfully performing these ceremonies through ignorance.[21] Finally, canon 17 from the Council of Auxerre forbade offerings and prayers for those who voluntarily took their own life.[22]

These texts, therefore, were well known in northern France. Robert included c.16 of the First Council of Braga which was included by both Bartholomew and Gratian.[23] Robert, however, would include additional texts not found in the penitential of Bartholomew. Found in Ivo's *Decretum* (10.5, 10.6, and 10.7), the additional texts emphasized that those who kill themselves in whatever manner—such as by drowning or by hanging from a noose akin to a traitor—were not revered as martyrs. They warrant neither a mass, the singing of the psalms, prayers, nor alms given in their name.[24] They stem from the false capitularies of Benedictus Levita (2.70),[25] the Council of Auxerre (c.17), and Augustine's letter against Petilianus, respectively.

21 A. Murray, *Suicide in the Middle Ages, Vol. 2: The Curse of Self Murder* (Oxford, 2000), 183, for an analysis of the transmission of the text, see pp. 271–274 where he notes that at some point *voluntarie* (of their own free will) was added to the original canon. This text had a wide circulation, being included in GD C.23 q.5 c.12 along with 19 other pre-1140 collections. Of those 19 collections, 7 were compiled in northern France: *Collectio Atrebatensis*, 290; *Collectio Sancte Genoveve*, 4.3.122; ID 15.140; *Liber canonum diversorum sanctorum patrum (Collecto Sancte Marie Novelle)*, 92.15; *Quadripartus*, 4.97; *Collectio IX voluminorum Sangermanensisis*, 7.51; Cdp 1.54.5.

22 Murray, *Suicide in the Middle Ages*, 2.184. Twelve collections contain the canon, but only two collections include it with the correct inscription: ID 10.6 and Paris Arsenal MS 713, 1355. Interestingly, seven collections attribute the canon to a council held at Châlons-sur-Marne (c.5): Burchard of Worms, *Decretum*, 19.131; the second version of the *Collectio Caesaraugustana*, 252; *Collectio Sancte Genoveve*, 4.3.123; ID 15.141; the original version of *Collectio XII partium*, 9.72; augmented version of the *Collectio XII partium*, 7.65; the latter part of the *Collectio II librorum/VIII partium*, 8.1.24.

23 Flamborough 5.2.1: "Placuit ut his – 'impoenitentes' subaudiatur." Firth notes that the text as it appears in Robert's penitential appears only in Bartholomew c.51 and GD C.23. q.5 c.12, see ed. Firth, 211 n. 51.

24 Flamborough 5.2.1 §243 "De eo qui – sibi collum ligauerunt."

25 Murray, *Suicide in the Middle Ages*, 2.261–262:

> De eo qui semetipsum occidit, aut laqueo se suspendit, consideratum est ut, si quis compatiens velit elemosinam dare, tribuat, et orationes in psalmodiis faciat, oblationibus tamen et missis careant. [Concerning the man who kills himself or hangs himself with a noose. It is considered [proper] that if anyone, from compassion, wishes to give alms, let him do so and make prayer in psalmody. But let there be no oblations or Masses for these people; for the judgements of God are incomprehensible and none can enquire into the depth of his counsel].

Gratian did not include this particular text, and it is found in only 2 pre-1140 collections: ID 10.5 and *Collectio canonum* in Paris Arsenal MS 713, 1354.

Even though Robert drew upon Bartholomew's penitential as a key source, why might he have dealt with suicide at the very beginning of his section on homicide when Bartholomew did not address it until midway through his section on the same subject? Why would he have included additional legal texts? After all, Hammer's examination of crime in Oxford in the 1340s suggested to him that suicide rates were "without [a] doubt low,"[26] and Schmitt's study of 54 cases of suicide in medieval Paris found that of the 31 victims for whom professions were listed, six (19%) were men of the Church.[27] Yet, William Courtenay observed that while the number of deaths—he pointed to accidents, illness, and violence—among students would have been comparably small to the overall population of the city, that number would still have been significant enough to have an impact.[28] While not an overwhelming percentage, suicide was not something that Robert could take for granted and ignore.

Thus, the answer to both questions may lie in the environment in which he worked. First, he, as *penitentiarius*, heard the students' confessions. Students are a vulnerable population subject to the stresses of university life, and there is no reason to think that this was not the case in the Middle Ages as well. Those stresses can lead to isolation and broken social ties with one's community, whoever was considered to be a part of that community. Those feelings could lead to suicide.[29] Second, conflicts between town and gown occurred as students and residents of the city designated as the center of the Capetian dynasty's administrative activity. While Hammer maintains that *clerici* (scholars) of Oxford participated in less than one-third of the assaults and comprised no more than one-quarter of the assailants, he did point to the lawlessness of town and disorder. Tavern brawls, sharp tongues, quick tempers, and weapons (esp. knives) led to problems.[30] Students might know of someone who died from a beating, knife wounds, or illness.[31] In Paris, this was without question the case. A scuffle erupted in 1200 involving an innkeeper and the servant of Henri de Jauche, a German who was a master at the university and in contention for the episcopal see at Liège, over the purchasing of wine. As the English chronicler Roger Howden (fl. 1174–1201) recounted, the servant was clubbed, and Henri de Jauche and his household sought to avenge the beating. Tasked with quelling upheaval and maintaining order, the prévôt (provost) of Paris, Thomas, accompanied by armed citizens of Paris, descended on the

26 C. I. Hammer, "Patterns of Homicide in Medieval University Town: Fourteenth-Century Oxford," *Past & Present* 78 (1978): 3–23, here 10.

27 J.-C. Schmitt, "Le suicide au Moyen Âge," *Annales ESC: Économies, sociétés, civilisations* 31, no. 1 (1976): 1–28, here 6.

28 W. J. Courtenay, *Rituals for the Dead: Religion and Community in the Medieval University of Paris* (Notre Dame, 2019), 8.

29 Schmitt, "Le suicide au Moyen Âge," 18.

30 Hammer, "Patterns of Homicide in Medieval University Town," 16, 20.

31 Courtenay, *Rituals for the Dead*, 7.

residence of Henri and his household which resulted in their death.[32] The king ordered that Thomas serve a sentence of life in prison, in close confinement with meager fare, unless he wished to undergo a trial by water. Should he be vindicated, he would be released but never to serve as provost again anywhere. The remaining perpetrators were to suffer the same fate—life in prison with the ability to be vindicated by trial by water. Those who fled punishment were condemned and to be hunted down and returned to Paris.[33]

A second example illustrating the environment in which a *penitentiarius* worked occurred at the end of February 1229. On the eve of Ash Wednesday and the start of Lent in the quarter of Saint Marcel, a bar fight would result in the Great Dispersion whereby teaching was essentially halted from 1229 until 1231 as the masters and students of the university left Paris. Students had been drinking heavily when a disagreement about the price of wine ensued with the tavern owner, resulting in a physical altercation. The students were beaten and thrown into the streets. The next day, seeking revenge, the students returned in larger numbers armed with wooden clubs, broke into the tavern, beat the offenders, and destroyed the establishment. Other shops were damaged in a subsequent riot which spilled into the streets. The tavern owner sought redress from the papal legate, Romano Frangipani, and the bishop of Paris, William of Auvergne. William deferred the matter to Queen Blanche of Castile, who was serving as regent during Louis IX's minority, despite the clerical status of the students and their privilege which exempted them from secular justice. Blanche had no tolerance for student violence and demanded retribution. Secular authorities were charged with punishing the students involved, and they did punish students, even killing several of them, yet it was uncertain that those killed were, in fact, involved in the original incident.[34]

The high justice administered as a result of such conflicts between town and gown could lead to a point where suicide was considered as an alternative to punishment. Overlapping authorities possessed the right of high justice in Paris, a right that normally entailed having some form of prison where punishment could be served or those condemned could be held prior to their execution. Alexander Murray noted a small group of approximately six monasteries around Paris that possessed seigneurial jurisdiction, which included high justice, exercised by the abbey's *officialis*. An *officialis* heard all ordinary criminal or ecclesiastical prosecutions against scholars. He may also hear civil cases in

32 P. Bermon, trans., *La foundation de l'Université de Paris (1200–1260)* (Paris, 2019), 63–64 with commentary on p. 58.

33 Bermon, *La foundation de l'Université de Paris (1200–1260)* (Paris, 2019), 53–54 with commentary on pp. 57–58.

34 Bermon, *La foundation de l'Université de Paris*, 147–153 with commentary on pp. 153–162. Of the different chronicles that recorded the event, that of Matthew of Paris is the most detailed. See also N. Gorochov, *Naissance de l'université: Les écoles de Paris d'Innocent III à Thomas d'Aquin (v. 1200–v. 1245)* (Paris, 2016), 397–414.

which a scholar was the defendant or plaintiff. As the twelfth century progressed, appeals to the crown increased courtesy of the growing power of the Capetian dynasty, the Church's long-standing relationship with the monarchy, and the revival of Roman law.[35] These trends led to the prévôt of Paris and his court, the châtelet (Conservator of the Royal Privileges of the University), as the main rival to the monasteries' jurisdiction. The prévôt tried civil actions in which a member of the university was involved, such as those cases involving real property, and the prisons in Paris fell under prévôt's oversight.[36] Should a student who normally fell under ecclesiastical jurisdiction become mixed up in jurisdiction disputes, suicide to avoid incarceration or punishment may have become a factor.

Be it the stress of university life or the result of a sentence, suicide was tied to connections between the emotions of *ira* (anger), *desperatio* (desperation), *tristitia* (sadness), and *acedia*. *Acedia* was a sense of weariness of the soul, a sense of worthlessness, and a general weariness of life that springs from deep sadness (*tristitia*) and leads to despair (*desperatio*). *Acedia* was powerfully associated with suicidal impulses in the medieval world.[37] For example, canon 4 of the Sixteenth Council of Toledo (693), *De desperantibus*, focused on the attempted suicide of those condemned to punishment—be it execution or incarceration—and pointed to a contagion of despair that the priest needed to root out.[38] In his commentary on the First Council of Braga in Raymond of Peñforte's *Summa penitentialis*, John of Freiburg (ca. 1300) would note that for a suicide to be guilty one must arise from "despair, indignation or anger [*desperatio, indignatio vel iracundia*] as distinct from frenzy or mischance [*secus si ex furore vel a casu*]."[39] Robert, as *penitentiarius*, along with all confessors, had to be alert to these emotions in the confessional where the "depths of the soul was probed."[40] They had to ferret out these emotions, emotions of particular concern for a university population, to prevent suicide. Should they not be successful, and a self-murder was committed, the implications were clear.

Bartholomew, as archdeacon and then bishop of Exeter, was not in the same position as Robert of Flamborough who was hearing confessions of students. As such, he may not have seen suicide with the same level of threat.

35 Murray, *Suicide in the Middle Ages*, 1.140, 142. Murray did not list the monasteries, and notes for his discussion of seigneurial justice were lacking.

36 Murray, *Suicide in the Middle Ages*, 1.185–186; H. Rashdall, *The Universities of Europe in the Middle Ages*, new edn. in 3 vols, eds. F. M. Powicke and A. B. Emden (Oxford, 1936), 1.411–412.

37 J. Feros Ruys, "'He who kills himself liberates a wretch': Abelard on Suicide," in *Rethinking Abelard: A Collection of Critical Essays*, ed. B. S. Hellemans (Leiden, 2014), 230–249, here 238–239.

38 Mansi 12:71–72; Murray, *Suicide in the Middle Ages*, 2.185. For whatever reason, this text does not seem to have circulated in the canonical tradition. A search of the *Clavis canonum* database does not list any pre-1140 collection that included the canon.

39 Murray, *Suicide in the Middle Ages*, 2.274.

40 Schmitt, "Le suicide au Moyen Âge," 16.

As Sara Butler has shown, suicide was very much a regional phenomenon in England, with some regions showing greater concern than others. The corner rolls from the fourteenth-century county of Devon, which is where Exeter is located, record fourteen suicides. By contrast, the county of York records 135 suicides, the county of Lincoln and Northamptonshire 43 suicides each, and the county of Nottingham 36. The county of Sussex records six; Surrey, Hereford, Buckingham, and Worchester four suicides each; and Berkshire records nine suicides.[41] Furthermore, bishops in England typically did not deal with suicide. Questions of burial fell to the parish priest. Coroners and justices in eyre rendered verdicts of suicide as they opened the door for the English crown to augment its treasury through confiscation. Bishops might become entangled in such verdicts only when there was a discrepancy of jurisdiction over clerical suicides and their inheritance.[42] Bartholomew's encounters with suicide, and those of his parish priests, would be very different from Robert's in Paris. The topic needed addressing, but not at the outset of his section on homicide, and it certainly did not warrant stressing with additional texts.

Violence Against and By Clergy

As violence between the Parisian bourgeoise and university students resulted in the death of clerics, it is no surprise that this was the second topic Robert addressed in his section on homicide. Private violence, that is, illegitimate violence, toward clerics had been addressed by Pope Innocent II at the Second Lateran Council (1139), thus establishing a *privilegium canonis*. Canon 15 decreed that anyone who laid violent hands on clergy or monks was automatically excommunicated and had to appear in person before the papal curia to receive absolution.[43] While Robert seems to have drawn upon Bartholomew for almost half of the texts on the subject, he turned to Burchard of Worms or Ivo of Chartres to provide individual texts particular to his penitential that elaborated on the penalties for willfully killing a *sacerdos*, a cleric in a major order. He who has done so may neither eat meat nor drink wine for the remainder of his days. He shall fast until evening, with the exception of feast days and Sundays. He may neither take up arms nor ride a horse. He may not enter a

41 S. Butler, "Degrees of Culpability: Suicide Verdicts Mercy and Jury in Medieval England," *Journal of Medieval and Early Modern Studies* 36, no. 2 (2006): 263–290, here 267 and Table 1 on p. 268. See also S. Butler, "Cultures of Suicide?: Suicide Verdicts and the 'Community' in Thirteenth- and Fourteenth-Century England," *The Historian* 69, no. 3 (2007): 427–449.

42 Murray, *Suicide in the Middle Ages*, 1.132–134, 138.

43 On private violence, see G. Halsall, "Violence and Society in the Early Medieval West: An Introductory Survey," in *Violence and Society in the Early Medieval West*, ed. G. Halsall (Woodbridge, 1998), 1-45, here 7-16. On c.15 of the Second Lateran Council, see R. H. Helmholz, "'Si quis suadente' (C.17 q.4 c.29): Theory and Practice," in *Proceedings Cambridge 1984*, ed. Peter Linehan (Vatican City, 1988), 425–438.

church for five years but only stand before the doors. After five years, he may enter the church but may not stand among those who take communions, but must stand with those only hearing the mass. After 12 years have passed and so long as he has amounted to his sins, others may communicate with him.[44] One of the most substantial additions, quite possibly taken from Burchard's *Decretum* (6.5) but originating with the Council of Thoinville (ca. 813),[45] set for the specific number of rounds of 40-day penance needing to be served and the price to be paid to the bishop (the *episcopalis bannus*) according to the rank of the cleric, that is, whether he is a subdeacon, deacon, priest, or bishop. For each rank, the associated penance and price were set forth depending upon whether he recovered from the physical injury or whether he died.[46]

Despite the subheading that puts the onus on the one who causes physical harm or injury to the cleric, the subheading also addresses clerics who commit murder. As the jurisdiction of cases and the associated punishments that could be meted out became muddled, Robert sought to ensure that ecclesiastical jurisdiction remained in its lane. He drew upon Bartholomew for a handful of texts prohibiting clerics from being involved in high justice. Canon 31 of the Fourth Council of Toledo (633) decreed that princes oftentimes princes entrust their business pertaining to high treason to priests. However, because priests have been elected by Christ to the administration of well-being, an oath should be sworn, exempting them from trials involving high justice should they serve as a king's judge. Should a cleric serve as a judge in such unsuitable trials against this prohibition, he is guilty before Christ of spilling blood, and before the Church, he may lose his particular rank.[47] That is, clerics could neither be involved in trials where bloodshed was a possible outcome nor participate in executions. Misattributed to a council held at Mainz, the canon decreed that it is not proper for those who handle the sacraments of the Lord to be involved in a trial where the judgment passed could be blows, which could lead to death or mutilation. Should anyone in the service of the Church be negligent of these precepts, he is to be stripped of his honor and rank and be held in the perpetual prison of damnation. He could, however, receive communion on his death-bed.[48] These same concepts are also reflected in Book 3 of Robert's penitential which addresses impediments to the order and execution of the order. Robert identified as voluntary homicide: the offering one's council, aid, support, or

44 Flamborough 5.2.2 §250 "Qui sacerdotem voluntarie–purificari mereatur," p. 216.

45 MGH LL 2, Table 2 spurious capitula on pp. 5–6.

46 Flamborough 5.2.2 §248, pp. 214–215.

47 Flamborough 5.2.2 §250 "Saepe princeps contra – perdat gradum," p. 216; Bartholomew c.47, pp. 214–215 ll. 33ff.

48 Flamborough 5.2.2 §247, p. 214; Bartholomew c.47, p. 214 ll. 17–32; XI Council of Toledo (675), c.6.

serving as an advocate or witnesses in cases resulting in death, mutilation, or trials or blood; as well as those who carry weapons and kill another. Such cases negated the ability to execute one's office without papal dispensation.[49]

The legal texts that Robert includes that are particular to his collection stress the importance of punishing the cleric according to his rank. A bishop should be punished more than a priest, a priest more than a deacon, and a deacon more than a subdeacon.[50] In cases where the cleric, such as a priest, has been suspected of murdering another cleric, such as a deacon, a panel of co-bishops and brothers from neighboring areas are to convene and ascertain his culpability. Should it be found that the priest's blow did not cause death but another factor, such as falling from a horse, had done so, the panel was to issue the appropriate penance, and the priest should be suspended from his office until he has served his penance. At that point, with satisfaction made, he may return to his duties. Should the panel find that the priest's blows were fatal, he was condemned because, although he did not intend to kill, his violent motions stemmed from anger and indignation, and resulted in death. But if the panel's inquiry finds that the cleric sought to harm him, his benefice was conceded to the deacon's church so that he and his were able to have sufficient substance for comfort.[51] Though not explicitly stated, the presumption is that injury inflicted with intent resulted in the loss of benefice. Whether or not he was degraded or simply demoted was left unaddressed.

While Robert emphasizes violence done to clerics and slips in violence perpetrated by clerics, Bartholomew directly confronts clerics who commit murder as a distinct theme. He, followed by Robert, included Pope Alexander II's decretal outlining what penance should be served and the number of years it should be served for a cleric who murdered another.[52] Yet, Bartholomew also includes texts—possibly taken from Ivo of Chartres's *Decretum*—that Robert chose to omit, texts which largely call for the cleric to be removed from office. He includes the beginning portion c.11 from the Council of Tribur (895), which stated that deposed a priest or deacon for committing murder even if compelled to do so.[53] Bartholomew omits the remainder of the canon, found in Ivo's *Decretum* (10.174), which includes a justification for this punishment grounded in the Scriptures, along with the qualification that if a cleric was present but neither consented nor was consulted he may remain in his office. If he is among the lower order, he may progress into the major orders if he should be worthy.[54]

49 Flamborough 3.3 §103, §105–§106, pp. 119–121.
50 Flamborough 5.2.2 §249, p. 216.
51 Flamborough 5.2.2 §251, p. 217. The decree of Pope Nicholas I is also found in ID 10.24.
52 Bartholomew c.47, pp. 213–214 ll. 29ff; Flamborough 5.2.2 §246, pp. 213–214; JL 4572.
53 Bartholomew c.47, p. 213 ll. 14–16.
54 ID 10.174. See Larson, "Killing a Career," 273–274.

Canon 45 of the Fourth Council of Toledo (633) decreed that clerics who willingly took up arms against someone and have been discovered doing so are dismissed from their position and handed over to a monastery.[55] Pope John VII's letter to the bishop of Venice stated that no one was permitted to minister as a priest after committing a murder. The priesthood having been denied ought to wash the shame of tears as a vast spring so that, having been cured to health, he is able to find judgment from such remedies.[56] Pope Gregory I barred a priest from the administration of his office for two months for having beaten a woman with a club who later died.[57] Bartholomew felt more inclined to take a direct stance regarding clerical homicide whereas Robert was content to weave the subject into his first concern, which was violence committed against clerics.

Clerical homicide occurred, but where did the law stand on criminous clerics? Could they return to office? Conciliar canons of the twelfth and thirteenth centuries continued to suggest that one of the most common failings of the clergy was that they frequented taverns and engaged in playing with dice and gambling. Compounding matters was that clergy went about armed with daggers, swords, spears as well as weapons of other kinds, and they did not hesitate to use them.[58] As we saw with the students of the University of Paris, an evening drinking at a tavern could lead to murder. Distinction 50 of Gratian's *Decretum* argued that those in the major orders who committed capital crimes, gave false testimony, or made a false claim were to be deposed of their honor and put into a monastery where they receive communion as a layman.[59] In such cases, clerics were degraded and prohibited from advancing.[60] Yet, a qualification was made to take intent into consideration and whether the cleric intended to kill the individual. Pope Nicholas I allowed clerics who killed a pagan defending themselves to return to their rank and progress to another after penance was served. Though he did point out that under normal circumstances, it

55 Bartholomew c.47, p. 213 ll. 16–18. This canon also appears in GD C.23 q.8 as c.5. The context of the discussion taken up in GD C.23 q.8 c.1–c.6 is within the context of war. This string of canons, which included that from the council of Toledo, also included by Bartholomew, curtailed the ability of the feudal-bishop to serve in a secular capacity in favor of his spiritual functions.

56 Bartholomew c.47, p. 213 ll. 20–29.

57 Bartholomew c.47, p. 215 ll. 5–10.

58 R. W. Collins, "The Parish Priest and His Flock as Depicted by the Councils of the Twelfth and Thirteenth Centuries," *Journal of Religion* 10, no. 3 (1930), 313–332, here 313–319.

59 GD D.50 c.7: "Si episcopus. Presbiter aut diaconus capitale crimen commiserit; aut cartam falsauerit; aut falsum testimonium dixerit; ab honoris offitii depositus; in monasterio detrudatur. Et ibi quamdiu vixerit; laicam tantum communionem accipiat."

60 GD D.50 d.a.c.1: "Et utique variis criminibus detentos a propriis ordinibus deiciuntur multorum auctoritatibus probatur, necnon a maiorum progressu arceri."

was in no way lawful to kill a man.[61] In another example, a cleric who committed murder when besieged with no hope of escape could be purged by a two-year penance of vigils, prayer, and alms, after which point he could return to his office and communion.[62] In neither case was the cleric's intention to commit murder, but rather he had to do so out of necessity. A series of examples were offered—Maria being cured of her leprosy, Peter denying Christ and yet remaining an apostle, and those reunited to faith falling into heresy and eventually becoming bishops—to show that it was possible to return to one's rank after penance.[63] If a cleric committed murder by accident (*casu*), he was permitted to retain his office after being granted a dispensation.[64] Those who fell were admonished and, after having accepted that admonishment, had the possibility to stand up again.

As suggested in Chapter 5 of this book, the key issue for Gratian was whether the cleric came to penance, was forced to penance, or performed penance for self-serving reasons. If he came to penance, he could be restored. If he was forced to

61 GD D.50 c.6:

> De his clericis pro quibus consuluistis, scilicet qui se defendendo paganum occiderunt. Si postea penitentiam emendati; possint ad pristinum gradum redire, aut ad altiorem scandere. Scitote nos nullam occasionem dare; nec ullam eis tribuere licentiam quemlibet hominum quomodolibet occidendi. Verum si contigerit; ut clericus sacerdotalis ordinis saltim paganum occiderit; multum sibi consulit; si ab offitio sacerdotali recesserit. Satiusque illi est; in hac vita sub inferiori habitu inreprehensibiliter famulari, quam alta indebite appetendo; dampnabiliter in profundum dimergi.

62 GD D.50 c.36:

> … Quod si in hoc inciderint, tam offitio quam communione priventur duobus annis ita ut duobus annis vigiliis, ieiuniis, orationibus et elymosinis pro viribus, quas Dominus donaverit, expientur; et ita demum offitio vel communioni reddantur. ea tamen ratione, ne ulterius ad offitia potiora promoveantur.

63 GD D.50 d.p.c.12:

> Econtra post per actam penitentiam; et exemplis et auctoritatibus admittendi probatur, et ad maiores promovendi. Maria soror aaron postquam lepra percussa est, quia in moysen murmurauerat; acta penitentia mundata est; et pristinam gratiam prophetandi receipt; aaron post vitulum conflatum in summum sacerdotem est consecratus; david post adulterium et homicidium spiritum prophetię recepit; …et ut multa ueterorum exempla pretereamus; petrus christum negavit. et factus est tamen apostolorum princeps. Paulus stephanum lapidavit. et tamen a deo in apostolum electus est.

64 GD D.50 d.p.c.36: "Casu quoque si homicidium clericus fecerit, in proprio gradu ex dispensatione permittitur." See also Larson, "Killing a Career," 227.

penance or performed it for self-serving reasons, then he could not be restored.[65] In other words, those called to, that is, ordered to do, penance for any crime could not be accepted into or remain among the clergy. Likewise, if one was moved to penance in the spirit of pride after the crime was found out, he was not to be admitted to the clergy after penance. Those who offered false penance out of fear of poverty (i.e., losing their benefice) or ambition were not to be restored to their former grade because they did not perform their penance out of disgust of the crime. However, those who *offered* penance to God for crimes were able to return to their rank. It was a question of the motive driving the penance. While one could return to his rank if he performed solemn penance, which should only be performed once, then he could not advance to or within the major orders.[66] Gratian thus concluded that those who had lapsed were able to be restored to their orders after penance. Yet, it was entirely prohibited for them to advance higher.[67]

On the cusp of the thirteenth century, decretal law took a tone that, at first blush, seemed to echo that set forth in the *Decretum*: with penance served, a cleric could return to his duties but could not advance. Pope Honorius III decreed that if a cleric fighting against the enemies of the Catholic faith happens to strike a fatal blow and his conscience nags him for having killed the man, he ought to abstain from ministering at the altar.[68] Presumably, he could return to his ministry once penance had washed away his guilt. Pope Alexander III stated that a deacon having caused the death of another was not to move forward into the priesthood.[69] A common thread between the *Decretum* and decretal tradition was that clerics guilty of murder were not able to advance in the ecclesiastical ranks.

Yet, examples point to a developing jurisprudence that took into consideration willful intent, accident, and poor judgment, particularly as the papacy became the final arbiter. For example, in the case of the cleric whose stubborn horse burst into a run and inadvertently killed a woman who was crossing his path, Pope Innocent III decreed that he should serve penance as a precaution and minister in the minor orders but he remained eligible for promotion into the major orders.[70] Papal rescripts show that clerics were being reinstated after

65 GD D.50 d.p.c.24:

> Qualiter igitur haec auctoritatum dissonantia concordiam ualeat; videamus. Sunt non nulli quos non odium criminis. set timor vilitatis. amissio proprii gradus, et ambitio celsioris ad penitentiam cogit. hos sacri canones irrecuperabiliter deiciunt, quia qui simulatione penitentię autem honoris affectione adeo non consequitur veniam; nec ab ęcclesia reparationem meretur.

66 GD D.50 d.p.c.53, d.p.c.61–c.63, d.p.c.64–c.66.

67 GD D.50 d.p.c.51: "Premissis auctoritatibus, lapsis permittitur, ut post penitenciam in suis ordinibus reparari valeant; ad maiorem autem conscendere post lapsum nulla eis auctoritate permittitur, immo penitus prohbetur."

68 V Comp. 5.6.4 (X 5.12.24).

69 I Comp. 5.10.10 and I Comp. 5.10.7 (X 5.12.11).

70 III Comp. 5.7.4 (X 5.12.16). See also Larson, "Killing a Career," 284–285.

their penance, but they were being downgraded as well. Pope Alexander III responded to the Archbishop of Cosenz's quandary of deciding a case involving a deacon and accidental homicide. The deacon along with some other clerics had been clearing the vineyards of a church, some distance from where they lived. After completing their work, they engaged in a game travelers would play as a way to make the time pass more quickly. The game involved throwing a walking stick down the path to try and hit the club of the other. The cleric would then run down the path to fetch the stick. In this particular case, a layman sprung upon the cleric and was inadvertently wounded when he banged into the sickle that was hanging on the belt of a deacon. The layman would die eight days later. The Pope declared that not only could the deacon not advance without papal permission, but he was also demoted from his current position of deacon though he was able to administer the office of the subdeaconate. Even though this was an accident, commentators explained that the deacon did bear some blame as it was not permitted to play games with laymen and he should not have been playing with a sickle on his belt.[71] In another decretal of Pope Alexander III, it was stated that a priest who struck a child in the head while disciplining him, resulting in the death of the child a few days later as a result of the wounds, both ought to be removed from all ministries at the alter and ought to be deposed from the priestly office.[72]

Robert and Bartholomew drew on similar legal sources to develop their stances toward clerical homicide. Both regarded engagement in high justice as worthy of being degraded. Both would have been of concern as connections between the prelacy and the Capetians around Paris were strong, just as were connections between the prelacy and Plantagenet kings in England. Both drew upon the older law found in Burchard of Worms and Ivo of Chartres, yet their emphasis seems to be placed differently. Like Gratian, Robert seems to tilt more toward instances in which the cleric could return to his previous rank with penance served and satisfaction made, despite not being able to advance in the orders. The environment of Paris may have warranted a sense of clemency. Following papal decretals that sought to explore every crevice of the cleric's culpability, even in cases where the murder was an accident, Bartholomew seems to tilt more toward instances in which a cleric was degraded or demoted after penance was served. After all, the clergy should be held to a standard higher than those whom they serve. While contrition, penance, and satisfaction washed away the sin of the crime, Robert and Bartholomew held slightly different views about the amount of residue that would coat a clerical career.

71 I Comp. 5.10.9 (X 5.12.8). See also Larson, "Killing a Career," 282–284.
72 I Comp. 5.10.8 (X 5.12.7).

With a Focus on the Laity: Murder of Spouse and the Intention Behind a Homicide

As opposed to Robert, who had as one of his principal concerns those with clerical status studying in the bustling environment of Paris, Bartholomew, whose interest lay with the penance in the diocese, chose to address with more force certain topics that pertained solely to the laity. One such topic was the killing of a spouse, which Bartholomew addressed earlier in his section on homicide and with more texts than Robert. Robert included but one text on the topic, a text probably drawn from Bartholomew but one in which Robert chose to abbreviate further. The text is a letter from Pope Stephen V to Astulph, who had killed his wife and then tried to justify his actions by accusing her of adultery without corroborating testimony from suitable witnesses. Robert's text simply stated that for having perpetuated the murder, he was to enter a monastery, a punishment that the pope conceded was certainly the lighter and easier choice. If, however, he decided to remain among the world and perform his public penance at home, this penance would be more onerous, difficult, and severe. For every day of his penance, he was not to drink any wine or strong drink. He could not eat meat at any time, with the exception of Christmas and Easter; he was to perform penance on bread, water, and salt. He was to persevere in fasting, vigils, prayers, and almsgiving perpetually. He was never to take up arms or fight anywhere. He was to take neither a wife, nor concubine, nor dare to commit adultery. He was never to bathe nor be present at any joyful celebrations. In church, he was to be segregated from other Christians and was to position himself outside the door and vestibule where he was to present himself and implore the prayers of all those entering and leaving. He was to consider himself unworthy to receive the Lord's body and blood for the rest of his life. Though, on his last day as he lay dying, he was conceded the right to receive the last sacrament, if he should merit it and if there was someone there to grant it to him.[73] Bartholomew included a longer version of this text which went on to state that many other things, suitably difficult and severe, would be added in accord with the great gravity of his sin. If he should undertake and complete all of the tasks set before him with a pure heart and God's help, it was for God's great clemency to grant him remission of his sins. So long as the Holy Church absolves him from the bond of sin on earth, he would be forgiven in heaven. If he should not complete the tasks set before him and he should despise the saving admonitions of the Holy Church, he would be bound in the Devil's snare. His blood would be upon his own head. Though separated from the Church, the Church, through God's assistance, would persistently implore His mercy daily for him and the salvation of all God's children.[74] In what appears to be a *dictum* on the aforementioned penance of Astulph, Bartholomew noted that when asked about the

73 Flamborough 5.2.9 §264, pp. 225–226.
74 Bartholomew c.50, pp. 218–220.

killing of his wife, it had been said that Astulph never led a wife in marriage according to the rigor of the canons. Furthermore, an indulgence for penance should be conceded to adolescents 15 years of age in cases of marriage.[75]

Bartholomew's interest in the laity likely drew him to address the killing of spouses in more detail and thus include additional texts that Robert would omit. Pope Pius had decreed that whoever killed his wife without right, cause, or certain proof and then took another must put aside his arms and do public penance. If he was contumacious and disobedient toward his bishop, he should be anathematized until he complied. The same law applied to one who killed his *senior*.[76] A council held near Granada (Eliberitano) decreed that if a woman killed her husband with poison because of fornication, she was relinquished to a monastery to do penance. The same punishment should hold true for the man.[77] Similarly, a council held at Mainz stated that if a husband killed his wife or a wife her husband, both were subject to the same justice.[78] A letter of Pope Nicholas I to Rudolph, the archbishop of Bourges, asserted that those who killed their wives without trial, since it was not indicated that the wives were adulteresses or anything like that, should be accounted as murderers subject to penance. They were absolutely forbidden to remarry unless they were young men. In this case, the rule of Pope Leo I was to be applied with mercy,[79] the point to which Bartholomew referred to above in his comment on Astulph's case. Bartholomew included a portion of Gratian's *dictum* which noted that though Pope Nicholas appeared in this canon to permit the killing of wives on account of adultery or similar crimes, it was not true.[80] Interestingly, Bartholomew did not include Gratian's full explanation, which was that

> ecclesiastical discipline commands that criminals be slain, not by a material sword, but by the sword with which Peter was ordered to kill and eat, this is the sword Christ speaks of in the Gospel, saying, 'I have not come to bring peace upon the earth, but a sword.'[81]

75 Bartholomew c.50, p. 220: "Hac premissa penitentia notandum est, quod cum de interfectore uxoris dicitur quod nunquam ducat uxorem, secundum rigorem canonum dicendum est. Adolescentibus enim perfecta quindecim annorum penitentia coniugii conceditur indulgentia."

76 Bartholomew c.50, p. 218; C.33 q.2 c.7.

77 Bartholomew c.50, p. 218 ll. 15–23.

78 Bartholomew c.50, p. 218 ll. 24–28.

79 Bartholomew c.50, p. 220 ll. 6–12; C.33 q.2 c.5. The decretal of Pope Leo I is contained in GD C.33 q.2 c.14.

80 Bartholomew c.50, p. 220 ll. 12–15: "Est etiam notandum quod in principio premissi capitula uidetur Nicholaus permittere maritis adulterii causa, uel alterius eiusmodi criminis, uxores suas inerficere, quod non est uerum"; GD C.33 q.2 d.p.c.5.

81 GD C.33 q.2 d.p.c.5: "Sed ecclesiastica disciplina spirituali gladio, non materiali criminosos feriri iubet; illo uidelicet gladio, quo Petrus iubetur mactare et manducare. De quo etiam gladio Christus ait in euangelio: 'Non ueni pacem mittere in terram, sed gladium.'"

Finally, Bartholomew included a letter Pope Nicolas I had written to Bishop Albinus stating that no one may lawfully kill his wife as an adulteress. God's Holy Church, however, is not subject to worldly law. It has no sword except the spiritual one and it does not kill; rather, it gives life.[82]

Bartholomew's focus on the laity also comes through in his discussion of how not all who kill are guilty of homicide, a topic that Robert did not address at all. Bartholomew likely took these texts from Causa 23 of Gratian's *Decretum*. Bartholomew is keen to show the importance of circumstances when considering one's guilt. He includes a text from John Chrysostom's commentary on Matthew where John muses that though Phinehas killed a man, he was considered righteous for doing so. Abraham not only killed a man but, far worse, killed his own child. Yet, this action pleased God. Peter wrought a twofold homicide, nevertheless it was considered a spiritual deed. Chrysostom concludes that we have to consider the acts but we must also examine the time, the cause, the mindset, the differences between the persons, and whatever other factors accompanied these deeds. It is only through this that we are able to arrive at the truth.[83] In the *Dialogues*, Pope Gregory I noted that Peter, who by his prayers raised up Tabitha and, by his reproach, sentenced Ananias and Sapphira to death for their lying. We do not read that he prayed for their death, but simply that he rebuked them for the sin which they had committed.[84] Pope Nicholas I's letter to the Bulgarians noted that Lent is a sacred time in which war should not be waged. However, if inevitable circumstances arise, such as the preservation of the faith, then it is permitted to do so.[85] Ambrose commented those who execute sentences, though killing a wicked man, are nonetheless ministers of the Lord.[86] Augustine made a similar observation in his *City of God*. Yet, those who lack public authority and maim or cause the death of a criminal, a thief, an impious individual, an adulterer, or a perjurer have usurped God's power and granted it to himself. He is judged no differently than those whom he maimed or killed. [87] The circumstances under which the killing took place, and the power granted to the individual to do so, needed to be taken into consideration. Even if the individual was granted the authority to do so, we must also consider the individual's heart and the motive behind the killing. As Augustine noted, it makes a great difference whether the act was done out of a desire to harm, to unjustly steal something, out of retribution, out of obedience to a judge, out of a necessity to escape, or to help someone. Sometimes, he who causes the death is less to

82 Bartholomew c.50, p. 220 ll. 15–21; GD C.33 q.2. c.6.
83 Bartholomew c.60, pp. 224–225 ll. 26ff; GD C.23 q.8 c.14.
84 Bartholomew c.60, p. 225 ll. 1–8; GD C.23 q.8 c.16.
85 Bartholomew c.60, p. 225 ll. 8–16; GD C.23 q.8 c.15.
86 Bartholomew c.60, p. 225 ll. 16–18; GD C.23 q.5 c.29.
87 Bartholomew c.60, p. 225 ll. 19–26; GD C.23 q.8 c.33.

blame than the one killed. At the forefront must be the consideration that the life was not taken out of vengeance but out of zeal for correction.[88]

Conclusion

The careers of Robert of Flamborough and Bartholomew of Exeter reflect differences and similarities in their approach to the use of the law. The former was a canon at St. Victor, a papal judge-delegate, the penitentiary to students of the University of Paris, and no doubt engaged in the political environment of the city. The latter was an archdeacon, bishop, and a papal judge-delegate. Both required a knowledge of law and for that knowledge to be rendered usable. Their *Libri penitentiales* tailored relevant legal theory to the *cura animarum*. A known jurist, Bartholomew of Exeter structured his penitential more akin to a law collection by including the material source. A known theologian, Robert was less inclined toward the inclusion of material sources, but that does not mean he was less inclined toward the sources of law. Robert drew not only upon Bartholomew but also upon a swath of sources from Burchard of Worms' *Decretum*, to Ivo of Chartres' *Decretum*, to Gratian's *Decretum*, to Huguccio's *summa* on Gratian as seen in chapter 2, to more recent papal decretals.

Penitentials should have a broad applicability across the social spectrum. Despite one of his principal functions as hearing the confessions of university students who held clerical status, Robert discussed marriage as his second book. The topic was important to address. Yet, the manner in which Robert and Bartholomew each approached homicide suggests that compilers could also have a particular audience in mind. Law had to be tailored to serve the audience in mind. Robert addressed suicide first, followed immediately by the murder of and murder caused by clerics. These topics might have been more of a concern for university students in a bustling administrative center. University life can be stressful for students. Suicide resulted from the *acedia*, a general weariness of life that springs from deep sadness (*tristitia*) and led to despair (*desperatio*). Conflicts between town and gown could lead to scuffles, with students facing high justice and life in prison. Bartholomew of Exeter, however, had less of a concern for suicide, though he did address it later. His principal focus was the laity, as evidenced by his deeper engagement with the murder of spouses and offering a justification of how those who kill might not always be guilty. He faced the reality of spousal conflict, particularly as it pertained to accusations of adultery. He faced the reality of those engaged in armed combat and the execution of secular justice. Robert and Bartholomew needed the law, but they needed to tailor the law to suit slightly different ends.

88 Bartholomew c.60, pp. 225–226 ll. 26ff; GD C.23 q.5 c.19.

7

THOMAS OF CHOBHAM

The Deadly Sin of Greed

Introduction

Throughout this work, we have studied theologians who adapted legal thought to their needs. They engaged in a dialogue about how people should behave in a specific situation and navigated the waters of offense and appropriate punishment based on the circumstances. Navigating such waters, as Frank Rexroth noted, necessitated moving between different areas of knowledge.[1] The canon law of what David d'Avray dubbed the "second decretal age," that is ca. 1200, adapted papal jurisprudence to respond to social changes.[2] Scripture likewise remained integral to grappling with society's increased complexities. Jason Taliadoros found that Ricardus Anglicus's use of Scripture in his *Distinctiones decretorum* (1196/1198) was "neither wholly canonistic, nor wholly theological, nor wholly exegetical…" The *distinctiones* in which he drew most heavily from Scripture dealt with marriage, excommunication, use of force, clerical property, and clerical testimony in court. Ricardus, like so many others, landed himself an administrative career. He was a student of the canonist Honorius of Kent at Paris and then served as a regent master at Bologna before joining the

1 F. Rexroth, "Kodifizieren und Auslegen: Symbolische Grenzziehungen zwischen päpstlich-gesetzgeberischer und gelehrter Praxis im späteren Mittelalter (1209/10–1317)," *Frühmittelalterliche Studien* 41 (2008): 395–414, here 399.

2 D. d'Avray, *Papal Jurisprudence, 385–1234: Social Origins and Medieval Reception of Canon Law* (Cambridge, 2022). Both decretal ages had a conception of canon law as separate from theological concerns. The thirteenth-century schools of Paris contributed further to the separation of law and theology, as it was there that questions of speculative theology were worked out. As a result, the papacy was not called upon as often to resolve theological differences. Contributing further were changes in intellectual leadership in Paris, which saw the collaborative relationship between law and theology fall by the wayside.

DOI: 10.4324/9781003465096-8

Augustinian house at Dunstable in 1202. As prior, he would also serve as a papal judge-delegate and as an advocate in the common law courts when the matter affected the priory.[3]

The pastoral theologians discussed so far, along with Thomas of Chobham to be discussed in this chapter, sailed in similar waters as Ricardus Anglicus. The students of Ricardus worked in practical (as opposed to academic) careers, serving in the ecclesiastical courts or in pastoral care. Scripture was important, but granularity was not paramount. A culture that valued the porous boundaries between law and theology was equally essential to the work of Peter the Chanter's circle. As administrators, they needed to be comfortable with the legal arena. As casuists, those who resolved moral problems by applying theoretical rules to particular instances, they needed to draw on both theology and canon law.[4] Similar Ricardus Anglicus, the students of Peter the Chanter saw the virtues of simplifying their rendering of the law.[5] Thomas of Chobham continued this tradition; as we have seen with Bartholomew of Exeter, confessors' manuals and pastoral works for parish priests were quite popular in England. According to Emily Corran, the moral dilemmas that appear in English confessors' manuals marked the beginning of a new genre of Catholic moral philosophy, which bears witness to the increasing emphasis on confession beginning in the twelfth century.[6] In some respects, one could see a complementary relationship between Thomas of Chobham's *Summa confessorum* and his *Summa de arte praedicatoria*, a work that emphasized the important connection between preaching and instruction. In teaching the method and shape preaching should take, Thomas drove home how preaching led the listener on the path of proper faith and good behavior.[7] The *Summa confessorum*, in turn, rendered canon law useable—often prefacing stances with "verba canonis," "dicit canon," "unde canon," "secundum antiquos canones," and, in one

3 J. Taliadoros, "Law, Theology, and the Schools: The Use of Scripture in Ricardus Anglicus's *Distinctiones decretorum*," in *Proceedings Toronto 2012*, eds. J. Goering, S. Dusil, and A. Thier (Vatican City, 2016), 1045–1089, here 1047–1049 and Table 1, p. 1052.

4 E. Corran notes that casuistry are cases of conscience exclusively dealing with practical concerns. They answered the question, "What should I do?", and favored occasions that arose in the course of care of souls in which the answer was not obvious. See "Moral Dilemma in English Confessors' Manual," in *Thirteenth Century England XVI: Proceedings of the Cambridge Conference, 2015*, eds. A. M. Spencer and C. Watkins (Woodbridge, 2017), 21–36, here 21–23.

5 Taliadoros, "Law, Theology, and the Schools," 1058–1059.

6 Corran, "Moral Dilemma in English Confessors' Manual," 22–23; C. Rider, "What to Ask in Confession: A List of Sins from Thirteenth-Century England," in *Pastoral Care in Medieval England: Interdisciplinary Approaches*, eds. P. D. Clarke and S. James (London, 2020), 67–99. Rider's edition and translation of the confessional treatise *Animetur primo* provides a good example of Catholic moral philosophy and its focus on confession and pastoral care.

7 G. R. Evans, "Thomas of Chobham on Preaching and Exegesis," *Recherches de théologie ancienne et médiévale* 52 (1985): 159–170, here 160, 170.

instance, "dicit quedam decretalis"—[8] thus enabling clerics to reflect on their own behavior while also ministering to the penitential needs of their flock.[9] It is very much a work that can be viewed through the lens of the interplay of Christian principles and people going about their daily lives.[10] In his treatment of greed, the focus of this chapter, Thomas of Chobham drew upon his experience as subdean and *officialis* of Salisbury to distill and apply legal thought in such a way that it could be applied to the murky waters categorized under theft and robbery, usury, and simony. The law on subjects that fell under this umbrella was becoming increasingly complicated and less clear in a burgeoning market economy.

Thomas of Chobham studied at Paris, probably under Peter the Chanter, and returned to England in 1189/92 after receiving the title of *magister*. His first ecclesiastical post upon return to England was in the service of the bishop of London. A member of the bishop's curia, he is noted as having witnessed charters of Bishop Richard Fitz Nigel and Stephen II, who served as master of St. Bartholomew's Hospital. By 1199, he was serving Herbert Poore, bishop of Salisbury (1194–1217). He was probably made subdean between October 1206 and ca. 1208, and he was still in the role in 1230 as he was named in an agreement reached between Chertsey Abbey and the community of Chobham, which wanted its own graveyard despite the abbey's objections. He presumably held the position of subdean until his death sometime between 1233 and 1236. Thomas also became a member of the chapter of Charminister in 1214 and held the prebend, which he may have received from King John after Herbert Poore resigned it when he became bishop. Thomas would serve as *officialis* of Salisbury between 1214 and 1217, during which time he may have written his *Summa confessorum*, possibly completed ca. 1215 and in circulation by ca. 1216.[11]

8 Examples include "verba canonis": 7.6.11.4, p. 508; "dicit canon": 7.6.6, p. 498; "unde canon": 7.6.6, p. 498; "secundum antiquos canones": 7.6.3.2, p. 493; and "dicit quedam decretalis": 7.6.11.6, p. 511.

9 M. B. Cels, "Interrogating Anger in the New Penitential Literature of the Thirteenth Century," *Viator* 45, no. 1 (2014): 203–220, here 206. Cels notes Thomas's complaint that few people confessed spiritual sins such as wrath, and few priests knew how to assign penances for them. He was a favored source for wrath, vengeance, conflict, and violence (203).

10 D. Copeland Klepper, *Pastoral Care and Community in Late Medieval Germany: Albert of Diessen's Mirror of Priests* (Ithaca, 2022), 4–10 for a fascinating discussion of "lived religion" as whatever intellectual, moral, theological, legal, or cosmological frameworks might be part of a particular religious tradition. Christianity, as practiced in the world, was shaped and informed by interaction with a written tradition and its institutional structures and expectations, and vice versa.

11 *Thomae de Chombham Summa confessorum*, ed. Revd. F. Broomfield (Louvain, 1968), xxvi–xxxviii; E. Corran, *Lying and Perjury in Medieval Practical Thought: A Study in the History of Casuistry* (Oxford, 2018), 90. G. R. Evans is the only scholar I have found to refer to Thomas as dean of Salisbury, see "Thomas of Chobham on Preaching and Exegesis," 159. See chapter 2 for how scholarship on the circulation of conciliar canons could factor into the dating of the *Summa confessorum*.

Revd. F. Bloomfield claimed in his critical edition of the *Summa confessorum* that it was unlikely that Thomas read law because he did not think himself a canonist or of his book as a canonical work, though Bloomfield did acknowledge that Thomas must have had the legal knowledge of an administrator since Herbert Poore (bishop of Salisbury, 1194–1217) appointed him *officialis*. He claimed that Thomas probably picked up knowledge in the canonical-theological school of Peter the Chanter and in the curiae of London and Salisbury.[12] As this work has demonstrated, the twelfth-century theologians who studied at Paris found a working knowledge of law useful. Northern France was rich in legal collections, and the environment made learning law easy and possible, even if it was not their primary area of expertise. These theologians were comfortable reading the law, drawing upon and adapting it when it suited their needs. David Smith likewise reinforced Thomas's working knowledge of the law: he held an inquest into the possession of lands and tithes in a dispute between Cirencester Abbey and the rector of a parish. Thomas also wrote to Master John of London, his counterpart as the *officalis* of the bishop of Winchester, concerning a matrimonial case.[13]

Precisely because Thomas compiled his *Summa confessorum* while serving as subdean and *officialis* of Salisbury, it is worth considering the nature of his administrative activities to set the stage for an analysis of how he used legal thought in his manual. As we have seen, university training and the title of *magister* became increasingly important to procuring a career in both secular and ecclesiastical service in the latter half of the twelfth century. Nobility such as Stephen of Blois, Richard II, and William the Conqueror employed clerics, often bestowing upon them the title of chancellor. Be it in secular or episcopal service, a *magister* wrote charters, held masses, served as tutors, and acted as ambassadors.[14] Remembering that Thomas held the prebend of Charminister adds to his administrative importance. Such benefices without the care of souls were seen as necessary to support bureaucrats who would serve as diocesan lawyers and councilors to aid the bishop in managing the church.[15] These posts would have proved critical for deans—and presumably subdeans—who were expected to maintain their residency as they served the spiritual and disciplinary needs of larger churches, engaging in both executive and judicial matters. They were known to oversee tribunals, summoning nearby clergy and, when

12 *Thomae de Chombham Summa confessorum*, xxxi.

13 D. M. Smith, "The 'Officialis' of the Bishop in Twelfth- and Thirteenth-Century England: Problems of Terminology," in *Medieval Ecclesiastical Studies in Honour of Dorothy M. Owen*, eds. M. J. Franklin and C. Harper-Bill (Woodbridge, 1995), 201–220, here 205.

14 J. Barrow, *The Clergy in the Medieval World: Secular Clerics, Their Families and Careers in North-Western Europe, c. 800–c. 1200* (Cambridge, 2015), 231–234, 246–247, 256–258.

15 M. Burger, *Bishops, Clerks, and Diocesan Governance in Thirteenth-Century England: Reward and Punishment* (Cambridge, 2012), 25–26.

necessary, the laity to answer for offenses against church law.[16] Peter of Blois served as *officialis* for—the deputy of—Richard of Ilchester, bishop of Winchester (1174–1188). By about 1210, most English dioceses had an *officialis*. As a member of the episcopal *familia*, his duties as an episcopal administrative assistant—an episcopal functionary—varied: holding inquiries and judicial activities, accompanying the bishop on travels or serving in the bishop's place when he was absent from the diocese, witnessing charters, keeper of the spiritualities (and sometimes of the temporalities) of vacant sees, supervising elections of monastic heads, instituting clergy to benefices, and bringing a clerk into the king's court if the bishop was not available.[17] The office of *officialis* underwent changes over the course of the thirteenth century. From ca. 1250 or so, the *officialis* came to designate the judge who headed the bishop's consistory court. Preoccupied with judicial cases, he became fixed to the episcopal city and was detached from the *familia*.[18]

Thomas's administrative positions as subdean and *officialis* are important to take into consideration when arguing for what his *Summa confessorum* was and was not. Broomfield argued that *summae confessorum* have been defined inadequately as works that are essentially canonical and casuistical in nature. There are those penitentials, he noted that of Robert of Flamborough, that show a legal bias and highlight aspects of trial and punishment; Thomas's does not. His *Summa*, rather, is a manual on pastoral care that applies the principles of theology and law that guide human activity within the Christian community. A confessor must deal with all possible deviations from the rule, which means having a sound grasp of the rule itself.[19] Bloomfield made an important observation here, the corollary of which is that Thomas needed to know the law in order to explain it—and how to deal with the deviations from it—to the users of his manual.

Recently, Emily Corran has argued that Thomas sought to create a manual that was accessible to a simple priest by making the lessons digestible and by

16 C. R. Cheney, *From Becket to Langton: English Church Government 1170–1213* (Manchester, 1956, rpt. 1965), 146–147; R. H. Helmholz, *The Oxford History of the Laws of England. Vol. 1: The Canon Law and Ecclesiastical Jurisdiction from 597 to the 1640s* (Oxford, 2004), 217; Barrow, *The Clergy in the Medieval World*, 301–304. Barrow notes that often the dean was a terminal position, though, on occasion, a dean could be elected bishop.

17 Smith, "The 'Officialis' of the Bishop in Twelfth- and Thirteenth-Century England," 201–220; Cheney, *From Becket to Langton*, 147–148; Helmholz, *The Oxford History of the Laws of England*, 1.140–141; R. Brentano, *Two Churches: England and Italy in the Thirteenth Century* (Los Angeles, 1988), 76–78.

18 J. Brundage, *The Medieval Origins of the Legal Profession: Canonists, Civilians, and Courts* (Chicago, 2008), 139–145; Burger, *Bishops, Clerks, and Diocesan Governance in Thirteenth-Century England*, 6. For an excellent analysis of the shift in the *officalis*'s duties and his place within the episcopal *familia* in the thirteenth century, see M. Burger, "Officiales and the familiae of the Bishops of Lincoln, 1258–99," *Journal of Medieval History* 16 (1990): 39–53.

19 *Thomae de Chombham Summa confessorum*, xvii–xviii, xxiv.

giving a run-down of the basics before citing the exceptions. In an example of adultery, Thomas provided a definition, explained how the sin of adultery should be compared to other sins, and listed the appropriate penances. Only after laying the foundation is there a chapter on "ambiguous cases." Despite his claim to simplicity, Corran stresses that Chobham made his reader aware of the limiting cases, that is, occasions when a priest would have to interpret the rules, thus acknowledging that many of the cases a confessor would encounter would not be straightforward.[20] A similar framework can be seen in his article on greed.

Thomas was not a canonist to be sure, but he was comfortable navigating the law, courtesy of the intellectual climate and the porosity of the disciplinary boundaries. The schools of Paris, like Lanfranc and Anselm of Bec long before, trained clerics to be administrators. As Charles Duggan noted, English clerics engaged tirelessly on diplomatic missions between England and almost every part of Western Europe on behalf of the Angevin kings. The monarchy's numerous councils and arbitrations afforded an ideal opportunity for the dissemination of material and ideas.[21] The scope of the work undertaken by these administrators required the ability to navigate both law and theology. Thomas was well trained for what would be required of him: as subdean, he was prepared to tend to the spiritual and disciplinary needs of a large church; as *officialis*, he had the breadth and depth of knowledge to serve the bishop in whatever judicial or administrative capacity needed of him. While the users of his *Summa confessorum* would not have necessarily needed the legal citations, they did need to know the legal, as well as theological, concepts. It was Thomas's responsibility as a subdean and as an *officialis* undertaking this work to ensure that they had the tools necessary to deal with ambiguous cases and care for the souls of their flock, while also avoiding these pitfalls themselves.

As noted above, Thomas used confession as a framework to instruct priests both in the penitential activity of caring for the spiritual well-being of their parishioners and in their duties as priests; the *Summa confessorum* thus provided the priests the tools to tend to their flock and to reflect upon their own behavior. The work's conversational tone engages the reader in the topics addressed. Thomas begins by erecting the scaffolding: describing what penance is (Article 1), delving into public and private penance as types of penance (Article 2), and laying bare the nature of sin as well as venial and moral sins for which penance is enjoined (Article 3). Thomas then treats the sacrament of penance and the circumstances surrounding it: the qualities of the priest tasked with issuing penance followed by a treatment of ordination, baptism, Eucharist, matrimony, confession, and extreme unction as sacraments (Article 4). Thomas

20 Corran, "Moral Dilemma in English Confessors' Manual," 28–30, 35–36.

21 C. Duggan, *Twelfth-Century Decretal Collections and their Importance in English History* (London, 1963), 150–151.

then moves to particular sins and their remedies along with binding, loosening, and the knowledge a priest should have (Article 5). Finally, Thomas turns attention to the penitent and penitential practice: obligations of the penitent and ways of remission (Article 6); and the various sins categorized according to the 7 Deadly Sins, sorcery, lying, vows, and scandal (Article 7). Each of the Articles, with the exception of Articles 1 and 2, is divided into distinctions delving into different questions. Sometimes, questions are further divided into chapters which drill into greater detail. At every level of the work, rubrics provide a summary of the topic to be discussed.

Having a practical orientation, Article 7 is quite interesting, grouping many sins under distinctions devoted to the 7 Deadly Sins—lust, gluttony and drunkenness, anger, greed, envy, sloth, and pride—with other distinctions on key freestanding topics. After an introduction to what follows in distinction 1, Thomas begins with distinction 2 on lust. Here he delves into sexual sins such as nocturnal emissions, fornication, prostitution, rape, adultery, relations with the clerical and religious, affinity, sins against nature, and pandering. Distinction 3 includes two questions, one on gluttony and another on drunkenness. Distinction 4 addresses anger through the lens of cursing someone, meritorious murder (e.g., judgments of blood, war, and whether Jews and heretics could be killed), and licit and illicit homicide. Stepping away from the 7 Deadly Sins, distinction 5 addresses sorcery, leaning heavily on Causa 26 of Gratian's *Decretum*. Distinction 6 returns to the 7 Deadly Sins to focus on greed, which serves as the case study of this chapter and will be dealt with in detail below. Distinction 7 introduces and distinctions 8 through 10 deal in turn with the sins of envy, sloth, and arrogance. With the 7 Deadly Sins thoroughly covered, Thomas uses distinction 11 to address lying, leaning heavily on Causa 22 of Gratian's *Decretum*; distinction 12 addresses vows; and finally, distinction 13 addresses scandal. Throughout the distinctions, a firm grounding of the legal tradition was warranted as Thomas addressed sins treated in both the external and internal fora. Principles from Gratian's *Decretum*, papal decretals included in the *Compilationes antiquae*, the earlier legal tradition represented by Ivo of Chartres (via the penitentials of Bartholomew of Exeter and Robert of Flamborough),[22] and Roman law were distilled in a manner that would allow the confessor to navigate the complexities of the situation.

The Faces of Greed

In the 1987 movie *Wall Street*, Michael Douglas's character Gordon Gekko, a corporate raider, famously stated: "Greed, for lack of a better word, is good." Greed "marked the upward surge of mankind." In an increasingly market economy, Thomas of Chobham seems to be addressing such assertions in Article 7

22 Quotations found in Chobham 7.6.6 dealing with penance for theft and sacrilege.

distinction 6 where he analyzes the practical categories that greed took: theft and robbery, usury, and simony.[23] Thomas frames each topic in the same manner. He begins by defining the concept and then delves into the weeds of specific examples. The manner in which Thomas treats these subjects and the examples that he incorporates very much have the feel of the social, economic, and cultural realities of daily life, people looking to get ahead through covert means, nefarious business dealings, and usurpation of the ecclesiastical.[24]

As noted, Article 7, distinction 6 uses the broad categories of theft, usury, and simony to delve into forms that greed can take and, by extension, the conflicts that a priest or an ecclesiastical judge would have to navigate. Having briefly introduced the types of greed in question 1,[25] questions 2 through 9 focus on theft and robbery. Subjects linked to question 2 on theft include: what constitutes theft; finding objects, treasure, or animals; theft from the rich; and restoration.[26] Subjects linked to question 3 on robbery, which Thomas considers worse than theft, include: what constitutes robbery; sanctuary; and why the church supports their corporeal punishment.[27] Sacrilege is the subject of question 5;[28] theft from the dead is the subject of question 7;[29] and taking of alms is the subject of question 8.[30] Rounding out the subject of theft and robbery are question 6, which addresses penance for theft and sacrilege,[31] and question 9, which addresses the restoration of illicit gains obtained by court officers.[32] Question 10 is an exceptionally short discussion of prescription,[33] a discussion which transitions into question 11 on usury. Thomas begins by defining usury but then quickly moves into murky cases, such as dealing with those whose livelihood depends upon usury, and buying and selling on credit by hedging profits against market uncertainties.[34] Equally lengthy as question 11 is

23 There is not a question 4 in either the Table of Contents or in the critical edition.

24 The framing of the topics falls in line with Corran's observations noted above. I am indebted to Klepper's *Pastoral Care and Community in Late Medieval Germany*, 22, 197, for giving me the "ah ha!" moment I needed. Her observation that pastoral manuals sit between canon lawyers/theologians and parish priests, a nexus between ideal and reality, describes Thomas of Chobham's *Summa confessorum* wonderfully.

25 Chobham, 487.

26 Chobham, 488–493.

27 Chobham, 493–494.

28 Chobham, 495–496.

29 Chobham, 499–500.

30 Chobham, 500–501.

31 Chobham, 496–499. While I will not delve into this question, Thomas of Chobham leaned largely on the penitential of Bartholomew of Exeter, which, as discussed in the previous chapter, which drew from the canonical collections of Burchard of Worms, Ivo of Chartres, and Gratian.

32 Chobham, 501–503. I will treat this question in conjunction with question 12 cap. 1 on simony as there is overlap.

33 Chobham, 503–504.

34 Chobham, 504–518. Thomas deals with a number of situations in this section; I will delve into a few of the more prominent ones as examples.

question 12 on simony. Following a description of simony as both the buying or selling of the spiritual or spiritually linked and the agreement about temporal things for the spiritual and vice versa, Thomas discusses the selling of justice; oblations for baptism, saying of mass, burial, prayers for the dead, chrism, and marriages; the priest's stipend; granting of benefices to one's relatives; a master receiving payment from students; the selling the right of patronage; laity withholding the tithe; buying and selling of the tithe; and the penalty for simoniacs.[35]

Throughout distinction 6, Thomas explicitly and implicitly engages with the breadth of the legal tradition. The Roman legal tradition can be felt, particularly with respect to theft, robbery, and usury. In terms of canonical law, the intellectual mindsets found in Gratian's *Decretum* and the twelfth- and early thirteenth-century conciliar tradition and papal decretals are echoed, as are the penitentials of Bartholomew of Exeter and Robert of Flamborough, which, in turn, used the canonical collections of Gratian, Ivo of Chartres, and Burchard of Worms. Hanging in the air, almost like a fog, are the episcopal acta of the diocese of Salisbury and the English common law tradition. While Thomas does not explicitly reference the traditions upon which he drew, he was very much engaged in similar conversations. Thomas's comfort with the legal arena may seem surprising at first, but when his role as *officialis* is taken into consideration the pieces seem to come into place.

Theft and Robbery

Theft and robbery set the foundation for the topics that make up distinction 6. Thomas defines theft in two ways. The first is to take something without the owner's consent, such as when one takes a cow and does not return it. Theft is also committed when one uses something without permission even though it might be returned. Thomas's definition pulls from Justinian's *Institutes*. Theft is the fraudulent intention to use or have possession of something. It is committed not only when someone removes something belonging to another to have it for himself, but whenever someone handles something belonging to another without the owner's consent.[36] Robbery, Thomas maintains, is a greater sin than theft because force is used to steal the item. This simple distinction has roots in both Roman and canon law.[37] To make amends for the sin of theft, Thomas leans into C.14 q.6 c.1 of Gratian's *Decretum*: what has been taken must be restored. If it is not possible to restore the item, the perpetrator must

35 Chobham, 518–533.
36 Chobham 7.6.2.1, p. 488; Inst. 4.1.1, 4.1.6.
37 Chobham, 7.6.3.1, p. 493; Inst. 4.2; GD C.14 q.5 c.13.

lament and grieve, and, at some point, make restitution by restoring it.[38] Once stolen, Thomas emphasizes that the object remains stolen no matter how many hands it passes onto. As soon as someone realizes that the object is stolen, he has the obligation to return it or be guilty of theft; the stain of sin cannot be removed unless it is returned to its rightful owner or his heir.[39] Such notions are seen throughout the canonical tradition. For example, Gratian included a text from Ambrose stating that another could not buy what is seized unless the intention is to return it.[40] The decretal tradition took the stance that objects, along with their fruits, were to be restored in order to make good the damages and to provide satisfaction for the injuries. Furthermore, thieves and robbers were to be denied the sacraments.[41]

With the conceptual foundation laid, Thomas turns to examples that an ecclesiastic would no doubt encounter: "I found it" and "He's rich and can afford to lose it." Making quick work of the latter, Thomas simply quotes the entire canon of C.14 q.5 c.3 of Gratian's *Decretum* to prove the point that nothing is to be taken away from the rich to be given to the needy.[42] Under the umbrella of "I found it," Thomas echoes Gratian's *Decretum*, making it clear that someone who finds something and does not return it has stolen it because theft is removing for the sake of profit. If the original owner could not be found, it should be given to the Church for distribution as it sees fit.[43] Within the context of whether alms are able to be given from interest, C.14 q.5 c.4 stated that if one who wishes to repent could not find the person from whom he extracted the interest, then he is to give it to the Church or to the poor.[44] A similar sentiment, also within the context of usury, was echoed by the Council of Paris (1212) which decreed that if it was not possible for usurers to restore what they extorted, it could be given to the bishop for distribution to the poor.[45] Should the owner discard the property and it is considered abandoned, Thomas states

38 Chobham, 7.6.2.1, p. 488; GD C.14 q.6 c.1. In general, C.14 q.6 deals with the idea that penance cannot be done unless the thing taken is restored. The question, however, is not addressing theft, per se, but rather usury. In C.14 q.5 d.p.c.12, however, Gratian made the connection between usury and theft: all illicit usurpation of another's things was understood by the name of theft. Rolandus echoed similar sentiments as Thomas; see Rolandus, *Summa decretorum*, ed. F. Thaner (Innsbruck, 1874), ad C.14 q.6.

39 Chobham, 7.6.2.7, pp. 492–493. A parallel thought is reflected in IV Comp. 2.3.3 (X 2.13.18): The receiver of something knowingly taken by a robber was obligated to restore it to the person robbed, even if ownership could not be proven.

40 GD C.14 q.5 c.5.

41 I Comp. 5.26.4 (X 5.18.2); II Comp. 2.7.5 (X 2.13.11).

42 Chobham 7.6.2.5. Broomfield notes that Gratian's text is also found in the penitentials of Bartholomew of Exeter and Robert of Flamborough.

43 Chobham 7.6.2.2, pp. 488–489. Thomas quotes GD C.14 q.5 c.6 and c.8 which note that theft occurs when something is found and not returned. In C.14 q.5 d.p.c.14 Gratian commented that sometimes things acquired poorly could be justly used to care for the poor.

44 GD C.14 q.5 c.4.

45 Council of Paris (1212), second part c.7 (Mansi 22:827).

that the finder could have it. His view has a basis in Roman law: if an owner abandoned something it could pass straight away to anyone who took possession of it. The law saw an object as abandoned when its owner threw it away, indicating that it was no longer his property.[46] The important element is the intention to discard. Pope Innocent III wrote to the bishop of Trent that should one enter property without knowing the owner to whom it belonged, the owner may repel the intruder, with force if necessary, as soon as he became aware of it.[47] The owner had not intentionally abandoned his property.

Treasure and animals also fell under the umbrella of "I found it." Juxtaposing the intention of the finder with the ownership of the property, Thomas delineates between someone who finds a hidden treasure in a field, in which case he can retain the whole treasure; someone who finds treasure by chance in a field belonging to another, in which case he can have half; and someone who searches the land belonging to another, in which case he can keep nothing. Roman law shared a similar framework. The Roman emperor Hadrian allowed someone who found treasure on his land to keep it, with the same ruling for chance finds on sacred or religious land. If one found a treasure by chance—that is, not by a deliberate search—on private land, the emperor allotted half to the owner and half to the finder. Similarly, one who found treasure on imperial property could keep half of it, with the other half allotted to the emperor. A find on fiscal or public land was divided equally between the finder and the exchequer of the town.[48] Noted in the *Codex* was that anyone who searched for and found a treasure on another's property shall turn it all over to the owner and shall be punished as a violator of the law. But if anyone accidentally found treasure while plowing or cultivating another's property, it shall be divided equally between the finder and the owner of the property.[49] Roman law also provided a basis for Thomas's stance on the theft of animals. Domestic animals must be returned, but wild animals could be retained so long as they returned to him. According to Justinian's *Institutes*, if someone caught a wild animal it remained in his possession until which time it recovered its natural liberty. Animals that by nature came and went remained in someone's possession so long as they continued to return through their homing instinct. When they lost that, they ceased to be in his possession.[50]

The finding of treasure and animals provided Thomas with an opening to comment on secular practice. He disagrees with kings and princes who said that whatever is in a field, be it treasure or animal, belonged to them. As he set

46 Chobham 7.6.2.2, pp. 488–489; Inst. 2.1.47–48.
47 III Comp. 2.6.2 (X 2.13.12).
48 Inst. 2.1.39.
49 Cod. 10.15.1.3–4.
50 Chobham 7.6.2.3, p. 490; Inst. 2.1.12, 15.

forth, Thomas maintained that one could keep hidden treasure found in his own field and he was not bound to give it to the prince,[51] a stance we saw espoused in the *Institutes*. Thomas's position was at odds with contemporary secular law. Glanville, for example, treated the concealment of the treasure trove as a criminal plea in his *Tractatus de legibus et consuetudinibus regni Anglie* (ca. 1187–1189). When such a charge was based on public notoriety, the law held that no one should be purged by ordeal unless it had been previously proved against, or admitted by, him in court that what was found and recovered from the place in question was something different from the contents of the treasure trove. He then was bound to purge himself by ordeal to show that he found and recovered nothing more from that location.[52] Thomas also disagrees with making inhabitants swear to abide by these rules and punishing them if they do not. In the case of animals, he does concede that if a person swore such an oath voluntarily, he must make restitution. If the oath was sworn under compulsion, however, he must do penance but he is not bound to restore the animal.[53]

Thomas seems to be taking issue with contemporary secular law and the concept of trespassing. Canon 8 of Henry II's 1170 "Inquest of Sheriffs Regarding the Forests" called for an inquiry to be held into those who trespassed in their forests and upon the deer, hinds, and other wild beasts. The findings should be written down carefully, including whether the foresters or bailiffs seized and arrested anyone, or by surety or pledge detained him and let him go of their own accord without judgment.[54] Forest law was a point of contention as woodlands were important economically for people, lay and clerics alike; they provided pastures, timber, wood, and reserves of arable land. For example, in 1135, Bishop Roger of Salisbury ordered the royal foresters of Yorkshire to allow Archbishop Thurstan of York and his men all easements and necessities in the woods of the archbishop, whom the king had included in his forest.[55] Issues regarding forest law centered on the requirement to swear to the king to protect the "venison and vert" (the deer and the vegetation on which they deer fed, bred, and sheltered), serve on hunting parties, and move

51 Chobham, 7.6.2.4, p. pp. 490–491.

52 Glanville, *Tractatus de legibus et consuetudinibus regini anglie/The Treatise on the Laws and Customs of the Realm of England*, ed. and trans. G. D. G. Hall (London, 1965), Bk. 14 chap. 2.

53 Chobham 7.6.2.4, pp. 490–491.

54 W. Stubbs and H. W. C. Davis, eds., *Select Charters of English Constitutional History* (Oxford, 1913), 177.

55 B. R. Kemp, ed., *English Episcopal Acta, Vol. 18: Salisbury 1078–1217* (Oxford, 1999), no. 40 p. 28. Other requirements included providing board and lodging for huntsman and their dogs; and prohibitions against carrying weapons, nets, or any "engines" that could catch deer. Furthermore, people were required to cut the toes of their own large dogs so they could not chase deer.

domestic animals out of the forests when deer were fawning.[56] In his countering of contemporary secular law on treasure and animals, Thomas is taking issue with the concept that all land could be privatized in the hands of one to the detriment of the many.[57]

Thomas provides two instances in which something taken does not have to be restored. The first is when a madman deposits items with a *bonum virum*. In addressing the gravity of lying, Gratian's *Decretum* addressed a man prone to madness who entrusted a sword to another who promised to return it. If the owner, in a fit of madness, demanded the sword back, it should not be returned to him until soundness of mind was restored to him lest he kill either himself or others. The one to whom the sword was entrusted and promised that he would return it was not at fault on account of the owner's mental state.[58] The second instance is when someone is owed for services rendered or some other unpaid debt. Should he secretly steal what he is owed, he is not bound to restore it. While Thomas acknowledges that this second option is not permitted under human law without a judge, he nonetheless believes that he is not bound to restore it though he stole it uncivilly. Thomas may be adapting a text, such as

56 On forest law, see J. Langton, "Forest Law in the Landscape: Not the Clearing of the Woods, but the Running of the Deer?," in *Deer and People*, eds. K. Baker, R. Carden, and R. Madgwick (Oxford, 2015), 218–230; M. Ley Bazeley, "The Extent of the English Forest in the Thirteenth Century," in *Internal Colonization in Medieval Europe*, eds. F. Fernandez-Armesto and J. Muldoon (Aldershot, 2008), 163–197; J. R. Birrell, "Hunting and the Royal Forest," in *L'Uomo e la foresta secc. XIII-XVIII: Atti della Ventisettesima Settimana di Studi, 8-13 maggio 1995*, ed. S. Cavaciocchi (Florence, 1996), 437–457; J. Birrell, "Forest Law and the Peasantry in the Later Thirteenth Century." *Thirteenth Century England, II. Proceedings of the Newcastle Upon Tyne Conference 1987*, eds. P. R. Cross and S. D. Lloyd (Woodbridge, 1988), 149–163.

57 Ralph Niger similarly noted concern for access to woodlands in his *Book of Kings*. He recounted King Louis VII's sensitivity to the plight of a poor peasant:

> Item cum in foresta Biera stagnum fieret multis laboribus et expensis regiis et opus presente rege plurimum serveret, accessit ad regem pauperculus rusticus dicens quia exheredaret eum de suo nemore restagnatione aque. Quippe habebat pauper ius quoddam in nemore usque ad constitutam metam non longe a sua domumcula, quatenus curtis eius extenderetur, ut sicca ligna perciperet ad focum et viridia ad refectionem domuum suarum. Respiciens itaque princeps pauperem et despicabilem rusticum, ait 'O quam turpe et graue dampnum si pro terrrula tua perderem terram viuentium.' Mandato igitur regis voce preconia, interdictum est opus uniuersum. Cumque mirarentur uniuersi regis zelum, accesserunt maiores ad rusticum et induxerunt eum ut gratis offerret regi ius suum, ne tantarum expensarum impediretur negotium per eum. Vix autem tandem acquievit rex ut, taxato iure pauperis usque ad iustum precium, multiplicata largitione, reciperet emptum et insuper pauperi et heredibus eius donavit ius simile in universo nemore quale habuit in paruula parte.
>
> (Lincoln, Cathedral Library Ms. 26, fol.140ra–140rb).

See also F. Lachaud, "Ralph Niger and the Books of Kings," in *Anglo-Norman Studies XL: Battle Conference on Anglo-Norman Studies, Paris, 2017*, ed. Elisabeth van Houts (Woodbridge, 2018), 125–146. I would like to thank Nicholas Vincent for the references.

58 GD C.22 q.2 c.14.

C.14 q.5 c.15 of Gratian's *Decretum* to justify the point that taking something from someone against their will did not always constitute unjust theft. Very often, people were unwilling to give due recognition to a doctor or wages to a workman. If they receive their wages from employers who were unwilling, they did not receive them unjustly; rather, it would be unjust if they were not given to them.[59]

As robbers were worse than thieves on account of the force used to exact the crime, Thomas grappled with what should be done with such violators. At stake were the issues of sanctuary and corporeal punishment. Public and highway robbers can take no refuge in the church but should be dragged from there if they do so. Yet, Thomas acknowledges this position is not upheld universally. In some regions, he can take refuge in the church no matter the crime, unless he committed the crime in that particular church. If the robber was discovered in the church, he should not be exposed to death. Rather, he should be placed in the tower and, having been scourged, be cast out from the city. If the man was a debtor of another's property or a servant, he was to be handed over to his creditor or owner with freedom from punishment of life and limb. The Church, Thomas states, should see to it that those who take refuge will not suffer physical punishment.[60]

The position that men are not to be seized from a church and rules for sanctuary represented a robust tradition. Biblical texts, such as from Exodus, Deuteronomy, and I and II Kings, set forth the concept of a safe space. Patristic texts, such as the writings of Augustine in particular, established the importance of episcopal intercession and penitential discipline as an act of divine mercy and a more beneficial form of correction than imperial justice. Roman law, particularly the *Theodosian Code* by way of the *Edictum Theodorici* (ca. 460), was important as canons on the protection of public debtors (c.71) and slaves (c.70) who fled to a church and capital punishment for those who harshly dragged someone from the church (c.125) entered the legal tradition.[61] Justinian's *Codex* held that no one shall abduct those who took refuge in churches, lest they be prosecuted for treason. Churches should be open to those who were in fear. This space included only the sacred altars and the oratory of the church, which were enclosed by the barriers of four walls, but also whatever space there was beyond that, as far as the outermost entrance of the church.[62] Causa 17 q.4 of Gratian's *Decretum* noted that those having

59 Chobham 7.6.2.6, p. 492: "Credimus tamen quod inciviliter facit si accipit, nec tenetur restituere si acceperit."

60 Chobham 7.6.3.2, p. 494: "…, ita tamen quod ecclesia habeat securitatem quod ille qui ad eam confugit non habeat damnum vitae vel membrorum."

61 K. Shoemaker, *Sanctuary and Crime in the Middle Ages, 400–1500* (New York, 2011), 19–21, 54, 59–62.

62 Cod. 1.12.2–3.

committed a crime who fled to a church should not be subject to punishment or death but rather be permitted to lawfully make amends for their misdeeds. Furthermore, those who violently seized someone from a church were prevented from entering one.[63] In the case of slaves who sought refuge in the church, once their security had been given, they were to be restored to their owners.[64]

Yet, Thomas's caveat of sanctuary unless the crime was committed in that church is important to bear in mind. It echoes a proposition posited for discussion at the Council of Westminster (1175) that prohibited a church or its territory from protecting a man who killed another man there.[65] Thomas's caveat also transitions to the paradox that in some countries there are those who are killed for robbery, though in antiquity divine law established that this should not happen. Thomas explains that this is done with great consideration because in some countries people are prone to theft or robbery and unless there is fear of death or mutilation of limbs, they would not stop stealing or robbing. It is for this reason that the Church supports the killing of robbers.[66] This position seems to be factoring in the exceptions that prohibited thieves and highway robbers from claiming sanctuary, exceptions echoed by Pope Innocent III.[67] Thomas was walking a tightrope. While setting up the position that there are different types of medicine—divine judgment and human judgment—Gratian stated that the Church ought to intercede, but not defend, the wicked before the princes.[68] The canons were clear: clerics could not judge cases in which corporeal punishment or death were at stake. Prelates could judge cases dealing with kidnapping and other crimes, yet they could not inflict bloodshed as that is the purview of secular justice.[69] The Council of Westminster (1175) decreed that clerics were neither to perform public functions nor deal with cases of blood, and that judgments of blood or of death were not to be carried out in either churches or consecrated places.[70] Yet, there also was a shifting mentality, echoed by Innocent III in a letter to the bishop of London regarding

63 GD C.17 q.4 c.8–c.10. See also Shoemaker, *Sanctuary and Crime in the Middle Ages*, 121–123.

64 GD C.17 q.4 c.32.

65 Council of Westminster (1175), proposition 32. See, M. Cheney, "The Council of Westminster 1175: New Light on an Old Source," in *The Material Sources and Methods of Ecclesiastical History*, ed. D. Baker (Oxford, 1975), 61–68. While this proposition did not result in a canon issued at the council, it does point to Thomas being aware of the topics of interest.

66 Chobham 7.6.3.3, p. 494: "Et ideo sustinet ecclesia quod fures occidantur."

67 III Comp. 3.32.1 (X 3.49.6). Shoemaker, *Sanctuary and Crime in the Middle Ages*, 129, see also p. 158 for the ordinary gloss of Gratian's *Decretum* excluding public thieves from sanctuary.

68 GD C.14 q.6 c.1–c.3, d.p.c.2: "Pro malis autem apud principes ecclesia debet intercedere, non eos temerario ausu defendere."

69 I Comp. 5.14.3 (X 5.17.4); Third Lateran Council, c.27 (COGD 2.1, pp. 145–147); Fourth Lateran Council c.18 (COGD 2.1, p. 177), c.42 (COGD 2.1, p. 186); Appendix of diocesan statutes c.6.

70 Council of Westminster (1175), c.3, c.6.

crimes committed by clerics, that it was in the public's interest that crimes did not go unpunished.[71] The tightrope Thomas seemed to be walking was that just because ecclesiastical judges could not be involved in cases of corporal punishment and death did not mean the Church did not support such cases from time to time, particularly as they involved robbery.

A special type of theft and robbery is the crime of sacrilege, which Thomas defines as when a sacred thing is stolen regardless of whether or not it is stolen from a sacred place. It is also sacrilege when something sacred is injured (such as a cleric), broken, burned (such as a church), or polluted.[72] The subject was dealt with extensively in the legal tradition. Sacrilege was defined in the *Codex* as disturbing, violating, or offending the sanctity of the divine law.[73] Gratian dealt with sacrilege extensively in the *Decretum*, devoting much of C.17 q.4 to the subject, with the subject of incendiaries being addressed in C.23 q.8 c.31–c.32.[74] The decretal tradition similarly treated the sacrilegious as the mistreatment of an ecclesiastic object or person.[75] Thomas concludes his definition of sacrilege by quoting a canon attributed to Bishop (Pope) Lucius anathematizing not only the sacrilegious but also those who support them as they consented to the actions.[76] The text provided a segway to accomplices of a theft or robbery. Such people approved in their mind, provided assistance,

71 III Comp. 5.21.8 (X 5.39.35): "...quum praelati excessus corrigere debeant subditorum, et publicae utilitatis intersit, ne crimina remaneant impunita, et per impunitatis audaciam fiant qui nequam fuerant nequiores ..."; Shoemaker, *Sanctuary and Crime in the Middle Ages*, 162–163.

72 Chobham 7.6.5.1, p. 495.

73 Cod. 9.29.1: "Qui divinae legis sanctitatem aut nesciendo confundunt aut neglegendo violant et offendunt, sacrilegium committunt."

74 Arnaud Fossier has argued that in C.17 q.4 d.p.c.29—"Qui autem de ecclesia vi aliquem exemerit, vel in ipsa ecclesia, vel loco, vel cultui, sacerdotibus, et ministris aliquid iniuriae inportaverit, ad instar publici criminis et lesae maiestatis accusabitur, et convictus, sive confessus, capitali sententia a rectoribus provinciae ferietur"—Gratian used the Roman qualification of "lèse-majesté" to argue that sacrilege should be judged as lèse-majesté. Thus, to hit and hurt a cleric, to violate a church or any place of worship was such a serious offense that it had to be judged *as if* it was a crime of lèse-majesté. Fossier, "Lèse majesté, Sacrilege, and Reserved Cases to the Pope" (paper presented at the XVII International Congress on Medieval Canon Law, University of Kent, 8 July 2024).

75 I Comp. 5.37.8 (X 5.41.7). See also I Comp. 5.14.5 (X 5.17.2) and I Comp. 5.14.6 (X 5.17.5) which deal with the burial of the sacrilegious and incendiaries.

76 Chobham 7.6.5.1, p. 495; GD C.17 q.4 c.5:

> Omnes ecclesiae raptores atque suarum facultatum alienatores a liminibus eiusdem matris ecclesiae anathematizamus, apostolica auctoritate pellimus, dampnamus atque sacrilegos esse iudicamus; et non solum eos, sed omnes consentientes eis, quia non solum qui faciunt rei iudicantur, sed etiam qui facientibus consentiunt. Par enim pena et agentes et consentientes conprehendit.

Bloomfield also notes the text can be found in the penitentials of Bartholomew and Robert of Flamborough.

suggested the crime, defended it, did not resist it, or did not rebuke or correct the crime after it happened.[77] The sacred must remain sacred without fear of desecration or illicit trafficking.

Thomas then turns to the natural extensions of sacrilege. The first is the plundering of the dead and dying. Clerics who dig up the graves of the dead are to be removed from the clerical orders and assigned three years penance, a text Thomas quoted most likely from Robert of Flamborough but originally found in Ivo of Chartres's *Decretum*.[78] Quoting from Turpin's *History of the Life of Charles the Great and Roland* to use a popular story to instill a message, Thomas maintains that by not executing a will as directed, one has essentially stolen the goods of the dead. A three-fold retribution is owed: to the heirs who should receive what was bequeathed, to the deceased for the failure to distribute, and to God whom he transgressed.[79] The legal tradition was quite clear on this matter: the executor of the will must execute the final wishes of the deceased. The *Institutes* addressed the trustee of estates as the person responsible for carrying out the will and how that should take place.[80] Gratian's *Decretum* emphasized that the last will of the dead ought to be served,[81] while also delving into denying the oblations of the dead to churches and the plundering of dying clerics.[82] The decretal tradition doubled down on the execution of a will, giving bishops the license to be more involved when the executor did not fulfill his duties.[83] A second extension of sacrilege is the priest, who is overwhelmed by prayers of the poor and does not give them anything when he can, actions which are contrary to the canonical tradition.[84] Priests are stewards of the goods that God has committed to them, and they cannot retain them for their own use unless necessary. With that said, priests should examine to whom they give and keep the Lord in mind; they should be judicious with their almsgiving.[85]

Thomas uses the subject of prescription to transition from robbery to usury and simony, yet he does not dwell on the topic at all, devoting only two short paragraphs to the subject. He defines prescription as when someone holds something for a long time and thus is not bound to restore it. He simply notes, without any explicit reference to the law, that prescription was once customary and established for people who held property to protect themselves. Such was

77 Chobham 7.6.5.2, pp. 495–496.
78 Chobham, 7.6.5.3, p. 496; ID 13.49; Flamborough 5.4.1 §312, p.253.
79 Chobham, 7.6.7, pp. 499–500.
80 Inst. 2.23 and 2.24.
81 GD C.13 q.2 c.4.
82 GD C.13 q.2 c.9–c.11; GD C.12 q.2 c.46–c.48.
83 I Comp. 3.22.11 (X 3.26.6); I Comp. 3.22.12 (X 3.26.3); X 3.26.17; X 3.26.19.
84 GD D.88 c.2 forbade clerics from impeding the care of widows and orphans, while the Council of Paris (1212), part 4 c.6 (Mansi 22:840) reiterated priests' duty to listen to the needs of the poor by providing alms and hospitality.
85 Chobham 7.6.8, pp. 500–501. Here, Thomas uses the first-person plural.

reiterated in decretal law.[86] Yet, he goes on to note that all this had been changed by a new policy. If a person acquired another's property in good faith, that is, he does not believe that the property is another's in some way, and if he holds it with just title as if by purchase or by gift, he is not bound to restore it. But should there be bad faith on behalf of the possessor and he knows that the property belongs to someone else, he is bound to restore it.[87] For Thomas, the policies on cultivating new land rendered prescription less of a matter of contention but simply a topic worthy of note.

Despite Thomas's downplaying of prescription, it was an important part of property and tithing rights. A prescription, whether as a type of contract or an enforcement of the status quo, was the acquisition of ownership (*uscapio*) of immovable property through continuous and uncontested possession or use for a fixed period of time. Stated another way, a prescription applied when one party had entered into an agreement with another whereby property was given for a predetermined amount of time, such as 30 years. At the end of the 30 years, the original owner must reclaim it, otherwise the second party would acquire permanent ownership. A prescription also applied when one party had farmed land or had exercised a right with no objections for a long period of time, such as 30 years. If no legal objections had been raised, the status quo was allowed to remain. Prescription—rights obtained through long usage—became a way for ecclesiastical entities to expand their holdings.[88] Litigation of property rights had become increasingly common in the twelfth century. The gradual distinction between episcopal holdings and cathedral patrimonies, the spread of reformed canons, and the proliferation of monastic orders compounded the need to enforce prescriptions. As previously unusable land became productive, more claims were made to pay various dues, particularly the tithes on goods produced for sale or personal use. For example, the Council of Westminster (1200), also known as the Council of London, declared that tithes on newly cultivated lands should be paid to parochial churches within the

86 See, for example, X 2.26.

87 Chobham 7.6.10, pp. 503–504. The Fourth Lateran Council c.41 (COGD 2.1, p. 186) decreed that no prescription, whether canonical or civil, was valid without good faith. A similar notion was expressed by Rufinus; see *Summa decretorum*, ad C.14 q.6 s.v. *Quod vero penitentia*, p. 344 and Stephan of Tournai, *Summa decretorum*, ed. J. F. von Schulte (Giessen, 1891), ad C.14 q.6 c.1 s.v. *Si rest aliena*, p. 220.

88 R. Helmholz, "The Creation of a Canon Law of Prescription," in *Prescriptive Formality and Normative Rationality in Modern Legal Systems: Festschrift for Robert S. Summers*, eds. W. Krawietz et al. (Berlin, 1994), 266–267. For more on this, see M. H. Eichbauer, "Law in Service of a Community: Property and Tithing Rights in Gratian's *Decretum* and Stephen of Tournai's *Summa*," in *The Use of Canon Law in Ecclesiastical Administration, 1000–1250*, eds. M. H. Eichbauer and D. Summerlin (Leiden, 2018), 69–88.

limits of that church's lands.[89] The scramble for increasingly limited land would impact the Church and the associated appurtenances, such as tithes, oblations, and farms.[90]

Usury

Theft and robbery laid the foundation for the topics in the remainder of the distinction, topics to which Thomas devoted a significant amount of time. The first was the subject of usury. The medieval economy was becoming more monetary, as exemplified by Bishop Roger of Salisbury's notification to Sheriff Aubrey de Vere and all present and future ministers of the king in London that King Henry I had granted Reading Abbey a moneyer in London so the abbey may have a mint and hold an exchange there. The moneyer (Edgar and those after him) shall be as free and *in manu* of the abbot and monks as if he dwelt at Reading. The moneyer shall pay the monks the same dues for the mint as the other London moneyers pay the king.[91] As the reliance on money increased, issues surrounding "passive income" were bound to arise. Falling under ecclesiastical jurisdiction, usury cases often began *ex officio* and were often addressed locally.[92]

Thomas begins again by setting the framework with ecclesiastical law's strict definition of usury: more is required or hoped for than was given, whatever that "more" may be. While Roman law allowed for the collection of modest

89 Council of Westminster (1200), c.9. See D. Whitelock, M. Brett, and C. N. Brooke, eds., *Councils & Synods with other documents relating to the English Church, Vol. 1, Part 2 (1066–1204)* (Oxford, 1981), 1066–1067. This concept was also included in the decrees of the Council of York (1195), c.11; the Council of Rouen (1190), c.23; the Council of Westminster (1175), c.13, and in GD C.16 q.7. c.6. On the decrees of the Council of Westminster (1200), see D. Summerlin, "Hubert Walter's Council of Westminster in 1200 and Its Use of Alexander III's 1179 Lateran Council," in *The Use of Canon Law in Ecclesiastical Administration, 1000–1250*, eds. M. H. Eichbauer and D. Summerlin (Leiden, 2018), 121–139.

90 D. Herlihy, "Church Property on the European Continent, 701–1200," *Speculum* 36, no. 1 (1961): 81–105, here 92–99; A. Boureau, "How Law Came to the Monks: The Use of Law in English Society at the Beginning of the Thirteenth Century," *Past & Present* 167 (2000): 29–74 here 36; G. Constable, *The Reformation of the Twelfth Century* (Cambridge, 2002), 223–225. See C. Wickham, "Ecclesiastical Dispute and Lay Community: Figline Valdarno in the Twelfth Century," *Melanges de l'Ecole francaise de Rome: Moyen- Age, Temps modernes* 108, no. 1 (1996): 7–93 for a case study involving the conflict between the parish of Figline and the canons of S. Bartolomeo (sometimes called S. Signore). The dispute centered around the patronage of churches, the dues and obedience owed by a parish church, and the location of mills and canals.

91 Kemp, ed., *English Episcopal Acta, Vol. 18*, no. 38, p. 27.

92 Richard H. Helmholz, "Usury and the Medieval English Church Courts," *Speculum* 61, no. 2 (1986): 364–380, here 365, 367, 369. Helmholz notes that usury cases often did not make it to the commissary court for the diocese of London.

interest,[93] canon law forbade the collection of any interest. Expecting more than originally given—whether monetary, wheat, wine, oil, or something else—is usurious.[94] Robert of Courçon remarked that sometimes usury meant any surplus received in addition to the capital, while other times it designated one who lent with the intention of receiving something in addition to capital. In whatever form, usury is a sin resulting from what one receives or aims to receive something in addition to the capital.[95] Thomas explains the situation in this manner. In the case of a *commodatum* contract—something lent for use, such as a horse, which will be returned exactly as it was lent—ownership (*dominium*) does not pass on a loan but remains in the power of the lender. In the case of a *mutuum* contract—money that can be counted, grain or wine that can be measured, or gold or silver that can be weighted—ownership (*dominium*) passes from one person to another: what is mine becomes yours. With a *mutuum* contract, the borrower is required to return not the exact same item, as is the case *commodatum* contract, but to repay the same quantity of a similar kind. Whether the contract takes the form of a *commodatum* or a *mutuum*, the lender will be repaid and thus he is only out time; money cannot be made on time. It is contrary to the commandment of the Lord for a lender to profit without any effort, to profit simply by sleeping.[96]

93 Cod. 4.32.26–28 set the rate of interest for ordinary loans at 6% and even to 4% if the lender was a *persona illustris*. Those involved in commercial transactions could ask for 8%, while maritime loans and loans of produce—loans in which the terms were shorter and risks were greater—could be at 12% or 12.5%. Interest higher than capital, however, was forbidden. Nov. 32 and Nov. 120 set the limit of interest on farm produce at 12.5%, the rate for monetary loans to farmers at 4%, and to churches and pious foundations at 3%. For more on usury in Rome, see R. Maloney, "Usury in Greek, Roman, and Rabbinic Thought." *Traditio* 27 (1971): 79–109, esp. 88–95.

94 GD C.14 q.3 d.a.c.1–d.p.c.4; GD C.14 q.4 c.4–c.7; I Comp. 5.15.12 (X 5.19.10). Helmholz, "Usury and the Medieval English Church Courts," 365–366; T. P. McLaughlin, "The Teaching of the Canonists of Usury," *Mediaeval Studies* 1 (1939): 81–147, here 95.

95 G. Lefèvre, ed. and trans, *Le Traité "De Usura" de Robert de Courçon: Texte et traduction publiés avec une introduction* (Lille, 1902), 3.

96 Chobham 7.6.11.1, p. 505: "Unde fenerator nihil vendit debitori quod suum est, sed tantum tempus quod dei est. Unde quia vendit rem alienam non debet inde aliquod lucrum habere. Preterea, fenerator vult consequi lucrum sine omnilabore etiam dormiendo, quod est contra preceptum domini…" See also McLaughlin, "The Teaching of the Canonists of Usury," 100. A. Berger, *Encyclopedic Dictionary of Roman Law* (Philadelphia, rpt. 1991), 399 defines *commodatum* as a gratuitous loan of a thing to be returned by the borrower to the lender on the terms fixed in the agreement or reasonably corresponding to the purpose of the loan; p.591 defines *mutuum* as a loan in which the borrower was obligated to return in due time the sum of money or the same quantity of fungibles of the same quality as was lent to him. During the time of the loan, the borrower becomes the owner of the things given to him for consumption. See also A. Sapir Abulafia, "The Role of Money in Medieval Christian-Jewish Relations," *Erasmus Forum Bulletin* 5 (2021–2022): 7–26, here 13–15.

Engaged in a burgeoning market economy,[97] Thomas had to confront the realities of those whose livelihoods were linked with usury. Each case necessitated a different framing of the legal tradition. Broaching the issue of the Jews' engagement in moneylending, Thomas navigated the canonical tradition—that Jews were forbidden from taking interest from Christians and yet the secular realm was charged with ensuring that what was taken was restored—by accentuating the good that comes from secular use of illicitly acquired funds.[98] He notes with surprise that the Church supports princes who reallocate the money of Jews for their use without punishment. Yet, the Jews have nothing except that acquired from usury and thus princes are partakers of usury and, by extension, are usurers. Thomas reconciles this moral quandary by settling on the stance that while they are not excused before God, the Church excuses them because they defend their subjects against the Jews and others who might expel them from the land if they could. Their providing of defense excuses secular lords of blame.[99]

In the case of whether a laborer could receive wages from a lender knowing that his earnings are derived from profits made from interest, Thomas concludes that if the laborer can find work elsewhere and does not, he commits a mortal sin. If he cannot and does not have the necessities of life, he is able to work for the lender and accept wages that stem from the profits of usury so that he is not tormented by hunger.[100] Such a stance may have been a qualification for alternative positions in circulation. For example, part 5 of the Council of Paris (1212), which Robert of Courçon convened on usury and robbery, decreed that robbers and all who worked for them were bound by excommunication.[101] Yet, in his tract on usury, Robert commented that soldiers who received little from princes other than what was acquired by usury or plunder were akin to doctors who had to resort to methods outside of the norm to

97 See, for example, J. L. Bolton, *Money in the Medieval English Economy: 973–1489* (Manchester, 2012) for the increase in commercialization between 1158 and 1351 which coincided with the use of silver and the availability of money between 1086 and 1300.

98 III Comp. 5.10.2 (X 5.19.12); IV Comp. 5.7.3 (X 5.19.18); Fourth Lateran Council, c.67 (COGD 2.1, p. 198).

99 Chobham 7.6.11.4, p. 510:

> Unde mirum est quod ecclesia sustinet quod principes impune convertunt in usus suos pecuniam iudeorum, cum iudei nihil babeant nisi ex usura, et ita tales principes sunt omnes participes usurarum et usurarii. Sed non punit eos ecclesia propter potestatem eorum, unde non excusantur apud deum. Dicunt tamen principes quod quia ipsi defendunt subditos suos contra iudeos et alios qui eos expellerent a terra si possent, ideo possunt licite accipere tantam pecuniam de bonis eorum.

See also Abulafia, "The Role of Money in Medieval Christian-Jewish Relations," 18–19 for traditional canonistic views.

100 Chobham, 7.6.11.2, p. 506.

101 Council of Paris (1212), part 5 c.6 (Mansi 22:851).

wage war on a grave illness.[102] As money lending was a form of robbery and yet necessity sometimes warranted extreme measures, Thomas may have wanted to ensure the spiritual well-being of those who had no other way in which to support themselves.

Similarly, what about the wife of a lender who had nothing except what her husband acquired from interest? Here, Thomas presents two viewpoints: (a) if he has neither friends nor knows any other skill, she may well withdraw from her husband; (b) as the Lord ate with sinners and robbers so that He may convince them to restore their faults, she may remain with her husband in the hopes of cajoling him to restore the interest he has taken or take less interest from the poor.[103] By staying with him, she labors on their behalf and thus licitly lives on the goods he takes illicitly. Though Robert of Courçon expressed the position in his treatise that a usurer's wife could not live with an incorrigible lender of a husband,[104] Thomas seems to echo a different position. The Council of Paris (1212), for example, held that a wife of a moneylender could live sparingly on the spoils of her husband's usury because she advocated for the betterment of the despoiled's cause by softening her husband's heart and inducing him to restore what had been taken away. But if she found that her husband's heart was unrepentant and incorrigible, she was obliged to seek separation from him, begging friends or others for food and clothing. If she had reached such a state of health that she was completely decrepit, leprous, or deserted by all so that no one wanted to give her bread, she may remain with her husband for the sake of necessity.[105] Both in the case of the laborer and the wife who was in need, we see the spirit of Gratian's words in C.14 q.5 d.p.c.14: that which was acquired poorly could be turned into good.[106]

A central focus for Thomas was actions *in fraudem usurarum*, dealings in which someone's love of greed resulted in the acquisition of usurious money through less-than-upright means. His framing lay in one determining factor: whether there is an unequal partnership, whether one benefits from the arrangement more than the other. For example, if someone has a dilapidated house and lends it to another so he can care for it lest it falls into further disrepair, there is no usury if there is equal benefit for both sides. However, if the person living in the house needs it more than the owner who wants the

102 Lefèvre, ed. and trans, *Le Traité "De Usura" de Robert de Courçon*, 41, 43.

103 Chobham 7.6.11.3, pp. 506–507.

104 Lefèvre, ed. and trans, *Le Traité "De Usura" de Robert de Courçon*, 43: "Verum uxor foeneratoris seorsum debet vivere, ut prædiximus, ex labore manuum et non cohabitare cum incorrigibili viro suo foeneratore in rapinis suis, et reddere debet ei debitum horis certis."

105 Council of Paris (1212), part 5 c.10 (Mansi 22:852).

106 GD C.14 q.5 d.p.c.14: "Que vero de malo sic acquiruntur in bonum possunt converti."

repairs, the latter is guilty of usury. He is taking advantage of a situation to have his house repaired.[107]

Balancing equity and the uncertainties associated with doing business led Thomas to walk another tightrope. Take, for example, instances in which someone buys grain as seeds so he can receive more at the harvest. Is he a usurer? It depends. If it can be determined with some sense of certainty—here Thomas refers to a *bonus vir* as the arbiter—that the market will be good based on the growing conditions and intends to sell at a higher price, he is a usurer. He is not a usurer if there is market uncertainty based on growing conditions. There is a distinction between buying now to sell higher later and hedging agricultural profits against the uncertainty of weather. He is also not a usurer if he proposes to sell the grain on a certain day at the market price for that day (whether more or less), and he ends up earning more.[108] Market uncertainty based on weather also applies to animal husbandry. A landholder was given 100 sheep and he paid 20 pounds yearly—or whatever was agreed upon—for the fruits of the sheep. At the end of the contract term, is it usury to make the landholder return the fruits in addition to the original 100 sheep? If the *bonus vir* determines that sickness, pestilence, or weak pasture put the landholder at risk but not the one who gave the sheep, it is usury. If the *bonus vir* determines that these conditions were not factors and the fruits of the sheep (i.e., lambs, wool, and cheese) reflected the agreed-upon price, there is no usury.[109] Thomas was, in a sense, dealing with the issue of rent charges, whereby for a cash payment a man buys the annual yield of a price of land, or a fixed annual revenue for an agreed-upon period of time. Such contracts were not usurious, provided the annual revenue would not, in the common opinion of men, exceed the returns that would have been received in outright purchase.[110]

107 Chobham 7.6.11.4, p. 507:

> Item, si aliquis habeat bn domum ruinosam et commodat earn alicui tanturnmodo ut custodiat eam ne amplius corruat... Ad hoc dicunt quidam quod...si tanta utilitas est ex una parte quanta ex altera, non est usura. Si vero maier utilitas by est eius qui in domo habitat ca quam eius qui concedit domum...usura es.

Roman law on usufructuary will play a role in setting up the next section on simony. In so far as it matters here, the *Institutes* (2.5.2) noted that one who has a use in a house has only a personal right of habitation. The *Digest* (7.1.13.4) delved further into the issue. An usufructuary cannot make the condition of the property worse, but he can improve it. If the usufruct of land was bequeathed, the usufructuary should not cut down fruit trees, demolish buildings, or do anything else to the injury of the property. And if the estate should happen to be one used for enjoyment and possesses pleasure gardens, lanes, or shady and pleasant walks laid out under trees that do not bear fruit, he should not cut them down to make kitchen gardens, or anything else designed to produce an income.

108 Chobham 7.6.11.6, pp. 511–512.

109 Chobham 7.6.11.9, pp. 516–517.

110 T. P. McLaughlin, "The Teaching of the Canonists of Usury," 120.

In its very essence, actions *in fraudem usurarum* encompassed hidden or "cloaked" usury: usury collected through shady practices. For example, one form of hidden usury was a gift in return for a loan. In this case, someone who has received a loan gives something "freely" to the creditor, yet "freely" was synonymous with feeling the compulsion to do so for fear of being without the loan entirely. Such constitutes usury, which is also the case when someone hosting a banquet sends for a merchant in order that he should be given a free cup of absinthe wine.[111] The merchant is being given something gratuitously for his past and future business dealings. Thomas and canon law reacted to an increasingly commercialized economy, and he tailored the legal atmosphere to the needs of his region and people. He made the complex relatable and understandable. Thomas again uses a question to set up a more complicated discussion: could a penalty be charged for a loan not repaid at the agreed-upon time and was that penalty considered usury? Thomas maintains that it is not usurious. The failure to repay at the agreed-upon time caused the lender great loss: he does not have the wherewithal to repay other debts owed.[112]

Under the umbrella of hidden usury, Thomas deals with the complications associated with buying and selling on credit (*venditio* and *emptio ad tempus/ad terminum*). *Venditio ad tempus/ad terminum* is when the seller defers payment, and on account of this delay, the article is sold at a higher price. With *emptio ad tempus/ad terminum*, payment is made now for goods to be delivered at a later date, and on account of the deferred delivery the price is higher at the time of payment than it would have been had the payment also been deferred.[113] Thomas states that when someone lends his cloth [or whatever] for a certain time for a greater price than it is worth, he commits fraud and is guilty of usury.[114] Thomas applies the same concept to apprenticeship. In some cities, a child is handed over to a merchant for a certain amount of money or for a certain amount of time to learn the trade. The child is to be fed and clothed at the merchant's expense, but at the end of the contracted time, the child would receive his wages from the merchant. If, however, the cost of food and clothing resulted in the child working in servitude, it is usury. The merchant benefited from the child's service.[115] Thomas also applies the concept to currency exchange. It is usurious if one sells a mark (*marca*) of silver for 50 solidi or 60

111 Chobham 7.6.11.4, p. 508; GD C.14 q.3 c.3. See also Helmholz, "Usury and the Medieval English Church Courts," 372–373; and E. Corran, "Moral Dilemma in English Confessors' Manual," 27. Thomas quoted different portions of GD C.14 q.3. c.3.

112 Chobham 7.6.11.7, pp. 512–513.

113 McLaughlin, "The Teaching of the Canonists of Usury," 117–118. On the sin of deceitfully buying low and selling high, see Rufinus, *Summa decretorum*, ed. H. Singer (rpt. Aalen, 1963), ad C.14 q.3 s.v. *Quod autem preter summam*, pp. 341–342.

114 Chobham 7.6.11.7 pp. 513–514.

115 Chobham, 7.6.11.9, p. 516.

of other currency, but the mark is worth only 40 solidi at the time of the transaction. Because *venditio* and *emptio ad tempus/ad terminum* contracts resulted in surreptitious profits which amounted to "cloaked usury," they were treated in the internal, not external, forum.[116] Though permitted in the external forum, Thomas assigned blame to the creditor who engaged in such contracts.[117] Presided over by Robert of Courçon, the Council of Paris (1212) and the Council of Rouen (1214) both decreed that those who sell goods *ad tempus/ad terminum* and the delay led to an increase of the price incurred both the guilt and penalties of usurers.[118] The Council of Paris (1212) had decreed that no one should serve as a clerk to a moneylender or write up his contacts.[119] Thomas was very much engaged in a wider dialogue taking place among ecclesiastics.

Hidden/"cloaked" usury had been a matter of concern since the pontificate of Alexander III. Essentially, lenders were seeking to concoct a complicated transaction merely to disguise a usurious loan. For example, simulated sale contracts were loans in which the debtor obtained a loan by "selling" a field to the creditor for a certain sum of money. The contract would stipulate the price and that the debtor may recover this land at a certain time; the price and time were calculated in such a way that the creditor would reap a profit from the fruits of the field. Hidden usury could also involve a mortgage, cases in which someone purchased land by taking a loan from the owner. In such cases, the owner would retain the land until the debt was paid and ownership was transferred. In the meantime, the owner could rent out the land for profit, even renting it to the purchaser without deducting the rent from the principal of the debt.[120] Pope Alexander III had condemned hidden usury at the Council of Tours (1163). No one within the clergy should lend money to the needy and take their possession as a pledge so that they may receive profits beyond the principal of the loan. Anything already received beyond the principal after deducting the expenses from the profits must be restored to the debtor.[121] Alexander III also addressed "cloaked" usury when he wrote to the archbishop of Genoa about people procuring pepper, cinnamon, or other goods. These goods, he noted, were then not worth more than five pounds, yet people promised to pay six pounds to those from whom they received them at a fixed term. While this form of contract was not usury per se, the sellers nevertheless

116 McLaughlin, "The Teaching of the Canonists of Usury," 119–120; Abulafia, "The Role of Money in Medieval Christian-Jewish Relations," 16–17.

117 Chobham 7.6.11.7, p. 513. See also Helmholz, "Usury and the Medieval English Church Courts," 369. Diocesan courts dealt only with "public" or "manifest" usurers; hidden usury fell into the realm of the confessional.

118 Council of Paris (1212), part 2 c.25 (Mansi 22:832); Council of Rouen (1214), part 2 c.28 (Mansi 22:911).

119 Council of Paris (1212), part 5 c.3 (Mansi 22: 850).

120 On hidden or "cloaked" usury, see McLaughlin, "The Teaching of the Canonists of Usury," 113–116, and Helmholz, "Usury and the Medieval English Church Courts," 371–372.

121 I Comp. 5.15.1 (X 5.19.1).

incurred a sin.[122] In a letter to the abbot and brothers of St. Laurentius, Alexander III stated that if they held the land as a pledge and had received their lot from its fruits, they must return the aforesaid land to the cleric.[123] One of the propositions proposed for discussion at the Council of Westminster (1175) was that land should not be taken as a pledge. Rather the fruits of the land harvested during the season should go toward repaying the principal (the lot).[124] Alexander III would address this matter in a decretal addressed to the archbishop of Canterbury and suffragan bishops. Those who held property or trees in pledge and had received the principal after deducting expenses were to restore the security for the debt (i.e., the pledge) without usury.[125] Pope Innocent III wrote to the bishop of Polignano on a similar matter in which the debtor was to "sell" his houses and olives for seven to nine years until he paid 40 ounces of tarens. Such an instrument of sale violated promulgations against usurers. The debtor was to be restored his houses and olives.[126] Innocent III wrote similarly to the subdeacon of Pisa. If a usurer bought the property with the agreement that he would return it to the seller after a time and he received something beyond the principal, this profit calculated was considered usurious.[127] In such instances, as Innocent III noted in another letter, if the creditor had received so much profit from the pledge that the principal had been satisfied, the pledge must be restored to the debtor. The fruits should be added to the payment of the principal.[128] Robert of Courçon paid particular attention to hidden usury in his tract on the subject. This occurred when someone received land, fields and vineyards, mills, and farms as a pledge. He offered the example of someone who left a farm, field, or vineyard to the other for 10 or 20 years in exchange for a loan of 100 or 1000 pounds. Once the period had expired, he would return the land, but in the meantime, he would receive all the royalties and all the products from the farm, field, or vineyard.[129] It was also usurious for buyers to pay 10 pounds cash for 20 measures of wheat and take delivery of these measures at harvest when they would be worth twice as much, which amounted to *emptio ad tempus/ad terminum*. Finally, it was usurious for a seller or the buyer to expect some additional advantage. Someone granting a loan or stipulating a price in a sales or purchase contract with the hope of receiving something in addition to capital committed usury.[130]

122 I Comp. 5.15.8 (X 5.19.6).
123 I Comp. 5.15.10 (X 5.19.8).
124 Council of Westminster (1175), proposition 27. Cheney, "The Council of Westminster 1175: New Light on an Old Source," 63. Cheney notes that the decretal could also have been addressed to the Bishop of Exeter, which would have been Bartholomew at the time.
125 I Comp. 5.15.4 (X 5.19.2).
126 III Comp. 3.14.1 (X 3.17.5).
127 III Comp. 3.17.1 (X 3.21.4).
128 III Comp. 3.17.3 (X 3.21.6).
129 Lefèvre, ed. and trans, *Le Traité "De Usura" de Robert de Courçon*, 61, 63.
130 Lefèvre, ed. and trans, *Le Traité "De Usura" de Robert de Courçon*, 57, 59.

Simony

Thomas followed his lengthy discussion of usury with another lengthy discussion, this one on simony. Simony was so-called from Simon Magus, who tried to bribe St. Peter into giving him the power to confer the Holy Spirit (Acts 8:9–24). In the language of the eleventh- and twelfth-century reformers, simony referred to giving money or goods in exchange for an office, fulfilling an obligation in exchange for an office, and finally, fulfilling a future promise in exchange for an office.[131] They were particularly concerned with the integrity of the ecclesiastical office, and they sought to curtail the appointment of church officials by forbidding secular rulers from investing, or bestowing the symbols on, the bishop or abbot with his spiritual authority at the same time as investing him with his secular authority. Gratian devoted the first causa of his *Decretum* to the issue of simony. In a lengthy q.1, he quickly condemned the purchasing of spiritualities and the one who had simoniacally ordained another. He spent the remainder of the question focused on the efficacy of the sacraments for the recipients if they were administered by a simoniac or one ordained by a simoniac. Thomas continues to pull on this thread by framing simony as having two prongs: the desire to buy or sell the spiritual or spiritually linked; and an agreement concerning temporalities for spiritualities or vice versa.[132] He analyzes these prongs through the lens of topics relevant to a subdeacon and *officialis*: oblations for baptism, saying of mass, burial, prayers for the dead, chrism, and marriages; selling of justice; the priest's stipend; granting of benefices to one's relatives; a master receiving payment from students; selling the right of patronage/advowson; laity withholding the tithe; and the buying and selling of the tithe.

Thomas emphasizes a distinction between the spiritual and the spiritual adjacent/spiritually linked. The spiritual are the sacraments, and these cannot be bought or sold by law. The grace of God signified by the sacraments is entirely priceless. The spiritually linked/spiritual adjacent are those items connected to the ecclesiastical but are not among the sacraments. Sacred vessels and vestments, for example, can be bought and sold to ecclesiastical persons. They can also be sold to the laity, so long as they are reduced from their current form, that is, they are melted down and no longer the vessel, or the threads are

131 See, for example, GD C.1 q.1 c.114 for simony by coin, favor, promise; Fourth Lateran Council c.64–c.65 (COGD 2.1, pp. 197–198) and X 5.3.9, 19–20, 25, 30, 36, 39, 41 which addressed simoniacal practices, including asking for money to enter a monastic life. The Council of Rouen (1214) part 3 c.12 echoed previously expressed positions in decreeing that there can be no simony with the ordination of clerics, the dispensing of benefices, the dedication of churches, the blessing of virgins, or with any remuneration in spiritualities for temporal service (Mansi 22:919).

132 Chobham, 7.6.12.1, p. 518: "Describitur autem simonia dupliciter, primo sic: simonia est studiosa voluntas emendi vel vendendi spirituale vel adnexum spitituali; vel sic: simonia est pactio de temporalibus propter spiritualia facienda vel e contra."

pulled so they are no longer vestments.[133] The reason for this treatment can be seen, for example, in Gratian's *Decretum*: the laity cannot possess ecclesiastical items.[134] But as we saw above in the section on usury, Thomas worked in an increasingly monetized climate, and here he finds himself threading the needle between the accumulation of (necessary) revenue and the sin of simony.

This distinction opened the door for Thomas to grapple with the realities of a priest needing to accept money for his services to support himself and those in need without being perceived as selling the spiritual, and thus being a simoniac who takes a gift from hand, from tongue, or from obligation. He solves this dilemma by focusing on the proper mindset of the priest. Priests rouse the hearts of the faithful when they preach. From that generosity flows profit. The support of temporalities is necessary for priests as they live from the fruits God provides. The temporal, however, should never be the endpoint of the spiritual, but rather, the spiritual should be the endpoint of the temporal. Preaching, and thus pastoral care, is only possible with the help of the temporal because God gives the temporal for necessity, consolation, trade, and to provide goodwill through his benefice. Thus, those who preach either for the delight of temporal profit, for favor, or out of vainglory are simoniacs. The proper priest appointed to the prebend must be one with the right mindset: when praying on behalf of the temporal, he is, in fact, praying that God may be served without hindrance. He distributes fruits given freely to the poor and does not require payment for the burial of dead, baptism, chrism, or betrothals, though such oblations are customarily given. Should something be given freely, such as to a poor priest who otherwise would not be able to support himself, it is best if he received the gift after the ceremony rather than before so as to avoid scandal and create the illusion that spiritual gifts are being bought. With the correct mindset, the priest may thus accept an offering given voluntarily and not through coercion, for his upkeep and the care of his flock.[135]

In essence, Thomas contextualized the law for the realities of pastoral care. For example, Gratian's *Decretum* included canons forbidding the coercion or acceptance of payment for burial. Furthermore, no price is required for baptism.[136] Pope Alexander III at the Council of Tours (1163) decreed that it was simony to receive a payment for entering into religion, for granting priories or chapels, for establishing prelates, for burial, for chrism, for the holy oil, for the blessings of marriage, or other sacraments.[137] The Third Lateran Council

133 Chobham 7.6.12.1, pp. 518–519; 7.6.12.7, p. 526. Causa 1 q.1 of Gratian's *Decretum*, as noted above, was a lengthy analysis of the impacts of simony (and heresy more generally) on the efficacy of each of the sacraments as bestowed by the one simonically ordained and the one who did the ordaining simonically.

134 GD D.96 d.a.c.1–c.1.

135 Chobham 7.6.12.3–6, pp. 520–525; 7.6.12.9, pp. 526–527; 7.6.12.13, pp. 529–530.

136 GD C.13 q.2 d.p.c.11–c.15; C.1 q.1 c.99.

137 Council of Tours, c.6; I Comp. 5.2.7 (X 5.3.8).

(1175) continued this line of thought, decreeing that it was disgraceful that in certain churches trafficking is said to have a place. Charges were made for the enthroning of bishops, abbots or ecclesiastical persons, for the installation of priests in a church, for burials and funerals, and for the blessing of weddings or for other sacraments. He who needed such ceremonies could not obtain them unless he first made an offering to the person who performed them. Some think this was permitted because long-standing customs had given it the force of law. Rather, it was utterly forbidden that anything be demanded for the enthronement of ecclesiastical persons or the institution of priests, for burial of the dead, for blessing marriages, or any other sacraments.[138] A key factor in not falling into simony was the notion that the faithful gave freely and were not coerced to give.[139] The Fourth Lateran Council (1215) likewise focused on the notion of coercion: clerics could not demand and exhort payment for funeral rights for the dead, the blessing of those marrying, and the like.[140] For Thomas, compliance with the law—the avoidance of the heresy of simony and the sin of greed—hinged on the correct mental framework, the reason the priest was preaching, and the motives behind the care he provided.

Thomas continued to pull on the thread of spiritually adjacent as he addressed the selling of justice, the ability of a master to receive payment from students, and the granting of benefices to one's relatives. Thomas maintains that when a judge sells justice, justice is not undertaken for an advantage but for a just sentence.[141] Judges already receive large sums on account of their dignity, and they should receive nothing else. A judge who sells access sins because he is selling justice to someone who feels he has to buy access because he has no other option when, in fact, he is owed it. Advocates, however, can charge for their labor, but if he defends an unjust cause he sins mortally even though he does not commit simony. In such instances, he must restore whatever he received, and many say he owes restitution to the person he damaged.[142] Thomas sees the selling of access as a form of secret robbery. A judge, lawyer, councilor, or arbiter who is bribed must restore that which was given either to the Church, which distributes it to the poor, or to those who were damaged.[143] Specifically addressing the position of *officialis* within a judicial framework, Thomas reminds his readers that *officiales* are officers who call men to judgment and labor much in this area. As such, they essentially fall under the same provisions as both

138 Third Lateran Council, c.7 (COGD 2.1, pp. 132–133).
139 Council of Paris (1212), part 4 c.12 (Mansi 22:841).
140 Fourth Lateran Council, c.66 (COGD 2.1, p. 198).
141 Chobham 7.6.12.1, p. 519: "Cum autem dicitur quod iudex vendit iustitiam, non accipitur ibi iustitia pro virtute, sed pro iusta sententia."
142 Chobham 7.6.12.2, pp. 519–520.
143 Chobham 7.6.9, p. 501.

judges who cannot sell justice and lawyers who cannot take payment by violence or extortion. *Officiales* should be content with their wages.[144]

Thomas is engaged in what seems to be increasingly vocal conversations about whether ecclesiastics engaged in the legal arena should receive payment. Gratian's *Decretum*, as noted above, had synthesized the foundation laid by Augustine: that taking something from someone against their will did not always constitute unjust theft. Very often, people were unwilling to give the wages due to a doctor or wages to a workman, though not to do so would be unjust as they were owed them. However, the fact that the advocate was paid for providing a just defense and the legal expert (*iurisperitus*) for providing sound advice did not mean that a judge should receive money for a just judgment or a witness for giving true testimony. If it was not right to be paid for just and true judgments or testimony, taking money for unjust and false ones was certainly far more outrageous, even if the money was given voluntarily. Judgment ought not to be for sale. There were others who have less exalted public roles and received money from both sides without impropriety, such as *officialis* (!), because there were many roles necessary to human activity filled by people who are attracted to or retained by benefits of this sort.[145] Pope Alexander III at the Council of Tours (1163) tackled the issue head-on: despite being done in some places, it was forbidden for deans or archpresbyters appointed to administer on behalf of bishops or archdeacons to settle ecclesiastical cases for a fee.[146] Both the Third Lateran Council (1175) and the Fourth Lateran Council (1215) focused on ecclesiastics in secular justice. The former decreed that clerics in the subdiaconate and above, and also those in the minor orders, should not presume to become advocates in legal matters before a secular judge if they were supported by ecclesiastical revenues unless they happened to be defending their own case or that of their church, or acting on behalf of the helpless who could not conduct their own cases.[147] The latter decreed that every cleric was forbidden from laying claim to the rights of the laity, which included secular justice.[148]

Local councils picked up the baton passed by Pope Alexander III at the Council of Tours. The Legatine Council at St. Peter's (1195) decreed that all diligent effort should be placed to ensure that justice is rendered gratis and that

144 Chobham 7.6.9, pp. 502–503. Thomas seems to be interpreting the role of *officialis* as having an increasing legal capacity.

145 GD C.14 q.5 c.15. Thomas quotes from the canon but seems to counter the position that the *officialis* could receive payment, in part because he does not see it as a "less exalted" role. By his time the role of *officialis* had grown in importance and influence. Rufinus likewise seems to hold that *officiales*, like judges, should not receive payment; see Rufinus, *Summa decretorum*, ad C.14 q.5 c.15 s.v. *Isti* and s.v. *furtis, rapinis, calumpniis*, p. 344.

146 I Comp. 5.3.2 (X 5.4.2), Council of Tours, c.7.

147 Third Lateran Council, c.12 (COGD 2.1, p. 137).

148 Fourth Lateran Council, c.42 (COGD 2.1, p. 186).

no one presumes to accept a price for it in ecclesiastical cases to be completed, lost, hastened, or delayed.[149] The Council of Paris (1212) forbade a canon or other cleric having a sufficient ecclesiastical benefice to serve as an advocate. It also forbade lawyers who did not have ecclesiastical benefits from demanding or extorting excessive salaries.[150] Finally, it was forbidden for prelates or their ministers to demand anything for rendering justice, for speeding up the process, or for delaying it.[151] *Officiales* who have been defamed for selling justice shall be removed from that office by the bishop.[152] The Council of Rouen (1214) similarly decreed that *officiales* should be faithful and wise, without consideration of person, and exercise justice for free.[153] Thomas was very much engaged in the conversations taking place regarding who can and cannot engage in the legal arena, and who can and cannot receive fees from justice.

Equally contentious was how a master could charge his students and not be guilty of simony, but a chancellor who grants a license to teach is guilty of simony if he charges a fee. Thomas is quite clear: the license to teach cannot be sold because it is a gift of the Holy Spirit. There is also a practical aspect to consider. The master has no means of living comfortably without the fees associated with teaching; teaching is his livelihood. The chancellor, however, does not work by teaching and has other means from which to live sufficiently.[154]

The canonical tradition was very much concerned with whether masters could charge for their services. Canon law, like Thomas, argued that a fee could not be associated with bestowing a license to teach. Pope Alexander III wrote that nothing should be required or promised for the license to teach, and should it happen, the exact amount must be restored, and the promise returned.[155] Paying for a teaching license should not be required, irrespective of whether one argued that it was customarily done.[156] The Third Lateran Council (1175) would decree that a cathedral church must provide a benefice to the teacher, who teaches the clergy of the same church and other poor people free of charge. No one should demand any money for a license to teach, or under cover of some custom seek anything from teachers, or forbid anyone to teach who is suitable and has sought a license.[157] The Council of Paris (1212) echoed the position by forbidding anyone to demand or extort anything before, or after for permission to teach.[158] The Fourth Lateran Council (1215) extended

149 Legatine Council at St. Peter' s, York (1195), c.10.
150 Council of Paris (1212), part 1 c.6 (Mansi 22:820–821).
151 Council of Paris (1212), part 4 c.13 (Mansi 22:842).
152 Council of Paris (1212), additio c.3 (Mansi 22:845).
153 Council of Rouen (1214), part 3 c.11 (Mansi 22:919).
154 Chobham 7.6.12.15, pp. 530–531.
155 I Comp. 5.4.2 (X 5.5.2).
156 I Comp. 5.4.3 (X 5.5.3).
157 Third Lateran Council, c.18 (COGD 2.1, pp. 140–141); I Comp. 5.4.1 (X 5.5.1).
158 Council of Paris (1212), part 1 c.20 (Mansi 22:824).

the provision set forth at the Third Lateran Council farther. In each cathedral church, a suitable benefice should be provided for a master who shall instruct the clerics of the cathedral church and other poor scholars without charge. Furthermore, in churches with sufficient resources, a suitable master, elected by the chapter or by the greater and sounder part of it, shall be appointed by the prelate to teach grammar and other branches of study. The metropolitan should have a theologian to teach Scripture to priests and instruct them in caring for souls. Teachers should receive an income of one prebend so long as they teach.[159] By allowing masters to charge students, Thomas seems to take a position different from that of the Fourth Lateran Council. While it is certainly possible that he did not know what the council decreed, it is also possible he saw the realities on the ground. Not every teacher may be sufficiently supported by a prebend, and cases may arise where fees are necessary to ensure the teacher's livable income. In these cases, it is not greed that drives him to charge fees but simply the need to support himself.

Thomas then considers whether it is simony to give a spiritual benefice to a relative simply because he is a relative. This was an important matter because by the twelfth century, a *beneficium* included the church's property tithes, offerings, and oblations for baptism, funerals, etc.[160] While beginning under the premise that it is a sin but not simony as there is no intention of buying or selling something spiritual, he concludes that it is simony because he expects a temporal advantage from his kinsman for the spiritual advantage he gave him. Even though he did not receive money for it, the bishop who gave it to his kinsman receives fruits from the name of his kinsman, and thus he benefits from it.[161]

The connection of granting spiritual benefices to kin simply because they are kin with simony, and thus the sin of greed, brings into relief the canonical tradition that forbade the inheritance of benefices. The Council of Poitiers (1078) had forbidden the goods of the church to succeed by right of consanguinity.[162] Gratian's *Decretum* forbade the ability of one to obtain an office by way of blood relations.[163] The Council of Westminster (1175) emphasized the necessity for a bishop to prevent hereditary benefices and that sons should not succeed their fathers in churches.[164] The same provision was echoed and repeated at the Council of Paris (1212) and the Council of Rouen (1214). No one could claim any ecclesiastical benefice for himself by hereditary right, nor should it be conferred by the same right on the part of anyone else. Benefices cannot be held by hereditary right, and giving relatives rent or proceeds from

159 Fourth Lateran Council, c.11 (COGD 2.1, pp. 173–174); IV Comp. 5.3.1 (X 5.5.4).
160 For an excellent discussion, see A. Meyer. "The Law of Benefices," in *The Cambridge History of Medieval Canon Law*, eds. A. Winroth and J. Wei (Cambridge, 2022), 367–395, here 373.
161 Chobham 7.6.12.12, p. 528.
162 I Comp. 3.5.1 (X 3.5.1).
163 GD D.89 d.p.c.5–c.6.
164 Council of Westminster (1175), c.1, p. 984.

church property is also forbidden.[165] The Fourth Lateran Council (1215) condemned the bad practice of sons of canons being instituted in secular churches. Should it be done, the appointment was invalid, and he who had attempted to do this was suspended from their benefice.[166] Thomas was a part of an intellectual milieu in which these issues were discussed in different capacities.

As the discussion of giving benefices to relatives alludes, the spiritually linked intersects with agreements concerning temporalities for spiritualities or vice versa. Under this umbrella, Thomas addresses the right of patronage—and, by extension, advowson—followed by the tithe. Advowson—the right to recommend a member of the clergy for a vacant benefice—had two branches: appropriation and patronage. An advowson from appropriation arose in cases of a rectory church. The claimant possessed the right to present the vicar who would minister to the spiritual needs of the rectory's parishioners. The rectory of a church possessed a monetary value as the rector received the fruits and income from the endowments of his church. The claimant stood to benefit from these assets, yet, as Peter Smith noted, rectories frequently were transferred to monastic or other spiritual foundations, which would thereby obtain the income of the rectory "for their own use" (*in proprios usus*) and, over time, could reduce the financial benefits of the original claimant as patron.[167] Episcopal *acta* from Salisbury are riddled with examples of rectories being given to monks "for their own use" (*in proprios usus*). To offer an example, during the episcopate of Hubert Walter (1189–1193), the monks of Bec received the church of Ogbourne St. Andrew and the church of Ogbourne St. George with the license to convert for their own use its fruits and income, saving sufficient maintenance for the chaplain and others who serve in the church. They also received the church of Wantage, given by King Henry II, with license to convert for their own use its fruits and income, and having been given free administration of the church, to possess it freely in perpetuity, saving just and reasonable maintenance of a chaplain and others to serve in the church.[168] Thomas himself was party to a number of these transactions during the episcopate of Herbert Poore (1194–1217), often being listed as *magister*. He witnessed an *actum* conferring onto the monks of Sherborne the

165 Council of Paris (1212), part 1 c.20 (Mansi 22:824); Council of Rouen (1214), part 1 c.23 (Mansi 22:903–904); Council of Rouen (1214), part 2 c.44 (Mansi 22:914).

166 Fourth Lateran Council, c.31 (COGD 2.1, p. 182).

167 P. M. Smith, "The Advowson: The History and Development of a Most Peculiar Property," *Ecclesiastical Law Journal* 5, no. 26 (2000): 320–339, here 327–328. In Roman law, usufruct is the right to the use and fruits of another person's property, with the duty to preserve its substance (Inst. 2.5). The right of use is a more restricted right than usufruct. Someone with the right of use may only take vegetables, fruit, flowers, hay, straw, and firewood for day-to-day needs. He may remain on the land if he does not cause trouble to the owner or get in the way of those doing the farm work. He has no power to sell or to hire out what he is entitled to, nor is he able to grant a gratuitous license. A usufructuary can do all these things (Inst. 2.5.1).

168 Kemp, ed., *English Episcopal Acta, Vol. 18*, nos. 159–161, pp. 125–127.

churches of Aldermaston and Padworth for their own use, saving the perpetual vicarages that the bishops of Salisbury may tax in the future.[169] As one last example, Thomas witnessed as *magister* and subdeacon an *actum* confirming on Montebourg Abbey the license to convert Loders church and Bradpole chapel for their own use when vacant, provided that they be served by suitable chaplains. They were also provided in perpetuity the constitution of the church and chapel as a prebend of Salisbury cathedral with the same liberties as other prebends enjoy, the abbot having a place and stall in the cathedral to be served by a priest-vicar, to whom the abbey would pay an annual stipend of 40 shillings from the goods of the prebend.[170]

The second branch of advowson was the *ius patronatus*. Courtesy of the proprietary church system, donors—often lay but not always—essentially owned the churches they built and supported. They thus had the ability to appoint and dismiss the priest at will and to administer the church's endowments, which meant that they could sell, exchange, lease, and mortgage the property of the church they patronized. As an example, Bishop Herbert Poore granted and confirmed the infirm brethren of the hospital of Pont-Audemer, to whom the *ius patronatus* of Sturminster [Marshall] church belonged, 10 marks of silver annually from Sturminster church for their own use (*in proprios usus*), for the clothing of infirm of the house, and for the priest Richard de Fraxineto whom the bishop instituted as parson upon their presentation of him.[171] Even when canon law forbade a cleric from accepting a church from a layman in the eleventh and twelfth centuries, the lay donors continued to present their choice for a cleric to the bishop for admission and institution. Precisely because the advowson was seen as a form of property, the advowson could pass to another as would any other grant or inheritance of that manor. The result was that the manor could be sold, but the advowson was retained. Or, as was quite common, the advowson was sold while the manor was retained. The end result in either instance was to divorce the advowson from the land to which it originally attached.[172]

Thomas takes up the issue of whether selling the right of patronage constitutes simony. On the one hand, the laity possesses the right of patronage and, therefore, it can be sold. The right of presentation to the church, however, is

169 Kemp, ed., *English Episcopal Acta, Vol. 18*, no. 211, pp. 168–169.

170 Kemp, ed., *English Episcopal Acta, Vol. 18*, no. 214, pp. 171–172.

171 Kemp, ed., *English Episcopal Acta, Vol. 18*, no. 222, pp. 179–180. The *actum* went to state that the bishop granted and confirmed from Richard de Fraxineto's successors eight marks, and from Mr. Thomas of Chobham, whom he admitted to the perpetual vicarage at their presentation, and his successors two marks.

172 Smith, "The Advowson," 321, 324, 327. For Rufinus on the origins of *ius patronatus*—possession, construction, and enrichment—and whether it can be transferred to others, see ad C.16 q.7 c.26 s.v. *Pie mentis amplectenda devotio est*, pp. 368–371.

spiritual.[173] Thomas acknowledges the complexities of the issue: the right of patronage is mixed with temporal rights and spiritual rights.[174] He resolves this conundrum with the position that the right of patronage can pass (*transire*) with the corporate body (*universitas*). If someone sells a town in which there is the right of patronage attached to a church, he is not selling the right of patronage per se, but rather, he is selling the town and all that belongs to it. The right of patronage passes with the *universitatem*, with the rest of the corporate body.[175] The right of patronage cannot be sold alone but passes as part of a package deal: it passes with the community at large to the buyer of the town.

Thomas's position is rooted in the decretals of Pope Alexander III who granted patrons their due but only to a point. Involved in a messy case, the bishop of Worchester had consulted the pope, who maintained that new patrons could not change the institutions in patronized churches, nor can the vicissitudes of churches be affected by them.[176] In a letter to the bishop of Hereford and abbot of Ford regarding a case in which a soldier bought a town—which included a church—from a female abbey in Winchester, the pope maintained that the right of patronage/advowson passed to the buyer unless it was explicitly excluded.[177] The right of patronage, Alexander wrote to the archbishop of Canterbury, could not be sold per se.[178] A patron, he noted in a letter to the archbishops and bishops of England, could not alienate the right of patronage by his own authority, nor could he demand anything temporal from the church unless, at the time of its foundation, it was reserved to him by the diocese.[179] Should a disagreement arise between parties as to who had the right of patronage and multiple candidates were put forward to serve a church, the bishop had the right to determine who would serve the church if the matter had not been settled within three months.[180] Yet, as Peter Smith noted, though the Church claimed the jurisdiction to decide the right of patronage, the right to decide advowson fell to the king's court despite the Church's objections. Canon 1 of the Constitutions of Clarendon (1164) held that if a controversy concerning advowson and presentation of churches arise between laymen, or

173 Chobham 7.6.12.14, p. 530: "…quia possidetur a laicis et ideo videtur posse vendi, et tamen ius presentandi ad ecclesiam est spirituale." Thomas restates this point in 7.6.12.18, p. 532: "Videtur quod non, quia spirituale est presentare aliquem clericum ad aliquod beneficium. Salus enim episcopus dat omnia beneficia spiritualia in episcopatu suo, sed laici presentant…"
174 Chobham 7.6.12.18, p. 532: "Est igitur ius patronatus, sicut dicunt multi, mixtum cum iure spirituale et seculari."
175 Chobham 7.6.12.18, pp. 532–533. Thomas is not exact in his verbiage. In 7.6.12.14, p. 530, he does say it can be sold, using the verb *venire*. The implications in both chapters remain the same, however.
176 I Comp. 3.33.11 (X 3.38.9).
177 I Comp. 3.33.9 (X 3.38.7).
178 I Comp. 3.33.30 (X 3.38.16).
179 I Comp. 3.33.29 (X 3.38.23).
180 Third Lateran Council, c.17 (COGD 2.1, p. 140); I Comp. 3.33.4 (X 3.38.3).

between laymen and clerks, or between clerks, it should be treated of and terminated in the court of the lord king.[181] Glanville echoed this position in Book 4 on advowson in the *Tractatus de legibus et consuetudinibus regni Anglie*. When issues of advowson arose, the king's court decided which of the parties possessed the right to recommend a member of the clergy for a vacant benefice or to make an appointment. If someone brought the case before an ecclesiastical judge, it was moved to the king's court.[182] Thomas conveniently sidesteps this.

If the *ius patronatus*, right of advowson, could not be sold individually, what of the tithe? Does buying and selling of the tithe constitute simony? Thomas sets the stage by first addressing briefly the issue of laity withholding the tithe. Laymen cannot possess the right to receive (*ius percipiendis*) the tithes as they cannot possess the right of patronage (*ius patronatus*) without the involvement of the Church.[183] With that being said, while the Church has conceded the fruits of the tithes to the laity, it has conceded neither the right of receiving (*ius percipiendis*) them by the patron of the church on behalf of some priest preaching nor the right to present (*ius presentandi*); only a bishop, not the laity, grants the right of tithes and of the churches.[184] In essence, the Church can grant the laity the product from the act of tithing, but the laity cannot be granted the right to collect or distribute the tithe.

Thomas's position reflects the realities on the ground that saw the concept of tithing becoming more complicated and the tithe itself being frequently reallocated. The tithe was transforming to include: tithes levied on monetized products, such as cereals and wine grapes; tithes comprised agricultural products typically consumed locally, such as hay, vegetables, and fruit from orchards and gardens; tithes on animals which was collected from the increase of the flock or on fishing and hunting; and the distinction between ordinary tithes and "new" tithes (*novalia*) levied, often at a different rate, on lands newly cultivated by clearing.[185] The *acta* from Salisbury reveal multiple cases in which the tithes were being transferred from one entity to another. Bishop Hubert Walter

181 Smith, "The Advowson," 331; for Constitutions of Clarendon, c.1; see https://avalon.law.yale.edu/medieval/constcla.asp.

182 Glanville, *Tractatus de legibus et consuetudinibus regini anglie*, Bk. 4 (pp. 43–53) is entirely about advowson as it is treated in the king's court.

183 Chobham 7.6.12.16, p. 531. Thomas again referenced Alexander III's viewpoint expressed in Third Lateran Council, c.17 (COGD 2.1, p. 140) and in I Comp. 3.33.4 (X 3.38.3).

184 Chobham 7.6.12.16, p. 531: "Verumtamen videtur quod ecclesia ex permissione sua concesserit laicis fructus decimarum, non ius percipiendi, et patrono ecclesie potestatem orandi pro aliquo clerico, et non ius presentandi, quia solus episcopus dat ius decimarum et ecclesiarum, non laicus." See also II Comp. 1.16.4 (X 1.36.9) where Pope Lucius III writes against a layman who obtains the right of presentation, while the religious receive a new or greater share in the church, in which they used to have no or a smaller portion before.

185 C. de Miramon, "Ecclesiastical Property, Tithes, *Spiritualia*," in *The Cambridge History of Medieval Canon Law*, eds. A. Winroth and J. Wei (Cambridge, 2022), 345–367, here 360–362.

granted and confirmed the demesne tithe and all appurtenances to the canons of Notley of the church of Maiden Bradley with the chapel of Horningsham so they may convert the fruits for their own use (*in usus proprios*).[186] Bishop Richard Poore (1217–1228) granted as a benefice in perpetuity to the prior and convent of Beamore Priory half of the corn tithes of the parish of the church of Ebbesborne Wake, with the other half and all other tithes to be received by the church's parson who would be appointed by the bishop of Salisbury.[187] Thomas himself witnessed many of these arrangements as *magister*. For example, he witnessed an *actum* conferring onto the monks of Sherborne the churches of Aldermaston and Padworth. The *actum* also confirmed for their own use the tithes in Sotwell, land given as a gift by Adam de Port.[188] Bishop Herbert Poore had granted to the prior and monks of Hurley priory, for the office of the sacristy, all corn tithes of Waltham (St. Lawrence) throughout the year, and Roger, the chaplain at Longueville Abbey, was granted all of the demesne tithes of Wittenham.[189]

At its core, canon law held, however, that the laity could not withhold or collect the tithe while it fell to the bishop alone to distribute the tithe. Gratian's *Decretum* was clear that those who did not pay the tithes to priests incurred guilt and were to be excommunicated. Ecclesiastical goods, of which tithes were included, could only be distributed by the bishop's authority; neither laity, princes, nor the religious could take possession of goods without his permission.[190] Pope Alexander III continued to emphasize the position that the tithe could not be given to laymen and could not be granted as an inheritance. Furthermore, a patron could not confer the tithes to the church or anything spiritual without the consent of the bishop or the pope, even to a monastery.[191] The conciliar tradition likewise legislated on this matter. The Council of Westminster (1175) called for the excommunication of anyone who detained the tithes from wool, linen, and the like.[192] The Council of Paris (1212) likewise decreed that tithes taken from churches should be returned under pain of excommunication. Furthermore, the laity were to pay the tithes on newly cultivated lands.[193] The Fourth Lateran Council (1215) decried the custom of patrons claiming the incomes from churches for themselves, leaving the priests

186 Kemp, ed., *English Episcopal Acta, Vol. 18*, no.176, pp. 138–139.
187 B. R. Kemp, ed., *English Episcopal Acta, Vol. 19: Salisbury 1217–1228* (Oxford, 2000), no. 267, pp. 234–235.
188 Kemp, ed., *English Episcopal Acta, Vol. 18*, no. 211, pp. 168–169.
189 Kemp, ed., *English Episcopal Acta, Vol. 18*, no. 203, pp. 161–162; no. 209, pp. 167–168.
190 GD C.16 q.1 c.58–c.59, c.65–d.p.c.67; C.16 q.7 d.a.c.1–c.1, c.3–c.8. See also Rolandus, *Summa decretorum*, ad C.16 q.7, pp. 56–58.
191 I Comp. 1.36.7 (X 3.30.15); II Comp. 3.17.2 (X 3.30.17); I Comp. 3.33.21 (X 3.38.17).
192 Council of Westminster (1175), c.13, pp. 988–989.
193 Council of Paris (1212), additio c.14 (Mansi 22:846); item, *De usurariis* c.3 (Mansi 22:853).

barely able to sustain themselves. A sufficient portion of revenues must be assigned to the priest.[194]

With the secular realm's obligation to pay the tithe and the ecclesiastical realm's obligation to collect and distribute the tithe both affirmed, Thomas turns to the buying and selling of the tithe. If the Church can sell houses and properties, why are they not able to sell the tithes with their rights? Or, if the right to receive (*ius percipiendi*) tithes is purely spiritual, why do the laity possess the tithes and then grant or sell them to whomever they please? Thomas reminds his readers that tithes are purely spiritual, instituted by God, and given to his ministers so they might be able to support themselves. To that end, only ministers of the Church are able to possess the right of the tithes (*ius decimarum*). As a result, a cleric is able to sell the fruits of the tithes at the market or wherever he wants without simony. If a cleric sells a layman the tithes in relation to a field for a year or two, he is not able to sell him the right to receive the tithes (*ius percipiendi*) so that the laymen could curtail the peasants from paying them.[195] In essence, Thomas maintained that one could sell the fruits that came from the tithe of the field, but one could not sell the right to collect the tithe.

Thomas deftly balanced canon law against a burgeoning market economy. As Ben Dodds has shown, religious institutions appropriated the tithe for their own ends by choosing either to collect their tithes from the fields and prepare the grain for sale or consumption, or they could sell before collection in the field with the buyer agreeing to pay for the tithe grain on a specified day the following year. The tithe buyer only needed to collect the tithes at harvest time, dispose of the grain, and make the payments on the appointed days. Tithes were often sold annually but could be leased for a number of years.[196] Canon law was keen to legislate against the misappropriation of the tithe, particularly as the distinction between personal (payable upon receipt of the sacraments) and praedial (land-based) tithe came into the mix by the latter half of the

194 Fourth Lateran Council, c.32 (COGD 2.1, pp. 182–183). By decreeing that the priest must have sufficient revenues, the council seems to concede the reality that patrons in fact claimed the incomes from churches for themselves.

195 Chobham 7.6.12.19, p. 533:

> Fructus autem decimarum, sicut oblationes altaris potest clericus vendere in foro vel ubicumque voluerit sine omni simonia. Si autem clericus vendit decimas in agro alicui laico per unum annum vel per duos me, non potest ei vendere ius percipiendi decimas, ut scilicet coercere possit rusticos ad solutionem declmarum, sed solummodo fructus.

196 B. Dodds, "Demesne and Tithe: Peasant Agriculture in the Late Middle Ages," *Agricultural History Review* 56, Part II (2008): 123–141; idem, "Managing Tithes in the Late Middle Ages," *Agricultural History Review* 53, Part II (2005): 125–140, esp. 125–126, 136.

twelfth century.[197] Gratian's *Decretum* presented a simplistic approach; he did not distinguish between personal and praedial tithes. Bishops were guilty of simony if they distributed the tithes for either money or to the laity as opposed to clerics.[198] Yet, circumstances seemed to be shifting by the time of Pope Alexander III when it was decreed at the Third Lateran Council (1175) that laymen could not transfer the tithe to another layman, even if he possessed it with a title.[199] A byproduct of the *ius patronatus*, the tithe was not only possessed by the laity but like advowson, it was treated as a commodity to be bought and sold as it benefited the possessor. Church councils issued decrees forbidding the clergy from engaging in the commodification of the tithe. The Council of Paris (1212) decreed that if a prelate or any person bought the tithes, parishes, or other spiritual goods belonging to the priors, the contract was declared null and void since they could not be sold by law.[200] The Council of Rouen (1214) forbade abbots, priors, and other ecclesiastical persons to commit the tithes or offerings of the churches' lands to laymen.[201] The Fourth Lateran Council (1215) confirmed that regulars and secular clerics could not prejudice parish churches by adding a proviso to the contract that tenants and vassals shall pay the tithes to them and shall choose to be buried on their ground when they lend houses or grant fiefs.[202] The tithe had to be preserved for its intended uses.

Conclusion

Thomas of Chobham devoted Article 7 distinction 6 to the deadly sin of greed. Echoing the observations made by Emily Corran, Thomas began the broader subject with a treatment of traditional topics of theft and robbery—basic concepts—and then delved into the complications that he treated under usury and simony.

Woven into a fairly standard definition of theft and robbery, Thomas took the opportunity to comment on contemporary trends. One such trend was secular law's position toward finding treasure and forest law. Contrary to that set forth in Roman law, English law allowed for the king to retain the entire treasure. He also disagreed with the English law on wild animals, particularly deer, as property of the king alone. As a diocesan administrator, he would have had

197 A. Lewis, "Tithe Personal and Praedial," *The Journal of Legal History* 42, no. 2 (2021): 123–146 notes that Rolandus, Stephan of Tournai, and Hostiensis grappled with the distinction between personal and praedial tithes. Popes Celestine III and Innocent III grappled with the calculation of tithe payments vis-à-vis business expenses.

198 GD C.1 q.3 c.13–c.14. See Lewis, "Tithe Personal and Praedial," 126–128.

199 Third Lateran Council, c.14 (COGD 2.1, pp. 137–138); I Comp. 3.26.23 (X 3.30.19).

200 Council of Paris (1212), additio c.2 (Mansi 22:846).

201 Council of Rouen (1214), part 3 c.30 (Mansi 22:922).

202 Fourth Lateran Council, c.56 (COGD 2.1, p. 193).

a firm grasp of secular rulings that impacted the people in his care. Thomas also kept pace with current canon law which denied sanctuary to robbers. He conceded the reality that robbers may have to suffer corporeal punishment as medicine...so long as it was not at the hands of ecclesiastical judges.

With issues surrounding prescription fading into the sunset, courtesy of the regulations put in place for the cultivation of new land, Thomas turned to the more threatening forms that theft and robbery were taking at the turn of the thirteenth century. *Commdatum* and *mutuum* contracts could, and were, being abused by the greedy interested in collecting more than they originally loaned. Rather than treating the borrower equitably, lenders were devising ways to collect hidden/"cloaked" usury, a transgression that fell under the purview of the internal forum. With the increase in trade and mercantilism, Thomas spent considerable time navigating when buying and selling on credit was usurious and when it was not.

Just as usury was taking different shapes in this new environment, so too was simony. Thomas's treatment of simony as greed was shaped by his knowledge of the law and his administrative experience as an *officialis*. Simony was both the buying or selling of the spiritual or spiritually linked and the agreement about temporal things for the spiritual and vice versa. It encompassed the selling of justice and a chancellor selling a teaching license, subjects that were personal to him. It encompassed those things that made up an ecclesiastical *beneficium*: oblations for baptism, saying of mass, burial, prayers for the dead, chrism, and marriages; the priest's stipend; selling the right of patronage/advowson; laity withholding the tithe; and the buying and selling of the tithe. At its core, Thomas's treatment of simony was rooted in the realities of the *beneficium* being parceled out to the highest bidder for the benefit of others, both ecclesiastical and lay.

In the end, Thomas's treatment of the subjects under Article 7 on the Deadly Sin of greed does show a legal bias indicative of the climate of the time, even if it was not as forward-facing as others in Peter the Chanter's circle such as that of Robert of Flamborough. He was familiar with the canon law of Gratian's *Decretum*, and the older law found in the penitentials of Robert of Flamborough and Bartholomew of Exeter. He was versed in decretal law and seems to be engaged in the same conversations taking place at regional councils such as those held in Canterbury and York, and presided over in Paris (1212) and Rouen (1214) by Robert of Courçon who was also a member of Peter the Chanter's circle and whose work Thomas knew. He had some grounding in both Roman law and English common law. Thomas most likely learned canon and Roman law while studying at Paris. He no doubt supplemented his knowledge while serving in London and kept abreast of decretal, conciliar, and secular law as his administrative duties as subdean and *officialis* demanded it. Such breadth and depth of knowledge would have proven useful in the legal arena of a diocese and as a diocesan administrator. His integration of the legal tradition into his pastoral manual adapted the ideal to reality. Thomas was a casuist, and the ability to navigate the law was necessary to teach and ensure that the clergy had the knowledge necessary to carry out their functions. With that said, Thomas knew his audience, and he deftly rendered the complicated understandable by integrating the law into the needs and desired outcomes of the internal forum that guided human activity within the Christian community.

CONCLUSION

Throughout this work, we have seen how theology and law in the twelfth and early thirteenth centuries occupied the same intellectual space and thus could be seen as two sides of the same coin. Pastoral care, on the one hand, and the realities of administrative service outside of the schools, on the other hand, made familiarity with the law advantageous. Lanfranc and Anselm did much to shape the intellectual climate of northern France during their abbatial tenures at Bec. Using reason (*ratio*) to prove the point through debate (*disputatio*) as a teaching technique, the dialectical method created a culture in which *litterati* drew upon sources and techniques important to both theology and law while also bringing attention to discordant sources. A common intellectual tradition coupled with a climate in which theologians and canonists engaged in discussions on similar topics resulted in drawing from a common source base that included Scripture and the writings of the Church Fathers. The interweaving of authorities and commentary, the compiling of a *Glossa ordinaria* as an authoritative text, and the utilization of *questiones* as new literary genres were manifestations of this culture, a culture in which the lines between theology and law blurred as academia fosters synergies. To that end, it was not uncommon for one to compile both canonical and theological works because of his training in dialectical methods.[1]

1 P. Fournier and G. LeBras, *Histoire des Collections Canonique en Occident: Depuis les Fausses Décrétales jusqu'au Décret de Gratien*, 2 vols. (Paris, 1932), 2:316–322, 351. Between the time of Ivo of Chartres and Gratian, law and theology overlapped significantly around the sacraments, especially marriage and the simoniacal priest. Canonistic thought strongly influenced theological thought on the sacraments and pastoral duties; see, A. García y García, "The Faculties of Law," in *A History of the University in Europe, Vol. 1: Universities in the Middle Ages*. ed. H. de Ridder-Symoens (Cambridge, 1992), 388–408, here 405.

DOI: 10.4324/9781003465096-9

Marriage serves as an excellent example of how a common intellectual tradition operated on the ground as both theologians and canon lawyers were deeply engaged in shaping its framework and regulations. The theologians Hugh of St. Victor and Peter Lombard, and the canonists Ivo of Chartres, the anonymous compiler of the *Collectio St. Victor*, Walter of Thérouanne who possibly compiled the *Collectio decem partium*, and Gratian all addressed similar themes: marriage as a sacrament, the definition of a legitimate marriage, when a marriage begins, the conjugal debt, clandestine marriages, the good of marriage, separation, marriage of unbelievers, and consanguinity and affinity. The topic of marriage also allows us to see the extent to which a similar source base provided a foundation and porous disciplinary boundaries fostered cross-pollination. Hugh of St. Victor found the sermons of Ivo of Chartres useful on occasion and he incorporated conciliar canons as they were useful to his discussion of consanguinity and affinity. Peter Lombard drew from Gratian's *Decretum* though he shaped the material to suit his needs. The role consent versus coitus played in the formation of a marriage preserves the implicit and explicit dialogue that theologians and canonists no doubt engaged as they discussed these topics. Ivo of Chartres leaned more toward consent as reflective of the theologians while Walter of Thérouanne seems to have struggled more with the precious role coitus should play. Taking a 30,000-foot view of marriage, the *Collectio St. Victor* covers the high points of marital law quickly and efficiently without delving into specific examples. While beginning from similar points, Hugh of St. Victor, Peter Lombard, Ivo of Chartres, the anonymous compiler of the *Collectio St. Victor*, Walter of Thérouanne, and Gratian engaged with the individual topics with their audience and their needs in mind.

Within this intellectual climate legal knowledge spread between colleagues as well as between master and student. Ivo of Chartres was integral to these efforts as he compiled legal collections, taught, and engaged with regional prelates. This network, which John Ott referred to as the "Band of Brothers," discussed, debated, and shared knowledge. Law and theology were important to their work. Also integral to the spread of legal knowledge and the proliferation of legal texts was the *Via Francigena*. The pilgrimage route between Canterbury and Rome, like networks, facilitated the spread of people, texts, and knowledge. Those in need of knowledge borrowed from the texts available to create a work that suited their purposes and filled their needs.

Peter the Chanter can be seen as a parallel to Ivo of Chartres. He too created a "Band of Brothers," a network that included Robert of Courçon, Robert of Flamborough, and Thomas of Chobham. As *litterati* and as administrators in different capacities, they actively engaged in an intellectual environment where issues were discussed. Richard Poore, for example, served as dean of Salisbury from 1198 to 1214. Between ca.1208 and 1213, however, he lived and taught in Paris because he was out of favor with King John.

His tenure as dean of Salisbury coincided with that of Thomas of Chobham as subdean. Richard's exile in Paris could have kept Thomas in contact with happenings in and around Paris. In addition, Robert of Flamborough dedicated his work to Richard Poore,[2] a work that he completed by 1215, around the same time that Thomas of Chobham may have completed his. Book 4 of Robert of Flamborough's penitential is organized around the seven deadly sins, and, coincidently, so too is Article 7 of Thomas of Chobham's *Summa*. Finally, it must be remembered that Salisbury was in the archdiocese of Canterbury which received numerous decretals from Pope Alexander III. There was thus a culture and climate of a shared legal environment. The transmission of knowledge may not have been so much a→b or b→a, but rather a↔b.

Theologians thus studied, wrote, worked, and collaborated within this vibrant climate. They were not walled off from, but rather immersed in, legal thought. Not all theologians, however, had the same need for the legal texts. Hugh of St. Victor and Peter Lombard, for example, incorporated legal principles into their works, sparingly in the case of the former and more robustly in the case of the latter. The moral theology that grounded penitential manuals followed suit as they served practical needs. Such manuals represent a confessor who needed to be a "jack of all trades," competent in theology in order to instruct and guide the penitent, competent in canon law in order to deal with offenses that fell under church law, and competent in Roman law in order to draw upon principles not covered by canon law. All of these competencies, however, had to be distilled in a manner that would be rendered serviceable to the intended user.[3] That user might either not have been trained to read the technical material or not have had access to the source material to read it for himself.

It is important to remember that penitential books were by no means new to the twelfth and thirteenth centuries. Since the early Middle Ages, tariff books on penance had been the norm. Such works provided lists of sins with the penance to be "paid" to satisfy that transgression. Councils and synods likewise generated penitential canons as a way of regulating various offenses.[4] Joseph Goering, however, noted that the ancient canons prescribing a set penance for each sin gave way to discretionary penance. That is, there was a gradual shift from an overwhelming concern with satisfaction for sins to a concern with the penitent's contribution and confession of sins. The

2 Robert of Flamborough, *Liber poenitentialis: A Critical Edition with Introduction and Notes*, ed. J. J. Francis Firth (Toronto, 1971), 7–8; the Prologue p. 54 states *decane salesburienssis*.

3 Revd. F. Bloomfield, ed., *Thomae de Chobham Summa confessorum* (Louvain, 1968), xvi–xvii.

4 C. Vogel, *Les Libri Paenitentiales* (Turnout, 1978), 30.

description of sin and the contextualization of sexual offenses called upon the priest to use his best judgment.[5]

By extension, the manuals of Peter the Chanter and his circle focused on the questions and theological justifications pertaining to confession. *Libri penitentiales* and *Summae confessorum* were part of a climate between the Third Lateran and Fourth Lateran Councils (1179–1215) in which parochial ministry, the *cura animarum*, and the instruction of the priests for their duties in the confessional, were key areas of focus. The confessor should know the one confessing as a doctor knows his patients' bodies and cares for them.[6] These *Libri penitentiales* and *Summae confessorum* essentially systematized the remission of sin by focusing on the way in which confessors conducted confession. They helped the priests, such as those who heard confession and issued penance on behalf of the archdeacon, in their ministering to the laity. The laity, however, were not the only ones who gave confession. Rural deans, for example, were common in France and England. As a parochial priest, he was appointed by the bishop to supervise and hear the confessions of approximately a dozen parish priests. Charged with penitential discipline by the bishop, the *penitentiarius* heard the confessions of the clergy, adjudicated cases sent to the bishop from local confessors, and imposed public penances on behalf of the bishop.[7] *Libri penitentiales* essentially replaced the "tariff books" by providing confessors with a manual expounding on the theology, law, doctrine, and social problems underlying the sacrament of penance. *Summae confessorum* expounded on the procedure to which confessions should adhere.[8]

The administrative duties and the climate in which these theologians worked tell a lot about how, or if, they cited legal sources. As a teacher, Peter the Chanter could incorporate the essence of contemporary legal thought by providing a highly paraphrased citation if his purpose was simply to give the gist of an established and accepted legal principle. Sometimes, however, the need arose in which Peter felt that specific and detailed references were warranted, such as to the Third Lateran Council and the *Decretum* of Gratian. Entrenched in diocesan management, Bartholomew of Exeter tended to include an inscription to the material and the original source, rather than the formal, intermediary,

5 J. Goering, "The *Summa* of Master Serlo and Thirteenth-Century Penitential Literature," *Mediaeval Studies* 40 (1978): 290–311, here 297, 302. Jean Longère had made a similar observation, noting that their role was to discern and not blindly apply penance. See J. Longère, "Quelques 'Summa de poenitentia' à la fin du XIIe siècle et au début du XIIIe siècle," in *La piété populaire au Moyen Âge*, ed. E. Delaruelle (Paris, 1975), 45–58, here 57.

6 L. Boyle, "Summae confessorum," in *Les genres littéraires dans les sources théologiques et philosophiques médiévales: Définition, crique et exploitation. Actes du colloque internationale de Louvain-la-Neuve 25–27 mai 1981* (Turnhout, 1982), 227–237, here 230, 232–233.

7 Goering, "The Internal Forum and the Literature of Penance and Confession," in HMCL 2, 387–398.

8 Boyle, "Summae confessorum," 234; Vogel, *Les Libri Paenitentiales*, 13.

source for his texts. While Gratian's *Decretum* was important for Bartholomew, Robert of Flamborough continued to regard the *Decretum* of Burchard of Worms (ca. 1012–ca. 1022) and the *Decretum* of Ivo of Chartres (ca. 1195) as particularly useful in addition to the commentary of Huguccio and papal decretals. Robert of Courçon's reliance on the law, and his citation of it, depended on whether it was germane to the discussion. In some cases, where the law added to, but was not the center of, his point, he attributed a less specific reference. Phrases such as "cum auctoritas clamet," "dicit canon," "tradit decretales," or "dicit auctoritas" were common. As a papal legate, Robert may not have felt explicit references were needed as he expected his audience to know them. Though legal thought was in the air, Thomas of Chobham chose not to make any explicit references to the law. The closest one finds are loose phrases such as "in canonibus." As subdean and *officialis* in the diocese of Salisbury, Thomas knew his audience did not need the specifics but simply the concepts.

The topics covered in this work—topics such as marriage, excommunication, crusading and heresy, homicide, and greed—necessitated a knowledge of law, even if law was neither the author's first area of expertise nor their first area of interest. Each theologian's work and how he drew upon legal knowledge reflects the environment that occupied his thoughts. Peter the Chanter's *Summa* reflects his teaching career at Notre Dame. A study of his teachings on excommunication reflects his selective plucking of the law, and tweaking the tradition if need be, to instruct students on how to navigate difficult situations they could encounter while tending to the souls of the faithful. His treatment of the topic concerned its parameters for use, jurisdiction, offenses, sentences and their implications, communication with the excommunicated, and the ability to excommunicate those who have died. When it suited his purpose, Peter engaged with legal knowledge that was both firmly established and in the midst of change to offer pragmatic solutions for problematic questions that one engaged in pastoral care would face when ministering to his flock. Robert of Courçon, on the cusp of becoming a cardinal, was the most engaged in the institutional affairs of the Church of the moral theologians studied. With his principal duty to serve as a papal judge-delegate, his work takes the tone of someone waist-deep in the legal conundrums that came with crusading and the stamping out of heresy. Thinking critically about procedure and boundaries, he navigated both the interpretation of papal orders when the realities on the ground were a bit different, as well as the engagement of clerics in heresy trials. A canon at St. Victor, Robert of Flamborough served as *penitentiarius* for the students at the University of Paris. He arranged topics and supplemented them with legal sources that gave prominence to issues that catered to the community in which he served. In his consideration of the legal and penitential ramifications of homicide, both suicide and the murder of and murder caused by clerics weighed heavily on him. Conflicts between town and gown led the Church into jurisdictional quagmires as students, who held clerical status, faced high justice. Though Robert turned to the penitential of Bartholomew of Exeter on several occasions, Bartholomew's concerns were different from those of Robert. Rather than students, Bartholomew, serving as archdeacon followed by bishop, organized topics and drew upon the law in such a way as to cater to diocesan needs. His focus was upon the laity, as evidenced by his deeper engagement with the murder of spouses and offering a justification of how those who kill might not always be guilty; topics with which Robert did not concern himself. Thomas of Chobham was immersed in a burgeoning market economy. In his treatment of greed, he drew upon his experience as subdean and *officialis* of Salisbury to distill and apply legal thought in such a way that it could be applied to the murky waters of theft and robbery, usury, and simony. Thomas addressed the social, economic, and cultural realities of daily life: people looking to get ahead through covert means, cloaked usury, and negative impacts of advowson and the selling of the tithes. Each of these theologians needed to draw on legal knowledge to translate the ideal for humanity to the reality of their behavior.

Our *litterati* bear witness to the porous boundaries between penance and law as both were concerned with transgressions. The judge and the confessor both had to inquire into all the circumstances and decide the appropriate punishment.[9] Franz Kerff's study of the interplay between ecclesiastical criminal jurisdiction at the diocesan level and *Libri penitentiales* dating between the eighth and the twelfth century illustrates that together with the canon collections, penitentials set forth the norms and various procedures for ecclesiastical authorities who sat in judgment of offenses. *Libri penitentiales* were thus seen in connection with the ordinary jurisdiction of the bishop. In fact, Kerff maintained that penitentials probably conveyed a more precise picture of the norms pertaining to criminal procedure than did the thematically more comprehensive canon collections.[10] As Joseph Goering has noted, the penitential court (*forum penitentiae*) and the conception of the office of the confessor had come under the influence of the growing concern with law. The task of the confessor was largely judicial, and the court of penance followed a proper judicial procedure. This influence introduced a new era in the relationship between theology and law, a penitential law with a specific focus on the care of souls. The manuals, however, were written not specifically for lawyers but rather for pastors, and thus the structure of canonical texts and glosses was abandoned because they did not suit the practical needs of pastors.[11] For Kerff there was no

9 E. Corran, *Lying and Perjury in Medieval Practical Thought: A Study in the History of Casuistry* (Oxford, 2018), 106.

10 F. Kerff, "Libri Paenitentiales und kirchliche Strafgerichtsbarkeit bis zum Decretum Gratiani: Ein Diskussionsvorschlag," ZRG Kan. Abt. 75 (1989): 23–57, here 23, 32–33.

11 Goering, "The *Summa* of Master Serlo and Thirteenth-Century Penitential Literature," 305–306.

conceptual distinction between internal and external areas (*forum internum–forum externum*) until the beginning of the thirteenth century. The provisions of the *Libri penitentiales* were structured according to a uniform scheme: the definition of the offense is followed by the specification of the punishment. Since the same penalties applied to public and private criminal proceedings, the *Libri penitentiales* could be used in both.[12]

The late twelfth and early thirteenth centuries thus saw the same person serving as a judge in the external forum and as a confessor in the internal forum. Law and legal thought act as windows into a society's history, values, and daily life.[13] The *Libri penitentiales* of Peter the Chanter, Robert of Courson, Robert of Flamborough, and the *Summa confessorum* of Thomas of Chobham demonstrate the extent to which such works incorporated the law of the external forum of courts into the manuals of the internal forum of confession.[14] Theologians would incorporate into the internal forum of penance the more established and formal procedure from the courts. They would draw upon the Church's authority to restrain vice and foster virtue in the Christian community. As both Joseph Goering and Jason Taliadoros have noted, penitentials provided a vehicle for law to be applied to the practice of pastoral care. They exemplify both the spread of canonical doctrines beyond the schools of law as well as the application of legal knowledge to matters that were outside the ecclesiastical court. The overriding aim to resolve conflict through pragmatic, practical, and pastoral means crossed the disciplinary lines of law and theology.[15] Both canonists and theologians took an interest in penance and the divisions between the two disciplines in the schools were blurred. Whereas the former brought the law to bear, the latter realized the importance of teaching the confessor how to welcome, question, and advise the penitent. The judge dispassionately applied the law; the confessor discerned the penitent's intentions

12 Kerff, "Libri Paenitentiales und kirchliche Strafgerichtsbarkeit bis zum Decretum Gratiani," 40–41.

13 See the works of H. C. Lea, *History of the Inquisition of the Middle Ages*, 3 vols. (New York, 1888), *A Formulary of the Papal Penitentiary in the Thirteenth Century* (Philadelphia, 1892), and *A History of Auricular Confession and Indulgences* (Philadelphia, 1896). For a wonderful analysis of Lea's thought, see E. Peters, "Henry Charles Lea: Jurisprudence and Civilization," *Digital Proceedings of the Lawrence J. Schoenberg Symposium on Manuscript Studies in the Digital Age, Vol. 2, Issue 1: Lex Scripta: The Manuscript as Witness to the History of Law*, ed. L. Ransom (2010), article 2, pp. 1–14, available at https://repository.upenn.edu/ljsproceedings/vol2/iss1/2/.

14 On the relationship between the internal forum of confession and the external forum of court, see R. Eckert, "Peine judiciaire, pénitence et salut entre droit canonique et théologie (xiie s.–début du xiiie s.)," *Revue de l'histoire des religions* 4 (2011): 483–508, here 500–502.

15 J. Taliadoros, "Bartholomew of Exeter's Penitential: Some Observations on his Personal Dicta," in *Proceedings Esztergom 2008*, eds. P. Erdö and S. A. Szuromi (Vatican City, 2010) 457–473, here 471; J. Goering, "The *Summa de Penitentia* of John of Kent," BMCL 13 (1988): 13–31, here 28.

and heart.[16] While there was a uniform interest in law, there was not a uniform use of the law. Stated another way, compilers of penitentials did not use legal sources in the same way or for the same end. Each used legal sources in a way to suit their individual needs.

While questions have been raised about the extent to which we can consider *Libri penitentiales* and *Summae confessorum* as rooted in law, most notably by Cyril Vogel who cautioned us against reading law into the penitentials because they are not juridical documents possessing a didactic quality,[17] it is worth noting that penitentials were found in legal collections, the most famous of which was the *Corrector sive Medicus* which was included as Book 19 in Burchard of Worm's *Decretum*. Furthermore, law is not found simply in legal collections; it is found in literature, political writings, and penitentials. Jean Longère noted that while we should remember the personal nature of penance, it is worth paying attention to the law infused within penitentials.[18] Louis I. Hamilton has demonstrated that liturgy was steeped in law and that legal writings drew upon liturgical thought.[19] Joseph Goering, in turn, has argued that canon law was a body of jurisprudence that comprised lawyers, judges, and administrators who adjudicated crime as well as those who heard confessions and issued penance.[20] It cannot be denied that the theologians of Peter the Chanter, his circle, and the canonists occupied a similar intellectual milieu.

In the end, the separation between theology, penance, and canon law was not entirely distinct. Each was concerned with salvation, punishing infractions, and paving a road to bring sinners back to the right path. While the relationship between crime and sin was complex, they would remain linked as every crime was a sin, but not every sin was a crime.[21] With the *cura animarum* falling under the purview of both theologians and canonists, canon law and theology occupied an intellectual environment in which disciplinary specialization did not mean being walled off from other areas of knowledge. Penitentials were a part of this environment by addressing the pressing ethical questions that faced

16 Longère, "Quelques 'Summa de poenitentia' à la fin du XIIe siècle et au début du XIIIe siècle," 57.

17 Vogel, *Les Libri Paenitentiales*, 31, 36.

18 Longère, "Quelques 'Summa de poenitentia' à la fin du XIIe siècle et au début du XIIIe siècle," 45–58.

19 L. I. Hamilton, "'We receive the law on Mt. Sinai…when we study the sacred scriptures': Law, Liturgy and Reform in the Exegesis of Bruno of Segni," in *The Use of Canon Law in Ecclesiastical Administration, 1000–1234*, eds. M. H. Eichbauer and D. Summerlin (Leiden, 2018), 195–220.

20 Goering, "The Internal Forum and the Literature of Penance and Confession," 380, 427. Goering noted that the external forum of canonists and practices of ecclesiastical courts influenced the internal forum of penance practice.

21 I am grateful for insightful conversations with Greta Austin and Raphaël Eckert who helped shaped these ideas. See also Eckert, "Peine judiciaire, pénitence et salut entre droit canonique et théologie (xiie s.–début du xiiie s.)" 495–496.

confessors and the realities of their time. As we have seen, there was a significant grey area in practice between canon law and penance, between the external and the internal fora, and theologians worked in an environment where lay and ecclesiastical jurisdictions would overlap. As a result, law had a place in the service of theology and the practical needs of pastoral care.

BIBLIOGRAPHY

Primary Sources

Behrends, Frederick, ed. and trans. *The Letters and Poems of Fulbert of Chartres*. Oxford Medieval Texts. Oxford: Oxford University Press, 1976.

Bermon, Pascale, trans. *La fondation de l'Université de Paris (1200–1260)*. Sagesses Médiévales, 20. Paris: Les Belles Lettres, 2017.

Collectio canonum Sancto Victore. Paris, Bibliothèque de l'Arsenal, lat. 721, fol. 244r–277r.

Collectio decem partium. Berlin, Staatsbibliothek Preußischer Kulturbesitz, Phill. 1746. Available at https://digital.staatsbibliothek-berlin.de/werkansicht?PPN=PPN829071954&PHYSID=PHYS_0001

Conciliorum oecumenicorum generalium-que decreta, Vol. 2.1: *The Oecumenical Councils of the Roman Catholic Church: From Constantinople IV to Pavia-Siena (869–1424)*; Vol. 2.2: *From Basel to Lateran V (1431–1517)*, edited by Alberto Melloni et al. Corpus Christianorum. Turnhout: Brepols, 2013.

Cum omnia sacramenta II. In "Théologie et théologiens de l'école épiscopale de Paris avant Pierre Lombard," edited by F. P. Bliemetzrieder. *Recherches de théologie ancienne et medieval* 3 (1931): 273–291.

Denifle, Henricus, ed. *Chartularium Universitatis Parisiensis*, 4 vols. rpt. Bruxelles: Culture et Civilisation, 1964.

Diversorum patrum sententie sive Collectio in LXXIV titulos digesta, edited by John T. Gilchrist. Vatican City: Biblioteca Apostolica Vaticana, 1973.

Epitome Iuliani, edited by Simon Corcoran. "UCL Volterra Project." Available at https://www.ucl.ac.uk/volterra/texts/epitome-iuliani

Gilchrist, John T., trans. *The Collection in Seventy-Four Titles: A Canon Law Manual of the Gregorian Reform*. Mediaeval Sources in Translation, 22. Toronto: Pontifical Institute of Medieval Studies, 1980.

Cambrensis, Giraldi. *Symbolum Electorum*. Epist. 24 in *Opera*, Vol. 1, edited by J. S. Brewer. London: Longman, Green, Longman, and Roberts, 1861.

Glanville. *Tractatus de legibus et consuetudinibus regini anglie/The Treatise on the Laws and Customs of the Realm of England*, edited and translated by G. D. G. Hall. London: Thomas Nelson and Sons, 1965.

Gratian. *Concordia discordantium canonum (Decretum)*. In *Corpus iuris canonici*, Vol. 1, edited by Emil Friedberg. Leipzig: Tauchnitz, 1879.

Gregory IX, Pope. *Liber Extra (Decretales)*. In *Corpus iuris canonici*, Vol. 2, edited by Emil Friedberg. Leipzig: Tauchnitz, 1881.

Guérard, M. ed., *Cartulaire de l'église Notre-Dame de Paris*. Collection des cartulaires de France, 4. Paris: Crapelet, 1850.

Hugh the Chanter. *The History of the Church of York, 1066–1127*, edited and translated by Charles Johnson. London: Nelson, 1961.

Hugh of St. Victor. *On the Sacraments: A Selection of Works of Hugh and Richard of St. Victor, and of Peter of Poitiers*, translated by Hugh Feiss, OSB. Victorine Texts in Translation, 10. Turnhout: Brepols, 2020.

Hugh of St. Victor. *Hugh of Saint Victor On the Sacraments of the Christian Faith (De Sacramentis)*, translated by Roy J. Deferrari. Cambridge, MA: The Medieval Academy of America, 1951.

Hugh of St. Victor. Hugh of St. Victor. *De beatae Mariae virginitate*. In *L'oeuvre de Hugues de Saint-Victor*, Vol 2: *Super Canticum Mariae; Pro Assumptione Virginis; De beatae Mariae Virginiate; Egredietur virga, Maria porta*, edited by Patrice Sicard with introductory notes, and French translation by Bernadette Jollès. Sous la règle de saint Augustin series. Turnhout: Brepols, 2000.

Hugh of St. Victor. *De sacramentis Christiane Fidei*, edited by Rainer Berndt. Münster: Aschendorff, 2008.

Huguccio. *Summa decretorum*. Paris, Bibliothèque nationale de France, lat. 3892. Available at https://gallica.bnf.fr/ark:/12148/btv1b52502900f.

Ivo of Chartres. *Decretum*, edited by Martin Brett et al. Available at https://ivo-of-chartres.github.io/decretum.html

Kemp, B. R., ed., *English Episcopal Acta, Vol. 18: Salisbury 1078–1217*. Oxford: Oxford University Press for the British Academy, 1999.

Kemp, B. R., ed., *English Episcopal Acta, Vol. 19: Salisbury 1217–1228*. Oxford: Oxford University Press for the British Academy, 2000.

Le register de Lambert, évêque d'Arras (1093–1115), edited and translated by C. Giordangengo. Paris: CNRS Editions, 2007.

Lefèvre, Georges, ed. and trans. *Le Traité "De Usura" de Robert de Courçon: Texte et traduction publiés avec une introduction*. Travaux et Mémoires de l'Université de Lille, 10. Lille: L'Université de Lille, 1902.

Ministere de l'Instruction Publique et des Beaux-Arts. *Catalogue Général des Manuscrits des Bibliothéques de France, XI Chartres*. Paris, 1890.

Morey, Adrian, ed. *Bartholomew of Exeter, Bishop and Canonist: A Study in the Twelfth Century*. Cambridge: Cambridge University Press, 1937.

Munro, Dana Carleton, ed. *Translations and Reprints from the Original Sources of European History, Vol. 2: The Medieval Student*. Philadelphia: The Department of History of the University of Pennsylvania, 1895.

Panormia, edited by Bruce Brasington and Martin Brett. Available at https://ivo-of-chartres.github.io/panormia.html.

Pierre Le Chantre. *Summa de sacramentis et animae consiliis*, edited by Jean-Albert Dugauquier. Analecta Mediaevalia Namurcensia, 4. Lille: Librairie Giard, 1957.

Peter Lombard. *The Sentences. Book 4 On the Doctrine of Signs*, translated by Giulio Silano. Mediaeval Sources in Translation, 48. Toronto: Pontifical Institute of Mediaeval Studies, 2010.

Peter Lombard. *Sententiae in IV libris distinctae*, Vol. 2 [of 2]. Spicilegium Bonaventurianum, 5. Rome: Collegii S. Bonaventurae ad Claras Aquas Grottaferrata, 1981.

Robert of Courçon. *Summa penitentiae*. Paris, Bibliothèque nationale de France, lat. 14524. Available at https://gallica.bnf.fr/ark:/12148/btv1b100363481/f2.item.

Robert of Flamborough. *Liber Poenitentialis: A Critical Edition with Introduction and Notes*, edited by J. J. Francis Firth. Studies and Texts, 18. Toronto: Pontifical Institute of Mediaeval Studies, 1971.

Robert of Torigni. *Chronicle*. In *Chronicles of the Reigns of Stephen, Henry II, and Richard II*, edited by Richard Howlett, 4 vols. Rolls Series, London, 1884–1889; rpt. Wiesbaden: Kraus, 1964.

Rufinus von Bologna. *Die Summa decretorum*, edited by Heinrich Singer. Reprint, Aalen: Scientia, 1963.

Somerville, Robert, and Bruce C. Brasington, trans. *Prefaces to Canon Law Books in Latin Christianity: Selected Translations, 500–1245*, 2nd edn. Washington, D.C.: Catholic University of America Press, 2021.

Stephan of Tournai. *Summa decretorum*. Munich, Bayerische Staatsbibliothek, Clm 17162. Available at https://opacplus.bsb-muenchen.de/title/BV037455239.

Stubbs, William and H. W. C. Davis, eds. *Select Charters of English Constitutional History*. Oxford: Clarendon Press, 1913.

Die Summa magistri Rolandi nachmals Papstes Alexander III, edited by Friedrich Thaner. Innsbruck: Wagner, 1874.

Die Summa des Stephanus Tornacensis über das Decretum Gratiani, edited by Johann Friedrich von Schulte. Giessen: Emil Roth, 1891.

Tock, Benoît-Michel, ed. *Les Chartres des Évêques d'Arras (1093–1203)*. Collection de documents inédits sur l'histoire de France section d'historie médiévale et de philologie, série in-8, vol. 20. Paris: CTHS 1991.

Thomas of Chobham. Summa confessorum, edited by Revd. F. Broomfield, Analecta Mediaevalia Namurcensia, 25. Louvain: Éditions Nauwelaerts, 1968.

Walter of Thérouanne. *Vita domini oannis Morinensis episcopi*, edited by J. Rider. Corpus Christianorum Continuatio Mediaevalis, 217. Turnhout: Brepols, 2006.

Watson, Alan, trans. *The Digest of Justinian*, 4 vols. Philadelphia: University of Pennsylvania Press, 1985.

Whitelock, Dorothy, Martin Brett, and Christopher N. Brooke, eds. *Councils & Synods with other documents relating to the English Church*, Vol. 1, Part 1 (871–1066) and Part 2 (1066–1204). Oxford: Clarendon Press, 1981.

Secondary Sources

Abulafia, Anna Sapir. "The Role of Money in Medieval Christian-Jewish Relations." *Erasmus Forum Bulletin* 5 (2021–2022): 7–26.

Austin, Greta. "Were There Two Arsenal Collections? Arsenal 713B and the Ivonian Panormia." In *Canon Law, Religion, and Politics: Liber Amicorum Robert Somerville*, edited by Uta-Renate Blumenthal, Anders Winroth, and Peter Landau, 3–14. Washington D.C.: Catholic University of America Press, 2012.

Bähr, Andreas. "Between 'Self-Murder' and Suicide: The Modern Etymology of Self-Killing." *Journal of Social History* 46, no. 3 (2013): 620–632.

Baldwin, John. *Paris, 1200*. Standford: Stanford University Press, 2010.

Baldwin, John. *The Government of Philip Augustus: Foundations of French Royal Power in the Middle Ages*. Berkeley: University of California Press, 1986.

Baldwin, John. *Masters, Princes and Merchants: The Social Views of Peter the Chanter and His Circle*, 2 vols. Princeton: Princeton University Press, 1970.

Barrow, Julia. *The Clergy in the Medieval World: Secular Clerics, Their Families and Careers in North-Western Europe, c. 800–c. 1200*. Cambridge: Cambridge University Press, 2015.

Bazeley, Margaret Ley. "The Extent of the English Forest in the Thirteenth Century." In *Internal Colonization in Medieval Europe*, edited by Felipe Fernandez-Armesto and James Muldoon, 437–457. The Expansion of Latin Europe, 1000–1500, 2. Aldershot: Ashgate, 2008.

Bellomo, Manlio. *The Common Legal Past of Europe, 1000–1800*, 2nd edn. Translated by Lydia G. Cochrane. Washington, D.C.: The Catholic University of America, 1995.

Berger, Adolf. *Encyclopedic Dictionary of Roman Law*. Philadelphia: The American Philosophical Society, rpt. 1991.

Biller, Peter. "Northern Cathars and Higher Learning." In *The Medieval Church: Universities, Heresy, and The Religious Life: Essays in Honour of Gordon Leff*, edited by Peter Biller and Barrie Dobson, 25–53. Rochester: Boydell Press, 1999.

Bird, Jessalynn L. "Paris Masters and the Justification of the Albigensian Crusade." *Crusades* 6 (2007): 117–156.

Birrell, Jean R. "Hunting and the Royal Forest." In *L'Uomo e la foresta secc. XIII-XVIII: Atti della Ventisettesima Settimana di Studi, 8-13 maggio 1995*, edited by Simonetta Cavaciocchi, 437–457. Atti delle Settimane di Studi e altri Convegni, 27. Florence: Le Monn, 1996.

Birrell, Jean. "Forest Law and the Peasantry in the Later Thirteenth Century." *Thirteenth Century England, II. Proceedings of the Newcastle Upon Tyne Conference 1987*, edited by P. R. Cross and S. D. Lloyd, 149–163. Woodbridge: Boydell Press, 1988.

Blumenthal, Uta-Renate. "The Collection of S. Victor (=V), Paris: Liturgy, Canon Law, and Polemical Literature." In *Ritual, Text and Law: Studies in Medieval Canon Law and Liturgy Presented to Roger E. Reynolds*, edited by Kathleen G. Cushing and Richard F. Gyug, 293–307. Aldershot: Ashgate, 2004.

Bolton, Jim L. *Money in the Medieval English Economy: 973–1489*. Manchester Medieval Studies. Manchester: Manchester University Press, 2012.

Boureau, Alain. "How Law Came to the Monks: The Use of Law in English Society at the Beginning of the Thirteenth Century." *Past & Present* 167 (2000): 29–74.

Boyle, Leonard. "Summae confessorum." In *Les genres littéraires dans les sources théologiques et philosophiques médiévales: Définition, crique et exploitation: Actes du colloque internationale de Louvain-la-Neuve 25–27 mai 1981*, 227–237. Publications de l'Institute d'Études Médiévales, 2e série: Textes, Études, Congrès, 5. Turnhout: Brepols, 1982.

Brasington, Bruce. "Lessons of Love: Bishop Ivo of Chartres as Teacher." In *Teaching and Learning in Northern Europe, 1000–1200*, edited by Sally N. Vaughn and Jay Rubenstein, 129–147. Studies in the Early Middle Ages. Turnhout: Brepols, 2006.

Brasington, Bruce. *Ways of Mercy: The Prologue of Ivo of Chartres, Edition and Analysis*. Vita regularis: Ordnungen und Deutungen religiosen Lebens im Mittelalter, 2. Münster: Lit, 2004.

Brentano, Robert. *Two Churches: England and Italy in the Thirteenth Century*. Los Angeles: University of California Press, 1988.
Brett, Martin. "The Sources and Influence of Paris, Bibliothèque de l'Arsenal MS 713." In *Proceedings of the Ninth International Congress of Medieval Canon Law, Munich, 13–19 July 1992*, edited by Peter Landau and Jörg Müller, 149–167. Monumenta Iuris Canonici: Series C, Subsidia 10. Vatican City: Bibliotheca Apostolica Vaticana, 1997.
Brett, Martin. "The Collectio Lanfranci and its Competitors," In *Intellectual Life in the Middle Ages: Essays Presented to Margaret Gibson*, edited by L. Smith and B. Ward, 157–174. London: Continnuum, 1992.
Brundage, James. *The Medieval Origins of the Legal Profession: Canonists, Civilians, and Courts*. Chicago: University of Chicago Press, 2008.
Brundage, James. "Full and Partial Proof in Classical Canonical Procedure." *The Jurist* 67, no.1 (2007): 58–71.
Brundage, James. "Teaching Canon Law." In *Learning Institutionalized: Teaching in the Medieval University*, edited John Van Engen, 177–196. Notre Dame: University of Notre Dame Press, 2000.
Brundage, James. *Law, Sex, and Christian Society in Medieval Europe*. Chicago: University of Chicago Press, 1987.
Burger, Michael. *Bishops, Clerks, and Diocesan Governance in Thirteenth-Century England: Reward and Punishment*. Cambridge: Cambridge University Press, 2012.
Burger, Michael. "Officiales and the familiae of the Bishops of Lincoln, 1258–99." *Journal of Medieval History* 16 (1990): 39–53.
Butler, Sara. "Cultures of Suicide?: Suicide Verdicts and the 'Community' in Thirteenth- and Fourteenth-Century England," *The Historian* 69, no. 3 (2007): 427–449.
Butler, Sara. "Degrees of Culpability: Suicide Verdicts Mercy and Jury in Medieval England." *Journal of Medieval and Early Modern Studies* 36, no. 2 (2006): 263–290.
Cantarella, Glauco Maria. "L'evoluzione della normativa antiereticale di Innocenzo III dalla *Vergentis in senium* (1199) al IV concilio lateranense (1215)." *Bullettino dell'Istituto storico italiano per il Medio Evo* 106, no. 2 (2004): 207–240.
Cels, Marc B. "Interrogating Anger in the New Penitential Literature of the Thirteenth Century." *Viator* 45, no. 1 (2014): 203–220.
Cheney, Christopher R. *From Becket to Langton: English Church Government 1170–1213*. The Ford Lectures delivered in the University of Oxford in Hilary Term 1955. Manchester: Manchester University Press, 1956, rpt. 1965.
Cheney, Mary. "The Council of Westminster 1175: New Light on an Old Source." In *The Material Sources and Methods of Ecclesiastical History: Papers Read at the Twelfth Summer Meeting and The Thirteenth Winter Meeting of the Ecclesiastical History Society*, edited by Derek Baker, 61–68. Oxford: Basil Blackwell, 1975.
Chodorow, Stanley. *Christian Political Theory and Church Politics in the Mid-Twelfth Century: The Ecclesiology of Gratian's Decretum*. Berkeley: University of California Press, 1972.
Chodorow, Stanley. "Ecclesiastical Politics and the Ending of the Investiture Contest: The Papal Election of 1119 and the Negotiations of Mouzon," *Speculum* 46 (1971): 613–640.
Clanchy, Michael, and Lesley Smith. "Abelard's Description of the School of Laon: What Might it Tell Us about Early Scholastic Teaching?" *Nottingham Medieval Studies* 54 (2010): 1–34.
Clarke, Peter D. "Peter the Chanter, Innocent III and Theological Views on Collective Guilt and Punishment." *Journal of Ecclesiastical History* 52 (2001): 1–20.

Cobban, Alan B. *The Medieval Universities: Their Development and Organization*. London: Methuen, 1975.

Collins, Ross William. "The Parish Priest and His Flock as Depicted by the Councils of the Twelfth and Thirteenth Centuries." *Journal of Religion* 10, no. 3 (1930): 313–332.

Colish, Marcia. *Remapping Scholasticism*. The Etienne Gilson Series, 21. Toronto: Pontifical Institute of Mediaeval Studies, 2000.

Colish, Marcia. *Peter Lombard*, 2 vols. Brill's Studies in Intellectual History, 41. Leiden: Brill, 1994.

Constable, Giles. *The Reformation of the Twelfth Century*. Cambridge: Cambridge University Press, 2002.

Contreni, John J. "The Formation of Laon's Cathedral Library in the Ninth Century." In *Carolingian Learning, Masters and Manuscripts*, no. XIII. London: Variorum Reprints, 1992.

Coppens, Chris. "Teaching of Law in the University of Paris in the First Quarter of the 13th Century." *Rivista internazionale di diritto comune* 10 (1999): 139–173.

Corran, Emily. *Lying and Perjury in Medieval Practical Thought: A Study in the History of Casuistry*. Oxford: Oxford University Press, 2018.

Corran, Emily. "Moral Dilemma in English Confessors' Manual." In *Thirteenth Century England XVI: Proceedings of the Cambridge Conference, 2015*, edited by Andrew M. Spencer and Carl Watkins, 21–36. Woodbridge: Boydell & Brewer, 2017.

Courtenay, William J. *Rituals for the Dead: Religion and Community in the Medieval University of Paris*. The Conway Lectures in Medieval Studies, 2016. Notre Dame: University of Notre Dame Press, 2019.

Cushing, Kathleen. "Law and Reform: The Transmission of Burchard of Worms' *Liber Decretorum*." In *New Discourses in Medieval Canon Law Research: Challenging the Master Narrative*, edited by Christof Rolker, 33–43. Medieval Law and Its Practice, 28. Leiden: Brill, 2019.

d'Avray, David. *Papal Jurisprudence, 385–1234: Social Origins and Medieval Reception of Canon Law*. Cambridge: Cambridge University Press, 2022.

d'Avray, David. *Papacy, Monarchy and Marriage, 860–1600*. Cambridge: Cambridge University Press, 2015.

d'Avray, David L. *Medieval Marriages: Symbolism and Society*. Oxford: Oxford University Press, 2005.

De Smet, J. M. *De heilige Jan van Waasten en de Gregoriaansche hervorming in het bisdom Terwaan*. Université de Louvain, 1943.

Dahan, Gilbert. "Les interprétations juives dans les commentaires du Pentateuque de Pierre le Chantre." In *The Bible in the Medieval World: Essays in Honour of Beryl Smalley*, edited by Katherine Walsh and Diana Wood, 131–155. Studies in Church History, Subsidia 4. Oxford: Blackwell, 1985.

Dickson, Marcel, and Christiane Dickson. "Le Cardinal Robert de Courson: Sa Vie." *Archives d'histoire doctrinale et littéraire du Moyen Âge* 9 (1934): 53–142.

Dodds, Ben. "Demesne and Tithe: Peasant Agriculture in the Late Middle Ages." *Agricultural History Review* 56, Part II (2008): 123–141.

Dodds, Ben. "Managing Tithes in the Late Middle Ages." *Agricultural History Review* 53, Part II (2005): 125–140.

Duggan, Charles. *Twelfth-Century Decretal Collections and their Importance in English History*. University of London Historical Series, XII. London: University of London, The Athlone Press, 1963.

Dutton, Claire Maria. "Aspects of Institutional History of the Albigensian Crusade, 1198–1229." PhD diss. Royal Halloway and Bedford New College, 1993.

Eckert, Raphaël. "Peine judiciaire, pénitence et salut entre droit canonique et théologie (xiie s.–début du xiiie s.)." *Revue de l'histoire des religions* 4 (2011): 483–508.

Eichbauer, Melodie H. *Medieval Canon Law*, 2nd edn. Expanded and revised version of the First Edition by James A. Brundage. The Medieval World. London: Routledge, 2023.

Eichbauer, Melodie H. "A Desire for the Latest and the Greatest: Papal Decretals and Roman Law in the *Collectio decem paritum*." *Bulletin of Medieval Canon Law* 36 (2019): 195–208.

Eichbauer, Melodie H. "Law in Service of a Community: Property and Tithing Rights in Gratian's *Decretum* and Stephen of Tournai's *Summa*." In *The Use of Canon Law in Ecclesiastical Administration, 1000–1250*, edited by Melodie H. Eichbauer and Danica Summerlin, 69–88. Medieval Law and Its Practice, 26. Leiden: Brill, 2018.

Eichbauer, Melodie H. "Rethinking Causae 23–26 as the *Causae hereticorum.*" *Zeitschrift der Savigny-Stiftung fur Rechtsgeschichte*. Kanonistische Abteilung 101 (2015): 86–149.

Evans, Gillian R. *Law and Theology in the Middle Ages*. London: Routledge, 2002.

Evans, Gillian R. "Thomas of Chobham on Preaching and Exegesis." *Recherches de théologie ancienne et médiévale* 52 (1985): 159–170.

Evergates, Theodore. *Henry the Liberal: Count of Champagne, 1127–1181*. Philadelphia: University of Pennsylvania Press, 2016.

Fawtier, Robert. *The Capetian Kings of France: Monarchy & Nation (987–1328)*, translated by Lionel Butler and R. J. Adam. New York: St. Martin's Press, 1966.

Ferruolo, Stephen. *The Origins of the University: The Schools of Paris and Their Critics, 1100–1215*. Stanford: Stanford University Press, 1985.

Fiori, Antonia. "La 'Collectio Britannica' e la riemersione del Digesto." *Rivista internazionale di diritto comune* 9 (1998): 81–121.

Flood, John, James R. Ginther, and Joseph W. Goering, eds. *Robert Grosseteste and His Intellectual Milieu*. Toronto: Pontifical Institute of Mediaeval Studies, 2013.

Fournier, Paul. "Collections Issues du Décret de Burchard." In *Mélanges Paul Fabre: Études d'histoire du Moyen Age*, 199–203. Paris: Alphonse Picard, 1902.

Fournier, Paul. "Deux controverses sur les origins du Décret de Gratien. Primière Partie: Gratien et Pierre Lombard." *Revue d'histoire et de littérature religieuses* 3 (1898): 97–116.

Fournier, Paul. *Les collections canoniques attribuées a Yves de Chartres*. Paris: Alphonse Picard, 1897.

Fournier, Paul, and Gabriel LeBras. *Histoire des Collections Canonique en Occident: Depuis les Fausses Décrétales jusqu'au Décret de Gratien*, 2 vols. Bibliotheque d histoire du droit, 5. Paris: Sirey, 1932.

Fowler-Magerl, Linda. "The Collection and Transmission of Canon Law along the Northern Section of the *Via Francigena* in the Eleventh and Twelfth Centuries." In *Bishops, Texts and the Use of Canon Law Around 1100: Essays in Honour of Martin Brett*, edited by Bruce C. Brasington and Kathleen G. Cushing, 129–139. Church, Faith, and Culture in the Medieval West. Farnham: Ashgate, 2008.

Fowler-Magerl, Linda. *Clavis Canonum: Selected Canon Law Collections Before 1140*. Monumenta Germaniae Historica, Hilfsmittel, 21. Hannover: Hahnsche Buchhandlung, 2005.

Gaastra, Adriaan H. "Between Liturgy and Canon Law: A Study of Books of Confession and Penance in Eleventh and Twelfth Century Italy." PhD diss. Universiteit Utrecht, 2007.

García y García, Antonio. "The Faculties of Law." In *A History of the University in Europe, Vol. 1: Universities in the Middle Ages*, edited by Hilde de Ridder-Symoens, 388–408. Cambridge: Cambridge University Press, 1992.

Gaudemet, Jean. *Le marriage in occident: Les moeurs et le droit*. Paris: Les Éditions du Cerf, 1987.

Gaudemet, Jean. *Sociétés et mariage*. Recherches institutionelles: Institutions et Histoire, 4. Strasbourg: CERDIC, 1980.

Gaudemet, Jean. "Le droit romain dans la pratique et chez les docteurs aux XIe et XIIe siècles." *Cahiers de civilization médiévale* 8, no. 31–32 (1965): 365–380.

Gaudemet, Jean. "L'apport de la patristique latine au Décret de Gratien en matière de mariage." *Studia Gratiana* 2 (1954): 290–319.

Ghellinck, Jospeh de. *Le mouvement théologique du XIIe siècle: Études, rechercehs et documents*, 2nd edn. Bruges: l'Édition universelle, 1948.

Gilchrist, John T. "Changing the Structure of a Canonical Collection: The Collection in Seventy-Four Titles, Four Books, and the Pseudo- Isidorian Decretals." In *Iure Veritas: Studies in Canon Law in Memory of Schafer Williams*, edited by S. B. Bowman and B. E. Cody, 93–117. Cincinnati: University of Cincinnati Press, 1991.

Gillmann, Franz. *Die Notwendigkeit der Intention auf Seiten des Spenders und des Empfängers der Sakramente nach der Anschauung du Frühscholastik*. Mainz: Kirchheim, 1916.

Ginther, James R. "Peter Lombard (ca. 1100–1160)." In *The Rise of the Medieval World 500–1300: A Biographical Dictionary*, edited by Jana K. Schulman, 342–343. Westport: Greenwood Press, 2002.

Goering, Joseph. "The Scholastic Turn (1100–1500): Penitential Theology and Law in the Schools." In *A New History of Penance*, edited by Abigail Firey, 219–237. Brill's Companions to the Christian Tradition. Leiden: Brill, 2008.

Goering, Joseph. "The Internal Forum and the Literature of Penance and Confession." In *The History of Medieval Canon Law in the Classical Period, 1140–1234: From Gratian to the Decretals of Pope Greogry IX*, edited by Wilfried Hartmann and Kenneth Pennington, 379–428. History of Medieval Canon Law, 6. Washington D.C.: Catholic University of America Press, 2008.

Goering, Joseph. "The Internal Forum and the Literature of Penance and Confession." *Traditio* 59 (2004): 175–227.

Goering, Joseph. "The *Summa de Penitentia* of John of Kent." *Bulletin of Medieval Canon Law* 13 (1988): 13–31.

Goering, Joseph. "The *Summa* of Master Serlo and Thirteenth-Century Penitential Literature." *Mediaeval Studies* 40 (1978): 290–311.

Gorochov, Nathalie. *Naissance de l'université: L Les écoles de Paris d'Innocent III à Thomas d'Aquin (v. 1200–v. 1245)*. Études d'Histoire Médiévale, 14. Paris: Honoré Champion, 2016.

Gorochov, Nathalie. "L'évêque de Paris, le chapitre cathedral de Notre-Dame et l'université Moyen Âge." In *Notre-Dame de Paris, 1163–2013: Actes du colloque scientifique tenu au Collège des Bernardins, à Paris, du 12 au 15 décembre 2012*, edited by Cédric Giraud, 113–124. Turnhout: Brepols, 2013.

Gouron André. *La science du droit dans le Midi de la France au Moyen Age*. London: Variorum Reprints, 1984.

Graham-Leigh, Elaine. *The Southern French Nobility and the Albigensian Crusade*. Woodbridge: Boydell Press, 2005.

Große, Rolf. *Saint-Denis zwischen Adel und König: Die Zeit von Suger (1053–1122)*. Beihefte der Francia, 57. Ostfildern: Thorbecke, 2002.

Hallam, Elizabeth M., and Judith Everard. *Capetian France 987–1328*. 2nd edn. New York: Longman, 2001.

Halsall, Guy. "Violence and Society in the Early Medieval West: An Introductory Survey." In *Violence and Society in the Early Medieval West*, edited by Guy Halsall, 1–45. Woodbridge: Boydell Press, 1998.

Hamburger, Jeffrey F. *Color in Cusanus*. Stuttgart: Hiersemann Verlag, 2021.

Hamilton, Louis I. "'We receive the law on Mt. Sinai...when we study the sacred scriptures': Law, Liturgy and Reform in the Exegesis of Bruno of Segni." In *The Use of Canon Law in Ecclesiastical Administration, 1000–1234*, edited by Melodie H. Eichbauer and Danica Summerlin, 195–220. Medieval Law and Its Practice, 26. Leiden: Brill, 2018.

Hammer, Carl I. "Patterns of Homicide in Medieval University Town: Fourteenth-Century Oxford." *Past & Present* 78 (1978): 3–23.

Häring, Nikolaus M. "The Interaction between Canon Law and Sacramental Theology in the Twelfth Century." In *Proceedings of the Fourth International Congress of Medieval Canon Law, Toronto, 21–25 August 1972*, edited by Stephan Kuttner, 483–493. Monumental iuris canonici, Series C: 5. Vatican City: Bibliotheca Apostolica Vaticana, 1976.

Häring, Nikolaus M. "Chartres and Paris Revisited." In *Essays in Honor of Anton Charles Pegis*, edited by J. R. O'Donnell, 268–329. Toronto: Pontifical Institute of Mediaeval Studies, 1974.

Hartmann, Wilfied, and Kenneth Pennington, eds. *The History of Courts and Procedure in Medieval Canon Law*. The History of Medieval Canon Law. Washington, D.C.: The Catholic University of America Press, 2016.

Hartmann, Wilfied, and Kenneth Pennington, eds. *The History of Medieval Canon Law in the Classical Period, 1140–1234: From Gratian to the Decretals of Pope Greogry IX*. The History of Medieval Canon Law. Washington, D.C.: The Catholic University of America Press, 2008.

Helmholz, Richard H. "Citations and Construction of Procedural Law in the Ius Commune." In *The Creation of the Ius Commune: From Casus to Regula*, edited by John W. Cairns, 247–276. Edinburgh: Edinburgh University Press, 2012.

Helmholz, Richard H. *The Oxford History of the Laws of England*, Vol. 1: *The Canon Law and Ecclesiastical Jurisdiction from 597 to the 1640s*. Oxford: Oxford University Press, 2004.

Helmholz, Richard H. "The Creation of a Canon Law of Prescription." In *Prescriptive Formality and Normative Rationality in Modern Legal Systems: Festschrift for Robert S. Summers*, edited by W. Krawietz, Neil MacCormick, and Georg Henrik von Wright, 265–284. Berlin: Duncker & Humblot GmbH, 1994.

Helmholz, Richard H. "'Si quis suadente' (C.17 q.4 c.29): Theory and Practice." In *Proceedings of the Seventh International Congress of Medieval Canon Law, Cambridge, 23–27 July 1984*, edited by Peter Linehan, 425–438. Monumenta Iuris Canonici: Series C, Subsidia 8. Vatican City: Biblioteca Apostolica Vaticana, 1988.

Helmholz, Richard H. "Usury and the Medieval English Church Courts." *Speculum* 61, no. 2 (1986): 364–380.

Helmholz, Richard H. "Excommunication as a Legal Sanction: The Attitudes of the Medieval Canonists." *Zeitschrift der Savigny-Stiftung fur Rechtsgeschichte*. Kanonistische Abteilung 68 (1982): 202–218.

Herlihy, David. "Church Property on the European Continent, 701–1200." *Speculum* 36, no. 1 (1961): 81–105.

Hödl, Ludwig. *Die Geschichte der Scholastischen Literatur und der Theologie der Schlüsselewalt*, Teil I. Beiträge zur Geschichte der Philosophie und Théologie des Mittelalters, 38. Münster: Aschendorffsche, 1960.

Kalb, Herbert. *Studien zur Summa Stephans von Tournai: Em Beitrag zur kanonistischen Wissenschaftsgeschichte des späten 12. Jahrhunderts*, Forschungen zur Rechts- und Kulturgeschichte, 12. Innsbruck: Universitätsverlag Wagner 1983.

Kelly, Henry A. "Inquisitorial Due Process and the Status of Secret Crimes." In *Proceedings of the Eighth International Congress of Medieval Canon Law. San Diego, University of California at La Jolla, 21–27 August 1988*, edited by Stanley Chodorow, 407–427. Monumenta Iuris Canonici: Series C, Subsidia 9. Vatican City: Biblioteca Apostolica Vaticana, 1992.

Kennedy, V. L. "The Content of Courson's *Summa*." *Mediaeval Studies* 9, no. 1 (1947): 81–107.

Kennedy, V. L. "Robert of Courson on Penance." *Mediaeval Studies* 7, no. 1 (1945): 291–336.

Kerff, Franz. "Libri Paenitentiales und kirchliche Strafgerichtsbarkeit bis zum Decretum Gratiani: Ein Diskussionsvorschlag." *Zeitschrift der Savigny-Stiftung fur Rechtsgeschichte*. Kanonistische Abteilung 75 (1989): 23–57.

Kéry, Lotte. *Canonical Collections of the Early Middle Ages (ca. 400–1140): A Bibliographical Guide to the Manuscripts and Literature*. History of Medieval Canon Law. Washington, D.C.: Catholic University of America Press, 1999.

Kéry, Lotte. *Die Errichtung des Bistums Arras 1093/1094*. Beihefte der Francia, 33. Ostfildern: Thorbecke, 1994.

Klepper, Deeana Copeland. *Pastoral Care and Community in Late Medieval Germany: Albert of Diessen's Mirror of Priests*. Medieval Societies, Religions, and Culture. Ithaca: Cornell University Press, 2022.

Kouamé, Thierry. "The Institutional Organization of the Schools." In *A Companion to Twelfth-Century Schools*, edited by Cédric Giraud, 30–48. Brill's Companions to the Christian Tradition, 88. Leiden: Brill, 2020.

Kuttner, Stephan. *Gratian and the Schools of Law, 1140–1234*, 2nd edn. London: Routledge, 2018.

Kuttner, Stephan. "Rodoicus ou Rotbertus Modicipassus (Parvipassus)." In *Dictionnaire de droit canonique* (1965): 7.701–702.

Kuttner, Stephan. "Harmony from Dissonance: An Interpretation of Medieval Canon Law." In *Wimmer Lecture X, 1956, St. Vincent College*. Latrobe, PA: Archabbey Press, 1960.

Kuttner, Stephan. "Papst Honorius III. und das Studium des Zivilrechts." In *Festschrift für Martin Wolff: Beiträge zum Zivilrecht und internationalen Privatrecht*, edited by E. von Caemmerer et al., 79–101. Tübingen: J. C. B. Mohr, 1952.

Kuttner, Stephan, and Eleanor Rathbone. "Anglo-Norman Canonists of the Twelfth Century: An Introductory Study." *Traditio* 7 (1951): 279–358.

Kuttner, Stephan. "Les débuts de l'école canoniste française." *Studia et documenta historiae et iuris* 4 (1938): 193–204.

Kuttner, Stephan. *Kanonistische Schuldlehre von Gratian bis auf die Dekretalen Gregors IX*. Studi e testi, 64. Vatican City: Bibliotheca Apostolica Vaticana, 1935.

Kuttner, Stephan. "Zur Frage der theologischen Vorlagen Gratians." *Zeitschrift der Savigny-Stiftung fur Rechtsgeschichte*. Kanonistische Abteilung 23 (1934): 243–268.

Lachaud, Frédérique. "Ralph Niger and the Books of Kings." In *Anglo-Norman Studies XL: Battle Conference on Anglo-Norman Studies, Paris, 2017*, edited by Elisabeth van Houts, 125–146. Woodbridge: Boydell 2018.

Landau, Peter. "Kanonisches Recht und römische Form: Rechtsprinzipien im ältesten römischen Kirchenrecht." *Der Staat* 32, no. 4 (1993): 553–568.

Landgraf, Artur Michael. "Diritto canonico e teologia nel secolo XII." *Studia Gratiana* 1 (1953): 373–413.

Langton, John. "Forest Law in the Landscape: Not the Clearing of the Woods, but the Running of the Deer?" In *Deer and People*, edited by Karis Baker, Ruth Carden, and Richard Madgwick, 218–230. Oxford: Windgather Press, 2015.

Larson, Atria A. *Master of Penance: Gratian and the Development of Penitential Thought and Law in the Twelfth Century*. Studies in Medieval and Early Modern Canon Law, 11. Washington, D.C.: Catholic University of America Press, 2014.

Larson, Atria A. "Killing a Career: Homicide and the Development of Medieval Clerical Discipline." *The Jurist* 74 (2014): 265–288.

Larson, Atria A. "The Reception of Gratian's *Tractatus de penitentia* and the Relationship between Canon Law and Theology in the Second Half of the Twelfth Century." *Journal of Religious History* 37, no. 4 (2013): 457–473.

Lea, Henry Charles. *A History of Auricular Confession and Indulgences*. Philadelphia: Lea Bros. & Co., 1896.

Lea, Henry Charles. *History of the Inquisition of the Middle Ages*, 3 vols. New York: Harper, 1888.

Lea, Henry Charles. *A Formulary of the Papal Penitentiary in the Thirteenth Century*. Philadelphia: Lea Bros. & Co., 1892.

LeBras, Gabriel. "Alger of Liège et Gratien." *Revue des Sciences Philosophiques et Théologiques* 20 (1931): 5–26.

Leclerq, Jean. "The Renewal of Theology." In *Renaissance and Renewal in the Twelfth Century*, edited by Robert Benson and Giles Constable with Carol D. Lanham, 68–87. Medieval Academy for Reprints for Teaching, 26. Toronto: Medieval Academy of America, 1991.

Lefebvre-Teillard, Anne. "Un maître parisien: Pierre Peverel: In memoriam alii magistri Petri." *Bulletin of Medieval Canon Law* 36 (2019): 209–242.

Leff, Gordon. "The *Trivium* and the Three Philosophies." In *A History of the University in Europe*, Vol. 1: *Universities in the Middle Ages*, edited by Hilde De Ridder-Symoens, 307–336. Cambridge: Cambridge University Press, 1992.

Lewis, Andrew. "Tithe Personal and Praedial." *The Journal of Legal History* 42, no. 2 (2021): 123–146.

Longère, Jean. *Oeuvres Oratoires de Maitres Parisiens au XIIe Siècle: Études Historique et Doctrinale*, 2 vols. Paris: Études Augustiniennes, 1975.

Longère, Jean. "Quelques 'Summa de poenitentia' à la fin du XIIe siècle et au début du XIIIe Siècle." In *La piété populaire au Moyen Âge*, edited by Etienne Delaruelle, 45–58. Paris: Bottega d'Erasmo, 1975.

Lorenc, John. "John of Freiburg and the Usury Prohibition in the Late Middle Ages: A Study in the Popularization of Medieval Canon Law." PhD diss. University of Toronto, 2013.

Luscombe, D. E. *The School of Peter Abelard: The Influence of Abelard's Thought in the Early Scholastic Period*. Cambridge Studies in Medieval Life and Thought, New Series 14. Cambridge: Cambridge University Press, 1969.

Maloney, Robert. "Usury in Greek, Roman, and Rabbinic Thought." *Traditio* 27 (1971): 79–109.

Marmursztejn, Elsa. “Loi ancienne, loi nouvelle et normes chrétiennes dans la théologie scolastique du XIIIe siècle.” *Revue de l'histoire des religions* 228, no. 4 (2011): 509–539.

McDougall, Sara. “Women and Gender in Canon Law.” In *The Oxford Handbook of Women and Gender in Medieval Europe*, edited by Judith Bennett and Ruth Karras, 163–178. Oxford: Oxford University Press, 2013.

McLaughlin, T. P. “The Teaching of the Canonists of Usury.” *Mediaeval Studies* 1 (1939): 81–147.

Mews, Constant J. “The Schools and Intellectual Renewal in the Twelfth Century: A Social Approach.” In *A Companion to Twelfth-Century Schools*, edited by Cédric Giraud, 10–29. Brill's Companions to the Christian Tradition, 88. Leiden: Brill, 2020.

Mews, Constant J. “Law, Theology, and Praxis ca. 1140–1380: New Approaches to the Study of Law and Theology in Medieval Europe.” *Journal of Religious History* 37, no. 4 (2013): 435–440.

Meyer, Andreas. “The Law of Benefices.” In *The Cambridge History of Medieval Canon Law*, edited by Anders Winroth and John C. Wei, 367–395. Cambridge: Cambridge University Press, 2022.

Miramon, Charles de. “Ecclesiastical Property, Tithes, *Spiritualia*.” In *The Cambridge History of Medieval Canon Law*, edited by Anders Winroth and John C. Wei, 345–367. Cambridge: Cambridge University Press, 2022.

Monagle, Clare. “Theology, Practice, and Policy at the Turn of the Thirteenth Century: The Papacy and Peter Lombard.” *Journal of Religious History* 37, no. 4 (2013): 441–456.

Montaubin, Pascal. “Eugenius III and France: The Protected Protector.” In *Pope Eugenius III (1145–1153): The First Cistercian Pope*, edited by Iben Fonnesberg-Schmidt and Andrew Jotischky, 197–217. Church. Faith and Culture in the Medieval West. Amsterdam: Amsterdam University Press, 2018.

Montaubin, Pascal. “Innocent II and Capetian France.” In *Pope Innocent II (1130–43): The World vs. the City*, edited by John Doran and Damian J. Smith, 107–151. Church, Faith, and Culture in the Medieval West. London: Routledge, 2016.

Moraw, Peter. “Careers of Graduates.” In *A History of the University in Europe, Vol. 1: Universities in the Middle Ages*, edited by Hilde de Ridder-Symoens, 244–279. Cambridge: Cambridge University Press, 1992.

Morris, Colin. *The Papal Monarchy: The Western Church from 1050 to 1250*. Oxford History of the Christian Church; Oxford: Clarendon Press, 1989.

Müller, Wolfgang P. *The Criminalization of Abortion in the West: Its Origins in Medieval Law*. New York: Cornell University Press, 2012.

Müller, Wolfgang P. *Huguccio: The Life, Works, and Thought of a Twelfth-Century Jurist*. Studies in Medieval and Early Modern Canon Law, 3. Washington, D.C.: Catholic University of America Press, 1994.

Müller, Wolfgang P. “The Rediscovery of Justinian's Digest in the Middle Ages.” *Bulletin of Medieval Canon Law* 20 (1990): 1–30.

Murray, Alexander. *Suicide in the Middle Ages, Vol. 2: The Curse of Self Murder*. Oxford: Oxford University Press, 2000.

Murray, Alexander. *Suicide in the Middle Ages, Vol. 1: The Violent Against Themselves*. Oxford: Oxford University Press, 1998.

Nakashian, Craig M. *Warrior Churchmen of Medieval England, 1000–1250: Theory and Reality*. Woodbridge: Boydell Press, 2016.

Nicholas, Barry. *An Introduction to Roman Law*, Clarendon Law Series. Oxford: Clarendon Press, 1962.

Novikoff, Alan J. *The Medieval Culture of Disputation: Pedagogy, Practice, and Performance*. The Middle Ages. Philadelphia: University of Pennsylvania Press, 2013.

Novikoff. "Anselm, Dialogue, and the Rise of Scholastic Disputation." *Speculum* 86, no. 2 (2011): 387–418.

Ott, John. *Bishops, Bishops, Authority, and Community in Northwestern Europe c.1050–1150*. Cambridge Studies in Medieval Life and Thought, Fourth Series. Cambridge: Cambridge University Press, 2015.

Pennington, Kenneth. "Stephen of Tournai (Étienne de Tournai), 1128–1203." In *Great Christian Jurists in French History*, edited by Olivier Descamps and Rafael Domingo, 35–51. Law and Christianity. Cambridge: Cambridge University Press, 2019.

Pennington, Kenneth. "The Decretalists, 1190–1210." In *The History of Medieval Canon Law in the Classical Period, 1140–1234: From Gratian to the Decretals of Pope Gregory IX*, edited by Wilfried Hartmann and Kenneth Pennington, 211–245. History of Medieval Canon Law, 6. Washington, D.C.: Catholic University of America Press, 2008.

Pennington, Kenneth, and Wolfgang P. Müller. "The Decretists: The Italian School." In *The History of Medieval Canon Law in the Classical Period, 1140–1234: From Gratian to the Decretals of Pope Gregory IX*, edited by Wilfried Hartmann and Kenneth Pennington, 121–173. History of Medieval Canon Law 6; Washington, D.C.: Catholic University of America Press, 2008.

Pennington, Kenneth. "The 'Big Bang': Roman Law in the Early Twelfth-Century." *Rivista internazionale di diritto comune* 18 (2007): 43–70.

Pennington, Kenneth. "'Pro Peccatis Patrum': A Moral and Legal Problem of the Inquisition." *Church History* 47, no. 2 (1978): 137–154.

Peters, Edward. "Henry Charles Lea: Jurisprudence and Civilization." In *Digital Proceedings of the Lawrence J. Schoenberg Symposium on Manuscript Studies in the Digital Age*, Vol. 2, Issue 1: *Lex Scripta: The Manuscript as Witness to the History of Law*, edited by Lynn Ransom (2010), article 2, pp. 1–14. Available at https://repository.upenn.edu/ljsproceedings/vol2/iss1/2/.

Peters, Edward. "Crimen exceptum: The History of an Idea." In *Proceedings of the Tenth International Congress of Medieval Canon Law, Syracuse, 13–18 August 1996*, edited by Kenneth Pennington, Stanley Chodorow, and Keith Kendall, 137–194. Monumenta Iuris Canonici: Series C, Subsidia 11. Vatican City: Bibliotheca Apostolica Vaticana, 2001.

Petersen, Zina. "Hugh of St. Victor (1096–1141)." In *The Rise of the Medieval World 500–1300: A Biographical Dictionary*, edited by Jana K. Schulman, 226–228. Westport: Greenwood Press, 2002.

Phillips, Jonathan. *The Crusades, 1095–1204*, 2nd edn. London: Routledge, 2014.

Phillips, Jonathan. *The Fourth Crusade and the Sack of Constantinople*. New York: Penguin, 2004.

Poirel, Dominique. *Hugues de Saint-Victor*. Paris: Les Éditions du Cerf, 1998.

Porter, Jean. "Right Reason and the Love of God: The Parameters of Aquinas' Moral Theology." In *The Theology of Thomas Aquinas*, edited by Rik Van Nieuwenhove and Joseph Wawrykow, 167–191. Notre Dame: University of Notre Dame Press, 2005.

Radding, Charles. "The Geography of Learning in Early Eleventh-Century Europe: Lanfranc of Bec and Berengar of Tours Revisited." *Bullettino dell'Istituto storico italiano per il Medio Evo e archvio muratoriano* 98 (1992): 145–172.

Rashdall, Hastings. *The Universities of Europe in the Middle Ages*, new edn. in 3 vols, edited by F. M. Powicke and A. B. Emden. Oxford: Oxford University Press, 1936.

Reilly, James Patrick, Jr. "Saint Thomas on Law." In *The Gilson Lectures on Thomas Aquinas*, edited by James P. Reilly, Jr., 163–178. Etienne Gilson Series, 30. Toronto: Pontifical Institute of Mediaeval Studies, 2008.

Rennie, Kriston R. *Law and Practice in the Age of Reform: The Legatine Work of Hugh of Die (1073–1106)*. Medieval Church Studies, 17. Turnhout: Brepols, 2010.

Resnick, Irven M. "Marriage in Medieval Culture: Consent Theory and the Case of Joseph and Mary." *Church History* 69, no. 2 (2000): 350–371.

Rexroth, Frank."Kodifizieren und Auslegen: Symbolische Grenzziehungen zwischen päpstlich-gesetzgeberischer und gelehrter Praxis im späteren Mittelalter (1209/10–1317)." *Frühmittelalterliche Studien* 41 (2008): 395–414.

Reynolds, Philip L. *How Marriage Became One of the Sacraments: The Sacramental Theology of Marriage from its Medieval Origins to the Council of Trent*. Cambridge: Cambridge University Press, 2016.

Reynolds, Philip L. *Marriage in the Western Church: The Christianization of Marriage during the Patristic and Early Medieval Periods*. Texts and Studies of Early Christian Life and Language, 26. Leiden: Brill, 1994.

Reynolds, Roger E. "Penitentials in South and Central Italian Canon Law Manuscripts of the Tenth and Eleventh Centuries." *Early Medieval Europe* 14, no. 1 (2006): 65–84.

Rider, Catherine. "What to Ask in Confession: A List of Sins from Thirteenth-Century England." In *Pastoral Care in Medieval England: Interdisciplinary Approaches*, edited by Peter D. Clarke and Sarah James, 67–99. London: Routledge, 2020.

Rider, Catherine. *Magic and Impotence in the Middle Ages*. Oxford: Oxford University Press, 2006.

Rist, Rebecca. *Papacy and Crusading in Europe, 1198–1245*. London: Continuum, 2009.

Rolker, Christof, with contributions by Robert Somerville. *Canon Law in the Age of Reforms (c. 1000 to c. 1150)*. History of Medieval Canon Law. Washington, D.C.: Catholic University of America Press, 2023.

Rolker, Christof. *Canon Law and the Letters of Ivo of Chartres*. Cambridge Studies in Medieval Life and Thought, Fourth Series. Cambridge: Cambridge University Press, 2010.

Rolker, Christof. "The *Collection in Seventy-Four Titles*: A Monastic Canon Law Collection from Eleventh-Century France." In *Readers, Texts and Compilers in the Earlier Middle Ages: Studies in Medieval Canon Law in Honour of Linda Fowler-Magerl*, edited by Martin Brett and Kathleen G. Cushing, 59–72. Aldershot: Ashgate, 2009.

Rolker, Christof. "History and Canon Law in the Collectio Britannica: A New Date for London, BL Add. 8873." In *Bishops, Texts and the Use of Canon Law around 1100: Essays in Honour of Martin Brett*, edited by Bruce C. Brasington and Kathleen G. Cushing, 141–152. Church, Faith, and Culture in the Medieval West. Aldershot: Ashgate, 2008.

Rorem, Paul. *Hugh of Saint Victor*. Great Medieval Thinkers. Oxford: Oxford University Press, 2009.

Rosemann, Philipp W. *Peter Lombard*. Great Medieval Thinkers. Oxford: Oxford University Press, 2004.

Rüegg, Walter. "Themes." In *A History of the University in Europe, Vol. 1: Universities in the Middle Ages*, edited by Hilde De Ridder-Symoens, 3–34. Cambridge: Cambridge University Press, 1992.

Ruys, Juanita Feros. "'He who kills himself liberates a wretch': Abelard on Suicide." In *Rethinking Abelard: A Collection of Critical Essays*, edited by Babette S. Hellemans, 230–249. Brill's Studies in Intellectual History 229. Leiden: Brill, 2014.

Saller, Richard P. "Pater Familias, Mater Familias, and the Gendered Semantics of the Roman Household." *Classical Philology* 94, no. 2 (1992): 182–197.

Schmandt, Raymond H. "The Fourth Crusade and the Just-War Theory." *Catholic Historical Review* 61, no. 2 (1975): 191–221.

Schmitt, Jean-Claude. "Le suicide au Moyen Âge." *Annales ESC: Économies, sociétés, civilisations* 31, no. 1 (1976): 1–28.

Schumacher, Lydia, and David d'Avray, "Aquinas and the Place of Canon Law in Legal History." *Archivum Fratrum Prædicatorum* 5 (2020): 29–44.

Sdralek, M. *Wolfenbüttler Fragmente: Analekten zur Kirchengeschichte des Mittelalters aus Wolfenbüttler Handschriften*. Kirchengeschichtliche Studien, 1.2. Münster: Schöningh, 1891.

Sedano, Joaquín. "The *Collectio decem partium*'s Distinctive Sections: Parts 4 and 10." In *Proceedings of the Fourteenth International Congress of Medieval Canon Law. Toronto, 5–11 August 2012*, edited by Joseph Goering, Stephan Dusil, and Andreas Thier, 31–60. Monumenta Iuris Canonici: Series C, Subsidia 15. Vatican City: Bibliotheca Apostolica Vaticana, 2016.

Sedano, Joaquín. "The Manuscript Tradition of the *Collection in Ten Parts*." In *Proceedings of the Thirteenth International Congress of Medieval Canon Law, Esztergom, 3–8 August 2008*, edited by Cardinal Péter Erdő and Szabolcs Anzelm Szuromi, 261–272. Monumenta Iuris Canonici: Series C, Subsidia 14. Vatican City: Bibliotheca Apostolica Vaticana, 2010.

Sedano, Joaquín. "A Comparative Analysis of the *Panormia* and the *Collectio X partium*." *Zeitschrift der Savigny-Stiftung fur Rechtsgeschichte*. Kanonistische Abteilung 96 (2010): 80–110.

Shoemaker, Karl. *Sanctuary and Crime in the Middle Ages, 400–1500*. Just Ideas. New York: Fordham University Press, 2011.

Silano, Guilio. "Peter Lombard." In *Christianity and Family Law: An Introduction*, edited by John Witte, Jr. and Gary S. Hauk, 146–160. Cambridge University Press, 2017.

Simons, Walter. "Jean de Warneton et la Réforme Grégorienne." *Mémoires de la Société d'histoire de Comines-Warneton et de la region* 17 (1987): 35–54.

Smalley, Berly. *The Study of the Bible in the Middle Ages*, 3rd edn. Oxford: Clarendon Press, 1940; rpt. Notre Dame: Notre Dame University Press, 2006.

Smith, David M. "The 'Officialis' of the Bishop in Twelfth- and Thirteenth-Century England: Problems of Terminology." In *Medieval Ecclesiastical Studies in Honour of Dorothy M. Owen*, edited by M.J. Franklin and Christopher Harper-Bill, 201–220. Woodbridge: Boydell & Brewer, 1995.

Smith, Peter M. "The Advowson: The History and Development of a Most Peculiar Property." *Ecclesiastical Law Journal* 5, no. 26 (2000): 320–339.

Somerville, Robert. "The Letters of Pope Urban II in the *Collectio Britannica*." In *Proceedings of the Seventh International Congress of Medieval Canon Law, Cambridge, 23–27 July 1984*, edited by Peter Linehan, 103–114. Monumenta Iuris Canonici: Series C, Subsidia 8. Vatican City: Bibliotheca Apostolica Vaticana, 1998.

Somerville, Robert, "Papal Excerpts in Arsenal MS 713B: Alexander II and Urban II," in *Proceedings of the Ninth International Congress of Medieval Canon Law*, edited by Peter Landau and Jörg Müller, 169–184. Monumenta Iuris Canonici: Series C, Subsidia 10. Vatican City: Bibliotheca Apostolica Vaticana, 1997.

Somerville, Robert. *Pope Alexander III and the Council of Tours*. Center for Medieval and Renaissance Studies, UCLA. Berkeley: University of California Press, 1977.

Somerville, Robert. *Councils of Urban II, Vol. 1: Decreta Claromontensia*. Annuarium historiae conciliorum. Supplementum, 1. Amsterdam: Hakkert, 1972.
Soria, Myriam. "Alexander III and France: Exile, Diplomacy and the New Order." In *Pope Alexander III (1159–81): The Art of Survival*, edited by Peter D. Clarke and Anne J. Duggan, 181–201. Church, Faith, and Culture in the Medieval West. Farnham: Ashgate, 2012.
Southern, Richard W. *Scholastic Humanism and the Unification of Europe, Vol. II: The Heroic Age*. Oxford: Blackwell, 1997.
Summerlin, Danica. "Hubert Walter's Council of Westminster in 1200 and It's use of Alexander III's 1179 Lateran Council." In *The Use of Canon Law in Ecclesiastical Administration, 1000–1250*, edited by Melodie H. Eichbauer and Danica Summerlin, 121–139. Medieval Law and Its Practice, 26. Leiden: Brill, 2018.
Summerlin, Danica. "Three Manuscripts Containing the Canons of the 279 Lateran Council." *Bulletin of Medieval Canon Law* 30 (2013): 21–43.
Taliadoros, Jason. "Law, Theology, and the Schools: The Use of Scripture in Ricardus Anglicus's *Distinctiones decretorum*." In *Proceedings of the International Congress of Medieval Canon Law, Toronto 5–15 August 2012*, edited by Joseph Goering, Stephan Dusil, and Andreas Thier, 1045–1089. Monumenta Iuris Canonici: Series C, Subsidia 15. Vatican City: Bibliotheca Apostolica Vaticana, 2016.
Taliadoros, Jason. "Law, Theology, and Morality: Conceptions of the Rights to Relief of the Poor in the Twelfth and Thirteenth Centuries." *Journal of Religious History* 37, no. 4 (2013): 474–493.
Taliadoros, Jason. "Bartholomew of Exeter's Penitential: Some Observations on his Personal Dicta." In *Proceedings of the Thirteenth International Congress of Medieval Canon Law. Esztergom, 3–8 August 2008*, edited by Peter Erdö and Anzelm Szuromi, 457–473. Monumenta Iuris Canonici: Series C, Subsidia 14. Vatican City: Biblioteca Apostolica Vaticana, 2010.
Taliadoros, Jason. *Law and Theology in Twelfth-Century England: The Works of Master Vacarius (c.1115/20-c.1200)*. Disputatio, 10. Turnhout: Brepols, 2006.
Teillard, Lefebvre. "L'école de droit parisienne (fin XIIe-début XIIIe siècle)." *Zeitschrift der Savigny-Stiftung fur Rechtsgeschichte*. Kanonistische Abteilung 136 (2019): 45–54.
Teillard, Lefebvre. "Un précieux témoin de l'École de droit canonique parisienne à l'aube du XIIIe siècle: Le manuscrit 649 de la bibliothèque municipale de Douai." *Revue historique de droit français et étranger* 95 (2017): 1–57.
Theron, Stephen. "Justice: Legal and Moral Debt in Aquinas." *American Catholic Philosophical Quarterly* 78, no. 4 (2004): 559–571.
Thijssen, J.M.M.H. "Master Amalric and the Amalricians: Inquisitorial Procedure and the Suppression of Heresy at the University of Paris." *Speculum* 71, no.1 (1996): 43–65.
Tock, Benoit-Michel. "Jean de Warneton, Évêque de Thérouanne (1099–1130): Un Grégorien." In *Le diocese de Thérouanne au Moyen Age: Actes de la journée d'études tenue à Lille, 3 mai 2007*, 107–118. Arras: Commission départementale d'histoire, 2010.
Turley, Thomas. "History and Legitimacy in the Dominican Responses to John of Pouilly." In *Inventing Modernity in Medieval European Thought ca. 1100–ca. 1550*, edited by Cary J. Nederman and Bettina Koch, 53–70. Studies in Medieval and Early Modern Culture, 63. Kalamazoo: Medieval Institute Publications, 2019.
Ubl, Karl, *Inzestverbot und Gesetzgebung: Die Konstruktion eines Verbrechens (300–1100)*. Millennium-Studien. Berlin: De Gruyter, 2008.

Ullmann, Walter. "The Significance of Innocent III's Decretal *Vergentis*." In *The Papacy and political Ideas in the Middle Ages*, edited by W. Ullmann, 729–741. Variorum Collected Studies Series, 44. London: Variorum, 1976.

Uruszczak, Waclaw. "Albéric et l'enseignement du droit roman à Reims au XIIe siècle." In *Confluence des droits savants et des pratiques juridiques: Actes du colloque de Montpellier: Colloque tenu du 12 au 14 décembre 1977, sous le patronage et avec le financement du C.N.R.S. / Max-Planck-Institut für europäische Rechtsgeschichte, Istituto di storia del diritto italiano (Università degli Studi di Milano), Institut d'Histoire des anciens pays de droit écrit (Université de Montpellier I)*, 39–68. Milan: Giuffrè, 1979.

Van Engen, John. "From Practical Theology to Divine Law: The Work and Mind of Medieval Canonists." In *Proceedings of the Ninth International Congress of Medieval Canon Law: Munich, 13–18 July 1992*, edited by Peter Landau and Jörg Müller, 873–896. Monumenta Iuris Canonici: Series C, Subsidia 10. Vatican City: Bibilioteca Apostolica Vaticana, 1997.

Van Engen, John. "Observations on *De consecratione*." In *Proceedings of the Sixth International Congress of Medieval Canon Law, Berkeley 28 July–2 August 1980*, edited by Stephan Kuttner and Kenneth Pennington, 309–320. Monumenta Iuris Canonici: Series C, Subsidia 7. Vatican City: Biblioteca Apostolica Vaticana, 1985.

Vaughn, Sally. "Lanfranc at Bec: A Reinterpretation." *Albion* 17, no. 2 (1985): 135–148.

Verger, Jacques. "The First French Universities and the Institutionalization of Learning: Faculties, Curricula, Degrees." In *Learning Institutionalized: Teaching in the Medieval University*, edited John Van Engen, 5–19. Notre Dame: University of Notre Dame Press, 2000.

Verger, Jacques. "A propos de la naissance de l'université de Paris: Contexte social, enjeu politique, portée intellectuelle." In *Schulen und Studium im Sozialen Wandel des Hohen und Späten Mittelalters*, edited by Johannes Fried, 69–96. Vorträge und Forschungen. Ostfildern: Jan Thorbecke, 1986.

Verger, Jacques, and Charles Vulliez. "Naissance de l'Université, and Enseignement et culture universtiaires (jusque vers 1350)." In *Les Universités Au Moyen Age*, edited by Jacques Verger, 17–75. Paris: Presses Universitaires de France, 1973.

Vincent, Nicholas. "Albion Adrift: The English Presence in Paris and its Environs after 1204." In *Thirteenth Century England XVIII: Proceedings of the Cambridge Conference, 2019*, edited by Andrew Spencer and Carl Watkin, 209–246. Woodbridge: Boydell Press, 2023.

Vodola, Elisabeth. *Excommunication in the Middle Ages*. Berkeley: University of California Press, 1986.

Vogel, Cyril. *Les Libri Paenitentiales*. Typologie des Sources du Moyen Âge Occidental, 27. Turnout: Brepols, 1978.

Waelkens, L., and D. Van den Auweele. "La collection de Thérouanne ex IX livres à l'abbaye de Saint-Pierre-au-Mont-Blandin: Le codex Gandavensis 235." *Sacris erudiri: Jaarboek voor Godsdienstwetenschappen* 24 (1980): 115–153.

Watt, Jack. "Parsian Theologians and the Jews: Peter Lombard and Peter Cantor." In *The Medieval Church: Universities, Heresy, and Christian Life: Essays in Honour of Gordon Leff*, edited by Peter Biller and Barrie Dobson, 55–76. Studies in Church History, Subsidia 11. Woodbridge: Boydell and Brewer, 1999.

Wayno, Jeffrey M. "Rethinking the Fourth Lateran Council of 1215." *Speculum* 93 (2018): 611–637.

Wei, John C. "Of Scholasticism and Canon Law: Narratives Old and New." In *New Discourses in Medieval Canon Law Research*, edited by Christof Rolker, 105–126. Medieval Law and Its Practice, 28. Leiden: Brill, 2019.

Wei, John C. *Gratian the Theologian*. Studies in Medieval and Early Modern Canon Law, 13. Washington, D.C.: Catholic University of America Press, 2016.

Wei, Ian P. *Intellectual Culture in Medieval Paris: Theologians and the University c.1100–1330*. Cambridge: Cambridge University Press, 2014.

Weigand, Rudolf. "The Transmontaine Decretists." In *The History of Medieval Canon Law in the Classical Period, 1140–1234: From Gratian to the Decretals of Pope Gregory IX*, edited by Wilfried Hartmann and Kenneth Pennington, 174–210. History of Medieval Canon Law. Washington, D.C.: The Catholic University of America Press, 2008.

Weigand, Rudolf. *Glossatoren des Dekrets Gratians*. Bibliotheca eruditorum, 18. Keip: Goldbach, 1997.

Weigand, Rudolf. "Die Dekretabbreviatio 'Exceptiones ecclesiasticarum regularum' und ihre Glossen." In *Christianità ed Europa: Miscellanea di studi in onore di Luigi Prosdocimi*, edited by Cesare Alzati, 1.511–529. Rome: Herder, 1992.

Weigand, Rudolf. "Studien Zum Kanonistischen Werk Stephans von Tournai." *Zeitschrift der Savigny-Stiftung fur Rechtsgeschichte*. Kanonistische Abteilung 72 (1986): 349–361

Weisweiler, Heinrich. "Die Arbeitsmethode Hugos von St. Viktor: Ein Beitrag zum Entstehen seines." *Scholastik* 20, no. 24 (1949): 59–87 and 232–267.

Werckmeister, Jean. "La fidélité conjugale dans le droit canonique medieval." *Revue de droit canonique* 44 (1994): 17–34.

Werckmeister, Jean. "Le Mariage sacrament dans le Decret de Gratien." *Revue de droit canonique* 42 (1992): 237–267.

Wickham, Chris. "Ecclesiastical Dispute and Lay Community: Figline Valdarno in the Twelfth Century." *Melanges de l'Ecole francaise de Rome: Moyen- Age, Temps modernes* 108, no. 1 (1996): 7–93.

Wieruszowski, Helene. *The Medieval University: Masters, Students, Learning*. Princeton: Van Nostrand, 1966.

Williams, J. R. "Cathedral School of Reims in the Time of Master Alberic, 1118–1136." *Traditio* 20 (1964): 93–114.

Winroth, Anders. *The Making of Gratian's Decretum*, Cambridge Studies in Medieval Life and Thought, Fourth Series. Cambridge: Cambridge University Press, 2000.

Young, Spencer E. *Scholarly Community at the Early University of Paris: Theologians, Education and Society, 1215–1248*. Cambridge Studies in Medieval Life and Thought, Fourth Series. Cambridge: Cambridge University Press, 2014.

Zemler-Cizewski, Wanda. "*Lex* and *ius* in the *Summa Theologiae* of Thomas Aquinas: A Review of the Nuances." In *Proceedings of the PMR Conference, 19–20*, edited by Karl A. Gersbach, Frederick Van Fleteren, and Joseph C. Schnaubelt, 215–224. Villanova: Villanova University, 1997.

INDEX OF LEGAL AND THEOLOGICAL CITATIONS

Collectio Sancte Victor (CSV)

Gratian, *Decretum* (GD)

Roman Law

Theodosian Code

Epitome Juliani

GENERAL INDEX

Note: Dates listed after a proper name indicate lifespan. Dates listed after a title indicate length of term. For example, Alexander III, Pope (1159–1181) indicates that Alexander was pope from 1159 to 1181.

Pages in **bold** refer to tables and pages followed by "n" refer to notes.

www.ingramcontent.com/pod-product-compliance
Ingram Content Group UK Ltd.
Pitfield, Milton Keynes, MK11 3LW, UK
UKHW020150200926
475702UK00016B/2633
* 9 7 8 1 0 3 2 7 3 6 0 8 2 *